Farmers in the Forest

Farmers in the Forest

Economic Development and Marginal Agriculture in Northern Thailand

edited by
Peter Kunstadter
E. C. Chapman
Sanga Sabhasri

ꕔ *An East-West Center Book*
from the East-West Population Institute

Published for the East-West Center
by The University Press of Hawaii
Honolulu

Library of Congress Cataloging in Publication Data
Main entry under title:

Farmers in the forest.

   "An East-West Center book."
   "This book grew out of a conference on upland
agriculture in northern Thailand, organized by the
editors and held on the campus of Chiang Mai University
in January 1970."
   Bibliography: p.
   Includes index.
   1. Shifting cultivation—Thailand. 2. Hill farming
—Thailand. 3. Land use, Rural—Thailand. 4. Rural
development—Thailand. I. Kunstadter, Peter.
II. Chapman, E. C. III. Sanga Sabhasri.
IV. Mahāwitthayālai Chiang Mai.

S602.87.F37   333.7'6'09593   77–27263
ISBN 0–8248–0366–3

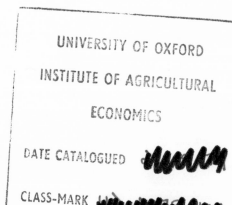

Contents

Contributors

Banijbatana, Dusit — Former Director General, Royal Forest Department, Bangkok, Thailand

Chapman, E. C. — Reader, Department of Geography, School of General Studies, Australian National University, Canberra, A.C.T., Australia

Charley, J. L. — University of New England, Armidale, N.S.W., Australia

Hinton, Peter — Department of Anthropology, University of Sydney, Sydney, N.S.W., Australia

Keen, F. G. B. — Agricultural Advisor, Northern Agricultural Centre, Ministry of Agriculture, Thailand

Komkris, Thiem* — Late Dean, Faculty of Forestry, Kasetsart University, Bangkhen, Bangkok, Thailand

Kunstadter, Peter — Research Associate, East-West Population Institute, East-West Center, Honolulu, Hawaii, U.S.A.

McGarity, J. W. — University of New England, Armidale, N.S.W., Australia

Pelzer, Karl J. — Professor, Department of Geography, Yale University, New Haven, Connecticut, U.S.A.

Ratanakorn, Sophon — Judge, Supreme Court of Thailand

Sabhasri, Sanga — Secretary General, National Research Council of Thailand, Bangkhen, Bangkok, Thailand

Smitinand, Tem — Curator, Royal Forest Herbarium, Bangkhen, Bangkok, Thailand

Zinke, Paul J. — Associate Professor, School of Forestry and Conservation, University of California, Berkeley, California, U.S.A.

* Deceased

Preface

Inability of food production to keep pace with population growth, and environmental degradation associated with use of marginal lands for agriculture are common problems in much of the tropical world. Slash-and-burn farming, shifting cultivation, or, as it is now generally referred to in scientific literature, swidden agriculture, in which fields are cleared for temporary use and then left for a relatively long fallow period, is a common feature of upland areas in northern Thailand, as well as on much of the unirrigated land in other parts of Southeast Asia. These are agricultural frontiers, frequently occupied by members of minority groups but increasingly the destination of landless migrants from the dominant ethnic groups in Thailand and many other countries.

The purpose of this book is to bring together some detailed accounts showing the range of variation in types of shifting cultivation, as well as to consider the implications of swiddening for the future of the people and the environment of Thailand. Throughout, we have attempted to integrate social and ecological aspects of these widespread land-use systems, as seen from the perspectives of soil, agricultural, and forestry sciences, law, administration, and, to the extent possible, through anthropological studies, to present the views of the forest farmers themselves. We have emphasized the description of traditional systems, and their adaptations to stresses imposed by population growth and economic development. Because shifting cultivation is not confined to northern Thailand, we have provided additional historical and geographic perspective by including a discussion of successful commercial use of shifting cultivation in Indonesia.

Acknowledgments

This book grew out of a conference on social, economic, and ecological aspects of upland agriculture in northern Thailand, organized by the editors, and held on the campus of Chiang Mai University in January 1970. The conference was sponsored by the Ford Foundation, Chiang Mai University, the Department of Land Development, the Faculty of Forestry of Kasetsart University, the Thai-Australian Land Development Project, the Tribal Research Centre, and the Department of Public Welare.

The conference included reports of studies done in the late 1960s on shifting cultivation in northern Thailand. This volume also includes several additional papers on related topics. The enthusiasm of the late Dr. Chaiyong Chuchart for humane, just, and technically sound development of the upland resources of Thailand was a major factor in the conference.

The Ford Foundation assisted in defraying the costs of preparing the manuscript for publication, as did the East-West Center. Publication was made possible through the support of the East-West Center.

The manuscript was typed at the stenographic pool of the East-West Population Institute, under the direction of Mrs. Lynette Tong. The drawings were made in the cartography section of the East-West Population Institute, under the direction of Mr. Gregory Chu, and in the Department of Geography, School of General Studies, Australian National University. Most of the photographic enlargements were made by Vichai Photo in Chiang Mai. Mrs. Elizabeth Bushnell did a patient and skillful job of copy editing. Mr. William Heaney and Ms. Brigid Donnelly assisted with the index.

We gratefully acknowledge the contributions and support of all the individuals and institutions who made this book possible, including the assistance of the people whose agricultural practices are described herein.

A Note on Units of Measure

In general we have used the metric system, with the exception of measures of area *(rai)* and yield *(tang)* in Thailand (which are readily converted to metric units). The conversion table below gives the equivalents of Thai, metric and English units.

Area

Acre = 43,560 sq ft = 4047 sq m = 0.405 ha = 2.531 *rai*
Hectare (ha) = 10,000 sq m = 2.47 acres = 6.25 *rai*
Rai = 1600 sq m = 0.16 ha = 0.395 acre

Length

Inch = 2.540 cm
Foot = 30.480 cm
Centimeter (cm) = 0.39 inch
Meter (m) = 39.37 inches

Weight

Pound (lb) = 0.373 kg
Kilogram (kg) = 2.2046 lb
Ton (metric) = 1000 kg = 2,204.6 lb

Volume

Bushel = 35.238 liters = 1.762 *tang*
Tang = 20 liters = 0.5676 bushel
Liter = 1.057 quarts

PART I

INTRODUCTION

1

Problems of Shifting Cultivation and Economic Development in Northern Thailand

Peter Kunstadter
E. C. Chapman

Rapid population growth in the tropics makes it essential to examine and evaluate the allocation of natural resources and the distribution of costs and benefits of these resources. In Thailand one of the primary resources is the forest-covered land of the hills and foothills of the North (chapter 2). Thai and "tribal" people have practiced unirrigated farming for centuries on this land using methods variously referred to as slash and burn, bush or forest fallow, swidden, *rai*, or shifting cultivation.[1] This book considers four kinds of social and economic problems in these marginal agricultural areas of northern Thailand: problems arising from sustained population growth; problems resulting from socio-economic inequalities of the marginal agricultural areas; problems of relatively low productivity per unit area of swidden cultivation; and problems of conserving soil, watershed, and forest resources. All of these are problems of the whole region of northern Thailand; they are not confined to remote foothill and upland villages.

"Shifting" cultivation does not necessarily imply that the cultivators themselves are nomadic. Some swiddeners live in villages that have been settled for hundreds of years and make repeated cyclical use of the same fields; others live in temporary villages which are abandoned as the fields become exhausted after a few years or a few cycles of cultivation and fallow; some farmers combine or supplement their use of permanent irrigated fields with shifting cultivation, especially where irrigable land is scarce.

Swidden cultivation is a marginal system in several respects. Yields per unit area (including fallow land), per unit of labor, or per unit of seed are often lower than in irrigated fields; swidden fields are usually located at some distance from markets, generally on land that is considered marginal or submarginal for annual or multi-crop farming. Swiddening is often carried out primarily as a subsistence operation, or even a supplementary subsistence operation, rather than as a source of cash crops, and swidden cultivators are often socially and economically marginal to the nation within which they live.

All of the northern provinces of Thailand are mountainous, with relatively small areas of valley land, as compared with the central plains provinces. They have a monsoonal climate, with a rainy season beginning in May or June and lasting until October or November. Almost no rain falls during the cold season, in December and January, and the hot season, beginning in mid-February and lasting until the rains start in May or June. The swidden growing season is strictly limited by the availability of water from rainfall and the small amount of moisture retained during the dry season. Production may be further limited because upland soils are generally well drained, and crops may suffer when monsoon rains are irregular.

The rural lowland people in the North are generally speakers of the Northern Thai dialect, while the hills are occupied by a variety of upland minority peoples ("hill tribes") including the Karen, Lua', Hmong (Meo),[2] Yao (Iu Mien), Akha (Ikaw), and Lahu (Musser). Swiddening is often thought of as a "hill-tribe" characteristic, but in fact both Thai and non-Thai people may engage in it in both the hills and the lowlands (see part IV).

The problems considered in this book are characteristic of much of Southeast Asia, and similar problems exist on the margins of intensively irrigated regions throughout the tropical world. In a comprehensive study, Spencer emphasized that shifting cultivation is the most widespread cropping system in South and Southeast Asia, although it dominates now only in Borneo and the hills of Thailand, Burma, Laos, Viet Nam, Cambodia, and southwestern China (Spencer 1966:4). Throughout these areas swidden farming is gradually giving way to more productive permanent systems of land use under the stress of economic necessity as populations grow, but there is also a countervailing tendency to force more people into this marginal form of agriculture as land:people ratios decline.

The problems of economic development of shifting cultivators in northern Thailand are *regional* in nature, that is *they are not limited to the plight of the individual subsistence farmer, nor to the condition of an isolated village, nor to any single ethnic group or ecological position.* The contributors to this book show clearly that shifting cultivation is practiced by both Thai and non-Thai peoples in northern Thailand, and by valley dwellers as well as hill villagers. The succeeding chapters also show clearly that the practitioners of shifting cultivation participate in many phases of the economy of the North beyond the confines of their own villages—in marketing their agricultural products, trading for supplies, and most notably, in the wage labor market of the region.

The forest fallow farmers of Northern Thailand participate both in the rapid population growth which is characteristic of all parts of Thailand, and in the complex pattern of internal population movements in recent years. In many instances hill people (e.g., Lua' and Karen; see chapters 6–9) work in the lowlands and, very commonly, Thai lowland swidden farmers move in fairly large numbers to seasonal jobs in other provinces for two to four months each year. Population growth throughout Thailand and the rapid occupation of remaining forested lowlands in the 1950s and 1960s, when the largest irrigation projects were completed, makes further absorption of population surpluses from marginal areas more difficult than in the past. In the absence of some basic economic changes, relief from mounting population pressure is often not readily available. This demographic consideration alone is sufficient to make it obvious that the economic problems of shifting cultivators are regional, and not limited to isolated villages.

HISTORICAL BACKGROUND

Contemporary relationships between population, natural resources, and the variety of agricultural technologies in northern Thailand are products of a long history of intensification of food production and population expansion. Two theories have been proposed regarding the origins of agriculture in Southeast Asia. In chapter 15 Pelzer discusses some of the basic ecological effects of the extensive use of fire in the development of forest farming. He outlines the view that root and tree crops, planted along watercourses in the lowlands and coastal regions, preceded the development of seed and grain crops on the hill slopes and in irrigated fields. A second theory, suggested by archaeological evidence which is beginning to accumulate from northern and northeastern Thailand, is that the tending of seed plants may have been practiced as early there as anywhere in the world, and may have preceded the domestication of root and tree crops (Gorman 1969, 1971*b*). Whichever sequence is correct, it is clear that some form of hill farming has been practiced in Southeast Asia for a very long time, and has resulted in extensive modification of vegetation in many areas. The demographic conditions accompanying this pattern of agriculture are as yet unknown. There is no evidence that would allow us to judge in detail the interaction of technological innovations (improved tools and crop plants) with population size, but it is evident that traditional technology could not have supported the current level of population.

The development or introduction of the metal knife, ax, hoe, and weeding tool blades allowed human populations to spread in space and expand in numbers, by making heavily forested lands available for more intensive agricultural use. The domestication of grain plants and the eventual development of irrigation technology must have allowed further increase of population and also resulted in concentration of population in the lowlands. This led to social differentiation: sizeable towns, formal governments, and other attributes of civilization developed in the valleys while swiddeners remained in marginal areas, living in relatively small and dispersed villages, affected more slowly and less directly by the development of valley-based civilizations.

New World crop plants have had major effects both in the subsistence economy and in the development of cash crops and plantation systems. Maize, manioc, and potatoes were introduced throughout Southeast Asia probably by the sixteenth and seventeenth centuries and had a profound effect on upland population size and distribution. Some groups, such as the Hmong (chapter 11), have a domestic economy based largely on maize, and their style of life must have been radically different before this crop became available. Other groups, such as the Lua' and Karen (part III), who are primarily rice growers, now depend heavily on maize as the earliest ripening starchy food, to tide them over for several months in the rainy season after their previous year's rice supply is exhausted and before the new rice ripens. Such alternative or supplemental food crops have allowed swidden populations to increase in numbers and expand in territory, a tendency which has also been supported by increasing opportunities for wage labor and by the spread of a cash economy.

Rapid population growth, urbanization, and the application of science and technology to agriculture are having profound effects on relationships between shifting cultivators and their natural and social environments. Thailand's population has grown rapidly, especially since the second world war, reaching a rate of over 3 percent per year in the early 1960s. The national growth rate has declined slightly in the 1970s but apparently remains high in the hill areas and the parts of the North where shifting cultivation is most widespread. The exact causes of the growth are not completely understood. They probably include a general rise in the level of public health and sanitation in areas where people are concentrated, control of a few important diseases (cholera, smallpox, and perhaps malaria), and absence of major political disruptions, all combined with general improvements in communication, transportation, and marketing.

The recent development of improved high-yield strains of rice will make great changes in Thailand's economy. The national agricultural economy has depended for many years on the production of rice for local subsistence as well as for export. The rice "premium" is the difference between the price of rice in Thailand and the price on the world market; it has been a primary source of government income while allowing local prices to remain low. This strategy worked well during the 1950s and early 1960s, when international rice prices were high. With the advent in the 1960s of the technology-intensive "green revolution," prices fell rapidly in Thailand's traditional markets, though exports remained high. Rapidly rising fertilizer costs, associated with the worldwide energy crisis in the early 1970s imply rising costs and rice prices (cf. Hirst 1974; Pimentel et al. 1973; Steinhart and Steinhart 1974). The total effect in the past few years has been increased uncertainty and rapid agricultural price fluctuations. The situation brings into question all plans for the economic development of Thailand based on intensification of rice agriculture for international exchange. This, along with sustained population growth and a rapid increase in landlessness among lowland farmers, diminishes the hope that surplus upland populations will be absorbed in the expanding intensive commercial rice agriculture in the lowlands.

Meanwhile, modernization and urbanization are proceeding rapidly and economic opportunities increasingly require formal education and nonrural skills. The result is a widening gap between the people of modernizing urban areas and those of rural areas, especially subsistence swidden farmers.

Unlike the earlier innovations (new tools, new crop plants), few if any of the modern innovations are directly applied to shifting cultivators. Except for malaria control and sporadic smallpox vaccination, these people are unlikely to have received much modern medical attention, though they may have been protected from contagious diseases by epidemic controls applied to the more accessible segments of the populations. Nor have they benefited much from the improved strains of crop plants or improved methods of cultivation, since these have been developed for lowland environments where purchase of fertilizer and pesticides and control of water are possible. Although starting in the early 1960s public schools were beginning to be made available in the upland areas, few if any of the children of shifting cultivators have yet progressed through high school. Despite the lack of direct modernization, the populations of the more marginal areas of shifting cultivation seem to be growing just as fast as, or faster than, those in the irrigated lowlands and in the cities (Kunstadter 1971).

VARIETIES OF UPLAND CULTIVATION SYSTEMS IN NORTHERN THAILAND

Assumptions concerning ethnic categories and their relationship to environment, economy, and social structure have important implications for public policy. Incorrect assumptions concerning ethnic categories include the ideas that only hill tribes practice swiddening and only Thais practice irrigated cultivation. Leach (1954) demonstrated that ethnic categories, environment, economic type, and social structure are not bound into an inevitable permanent pattern in mainland Southeast Asia. Nonetheless, land use in northern Thailand has usually been classified by ethnic group (cf. Van Roy 1971, especially chapters 2 and 3). When we look carefully at land use and ethnic distributions in northern Thailand we find almost as much variation in land use *within* some ethnic categories as between them. We find variations of land use within ecological zones, and we also find people from one ethnic category moving from one type of ecological zone and land use to another, sometimes without changing their ethnic identity (fig. 1.1; photos 14–19, 39, 118, 125).

Thus we have preferred to classify types of forest farming on the basis of relationships between cultivation and fallow periods. We have attached ethnic labels to these types only as aids to memory and they should be understood as such. It is evident from the descriptions of cultivation systems in the chapters which follow that variations in patterns of land use are associated with variations in physical and social environment, population density, major crop plants, and balance between subsistence and cash operations, as well as cultural traditions. The farmers alter their patterns of land use in response to these variations.

It is useful to think in terms of three types of swidden cultivation land use and one type of permanent upland cultivation: (1) short cultivation–short fallow (often used by Northern Thai); (2) short cultivation–long fallow, or "forest fallow" (often used by upland Karen and Lua'); (3) long cultivation–very long fallow or abandonment (often used by Hmong and other opium growing hill groups); (4) permanent field tree crops, associated with use of forest for swidden rice and fuel. Table 1.1 outlines the relationships between important variables and these land-use types.[3]

SHORT CULTIVATION–SHORT FALLOW ("NORTHERN THAI")

The Northern Thai system is one of short periods of cultivation, with short fallow periods (chapter 12). Secondary growth tends to be of the low tree and scrub type rather than a return to forest cover. Under primitive clearing and cultivating techniques the soil tends to lose fertility under this system, because the regrowth period is not long enough to allow the plants to bring sufficient nutrients above the soil surface, where they can be made available for agriculture by cutting and burning. In some cases the clearing and burning that precedes the planting of an unirrigated crop is preparatory to leveling and irrigating the field for annual cultivation. Use of these fields is often considered only supplementary to the "normal" irrigated form of agriculture in areas of high population: cultivable land ratio where there is insufficient irrigated or irrigable land, such as the foothill and terrace lands near Sa, Nan Province (chapter 12), or in the hills around Mae Sariang town.

The land that is swiddened may or may not be claimed by a village unit as a whole; individuals may retain use-rights for several periods of cultivation, or they may simply abandon their fields after using them temporarily. Fields are made wherever suitable land is available, usually in areas where the characteristic vegetation is of the Mixed Deciduous or Dry Dipterocarp type on relatively sandy or rocky soil. This is a very widespread pattern in the transitional zones between valley and hill lands, at elevations between 300 and 600 meters.

The principal crop is upland glutinous and nonglutinous rice, supplemented by various cash or catch crops (vegetables, cotton, maize, beans, chilies, etc.) planted after cultivation of the main crop. Because of the transitory and

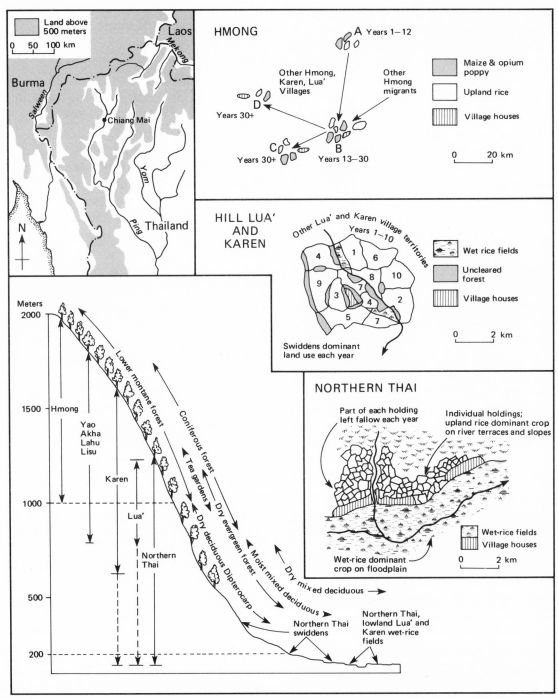

FIGURE 1.1   Land forms, land-use systems, and vegetation in northern Thailand.

marginal nature of much of this activity it is impossible to estimate the numbers of people involved. The number must be substantial; Judd estimated that more than a million people in northern Thailand were engaged in one or another type of shifting cultivation (1964:5).

SHORT CULTIVATION–LONG FALLOW
("HILL LUA' AND KAREN")

Upper terraces and foothills are often separated by relatively steep slopes from the rolling hills of the middle elevations, which range from 700 or 750 meters to well above 1,000 meters. In this zone the Lua' and Karen practice a forest fallow system of cultivation, with cultivation periods of only one year, and relatively long fallow periods of at least 6 or 7 years, up to 12 or 15 years in areas where land is plentiful (chapters 6–9). During the fallow period the forest cover and the soil normally rejuvenate to approximately the same condition as before the period of cultivation.

Native vegetation in these areas is often Dry Evergreen or Mixed Deciduous Forest on red clay or lateritic soils. Where swiddens have been cut, the primary climax forest is replaced with a secondary forest composed of fire-resistant species. Where population pressure is not already too great, this can be a stable system for an indefinite period of time, limited only by population growth or changes external to the system (such as changes in land laws, invasions by other populations, or changes in the aspirations of the villagers as a result of contact with new external conditions). These people live in permanent villages, some of which have been settled for generations or even hundreds of years.

The major crop is nonglutinous, slow ripening rice, which is raised primarily for subsistence. Numerous other crops (maize, sorghum, millet, chilies, beans, herbs, manioc, taro, sesame, etc.) are planted in the same fields. The people earn cash by selling small quantities of rice, garden or jungle products, or domestic animals, and by wage labor.

Characteristically the Lua' and Karen believe that the swidden land they cultivate belongs to the community, with individual household claims to use-rights. Community claims to the land usually go back several generations, and some were formally granted by the northern Thai princes (Nimmanahaeminda 1965), but these claims are no longer recognized by the Thai government. The land is worked by individual households, with cooperative (exchange) labor during times of heaviest work. Cooperation in agriculture is based primarily on kinship ties; within the village there is little or no work for wages in cash, and only small amounts of work for payment in rice. Almost all individuals and all families in the villages are directly involved in agriculture, but many of them supplement their incomes with wage labor away from the villages, especially during the slack agricultural seasons. Many upland Lua' and Karen villages also have irrigated fields, but because of the terrain the bulk of their land is used for hill farming. There are probably at least 100,000 Lua' and Karen participating in this type of system in northern Thailand (United Nations Survey Team 1967:56).

When unoccupied land was plentiful, Karen villages often split if their populations grew too large for convenient access to swidden fields. The upland Karen population has expanded very rapidly during the past century, and most of the suitable land has been occupied. The population continues to grow, and hard-pressed individuals or families who choose to remain as subsistence farmers must seek land in established villages where they have relatives, or accept a lowered standard of living. Others move temporarily or permanently to the lowlands, where wage work may be available.

TABLE 1.1   Characteristics of Four Types of Upland Cultivation

Type	Settlement Pattern and Migration	Location, Elevation (meters)	Major Crop Plants: Subsistence/Cash	Cultivation/Fallow Cycle (years)
Short cultivation, short fallow ("N. Thai")	Permanent lowland villages; individuals move between lowland villages	Uncleared valley terraces, foothills (300–600 meters)	Rice/peanuts, soy beans, mung beans	1/2+
Short cultivation, long fallow ("Hill Lua' and Karen")	Permanent villages; individuals move between hill villages and to lowlands	Middle elevations in hills (500–1000 meters)	Rice/rice	1/7–1/12
Long cultivation, very long fallow ("Hmong")	Temporary agglomerations split and move when soil is exhausted	Higher elevations in hills (1000+ meters)	Maize/opium	3–4/40+
Permanent field tree crops ("Tea gardens" of N. Thai and others)	Permanent villages; individuals move in from upland and lowland	Hillsides (600–1300 meters)	Rice/tea, fermented tea	Rice on variable swidden cycle, tea continuous, firewood considered "free good"

LONG CULTIVATION–VERY LONG FALLOW ("HMONG")

There is no sharp upper elevation boundary to the system just discussed, but there is a general tendency for elevations above 1,200 to 1,500 meters to be unused or to be occupied by Hmong (Meo), Yao (Iu Mien), Lahu (Musser), Lisu (Lisaw), Akha (Ikaw), and Yunnanese Chinese (Haw), most of whom are relative newcomers to the areas they now occupy. The system of shifting cultivation used by many Hmong farmers is one of long periods of use of a single field (up to five years or more), followed by abandonment when the soil fertility is exhausted or when secondary growth of grasses makes further cultivation impossible. Limestone-based soils are often deliberately selected and highly prized for their ability to sustain intensive cultivation for several years. The Hmong system is the most notorious in Thailand, both because the principal cash crop is opium, and because of the apparent destructiveness of the method to forest and watershed resources. As we have indicated, it is not typical of swidden systems in northern Thailand. Including Hmong, Lahu, Lisu, Akha, and Haw, more than 100,000 people practice shifting cultivation of this type (United Nations

TABLE 1.1 *(continued)*

Cultivation Techniques	Effects on Soil Fertility	Land Acquisition	Individual Land Tenure	Wage Labor
Clearing and weeding by hand tool (rice), hoeing (peanut)	Gradual decline with inadequate fallow	Squatting	Use-rights recognized within community	Wage work common to supplement farm income
Clearing and weeding by hand tool, no hoeing	Stable with adequate fallow	Ancestral claims recognized by prince, no legal claim now	Use-rights heritable within communally held area	Wage work common to supplement farm income
Deep hoe cultivation, clean weeding, crop rotation (corn-opium)	Long term decline, grass replaces forest	Purchase from previous owners, if any, squatting	Individual ownership until field is abandoned	Consumers, not sellers of wage labor
Rice weeded by hand tool; tea, selective thinning, grazing to clear underbrush	Under rice, dedendent on fallow cycle; under tea, stable if not overgrazed	Squatting, purchase, government lease, tenant farming	Use-rights recognized within community, some fee simple, some tenant farming	Individual entrepreneurs, wage labor, share cropping

Survey Team 1967:9; Young 1962:89), but this is probably only about 10 percent of the total number of shifting cultivators in the region.

These people are relative newcomers in Thailand, most of whom have arrived only since the turn of the century. Because they have had no access to the more fertile lands suited for permanent field cultivation, and because they are often involved in the illegal cultivation of opium, they have generally farmed in remote areas at higher elevations.

In areas that have been cultivated in this fashion, the forest cover almost never returns within a human lifetime. The secondary growth is usually some semipermanent or permanent form of grass which is less easily cleared (see chapter 2). It follows that land tenure in this system is not permanent. Evidently land is viewed by these farmers as a relatively free consumable good over which only temporary use-rights are appropriate. These people tend to live in less permanently settled villages, or villages that split or move from time to time. Land claims are not recognized after the fields are fallowed or abandoned (see Kickert 1969:36 for an example of land concepts of the Akha).

The main subsistence crop is maize or rice, and the primary cash crop has been opium,

though Hmong in the Mae Tho area on the eastern border of Mae Sariang District, Mae Hong
Son Province, have experimented with potatoes
and other truck garden products as supplements
or substitutes for opium, and in the 1970s coffee
has also been tried on an increasing scale.
Hmong farmers in northern Thailand are often
not self-sufficient for their subsistence and must
buy rice in large quantities from nearby Lua'
and Karen villages. The opium and maize fields
are usually on slopes, ridges, or peaks at relatively high elevations (1,000 meters or more).

Hmong have been in the far north of Thailand
(Chiang Rai Province) for at least 80 years and
have gradually spread south; there are now settlements in central Tak Province and Phitsanulok Province. The numbers of Hmong in
Thailand have expanded due both to very rapid
natural increase and, especially since mid-1975,
to extensive migration from Laos. Hmong have
had to obtain land from previous owners in
many of the areas to which they have moved
recently, and, according to Karen and Lua' informants, they have done so by purchase or by
threat, or by a combination of the two. Lua' and
Karen landowners are afraid to let the Hmong
into their area because they fear the effect of
Hmong cultivation practices on their watershed,
and also because they do not want to become involved in the opium business.

In some areas the Hmong are reported to base
their choice of new settlement sites on the availability of Lua' or Karen labor, as well as on the
quality of the soil required to grow maize and
opium. In the Mae Tho area and other parts of
Mae Chaem District it is clear that Hmong settlements depend heavily on labor from other
ethnic groups to assist in raising and marketing
their opium crops. They also depend on these
other ethnic groups as consumers of opium. The
Hmong evidently prefer to pay wages in opium

rather than cash. In recent years some Hmong in
the Mae Tho area also have tried to finance their
opium cultivation by mortgaging their opium
crops to Lua' villagers.

The Hmong system of cultivation is more
complex and more labor intensive than that of
the Lua' and Karen or Northern Thai. The soil is
much more thoroughly prepared, by hoeing
twice before the crops are planted. In the
agricultural system around Mae Tho, maize is
planted in May and harvested by August. The
opium, planted in the maize fields late in
August, matures in December and January. This
pattern of cropping may be repeated for several
years until the soil is exhausted or the grasses in-
vade the field and make it impossible to cultivate. The relatively deep, clean cultivation with
hoes makes it possible to continue planting for
several years, but also contributes to soil erosion
(photo 124). By contrast, the Lua' and Karen
weed their fields using a sickle-like tool, which
disturbs only the top centimeter or so of the soil
(photo 41) and would have little or no effect in
making subsurface soil nutrients available at the
surface. The Northern Thai use a narrow-bladed
spade *(siem)* for chopping weeds and roots on
their rice swiddens, but they use hoes in cultivating peanuts.

Ultimately the soil fertility is lost under the
Hmong system, and the fields are abandoned by
their owners. Individual household heads then
look for new fields, and if the fields of most of
the area near the village have been exhausted or
are otherwise unsuitable, the village may break
up, or move as a whole to other favorable spots.[4]

PERMANENT TREE CROPS ("TEA GARDENS")

A fourth system of upland cultivation is practiced on hill slopes in the middle elevations
(chapter 14). Fermented and cured tea are produced for the local market under several dif-

ferent land tenure and labor arrangements, primarily by people who identify themselves as Northern Thai. Their tea orchards usually start through selection of native tea plants growing wild in the area. Often the people cultivate subsistence rice swiddens to supplement cash income from tea, and raise cattle which they use to transport fermented tea to market or to a roadhead. They must cut substantial amounts of firewood, which is needed in tea processing; so their total land-use pattern includes cultivation of plantations and swiddens, maintaining grazing lands, and cutting firewood from the forest.

The communities are usually composed of people (or their descendants) who have moved out of the valleys, usually because of limited irrigable land and shortage of wage work opportunities in the lowlands. No comprehensive population figures exist for this type of population, but substantial numbers of people are involved, perhaps equaling the number of non-Thai "hill tribesmen" whose environment they share.

The effects of these systems on the environment, and their relationship to the lives and the livelihood of their practitioners are quite variable, and any generalization with respect to the upland cultivators in northern Thailand must take into consideration these variations. Nonetheless, we can say that in general the upland farmers are marginal to the national economy, are relatively poor, and have few sources of capital to promote their own economic development.

PRODUCTIVITY OF SHIFTING AGRICULTURE

Upland cultivation is probably inherently more variable in productivity than is irrigated agriculture because of variations in slope, aspect, and orientation of the hill fields, as well

as the uncertainty of rainfall. The accumulated data on swidden cultivation reveal tremendous variability in reported production. Climatic factors, soil type, state of soil fertility as related to vegetation type and length of time since previous cultivation, seed quality, cultivation techniques, insects and other pests have been offered as explanations, but available data do not yet allow a quantitative evaluation of the variability (table 1.2).

In Southeast Asia the reported range of rice production is from a low of 500–700 kg/ha among the Ma of South Viet Nam (Champsoloix 1960:50–53), or about 800 kg/ha among the Iban of Borneo (Freeman 1955), to a high of 4,500 kg/ha among the Rhade of Buon Kmrong Prong, on red soils in South Viet Nam (Maurice and Proux 1954), and up to 7,500 kg/ha projected from a small sample in Houei Khong, Laos (Bordsen 1968). Average yields in irrigated fields in Thailand are between 1,900 and 2,200 kg/ha, while in nonirrigated, rainfed fields, the average is between 630 and 940 kg/ha (Asian Development Bank 1969:160). The nonirrigated fields referred to here are probably mainly rainfed paddy fields, not hill fields. Our search of the literature, as well as the research reported in this book, indicated a range of from 814 kg/ha for Northern Thai farmers on frequently used soils in Nan Province (chapter 12) to 1,849 kg/ha for Yao farmers on good soil in Chiang Rai Province (Miles 1967).

Comparisons of production statistics from swidden farming and between swidden and irrigated agriculture are somewhat uncertain because so little effort has been devoted to standardized, repeated, large-scale measurements in swidden fields. Studies of production of shifting cultivation have used many different methods and a wide variety of units. In computing the entries of table 1.2, we have converted all pro-

TABLE 1.2 Productivity of Upland Agriculture*

Ethnic Group	Location	Rice Yield (kg/ha)				Source and Comments
		1st yr	2d yr	3d yr	4th yr	
BORNEO						
Iban		810				Freeman (1955:94–99)
Land Dyak		1,085				Geddes (1954:68)
LAOS						
Lamet	North Laos	1,335				Izikowitz (1951:287)
not stated	Houei Kong	3,550				Bordsen (1968:table 2) Mean of 10 locations; range: 1,000–7,500.
not stated	Sedone Province	4,340				Bordsen (1968:table 3) Mean of 7 locations; range: 2,620–6,820.
THAILAND						
N. Thai	Nan Province	814				Chapman (ch. 12)
Akha	Chiang Rai Province	840				Scholz (1969:96)
Skaw Karen	Mae Hong Son Province	959				Kunstadter (ch. 6)
Lua'	Mae Hong Son Province	1,032				Kunstadter (ch. 6)
Lahu Nyi	Chiang Mai and Chiang Rai Provinces	1,293				Walker (1970:494; 1976:181–182)
Pwo Karen	Mae Hong Son Province	1,464				Hinton (ch. 9)
Yao	Chiang Rai Province	1,849				Miles (1967:15)
SOUTH VIET NAM						
Jarai	Pleiku, Phu Bon	2,000–2,300	1,500	500–800		Lafont (1959:56, 1967:45–46) From forest.
		1,200–1,500	500–750			After 5–7 years fallow.

Group	Location					Source and notes
Koho (Ma and Cil)	Haut Donnai, Djiring Valley	over 1,500				Bertrand (1952:270) Ranges: 3,000 on good earth well cleared to 500 on poor earth sown late.
Ma	Bao Loc Plateau	1,500	1,500	800–1,000		Lafont (1967:45) From forest.
Ma	Blao Plateau	1,500				From shrubbery (first and only year). Boulbet (1966:87)
	Basaltic area	800–2,400	600–3,000			
	Alluvial plains	1,000–3,500				
Ma	South Tuyen Duc Province	500–750	600–700			Champsoloix (1960:50–53)
Rhade	Ban Me Thuot area	2,300	1,500–1,700	800–1,000		Lafont (1967:45) From forest, on basaltic, red earth soils. From secondary growth, black, sandy soils, rarely used 3 years.
Rhade	Ban Me Thuot area	1,500	1,000	600		Maurice and Proux (1954:195–196) Good year, average year, poor year.
Rhade	Buon Emap village, N of Ban Me Thuot	2,400–3,000	900–1,200			
	near Ban Me Thuot	1,500–2,250				
Rhade	Buon Aring, Buon Brieng, Buon Pok 25 km NE of Ban Me Thuot	2,500	1,700	1,000		Maurice and Proux (1954)
	Buon Puan, Buon Dang Kang, Buon Hang	2,500	1,667	833		Black and sandy soil.
	Red earth areas	2,783	3,333	2,500		Red earth.
	Buon Kmrong Prong	4,500	2,250	1,500		Black, sandy soil.
	Buon Kmrong Prong	3,000	2,250	1,500		Champsoloix (1960:58)
	Buon Ko M'Leo	880	920	840		From savanna.
	Buon Ko M'Leo	900	970	850	800	From secondary forest.

* Literature on agricultural production from South Viet Nam and Laos cited in this table was reviewed by Ms. N.D. Volk. See also Kalland (1976).

duction figures to kilograms per hectare. In Kunstadter's study of Karen and Lua' rice production (chapter 6 in this volume), rice production was measured by volume and converted to weight using 12.4 kilograms/*tang* as the average field weight of upland rice.[5] This figure was derived empirically and has been used in converting to weight the figures given by other researchers in bushels, gallons, and *tang*. The mean weight of rice varies with moisture content (wetter rice weighs more) and the variety and shape of the grain. Relatively short grained rice, such as that commonly grown by the Lua', weighs more per unit volume than does long-grained rice. Weight per *tang* will increase with packing. Weight also varies with the cleanliness and care with which empty grains have been winnowed out. Because of these variables it would be preferable to determine production in terms of weight, rather than volume, and to convert *field* weight to *standard* weight by determining moisture content of the rice as measured in the field.

In some cases, notably Yao (Miles 1967), Ma (Boulbet 1966), Rhade (Lafont 1967; Maurice and Proux 1954), and in Laos (Bordsen 1968), upland rice cultivation may be as productive per unit of cultivated land per crop as in many irrigated areas. In other cases (Lahu, as reported by Walker; Lua' and Karen, as reported by Kunstadter; Northern Thai in Nan, as reported by Chapman) shifting cultivation may yield only 35 to 40 percent as much rice per unit of cultivated land. When the fallow period is taken into calculation, annual productivity per unit of land may fall by as much as a factor of ten.

In general, upland cultivation requires more labor in a given year than does irrigated agriculture because of the difficulties involved in clearing and weeding, but irrigated agriculture requires a much higher initial investment in labor per unit of land because of the necessity to

clear, level, dike, and develop dams and ditches. Productivity of shifting cultivation per unit of labor probably goes down very rapidly as the quality of the land declines, since weeding is the task that consumes the greatest amount of labor, and the amount of weeding that must be done is proportional both to the number of weeds per unit area, and to the total area covered. This helps to explain why there is an upper limit on the amount of land used by any one family group for swiddening in a given year: with a given amount of labor, farming a larger area will not increase the total yield.

POPULATION AND ECONOMIC DEVELOPMENT

Two contrasting theories describe the relationship between population growth and economic development. Both assume the socioeconomic and demographic systems are closed. One of these theories states that population growth is a requisite for economic development and that pressure on the land forces development of more productive economic systems (Boserup 1965). The other, sometimes spoken of as the neo-Malthusian theory, holds that population grows as a result of economic development and that population growth and population pressure may hamper economic development, because gains in productivity are continually offset by demands of the expanding population and because expanding populations contain a larger share of dependents, since their age distribution contains a much higher proportion of very young people than does a nongrowing population. The theories in fact may not be contradictory. We find some support for both. For example, among the Lua' and Karen the development of small irrigation systems in the hills (learned from lowlanders) has apparently enabled these people to support larger hill populations than does an economy based exclusively on shifting cultivation. On balance, however, there is evidence that the standard of living of the upland people is declining as a result of population growth and that many hill villagers are forced out of the hills to seek wage work because of the poor economic conditions. Conversely, Keen (chapter 14) reports lowlanders are forced into the hills because of shortage of irrigated land. Evidently neither the socio-economic nor the demographic system is closed.

Economic conditions are deteriorating in many parts of the hills, both in subsistence and cash cropping areas, and in areas using all different types of swidden cycles. Scholz (1969), for example, in discussing the economy of an Akha village in Mae Chan District, Chiang Rai Province, indicates that upland rice is the villagers' main staple and has become their main cash crop as well. They have abandoned opium production in recent years because of the large amount of labor required for its production, the relatively low yield, and the poor quality of soil in the area where they live. They are unable to produce enough rice for subsistence, but nevertheless must sell a portion of their crop to purchase tools and other necessities—as well as opium. Meanwhile their population continues to grow. Oughton and Niwat (1971) discuss the increasing economic problems among *miang* (tea) growers in the Chiang Dao area of Chiang Mai Province, as indicated by the low return for labor, decreasing availability of land in the hills, and high land rents in the hills. In later chapters of this book Kunstadter and Hinton document increasing populations and declining productivity among Lua' and Karen hill swidden farmers in Mae Sariang District of Mae Hong Son Province, and Chapman describes the effects of and potential remedies for increased pressure on the land among lowland Northern Thai swiddeners in Sa District of Nan Province. Economic change has not kept pace with population growth in these areas of northern Thailand.

The prospects for control of population growth depend in part on the motivations for reducing family size. Under conditions of shifting cultivation it appears that some household heads desire to maximize their economic productivity by maximizing the amount of land they can appropriate and use. The chief limiting factor on the amount of land they can use is in the labor supply they can organize for such tasks as weeding. Therefore, they may desire to have the largest possible number of children as a potential labor force, or they may seek to enlarge the size of their households by adoption or the formation of extended families. Farmers with higher capital investment and limited land resources (as in intensive irrigated agriculture) may not feel the same need for large numbers of children. This might suggest that motivation for large families will persist in shifting cultivation communities as long as this form of agriculture is labor intensive (as contrasted with capital or energy intensive), and as long as land is treated as a somewhat free good, to be allocated among members of the community in proportion to need as determined by family size.

Land, of course, is not a free good, and even if it were an unlimited resource, use of the uplands would affect (through loss of watershed and soil erosion) the land resources at lower elevations. Thus the population planning motives of individual swiddening families may not be in harmony with the needs of people living in other ecological zones, or even with their own needs or the needs of their descendants.

POPULATION DYNAMICS OF SHIFTING CULTIVATORS

Settlements of shifting cultivators range in size from two or three households with 10 to 20 persons in a tiny Karen hamlet up to 200 to 300 households with a population of 1,000 to 1,500 persons in large Lua' villages, such as Baw Luang. The upper limit of size is apparently set by the distance to the fields, an especially important consideration when no transportation or pack animals are available.

In the hill areas that have been studied to date, the populations are characteristically young (median age between 16 and 17 years), with relatively high birth and death rates, and with rapid population growth or potential for it. Reproductive performance in a number of upland Lua' and Karen villages in Mae Sariang District was between 3 and 4.4 *surviving* children born to each woman of completed fertility, for an average doubling of population size each generation. These rates have evidently been sustained for several generations, even in the absence of modern medical care. Now that some of the major diseases (smallpox, cholera, malaria) are somewhat under control, the rate of population growth can be expected to increase (Kunstadter 1971).

MIGRATION OF SHIFTING CULTIVATORS

The traditional method of handling the problem of surplus population in villages of shifting cultivators has been village or household fission and migration. Migration has been of two sorts: temporary migration for wage work, and permanent resettlement. Resettlement has been in two directions: into relatively sparsely settled hill areas, and into valley communities. Migration within the hills has required no modification of existing technologies or social organizations. In the past most upland and foothill areas of Thailand have not been heavily populated, and relatively unused areas were available for new settlements. As a result of population increase, this is evidently no longer true in some areas (for example eastern Mae Sariang Dis-

trict), and some hill areas can no longer absorb the surplus populations they are producing. One "escape route," especially for Lua' hill people in the past, has been to the lowlands, but the rapid rate of lowland population increase may make it increasingly difficult to absorb migrants from the hills. When Lua' and other similar migrants have moved from the hills they have changed culture and rapidly assimilated themselves into Northern Thai society. Thus upland population growth is contributing directly to the growth of the lowland Thai population.

The problems of population in relation to technology and social organization are evidently quite different among the different upland groups. The upland Lua' and Karen have developed a relatively nondestructive balance between their subsistence technology and the land, but they have failed to solve the problem of population growth within their own village socio-economic system. In the absence of technological change, upland subsistence agricultural systems such as those of Lua' and Karen appear to be unable to accommodate and respond to labor surpluses with a comparable increase in productivity. The upland Lua' and Karen are already heavily engaged in wage labor for lowland employers. Some of the wage labor is actually done in the hills (lumbering, mining), but in these cases it involves nonrenewed or nonrenewable resources, and at this point it cannot be considered as a long-range economic solution to the problem of population surplus.

By contrast, the Hmong agricultural system, with its emphasis on cash cropping, evidently requires a larger labor supply than most Hmong families can produce. They attempt to make up for the deficit in labor by various devices calculated to increase the size of their families (extended families, plural marriage, and adoption),[6] and the systematic recruitment of labor. The Hmong system, with its dependence on opium as a major cash crop, even if it were morally or politically acceptable, is not balanced with respect to its use of land resources (chapters 10, 11). In the absence of technological improvements, it leads to persistent changes in soil or vegetation which make long term, permanent settlement impossible. Hmong settlements are forced to relocate periodically, leaving behind them areas which for a generation or more are no longer suitable for cultivation or forest regrowth.

ECONOMIC DEVELOPMENT IN THE NORTH

The expansion of population implies a need for the expansion of economic opportunities for those who have traditionally been engaged in swidden cultivation. Expanding the areas under cultivation does not seem to be the answer, since population increase will ultimately lead to degradation of soil resources as the length of the fallow period is shortened. Likewise, more labor-intensive shifting cultivation of the Hmong type does not seem to be the answer, for similar reasons. These considerations imply the necessity for technological and social change.

A number of schemes for economic development have been tried in northern Thailand and elsewhere, with varying degrees of success. Numerous attempts have been made to improve subsistence farming techniques through the introduction of improved strains of livestock, vegetables, and crop plants. The remarkable development of high yielding varieties of rice ("miracle rice") has had little direct effect on shifting cultivators for two reasons: no strains have been developed which are suitable for dry cultivation,[7] and those strains which have been developed for irrigated fields require technical knowledge and heavy investment in fertilizers and pesticides, which has not been practical for the vast majority of the impoverished shifting cultivators. High yielding varieties of maize have been introduced in some upland areas (e.g., Chiang Rai Province), but transportation and marketing difficulties limit the commercial success of these operations. Uncertainties of land tenure, the absence of cash for investment, the absence of credit, and the lack of transportation and marketing facilities will probably limit the effectiveness of any program designed to introduce improved strains of grain plants as cash crops into the shifting cultivation areas.

Cash cropping in the irrigated lowland areas has had spectacular success in many parts of the North, especially since the early 1960s. This has chiefly involved garlic, fruit trees, truck crops, peanuts, and tobacco. This has happened particularly in the area near Chiang Mai, and to some extent in all the northern provinces where tobacco has been fostered as a dry-season crop. The usual pattern has been for the tobacco companies to furnish seed, fertilizer, and instructions to the farmer and to guarantee to buy the crop at a fixed price. As a result, second-cropping of this "upland" (nonirrigated) cash crop has expanded rapidly, probably with an improvement in soil quality because of the fertilizer which the tobacco companies have provided in order to control the quality of the product. Because most tobacco is grown during the dry season, the expansion of this crop has helped to absorb the seasonal surplus of unemployed agricultural labor.[8]

Similar methods have not yet been tried with rice and have not been very successful when tried with maize. It seems unlikely that the success of the tobacco scheme could serve as a model for improving the production of subsistence crops, even in the lowland areas where marketing and transportation networks are available. To do so would require reorganization and reorientation of the rice marketing system in this area, which seems unlikely until the farm price of rice rises, or until the cost of improved rice production falls low enough to compete successfully in world markets which have already been affected by the "green revolution" (see Staub and Blase 1971). It seems even less likely that the model can be applied to the hill areas because of difficulties in transportation.

The major emphasis and the major expenditures in the public sector for agricultural development in Thailand in recent years have been for enlarged irrigation systems. These have been designed to subjugate larger areas and to make double- and triple-cropping possible in areas which previously could be irrigated only in the rainy season. These projects might be able to absorb some of the surplus population from the shifting cultivation areas, but to date they seem to have had little effect in this regard. Some of the dams that were built have actually made necessary the relocation of significant numbers of people from previously irrigated land which is now flooded, and forced some of them into shifting cultivation in the hills or into nonagricultural occupations in other areas. Unless they are designed specifically for relocation of upland cultivators, and unless steps are taken to see that people from marginal agricultural areas actually receive the newly irrigated land, the large-scale irrigation projects will have no beneficial effect for the forest farmers. Failure to consider the entire population of the watershed and drainage system which is being dammed is undoubtedly a shortcoming in the planning of these projects. Increased and unrelieved population pressure in the shifting cultivation areas will lead to increased erosion and increased silting problems behind the dams. Dams may have other ecological consequences for those living downstream: by removing silt before it reaches the fields, dams may be responsible for reducing the fertility of irrigated fields; the characteristics of the ecologically important

wetlands may be detrimentally affected; if fish ladders are not provided various species of fish may become extinct (already reported for several species in the Chao Phraya drainage); and the greatly reduced flow of rivers in the dry season may increase pollution problems.

Projects are now underway in Nan and Lampang provinces directed at the clearing, improvement, and assignment of permanent title of land used by lowland Thai shifting cultivators. The results of these projects are reported by Chapman and by Charley and McGarity elsewhere in this book. The techniques used have wide applicability on flat or gently sloping terrace lands which have been used by Northern Thai for slash-and-burn farming. Because permanent use of the land implies more intensive use, this system of clearing may offer temporary relief from the problems of expanding populations in the valley and foothill zones. Hill-tribe resettlement centers (e.g., Ban Pa Klang near Pua in Changwat Nan) have recently been established on such terrace land. On steeper slopes, however, development of this kind is much more costly and difficult to implement. On steeper slopes in areas of high-intensity rainfall (such as all northern Thailand), the risk of soil erosion necessitates close spacing of contour channels or absorption banks, or the construction of agricultural terraces. To the problem of the substantial cost involved can be added problems of unclear land titles and of administrative jurisdiction. Steeper land usually must be reclassified for legal cultivation (see chapter 3).

Nonagricultural economic development that has clear implications for shifting cultivators includes work in forestry and industrial development, especially mining. The lumbering industry in Thailand has traditionally been entirely extractive; only recently has attention been paid to development of superior strains of trees, to reforestation of cut-over areas, and to deliberate planting of lumber and pulp "crops." Chapter 16 discusses the success of some of these efforts, their implications as regards removal of land from swidden cultivation, and the ability (or inability) of these forestry industries to support equivalent populations through wage labor.

Observations in the Samoeng area of Chiang Mai Province[9] indicate some of the effects of mining on upland farmers. In the area of the Baw Keo mines, population density has been increased by the presence of wage labor opportunities, and much of the local irrigated or irrigable land has been spoiled for cultivation by deposition of the waste from hydraulic mining. This has increased the pressure on swidden lands by local farmers. The pressure on swidden lands is further increased by the high local price of rice, especially during the rainy season, as a result of poor transportation and marketing facilities. Thus local economic development and wage labor opportunities have brought, unintentionally, an accelerated rate of destruction of soil resources. When the mineral resources of the Baw Keo mines are exhausted in a few years' time, the agricultural resources probably will also have been completely devastated.

The development of agricultural processing and manufacturing industries in northern Thailand is only beginning. Although this has had some effect on the wage labor picture, we have few data on the effect of industrialization on the surplus population of forest farmers. Such anecdotal information as is available suggests that industries in the North may rely on labor recruited from Bangkok, the Central Plain, or other areas outside the North, especially for the more skilled jobs. Few forest farmers have the skills or the education to qualify them for industrial jobs, even if the recruitment networks were available to them.

Road building has often been considered a primary means of bringing development to remote areas. The building of roads into upland areas of the North has been followed rapidly by a series of changes, including the proliferation of local transportation systems, changes in settlement patterns, increases in land values along the roads, and movement into the hills by lowlanders able to capitalize on the improved access to upland resources. On balance, it is probably the lowlanders who have benefited the most from these changes, although improved transportation has aided upland farmers located close to a road in getting their products to market.

KNOWLEDGE NEEDED FOR DEVELOPMENT

One crucial dimension of the economic problems of upland cultivators is that of population. At present we have no adequate measure of the total population involved in swiddening and only a sketchy idea of its geographical distribution in northern Thailand. Studies done to date indicate that the population of forest farmers is multiethnic, large, and growing at least as fast as the urban or lowland rural population dependent on irrigated agriculture. Better estimates of the total population of forest farmers and their population dynamics (birth, death, and migration directions and rates) are needed for rational planning. Research is also needed to develop and test hypotheses, such as those mentioned above, regarding the relationships between household size, economic productivity, and motivations for family planning.

The total area under swidden cultivation is not known, nor is the average length of the cultivation cycle. This information, as well as knowledge of the trends in total area and cultivation cycles in the recent past, are vital for rational planning. Assessment of population and land areas affected is probably most rapidly and inexpensively estimated by examination of existing aerial photographs, perhaps supplemented by new photographs of selected areas, combined with sample surveys made on the ground to determine length of fallow cycle and size of households. The basic methodology for such a study has been worked out by the National Statistical Office in the study of opium production undertaken for the UNESCO Division of Narcotics between 1964 and 1967 (United Nations Survey Team 1967:54–55), and has been used successfully in some upland areas of Laos for estimating population size and agricultural potential.

PROBLEMS OF SWIDDEN LAND TITLE

Control of land is basic to any agricultural system. Secure title to land is essential for any agricultural development which requires external financial assistance. The Northern Region contains almost 90,000 sq km of land, of which only 0.33 percent (300 sq km) had land certificates in 1967, while 11 percent had "land possession" registration (see chapter 3 for definition of these types of titles), and the remaining 89 percent was considered "forest, wasteland and other." The Northern Region figures for land certificate and land possession are the lowest for any region of Thailand (Royal Thai Survey Department 1969:8.2), and reflect both the mountainous nature of the area and the fact that much of the agriculture there is swidden cultivation. The large portion of the North which is customarily used for swidden cultivation is not recognized in the land registration system. Thus, under ordinary circumstances upland cultivators cannot proceed through the several stages of application, registration, and survey to insure their title to the land which they use.

Judge Sophon Ratanakhon has done invaluable service in describing the legal obstacles facing forest farmers if they should desire to stabilize their system of land tenure and land use

(chapter 3). Thai land law assumes as "normal" the individually held, annually cultivated, irrigated or fixed field agriculture in lowland areas not covered by forests. Apparently the authors of the law wanted to discourage what they assumed to be the destructive features of upland cultivation. Perhaps they were thinking only of the type we have described as "long cultivation–very long fallow," and did not recognize the legal rights, or even the existence in large numbers, of settled swiddeners who use a regular rotation system of cultivation and fallow.

Thus land law conflicts at many points with the traditional land-use and land-tenure systems associated with various kinds of shifting cultivation. When the current land law was passed in 1954, holders of untitled land had the opportunity to register their possessions, but few if any swidden cultivators did so. Villagers might have the legal right to organize themselves as "self-help" or "cooperative" communities, and seek title to their communally held lands, but apparently this was not done except in the case of government-sponsored settlements *(nikhom)*. The overall effect of the land laws (chapter 3), together with the forestry laws (chapters 4, 5), is to place virtually all swidden cultivators in violation of the law and subject to punishment, with little legal recourse to protect their traditional claims vis-à-vis other claimants or the government. Their rights are limited by the fact that their occupation of the land is probably illegal and not under protection of the government.

It is unlikely that any capital-intensive developments in shifting cultivation areas can become widespread until the question of land titles is clarified. The lack of clarity of title combined with increased population pressure is likely to increase instability of the shifting cultivators and to increase the frequency and violence of conflicts over land claims. Any capital-intensive developments will also depend on the development of agricultural credit and marketing systems appropriate to the upland environment.

Agricultural developments in the shifting cultivation areas must combine readily marketed cash crops with higher yielding subsistence crops, land-intensive cropping systems, and marketing and transportation facilities. Any one of these by itself will not solve the problems of increased population and relative decline in standard of living of the shifting cultivators. Even with extensive agricultural development, it is unlikely that this growth alone will be able to handle the economic and demographic problems of the region in the near future. The area will also need expanded wage-labor opportunities and recruitment networks coordinated with educational and training programs (cf. Staub and Blase 1971:122).

NOTES

1. This type of farming is now commonly designated in scientific literature as "swidden cultivation" (swidden: a cleared and burned field). The term "shifting cultivation" has the connotation, often untrue, of nomadism, for which reason the term "forest fallow," or the more neutral term "swidden," may be preferable. The Thai term *rai* and its Northern Thai cognate, *hai*, refer to unirrigated fields. In this book *rai* is reserved to designate the Thai unit of land measurement, equivalent to 0.16 hectare.

2. Throughout this book, the people referred to in popular and some earlier scientific literature as "Meo" and "Miao" are designated "Hmong," the term now becoming standard in scientific usage, and which is also the term the people prefer to use for themselves.

3. Conklin's distinction between "partial" and "integral" swidden systems and their subtypes is not followed here because people of any one community or ethnic group may engage in several different types, depending on availability of resources. The emphasis in our classification is on method of use of resources.

4. This description of the "Hmong system" is based largely on Kunstadter's observations and discussions with Karen, Lua', and Hmong informants in Mae Sariang and Mae Chaem districts. For other views of the Hmong see Geddes (1970, 1976) and chapter 11 in this book. For a description of the similar Lahu Nyi cultivation system see Walker (1970; 1976).

5. Lua' rice was well cleaned and dried when weighed. It was poured into a standard Thai *tang* measure (20 liters) and smoothed off at the top with a section of bamboo, according to the standard practice.

6. Methods of expanding household size among the Yao, especially through adoption of outsiders, are detailed by Kandre (1971) and Miles (1973).

7. The potential for developing high yield strains of upland rice may be limited since rice is apparently very dependent on adequate water supply for maximum yield.

8. Since large amounts of wood are required as fuel for drying the tobacco, the total ecological impact of tobacco growing is not clear.

9. Made by David H. Marlowe in 1967 (personal communication).

2

The Environment of Northern Thailand

Tem Smitinand
Sanga Sabhasri
Peter Kunstadter

Northern Thailand is that portion of the nation which juts northward from the great Central Plain. The hills of the North form the water catchments that provide the water to irrigate the nation's main rice producing area. Region Five, the administrative division of the North, contains the provinces *(changwat)* Mae Hong Son, Chiang Mai, Chiang Rai, Nan, Lamphun, Lampang, Phrae, and Uttaradit. The census definition of the North adds the provinces Kamphaeng Phet, Nakhon Sawan, Phetchabun, Phichit, Phitsanulok, Sukhothai, Tak, and Uthai Thani, which border on or extend into a region that geographically belongs to the Central Plain.

MOUNTAINS AND RIVERS

The area is one of hills and mountains with relatively narrow valleys. The Phi Pan Nam mountains and the Mekong River form a natural boundary along the frontier with Laos. The Thanon Thong Chai and Tanaosee ranges comprise the western frontier. The mountains and valleys of northern Thailand extend southward along the Burma border into Tak, Kanchanaburi, and

Ratchaburi provinces, and farther into the Isthmus of Kra, separating the large Chao Phraya plain draining into the Gulf of Siam from the Salween and Irrawaddy drainages of Burma to the west.

The headwaters of several major rivers are in the mountains and hills of the North. Watersheds are defined by the four north-south parallel mountain ranges known collectively as the Phi Pan Nam range. The Mae Kok in Chiang Rai province and the Mae Ing in Lampang, rising on the northern slopes of this range, flow northward into the Mekong on the Laos border. The Pai and Yuam rivers in Mae Hong Son, and the Mae Moei in Tak originate on the southern and western slopes of the Phi Pan Nam range and drain into the Salween River of Burma. The Ping, Wang, Yom, and Nan rivers, which begin on the southern and eastern slopes, are the main tributaries of the largest and longest river that is entirely in Thailand, the Chao Phraya. This is the major water resource of Thailand, feeding the rice bowl of the Central Plain. The Ping is the largest of the four tributaries, and its drainage includes several main branches, such as the Mae Taeng, Mae Faek, Mae Chaem, Mae Ngad, Mae Nam Li, and Mae Nam Tun.

The Ping River plain is the widest and longest relatively flat zone, while the other river basins are narrow and elongated. Elevations of the valley floors vary from 150 meters to 380 meters above sea level. Mountains of all the headwaters, especially to the west of the Ping valley and east of the Nan valley, are rugged. Limestone massifs in Chiang Mai and Lampang form scenic landscapes with barren, craggy ridges and many caves. Several peaks range from 1,500 to almost 2,600 meters. The highest peak in Thailand, Doi Inthanon (2,590 meters) lies to the west of the Ping, southwest of Chiang Mai. The highest peak in the northernmost portion of Thailand is Doi Pha Pok (2,296 meters). Doi Luang Prabang (2,115 meters) lies near the Laotian border to the east. A major karst exists in the Chiang Dao area.

The rolling hills between the major rivers are usually deeply cut by streams. Plateaus, in the true sense of the word, are not found in northern Thailand. Besides the major valley plains of the Ping, Wang, Yom, and Nan rivers, there are several small intermontane basins, especially in the western part of the region. Eroded terrace lands are found on the margins of many of the valleys. Construction of the Bhumiphol Dam at Sam Ngao in Tak Province has made the upper reach of the Mae Ping, from Ban Na in Tak to Hot in Chiang Mai Province, into a reservoir covering about 316 sq km. The dam now forms the northernmost point of wet-season river navigation from the sea.

SOILS

The largest part of the North is covered with rocks of the Kanchanaburi series of Silurian, Devonian, and Carboniferous age. There are smaller north-south bands of Triassic granites, plus small outcroppings of Ratchaburi limestones of Carboniferous and Permian age. The western portion of the North contains some of the Korat series of Triassic and Jurassic sedimentary and metamorphic rock, with small pockets of mafic and ultramafic gneiss and schist, and in the valleys, Quaternary alluvium and terrace deposits.

Mountain soils are generally dominated by red-brown podzolic soils and reddish brown lateritic soils. The Pai and Ping northern headwaters consist of steep land with some limestone crags and red-brown earth. The mountain soils of the Yuam drainage, on acid to intermediate rock, are mainly shallow red-yellow podzolic types. However, the lower-lying portions drained by the Yuam have red-yellow podzolic soil on old alluvium. Such soil is well drained, clayey and loamy, low in base, and low in fertility.

A variety of soil types is found in the valley plains of the Chao Phraya and Mekong tributaries. In the Ping, Nan, Kok, and Ing valleys, the soils near the rivers are alluvial, poorly drained, and clayey, with high to moderate fertility. Low-humic gley soils, mostly loamy and sandy, are found commonly in the Ping, Wang, and Yom valleys. Common to all valleys are old alluvium, red-yellow podzolic soils. Undifferentiated soils of lava and volcanic rock are found in the Wang and Yom valleys. Gray podzolic soil on old alluvium is scattered in the plains of the Ping, Wang, and Yom. Red-yellow podzolic soils on residuum and colluvium, formed from acid rocks, and of low fertility are occasionally found along the foothills. Maps of the distribution of soils and climate may be found in the resources atlas prepared by the Royal Thai Survey Department (1969).

Local variations in soil type are of crucial importance in upland agriculture, and upland farmers select the sites for their fields on the basis of subtle differences. Clayey soils may retain more water than sandy ones, allowing swidden crops to survive longer and better during a dry spell in the monsoon. Because opium thrives in limestone soils, opium growers seek even tiny pockets of limestone soil and have developed methods for keeping them in production for many years (see chapter 11).

CLIMATE

The monsoonal climate of the region is characterized by a distinct rainy season, with the peak of precipitation in July, August, and September, followed by a cool dry and then a hot dry season, ending with the return of the southwest monsoon rains in May or June. Rainfall is heavier in the mountains. The valleys, especially those at the northern margin of the Central Plain, are in a rain shadow. Lowland annual rainfall averages between about 1,200 and 1,700 mm, but the lowest annual minimum rainfall recorded in Thailand was at Tak in 1951, which had only 546.5 mm. Temperatures of the North represent the extremes for Thailand. The lowland absolute minimum of 0.1°C was recorded in Loei in January 1955, and the absolute maximum of 44.5°C was recorded at Uttaradit in April 1960. No upland weather stations have been in operation long enough to accumulate substantial records, but frost has been reported during the winter in the mountains, especially at levels above 1,500 meters.

The general pattern of the monsoon rain is regular, but precipitation may be spotty and the onset of rains is uncertain, varying by as much as a month or more. Thus, although irrigation is almost always assured downstream from large catchment basins, rainfed paddy fields, swiddens, and even irrigated fields in small upland valleys are subject to major variations in availability of moisture. This in turn makes production from these fields more variable and riskier than in the irrigated lowlands.

POPULATION

The total population of Thailand in 1970 was estimated at 34,397,374 in an area of 514,000 sq km, yielding an average density of 67 persons per sq km.[1] The 16 provinces grouped in the northern region for statistical purposes (table 2.1) had a total of 7,488,683 persons and an area of 170,009 sq km, for an average density of only 44 persons per sq km, that is, about a fifth of the nation's population in about a third of its area.

The reason for the relatively low density is the mountainous terrain of much of the North. Most of the population is concentrated in the valleys along the main rivers. Rural population distribution is very uneven, ranging from 2 persons per sq km in Um Phang, a hilly district in southwestern Tak Province, to 804 persons per sq km in Dok Kham Tai district, a small, intensively cultivated valley area in southern Chiang Rai Province. Population density in the mountains is generally below 25 persons per sq km, and is least dense in the mountainous western districts of Tak and Mae Hong Son provinces, which are inhabited primarily by ethnically non-Thai swidden farmers.

Annual national population growth between 1960 and 1970 is estimated from census data at 2.70 percent, while annual growth in the North was about 2.69 percent. Population growth was uneven within the area. Eleven provinces (Chiang Mai, Lampang, Lamphun, Mae Hong Son, Nakhon Sawan, Nan, Phichit, Phrae, Sukhothai, Tak, Uthai Thani, and Uttaradit) fall below the regional average. The highest annual growth rates of the region were in two provinces which are predominantly lowland and which border on the Central Plain (Kamphaeng Phet

TABLE 2.1 Population Size, Density, and Growth in Northern Thailand, 1960–1970

Northern Province	Area (sq km)[a]	Population 1960[b]		Population 1970[c]		1960–1970 Increase	Average Annual Increase (%)
		Total Number	No. per sq km	Total Number	No. per sq km		
Chiang Mai	22,991	798,483	35	1,026,450	45	227,967	2.51
Chiang Rai	18,809	811,771	43	1,111,607	59	299,836	3.14
Kamphaeng Phet	8,955	173,346	19	339,862	38	166,516	6.73
Lampang	12,518	471,699	38	583,378	47	111,679	2.12
Lamphun	4,408	249,820	57	310,836	71	61,016	2.19
Mae Hong Son	13,222	80,807	6	104,160	8	23,353	2.54
Nakhon Sawan	9,679	647,602	67	758,891	78	111,289	1.59
Nan	11,693	240,471	21	310,734	27	70,263	2.56
Phetchabun	11,165	319,611	29	524,791	47	205,180	4.96
Phichit	4,530	389,122	86	440,460	97	51,338	1.24
Phitsanulok	9,655	351,642	36	491,886	51	140,244	3.36
Phrae	5,848	299,369	51	365,509	63	66,140	2.00
Sukhothai	6,841	315,948	46	402,342	59	86,394	2.42
Tak	15,610	167,992	11	217,021	14	49,029	2.56
Uthai Thani	6,471	145,504	23	177,644	27	32,140	2.00
Uttaradit	7,614	259,919	34	323,112	42	63,193	2.18
Northern Total	170,009	5,723,106	34	7,488,683[d]	44	1,765,577	2.69
Thailand Total	514,000	26,257,911	51	34,397,374	67	8,139,463	2.70
Percent in North	33.08	21.80		21.77		21.69	

[a] Changwat-Amphoe Statistical Directory, Department of Local Administration, USOM, and National Statistical Office, Bangkok, 1965.
[b] Thailand Population Census 1960, Whole Kingdom, Table 1: "Total Population by Sex and Number in Population of Agricultural Households for Changwad and Region" (Thailand, Central Statistical Office, National Economic Board, 1962).
[c] 1970 Population and Housing Census, Thailand.
[d] The census reported that province figures for Nakhon Sawan, Phetchabun, and Phitsanulok provinces were incomplete at the time of Changwat tabulations; thus the total given for the northern regions is too low by more than 7,500.

and Phitsanulok), and in three provinces on the region's northern and eastern periphery (Chiang Rai, Nan, and Phetchabun). Some of this growth, especially in Kamphaeng Phet and Phetchabun, has resulted from migration from nearby provinces, as well as from the Central Plain and the Northeast. In some places, notably Nan Province, the population growth and shortage of irrigable land has forced large numbers of lowland ethnic Thai into supplementary or even permanent swiddening in the hills surrounding the few narrow valleys. The lowest estimated provincial growth rate in the region is reported for Phichit Province. Forest farming in northern

Thailand is associated with both low and high population density, and both ethnic Thai and non-Thai populations.

The degree of urbanization of the region is less than 6 percent as judged from the proportion of people living in administratively designated "municipalities." The only municipalities of population over 30,000 are Chiang Mai (83,729), Nakhon Sawan (58,751), Lampang (40,000), Chiang Rai (34,273), and Phitsanulok (33,883).

Ethnically and historically, only Chiang Mai, Lamphun, Lampang, Phrae, Mae Hong Son, Chiang Rai, and Nan provinces are considered

TABLE 2.2 Ethnic Minority Populations in Northern Thailand, 1972

Province	Ethnic Group										Total	Percent of Province Population
	Karen	Hmong	Lahu	Lisu	Yao	Akha	Lua'	Htin	Khmu'	Other		
Chiang Mai	59,904	7,125	7,646	4,412	395	305	5,279	–	–	–	85,066	8.3
Chiang Rai	1,982	6,557	5,870	3,080	14,712	9,611	132	–	–	825	42,769	3.8
Kamphaeng Phet	377	1,024	–	85	–	–	–	–	–	–	1,486	0.4
Lampang	2,437	560	113	2,453	–	–	–	–	–	–	5,563	1.0
Lamphun	12,262	–	–	–	–	–	–	–	–	–	12,262	3.9
Mae Hong Son	41,598	956	1,905	2,060	2,191	–	2,570	–	–	–	49,089	47.2
Nan	–	5,280	–	–	–	–	–	23,397	4,153	–	35,021	11.3
Phrae	5,749	–	–	–	–	–	–	–	–	–	5,749	1.6
Tak	28,328	5,806	855	574	–	–	–	–	–	–	35,563	16.4
Total	152,637	27,308	16,389	12,664	17,298	9,916	7,981	23,397	4,153	825	272,568	3.6

SOURCE: Directory of tribal villages in Northern Administrative Divisions: Chiang Mai, Chiang Rai, Kamphaeng Phet, Mae Hong Son, Nan, Lampang, Lamphun, Phrae, Tak. September 1972.

truly "northern." Although Central Thai is the standard dialect and is commonly used in administration and education, Northern Thai is still spoken at home, especially in rural areas, and local traditions reflect a past which included rule by local princes and occasional contact or conquest by principalities in Burma, the Shan States, and Laos.

The ethnic composition of the region is complicated by the presence of sizeable Central Thai and Chinese populations in urban places and market centers, and by non-Thai minorities ("hill tribes") mainly in the higher elevations (table 2.2). The largest minority is Karen, who live both in the lowlands and the hills and practice both swidden and irrigated subsistence rice farming. Lua' live in similar environments and have a similar economy, as do many Htin and Khmu'. Hmong (Meo), Lahu (Musser), Lisu (Lisaw), Yao (Iu Mien), and Akha (Ikaw), who live mostly in the hills and are almost entirely swidden farmers, supplement their subsistence cropping of maize and rice with cash crops, especially opium.

The hill tribe population was estimated in 1972 at 272,568, or about 3.6 percent of the region's total population (these figures exclude Phetchabun, Phitsanulok, and Uttaradit provinces, where no census of hill people has been taken). The upland minorities are concentrated in Chiang Mai (85,066), Mae Hong Son (49,089), and Chiang Rai (42,769) provinces. In some hill regions, like Um Phang District of northern Tak Province, "tribal" population is over 90 percent of the total. Mae Hong Son is the province with the highest estimated proportion of hill tribes in the North (47.2%).

TRANSPORTATION

Public transportation in northern Thailand includes bus, railroad, and air service. There is airplane service several times daily between Bangkok and Chiang Mai, and twice weekly to Mae Sot, Mae Hong Son, and Chiang Rai. A railway line of about 130 km connects Phrae, Lampang, and Lamphun with Chiang Mai, and joins with the main line leading from Bangkok to Phitsanulok. Daily express trains run in each direction between Bangkok and Chiang Mai, and a daily local train operates between Phitsanulok and Chiang Mai. Buses operate several times daily on the all-weather highway from Chiang Mai to Bangkok, making the almost 800-km trip in under 12 hours. Trunk roads of the North connect to all-weather highways from Chiang Mai, Chiang Rai, Mae Sariang, and Nan to the Central Plain. Lowland areas in the North are linked with frequent inexpensive buses which carry an ever-increasing load of passengers and even daily commuters from rural to urban areas. Local roads traversable by bullock carts in the dry season, and trails suitable for horses, elephants, and bearers link remote areas to the trunk roads. Nevertheless, some hill areas north, northeast, and northwest of Chiang Mai are nearly inaccessible in the wet season. The Ping, Wang, Yom, and Nan are generally navigable downstream, but upstream travel is possible only on the Ping.

The hill areas of the North have never been truly isolated from trade centers. For centuries caravan routes linking lowland towns of Thailand and Laos have crossed these hills, but until the development of rail and auto routes, the costs of transportation, except along the major river courses, were too high to allow profitable long-distance trade in bulky commodities. Highways crossing the hills have been an important stimulus to the development of trading and administrative centers in the valleys in recent years, and have encouraged the rapid exploitation of previously hard-to-reach lumber and mineral resources. Bus, minibus, and truck transport, often organized by small-scale entrepreneurs, becomes available as soon as a passable track has been created, and with trucks comes a profusion of manufactured goods. Because the road network is still poorly developed in the hills, it has had only localized and limited impact on agricultural development. For the most part it is still uneconomic to transport bulky low-value commodities from widespread places of production in the hills. With the exception of lumber, for which processing and marketing networks exist, no attempt has been made to reach dispersed resources with motorized transport.

FOREST TYPES OF NORTHERN THAILAND

The forest types of northern Thailand may be classified into two main categories, evergreen and deciduous, with further subtypes associated with differences in altitude, soil, rainfall, and land use. Details of the species distribution within the forest subtypes are listed in the following summary (most of the species mentioned below are illustrated by Pham Hoàng Hô 1970, 1972). The general pattern of distribution of the types is shown in figure 1.1.

There are three types of evergreen forests in northern Thailand: the Lower Montane, Coniferous, and Dry Evergreen forests.

The Lower Montane forest occupies the elevations from 1,000 meters upward, where annual rainfall is 1,500 to 2,000 mm, and there is constant high humidity. Tracts of this forest type still exist in the upper elevations of the mountains between Mae Sariang and Chiang Mai, and between Chiang Mai and Tak on red granitic or brown-black calcareous soils. Where a continuous closed canopy is found, it suggests the primary nature of this forest type.

The Lower Montane forest is two-storied. The upper story is composed of oaks, false chestnuts, laurels, birch, and others. Wherever the false chestnuts *(Castanopsis)* and birch *(Betula)* become dominant, they indicate the impact of man. These can be seen at Doi Suthep, west of Chiang Mai, where five species of *Castanopsis* have been identified, while the birch is now becoming dominant on the higher slopes. At Phu Langka, Chiang Rai Province, another false chestnut *(Castanopsis fissas)* forms a dense stand on the deserted cultivation grounds. The lower story consists of laurels and other species.

Shrubs of several genera are abundant. Herbaceous species form a rich ground flora. There are several genera of bamboos and a rich representation of ferns. Lianes are relatively infrequent.

Epiphytes are abundant on trees. Besides mosses, liverworts, and lichens, there are numerous epiphytic ferns and orchids. There are also a number of epiphytic shrubs.

Sphagnums are found in boggy areas at high altitudes. In the region where the summits and ridges are open and exposed, the vegetation is sparse, recalling a subalpine type of forest, with a number of temperate genera.

The Lower Montane forests are almost unusable as a source of economically valuable species because of lack of transportation. There are many valuable timber trees, but to date systematic exploitation has not been possible. Minor forest products have been collected on a small scale.

The Coniferous forest is an edaphic type which usually occupies steep slopes and exposed ridges subject to extensive erosion and leaching, on either grayish sandy, or brownish gravelly, and sometimes lateritic soils (photo 1). The annual rainfall is usually about 1,000 to 1,500 mm. It is a three-storied and rather open forest. The upper story is composed of the two-leaved pine *(Pinus merkusii)* and the three-leaved pine *(P. kesiya)*. The middle story is formed of oak and false chestnuts, together with other ever-green species. At lower elevations the middle story is mixed with dipterocarps. The lower story is formed of small trees and tall shrubs. (Photo 1.)

Ground flora is varied and mainly composed of tall grasses and a variety of herbaceous species.

The two species of pines occurring in the Co-niferous forest have been placed on the list of species reserved for purposes of national eco-nomic development: the two-leaved pine for oleo-resin, and the three-leaved pine for pulp and paper. Resinous pine wood is gathered lo-cally for torches and kindling.

The Dry Evergreen forest is found in scattered areas along the depressions on the peneplain and in humid valleys of the low hills, or forming galleries along streams and rivulets. The soil is either granitic or calcareous loam. Annual pre-cipitation ranges between 1,000 and 2,000 mm. Except where they occur in valleys between low ranges of hills, the present Dry Ever-green forests are remnants of a luxuriant and ex-tensive forest which once covered the peneplain. (Photo 2.)

The Dry Evergreen forests are three-storied. The upper story consists of *Anisoptera oblonga*, *A. costata*, and a number of dipterocarps and other species. The middle story is composed of *Chaetocarpus castanocarpus*, *Euphoria lon-gana*, and several other species. The lowest story contains smaller-statured trees of the genera *Aglaia*, *Amoora*, and others.

There are scattered palms and sparsely grow-ing bamboos. Lianes are abundant. Epiphytic orchids and ferns occur sporadically. Strangu-lating figs such as *Ficus altissima* and *F. drupacea* are frequent.

The dense undergrowth is composed of mem-bers of the ginger family, ferns, and a number of other plants.

Forests of this type are more accessible, and timber trees are occasionally exploited. "Eagle wood," caused by fungus attack on *Aquilaria crassna*, is seldom collected because of the scar-city of the tree. Bamboos and rattans are sources of building materials for the local inhabitants.

The Deciduous forests are of three types: Moist Mixed Deciduous, Dry Mixed Deciduous, and Dry Deciduous Dipterocarp forests.

The Moist Mixed Deciduous forest usually is confined to the higher elevations up to 600 meters above sea level. This is a three-storied forest which usually grows on loamy soil of either calcareous or granitic origin, where an-nual precipitation is between 1,000 and 1,500 mm. (Photo 3.)

The upper story contains teak, *Lagerstroemia tomentosa*, and many other species. The second story includes *Mitragyna brunonis*, *Premna tomentosa*, and many other species. The lower story is composed of *Cratoxylon cochinchi-nense*, *Mallotus philippinensis*, and several other species.

A few palms are scattered through this forest. Shrubs of several genera also occur. Lianes are scattered, bamboos abundant.

Epiphytes are less abundant; they include or-chids, epiphytic ferns, and other types.

The ground flora is composed of herbaceous species, *Kaempferia*, *Curcuma*, and others.

The Dry Mixed Deciduous forest is generally scattered in both lower and higher elevations, on sandy loam or lateritic colluvial soil. Annual precipitation is between 600 and 1,000 mm. (Photo 4.)

The upper story of this two-storied forest con-tains teak, *Xylia kerrii*, and several other species. The lower story contains *Dalbergia ovata*, *Millettia brandisiana*, and other species. Shrubs include species of *Memecylon*, *Helic-teres*, and other genera.

Bamboos are scattered. The ground flora is similar to that of the Moist Mixed Deciduous forests, but species of *Crotalaria, Desmodium,* and several other genera are also prominent.

Epiphytes, including ferns, orchids, and others, are frequent. Along ridges at elevations between 300 and 500 meters, the forests are more open because of high evaporation, excessive exposure, extensive surface erosion, and much leaching of the soil. Here xerophytic species are found scattered.

The ground flora in this forest type is subject to annual ground burning.

Mixed Deciduous forests have great economic value because many commercial species are abundant. Cutting and exploitation of these species is under government control. In addition, a number of other plants are used locally and marketed for food, medicine, bark (chewed with betel), manufacture of joss sticks, caulking, construction, etc.

The open, two-storied *Dry Deciduous Dipterocarp forest* (photo 5) derives its name from the fact that the predominant species belong to the family Dipterocarpaceae. This forest type is found on the undulating peneplain and ridges, where the soil is either sandy or lateritic and has been subject to extreme leaching and erosion, as well as annual burning. These conditions create a climax type of vegetation in which dipterocarps and other fire-resistant species prevail.

The upper story includes dipterocarps, *Quercus kerrii,* and *Melanorrhoea usitata.* The second story is composed of low shrubby trees including *Strychnos nux-vomica, S. nux-blanda,* and others. Generally, the height of trees in the upper story is between 20 and 25 meters, but only 15 to 20 meters in arid places.

The ground flora consists largely of tuber- and rootstock-bearing species, because of the selective effects of fire, and includes small bamboos, as well as members of herbaceous genera and others. *Dillenia hookeri* is common and forms clumps of low bushes.

Epiphytes are common in the Dry Deciduous Dipterocarp forests and include epiphytic ferns, orchids, and others.

In some localities the soil is podzolic, the forest floor is subject to inundation during the rainy season, and the annual plant community thus developed consists of species of *Eriocaulon, Habenaria, Spathoglottis,* and *Drosera.*

The Dry Deciduous Dipterocarp forests are also important in the regional economy. Even though there are relatively few marketable species as compared with the other deciduous forest types, trees in these forests are able to coppice freely, and thus their regeneration and availability for fuel are assured.

Commercial timber trees include the dipterocarps. Besides being used for construction, *Dipterocarpus tuberculatus* and *D. obtusifolius* provide an almost inexhaustible supply of commercially valuable firewood. *Melanorrhoea usitata* is the source of lacquer, an essential component in lacquer-wear manufacture, but its latex is very poisonous, causing dermatitis.

FOREST TYPES OF NORTHERN THAILAND

LOWER MONTANE (MOIST EVERGREEN) FOREST

Elevation: Above 1,000 m

Soil Types: Red granitic or brown-black calcareous

Location: Higher parts of western ranges of northern Thailand

Annual Rainfall: 1,500–2,000 mm, high humidity in undisturbed forest

Structure: Two-storied, dense

UPPER STORY

Trees. False chestnuts *(Lithocarpus, Castanopsis),* oaks *(Quercus),* laurels *(Cinnamomum, Neolitsea),* birch *(Betula alnoides),* and others—*Calophyllum,*

Carallia brachiata, Cephalotaxus griffithii, Fraxinus excelsa, Lophopetalum wallichii, Michelia rajaniana, Nyssa javanica, Paramichelia baillonii, Podocarpus neriifolia, Sapium baccatum, Schima wallichii, Toona ciliata

LOWER STORY

Trees. Laurels (*Lindera, Phoebe, Litsea, Machilus*), and others—*Anneslea fragrans, Ternstroemia japonica*; also *Abraema clypearia, Camellia confusa, Carpinus viminea, Elaeocarpus ganitrus, Engelhardia spicata, Garcinia speciosa, Gordonia dalglieshiana, Helicia nigilarica, Prunus arborea, P. cerasoides, Pyrenaria camelliflora, P. garrettiana, Rhododendron delavayi, R. moulmainense, Rhus rhetsoides, Sladenia celastrifolia, Symingtonia populnea, Symplocos henscheli, Tristania rufescens, Ulmus lanceifolius, Vaccinium sprengelii*

Shrubs (abundant). *Daphne, Wikstroemia,* and *Cornus, Cycas, Embelia, Maesa, Melastoma, Osbeckia, Osyris, Rapanea, Rhamnus*

Lianes (infrequent). *Gnetum montanum, Mucuna collettii*

Bamboos. *Melocalamus, Teinostachyum,* and *Dinochloa, Gigantochloa, Pseudosasa, Schizostachyum*

Palms. *Caryota urens, Livistona cochinchinensis, Phoenix humilis, Pinanga, Trachyspermum speciosum*

Ferns (abundant). *Athyrium, Asplenium,* and *Angiopteris, Blechnum, Bolbitis, Brainea, Cyathea, Dicranopteris, Dryopteris, Nephrolepsis, Osmunda, Phymatodes, Plagiogyria, Polypodium, Pteridium, Taenitis, Thelypteris, Woodwardia*

Tree Epiphytes (abundant)

Mosses: *Acrocrypheae, Brothera, Dicranoloma, Fissidens, Homaliadelphus, Papillaria, Rhynchostegiella, Rhynchostegium, Solsiella, Symblepharis,* etc.

Liverworts: *Bazzania, Calolejeunea, Chiloscyphus, Frullania, Herberta, Mastigobryum, Ptychanthus, Schistochila, Thysananthus,* etc.

Lichens: *Anaptychia, Arthonia, Arthopyrenia, Bacidia, Buellia, Catillaria, Graphis, Lecidea, Leptogium, Pannaria, Pertusaria, Pyxine, Ramalina, Sporopodium, Sticta, Usnea,* etc.

Epiphytic Ferns (numerous): *Drynaria, Crypsinus*

Orchids: *Dendrobium, Eria,* and *Armodorum, Bulbophyllum, Coelogyne, Cymbidium, Drymoda, Neogyne, Oberonia, Pleione, Porpax, Vanda*

Shrub Epiphytes. *Agapetes hosseana, A. parishii, A. variegata, Gaultheria crenulata, Hoya engleriana, Vaccinium ardisioides, Wightia speciosissima*

GROUND FLORA

Herbs. *Aneilema, Anoectochilus, Anthogonium, Asystasia, Boesenbergia, Calanthe, Catimbium, Curcuma, Forrestia, Globba, Habenaria, Hedychium, Liparis, Malaxis, Ophiorrhiza, Phajus, Pollia, Rungia, Streptolirion, Strobilanthes*

MODIFICATIONS AND SUBTYPES

Undisturbed primary forest type—portions with closed canopy

High altitude boggy areas—sphagnums

Open exposed summits and ridges—sparse vegetation resembling subalpine forests, containing temperate zone genera such as *Asparagus, Bupleurum, Ceratostigma, Circaea, Clematis, Cotoneaster, Delphinium, Gentiana, Geranium, Hypericum, Iphigenia, Iris, Kalanchoe, Lilium, Mahonia, Parnassia, Pedicularis, Primula, Ranunculus, Rhododendron, Saxifraga, Sedum, Selinum, Seseli, Silene, Sophora, Spiraea, Viola*

Areas disturbed by man—false chestnuts (*Castanopsis*) of several species including *C. fissa,* and birch (*Betula*) become dominant

ECONOMIC VALUE

Because of lack of transportation there has been little use of lumber from such valuable species as *Cinnamomum siamense, C. tamala, Michelia rajaniana, Lophopetalum wallichii, Calophyllum floribundum,* and oaks and false chestnuts; minor forest products are collected for trade or local use including the tannin-rich bark of *Quercus brandi-siana*, bamboos, rattans, and the nuts of *Castanopsis acuminatissima, C. tribuloides*, and *C. diversifolia* which are sold in lowland markets.

NOXIOUS SPECIES

Relatively few; include stinging nettle tree *(Dendrocnide basirostrata)* and several stinging nettles including *Laportea bulbifera* and *L. interrupta*; the latex of *Antiaris toxicaria* is reputed to be toxic and is locally used to poison darts.

CONIFEROUS FOREST

Elevation: Varies; this is an edaphic type which usually occupies areas subject to extensive erosion and leaching

Soil Types: Grayish sandy or brownish gravelly, sometimes lateritic

Location: Steep slopes and exposed ridges

Annual Rainfall: 1,000–1,500 mm

Structure: Three-storied, open

UPPER STORY

Trees. *Pinus merkusii* (two-leaved pine), *Pinus kesiya* (three-leaved pine = *P. khasya* = *P. ensularis*)

MIDDLE STORY

Trees. Oaks *(Quercus)*, false chestnuts *(Lithocarpus, Castanopsis)*, and other evergreens—*Anneslea fragrans, Schima wallichii*

LOWER STORY

Small trees and tall shrubs. *Phoenix humilis, Cycas pectinata*, and *Adinandra, Craibiodendron, Embelia, Lyonia ovalifolia, Maesa, Rhododendron, Styrax rugosum, Vaccinium bracteatum, Vaccinium sprengelii*

Epiphytes

Orchids: *Bulbophyllum, Coelogyne, Dendrobium, Eria*

Others: *Dischidia, Hoya, Usnea*, etc.

GROUND FLORA

Grasses. Tall grasses such as *Thysanolaena maxima* and *Themeda triandra*, and other grassy species including *Capillipedium assimile, Eulalia birmanica, E. phaeothrix, E. siamensis, Hyparrhenia fusca, Microstegium vagans, Panicum montanum, Polytoca wallichiana, Setaria lutescens, Themeda arundinacea*

Herbs. *Gentiana* and *Swertia*, and other genera including *Eriocaulon, Habenaria, Herminium, Lobelia, Osbeckia, Polygala, Polygonum, Spathoglottis*

MODIFICATIONS, SPECIAL SUBTYPES

At lower elevations middle story contains dipterocarps including *Dipterocarpus, Shorea, and Pentacme.*

ECONOMIC VALUE

Two-leaved pine is important to the national economy as a source of oleo-resins, and three-leaved pine as a source of pulp and paper; resinous pine wood is gathered locally for torches and kindling; *Schima wallichii* is rarely used despite its good lumber because of raphides in its bark and wood.

DRY EVERGREEN FOREST

Elevation: In depressions of the peneplain (300 m) and valleys of low hill ranges (500–1,000 m), and on either side of streams and rivulets

Soil Types: Granitic or calcareous loam

Location: Scattered in depressions in the peneplain, in humid valleys and low hills

Annual Rainfall: 1,000–2,000 mm

Structure: Three storied

UPPER STORY

Trees. *Anisoptera oblonga, A. costata*, dipterocarps and other species including *Acrocarpus fraxinifolius, Afzelia xylocarpa, Ailanthus triphysa, Alstonia scholaris, Antiaris toxicaria, Dipterocarpus alatus, D. costatus, D. macrocarpus, D. turbinatus, Holoptelea integrifolia, Hopea odorata,*

Lagerstroemia ovalifolia, Pterocymbium tinctorium, Shorea talura, S. thorelii, Tetrameles nudiflora

MIDDLE STORY

Trees. *Chaetocarpus castanocarpus, Cinnamomum iners, Diospyros brachiata, D. mollis, Euphoria longana, Irvingia malayana, Mangifera caloneura, M. sylvatica, Sapium insigne, Spondias pinnata, Vatica cinerea*

LOWER STORY

Trees and Shrubs. *Aglaia, Amoora,* and other smaller trees and shrubs including *Albizzia, Alchornea, Aporusa, Baccaurea, Celtis, Cleistanthus, Crataeva, Dillenia, Elaeocarpus, Eugenia, Holigarna, Knema, Macaranga, Mallotus, Melodorum, Memecylon, Millettia, Mitrephora, Pterospermum, Tarenna, Terminalia*

Palms (scattered). *Calamus, Areca,* and *Didymosperma, Livistona, Wallichia*

Bamboos (sparsely growing). *Bambusa, Dendrocalamus, Gigantochloa*

Lianes (abundant). Include *Phanera, Lasiobema,* and *Acacia, Artabotrys, Congea, Desmos, Derris, Entada, Gnetum, Hymenopyramis, Pisonia, Securidaca, Strychnos, Tetrastigma, Toddalia, Uncaria, Uvaria, Ventilago*

Epiphytes (occurring sporadically).

Orchids: *Aerides, Bulbophyllum, Coelogyne, Cymbidium, Dendrobium, Eria, Oberonia, Rhynchostylis, Sarcanthus,* etc.

Ferns (occurring sporadically): *Asplenium, Davallia, Dryania, Humata, Pyrrhosia,* etc.

Strangling Figs (frequent): *Ficus altissima, F. drupacea, F. microcarpa, F. maclellandii*

GROUND FLORA

Dense growth, including such members of the ginger family as *Curcuma, Boesenbergia,* and others such as *Alpinia, Catimbium, Ctenolophon*

Ferns. *Helminthostachys, Lygodium, Thelypteris,* etc.

Others. *Tacca, Strobilanthes,* and *Barleria, Capparis, Clausena, Crotalaria, Desmodium, Lourea, Micromelum, Moghania,* etc.

HISTORY

Except in valleys between low ranges of hills, these are remnants of extensive luxuriant forest which once covered the peneplain and has now been largely cleared for agriculture.

ECONOMIC VALUE

Timber is extracted from *Mangifera caloneura, M. sylvatica* (wild mangoes which also yield edible fruit), *Dipterocarpus* spp., *Hopea odorata, Anisoptera costata, A. oblonga, Vatica cinerea, Acrocarpus fraxinifolius, Toona ciliata,* and others; "eagle wood" caused by fungus attack on *Aquilaria crassna* is rare, but taken when found; bamboos and rattans are important sources of building materials.

NOXIOUS SPECIES

Similar to lower montane forest; in addition, leaves and flowering *Scleropyrum wallichianum* are reported to be highly toxic.

MOIST MIXED DECIDUOUS FOREST

Elevation: Above lowlands, up to 600 meters
Soil Types: Granitic or calcareous loam
Annual Rainfall: 1,000–1,500 mm
Structure: Three storied

UPPER STORY

Trees. *Tectona grandis* (teak), *Lagerstroemia tomentosa,* and *Acacia leucophloea, Adenanthera pavonina, Adina cordifolia, Afzelia xylocarpa, Albizzia chinensis, A. lebbek, A. procera, Anogeissus acuminata, Bombax anceps, B. insigne, Chukrasia velutina, Dalbergia cultrata, D. oliveri, Dillenia pentagyna, Gmelina arborea, Millettia leucantha, Pterocarpus macrocarpus, Terminalia bellerica, T. tripteroides, Xylia kerrii*

MIDDLE STORY

Trees. *Mitragyna brunonis, Premna tomentosa,* and *Albizzia lucida, Barringtonia racemosa, Callicarpa arborea, Careya arborea, Colona flagrocarpa, C. floribunda, Combretum quadrangulare, Cordia dichotoma, Diospyros montana, Ehretia laevis, Grewia microcos, Millettia brandisiana, Terminalia calamansanai, T. triptera, Vitex canescens, V. peduncularis, V. pinnata*

LOWER STORY

Trees. *Cratoxylon cochinchinense, Mallotus philippinensis,* and *Bauhinia racemosa, Casearia grewiaefolia, Croton hutchinsonianus, C. oblongifolius, Gardenia coronaria, G. obtusifolia, Piliostigma malabarica*

Shrubs. *Croton, Mallotus,* and *Bauhinia, Harrisonia, Memecylon, Premna, Randia*

Palms (scattered). *Calamus, Phoenix humilis*

Lianes (scattered). *Hymenopyramis brachiata, Congea tomentosa,* and *Artabotrys siamensis, Butea superba, Dalbergia rimosa, Desmos chinensis, Lasiobema horsfieldii, Phanera bracteata, Spathologium parviflorum*

Bamboos (abundant). *Dendrocalamus membranaceus, D. strictus,* and *Bambusa tulda, Cephalostachyum pergracile, Dendrocalamus longispathus, Gigantochloa albo-ciliata, G. nigrociliata*

Epiphytes

Orchids: *Dendrobium, Rhynchostylis,* and *Aerides, Ascocentrum, Bulbophyllum, Coelogyne, Cymbidium, Sarcanthus*

Ferns: *Platycerium, Drynaria*

Others: *Hoya, Dischidia*

GROUND FLORA

Grassy and herbaceous genera. *Capillipedium, Sporobolus,* and *Andropogon, Bothriochloa, Eragrostis, Hyparrhenia, Oryza, Reynaudia, Saccharum, Themeda, Thysanolaena*

Others. *Kaempferia, Curcuma,* and *Aristolochia, Boesenbergia, Brachycorythes, Carex, Ceropegia, Cyperus, Fimbristylis, Habenaria, Hibiscus, Pecteilis, Peristylus*

ECONOMIC VALUE

Teak and other valuable timber species are taken from this forest type.

DRY MIXED DECIDUOUS FOREST

Elevation: Scattered in higher and lower elevations
Soil Types: Colluvial, sandy loam or lateritic
Annual Rainfall: 600–1,000 mm
Structure: Two-storied

UPPER STORY

Trees. *Tectona grandis* (teak), *Xylia kerrii,* and others, including *Acacia leucophloea, Albizzia lebbekoides, A. procera, Bombax albidum, Dalbergia bariensis, D. cultrata, D. dongnaiensis, D. nigrescens, Dialium cochinchinensis, Lagerstroemia balansae, L. calyculata, L. macrocarpa, Pentacme burmanica, Pterocarpus macrocarpus, Shorea talura, Spondias pinnata, Terminalia alata, T. bellerica, T. chebula, T. corticosa, Xylia xylocarpa*

LOWER STORY

Trees. *Dalbergia ovata, Millettia brandisiana,* and others, including *Casearia grewiaefolia, Croton oblongifolius, Diospyros ehretioides, Grewia paniculata, Mallotus philippinensis, Phyllanthus embilica, Pterospermum semisagittatum, Strychnos nux-vomica, Vitex limonifolia*

Shrubs. *Memecylon, Helicteres*

Others. *Clerodendrum, Evodia, Grewia, Indigofera, Lespedeza, Micromelum,* etc.

Bamboos. *Bambusa spinosa, Gigantochloa albo-ciliata, Thyrostachys siamensis*

Epiphytes.

Orchids: *Aerides, Coelogyne, Dendrobium, Sarcanthus*

Others: *Dischidia, Hoya*

GROUND FLORA

Crotolaria, Desmodium and others, including *Barleria, Borreria, Brachycorythes, Clitoria, Derris, Eragrostis, Euphorbia, Hedyotis, Lygodium, Selaginella, Setaria, Uraria, Zornia*

MODIFICATIONS AND SPECIAL SUBTYPES

Along ridges between 300 and 500 meters, the forests are more open due to high evaporation, excessive exposure, extensive surface erosion, and much leaching of the soil; under these conditions xerophytic species are found such as *Dipterocarpus obtusifolius*, *D. tuberculatus*, *Pentacme siamensis*, *Shorea obtusa*.

SPECIAL CONDITIONS

Ground flora subject to annual ground fires

ECONOMIC VALUE

Great potential because of abundance of commercial species, including teak, *Xylia kerrii*, *X. xylocarpa*, *Pterocarpus macrocarpus*, *Lagerstroemia* spp., *Anogeissus acuminata*, *Afzelia xylocarpa*, *Dalbergia cultrata*, *D. oliveri* (rosewood), *Adina cordifolia*, and many others; bark of *Terminalia tripteroides* and *Pentacme burmanica* is collected for local consumption; mucilage-yielding bark of *Machilus* sp. is collected for a basic component in manufacture of joss sticks and for caulking coffins; ropes and cordage are made locally from fibrous bark of *Sterculia* sp.; fruits of *Terminalia chebula* and *T. bellerica* are collected for medicine and sold in urban markets; bamboos, including *Bambusa tulda* and *Dendrocalamus membranaceus*, are used in construction and wicker work; *Derris elliptica* is used locally as an insecticide and sold in the market, *D. scandens* is collected for medicine

NOXIOUS SPECIES

Scleropyrum wallichianum, *Trichosanthes bracteata* (seeds of which are highly poisonous), cow-itch (*Mucuna pruriens*) which irritates the skin, *Aphanamixis polystachya*, all parts of which are poisonous and cause vomiting

DRY DECIDUOUS DIPTEROCARP FOREST

Elevations: 300–1,000 m
Soil Types: Sandy or lateritic, subject to extreme leaching, erosion and annual burning

Location: On undulating peneplain and ridges
Annual Rainfall: Under 1,000 mm
Structure: Two storied, open upper story and low shrubby lower story

UPPER STORY

Trees. *Dipterocarpus obtusifolius*, *D. tuberculatus*, *Melanorrhoea usitata*, *Pentacme siamensis*, *P. suavis*, *Pterocarpus macrocarpus*, *Quercus kerrii*, *Shorea obtusa*

LOWER STORY

Trees. *Strychnos nux-vomica*, *S. nux-blanda*, and *Aporusa villosa*, *Canarium subulatum*, *Dalbergia kerrii*, *Diospyros ehretioides*, *Phyllanthus emblica*, *Symplocos racemosa*
Epiphytes.
  Ferns: *Drynaria*, *Platycerium*
  Orchids: *Aerides*, *Eria*, and *Ascocentrum*, *Bulbophyllum*, *Dendrobium*, *Sarcanthus*
  Others: *Dischidia minor*, *D. rafflesiana*, *Hoya kerrii*, *H. pachyclada*

GROUND FLORA

Chiefly tuber and rootstock-bearing species including small bamboos such as *Arundinaria pusilla* and *A. ciliata*, and vines, shrubs, and other low-growing species such as *Enkleia malaccensis*, *Linostoma persimilis*, *Phoenix acaulis*, *Pygmaeopremna herbacea*
Others: *Habenaria*, *Pecteilis*, and *Curcuma*, *Dillenia hookeri*, *Decachistia*, *Hibiscus*, *Kaempferia*

MODIFICATIONS AND SPECIAL SUBTYPES

Where the forest floor is subject to inundation during the rainy season and the soil is podzolic, the annual plant community consists of *Eriocaulon*, *Habenaria*, *Spathoglottis*, *Drosera*.

ECONOMIC VALUE

The Dry Dipterocarp forest has few trees of commercial importance as compared with the Dry Mixed Deciduous forest, but because trees are able to coppice freely, they are a continual source of firewood and their regeneration is perpetuated; commercial timber trees include *Dipterocarpus tuberculatus* and *D. obtusifolius* (both of which also supply firewood for railways, tobacco curing barns, and distilleries), *Shorea obtusa*, and *Pentacme suavis*; *Melanorrhea usitata* is the source of lacquer; *Shorea obtusa* yields dammar used for boat caulking; seeds of *Strychnos nux-vomica* are the source of strychnine and have been collected for export.

ECOLOGICAL EFFECTS OF SHIFTING CULTIVATION

The effect of shifting cultivation on the promotion or suppression of grasslands as secondary climax vegetation apparently depends on details of the cultivation methods, especially the length of continuous cultivation. One system, the long cultivation–very long fallow type (Hmong system), apparently promotes the development of grasslands, while what we have called the short cultivation–short fallow (Northern Thai) and the short cultivation–relatively long fallow (Lua' and Karen) systems appear to suppress the development of grasslands, or at least to allow the repeated development of forest or bush as secondary successions.

The Hmong and Sino-Tibetan-speaking peoples practice intensive agriculture at higher elevations, usually over 1,000 meters above sea level. They are traditionally maize and opium growers, and some grow dry rice only as a supplementary crop. After clearing and burning the forest, these people use the land intensively, often by growing two annual crops, maize and opium, on the same site during the same growing season for three to five years or more in succession, depending on local soil conditions. In addition to direct effects of the crop plants, clean cultivation exposes the soil throughout the year to solar radiation and to wind and rain which cause erosion and leaching. Soils on slopes are also subject to deep hoe cultivation, which makes subsurface nutrients available to crop plants, but which may increase the danger of erosion. Repeated weeding and burning tends to eliminate species which ordinarily go to make up the secondary growth in less intensively used areas, and uncontrolled grazing by farm animals intensifies this effect. As the cultivated area spreads, sources of seed are removed farther and farther from the now-abandoned original areas of cultivation, which, through lack of seed, repeated burning, and grazing, cannot reestablish their original forest cover (see chapter 11). When soil fertility is exhausted and the forest has become a grassland, the cultivation site is abandoned. Eventually, when all nearby land has been used, the villagers move to a new area where virgin forest or mature second-growth forest is available, and the process will be repeated.

The pattern of secondary growth associated with this system can be described roughly as follows. After the first year of two-crop cultivation, the fields will be covered with *Eupatorium odoratum*, interspersed with tall grasses such as *Thysanolaena maxima*, *Hyparrhenia rufa*, *Eulalia birmanica*, and *Themeda arundinacea*, together with seedlings of pioneer tree species, including *Albizzia chinensis*, *Engelhardia spicata*, *Garuga pinnata*, *Macaranga denticulata*, *Mallotus barbatus*, and a number of coppices from any remaining trees cut in the original clearing process.

The plots are kept under fairly continuous cultivation from the beginning of the rainy season in June through well into the dry season in December, when the opium crop harvest begins. When the first-year secondary growth is cut and burned, the soil does not receive much organic material as compared with the amount received after virgin forest or mature secondary growth has been burned prior to cultivation.

Most of the coppicing stumps and seedlings of pioneer species are killed in the second consecutive year of burning or by clean weeding and stump removal. *Eupatorium odoratum* is still prevalent after the second year, but begins to yield to Cogon or *kha* grass *(Imperata cylindrica)*, a hardy, fire-resisting species (photo 6).

After the third year of cultivation, *Imperata* is well established, and begins to supersede *Eupatorium*. There is less chance for any seedling of pioneer species to survive or become established, and coppicing stumps have all been dug out or killed by fire. As the site is subject to annual ground fire resulting from uncontrolled burning of areas adjacent to the cultivation sites, the pioneer species never have a chance to survive and become established. Only *Imperata* survives luxuriantly because of its underground rhizomes matted deeply in the soil. This grass completely bars any shallow-rooted species from the site, and a persistent grassland is formed.

The middle altitudes, above the valley floor and below about 1,000 meters, are populated by the Karen and Mon-Khmer-speaking peoples such as the Lua', and by Thai people, who are primarily subsistence rice growers (chapters 6, 9). These people grow only a single annual crop of dry rice in their swiddens, interplanted with a number of vegetables and root crops. After each season of cultivation they leave the site fallow for 5 to 10 years, following a more or less regular pattern of field rotation. To achieve this, the burning of slash on the cultivation site is under careful control, and fire is prevented from spreading into fallowed areas.

Because the crops are grown for a single year, the soil is directly exposed to solar heat, wind, and rain for only a short period. Harvest is completed at the end of the rainy season in November, and the fields are not weeded after early September. There is less erosion and leaching than under the more intensive system of land use, and the soil nutrients are better conserved. After harvest the land is covered with *Eupatorium* and grasses of the same species as occur in the maize-opium fields, together with seedlings of the pioneer tree species *Melia azedarach, Garuga pinnata, Mallotus philippinensis, Macaranga indica,* and other coppices from stumps.

If fires are kept out of the fallow fields, within 5 to 10 years pioneer species and coppices form a dense secondary growth canopy, suppressing *Eupatorium, Imperata,* and other grasses. Thus soil resources are conserved, plant nutrients are brought above the surface, and the secondary growth can be used repeatedly with the simple technology of forest fallow cultivation (see appendix to chapter 8 for details of species succession).

FIRES AND THEIR EFFECTS ON FOREST AND WATERSHED

During the period from February to May (before the monsoon rains begin), many fires in mountain forest and upland farming areas in northern Thailand are ignited for purposes *other than cultivation.* The extent of the burning is such that in February 1968 the authors observed that the forest floor all along the Chiang Mai–Mae Sariang highway was completely burned. Visibility is often poor, as smoke spreads over the region and there is little air movement or rain to disperse or precipitate the haze. Airplane flights are occasionally canceled into airports such as Chiang Rai and Mae Hong Son owing to poor visibility. Forest fires on the hillsides which appear to burn continuously can easily be seen at night during most of the burning season. Most of these appear to be deliberately set. Hunters burn the underbrush to drive out wild animals. Cattlemen burn off the forest floor to encourage regrowth of grass. Mushroom pickers burn, and then wait for the mushrooms to grow when the first rains come. Travelers who use trails in the forest sometimes start fires out of carelessness or loneliness, or in order to get rid of thorny bushes that block their way.

Fires can be beneficial as well as destructive to the forest. Destructive results are common in forested areas when the inner bark of trees is burned, increasing their susceptibility to insects and disease. Burning will greatly increase soil and water losses, especially if the forest floor is burned repeatedly. Forest soil in areas that are frequently burned is easily eroded and degraded, and it often becomes unstable (Komkris et al. 1969). On the other hand, controlled burning is a good practice for site preparation, and it converts nutrients which are tied up in vegetation to useable form for new growth. It assists in getting rid of slash, which under some conditions may pose a hazard for forest crown fires. Ground fires also may burn off grasses and weeds that compete with forest trees for soil moisture and nutrients. Furthermore, burning may be required for the germination of seeds of some fire-resistant tree species, and may favor the selection of some valuable species, such as teak.

Soil stability is essential to protect the watershed area so that soil moisture will be maintained and waterflow regulated in wet and dry seasons. Tall forest trees and an abundance of forest-floor vegetation maintain soil stability when the forest is undisturbed. Once the forest cover is removed, erosion and loss of storage capacity may soon take place.

Shifting cultivation and fire, no matter what its origin, have an impact on soil stability, which in turn affects the watershed. Degrees of erosion and of loss of water storage capacity, however, vary with the type of shifting cultivation and burning practices. It is incorrect to state that shifting cultivation causes no problems to watershed areas. It is also not true that all shifting cultivation seriously damages streamflow. The pattern of secondary growth must be taken into account. Where regrowth turns out to be of the grassland type, evaporation from the soil surface will be high (Sabhasri et al. 1968), the vegetation is less effective in conserving soil, and runoff will be more rapid (Sabhasri and Ruengpanit 1969).[2] The result is too much water in the wet season and too little in the dry season.

In an area that is farmed with the short cultivation–long fallow system, with a fallow period of at least seven years, a series of regrowth conditions will be found according to the points in the cultivation-fallow cycle which have been reached by the different plots. The area as a whole faces little erosion, and the effect on runoff is minimized. If the land is used for several years in succession, soil fertility and stability are depleted. The forest trees cannot regenerate, and the forest cover is replaced by grass, which results in more rapid runoff during the rainy season and decreased streamflow in the dry season.

NOTES

1. Unless otherwise specified, population figures presented in this section are based on published 1970 census figures (Thailand, n.d., 1970 Population and Housing Census). Land areas are based on unpublished data for 1970 from the Department of Local Administration, Ministry of the Interior.

2. This discussion does not involve water loss through transpiration, which is higher with forest cover than with grassland.

PART II

INSTITUTIONAL CONSTRAINTS ON FOREST FARMING

Introduction

Peter Kunstadter

The following three chapters deal with legal and administrative aspects of the setting within which forests are used in Thailand. Together they indicate the dilemma of those who have sympathy both for the traditional cultivators of forest farms and for Thailand's needs to preserve forest, soil, and watershed resources essential to life in the lowlands.

Judge Sophon Ratanakhon discusses the legal limitations placed on land use and land ownership in forested areas. As we have suggested in chapter 1, these laws seem inappropriate to the condition of the vast majority of upland farmers in northern Thailand today. Apparently these laws were designed by lowlanders who assumed that irrigated rice farming in the valleys was the normal and desirable form of agriculture; that individual holdings and permanent, continuous land use were essential to proper farming; that there was sufficient irrigable land in Thailand for all who needed it; and that upland and forested regions were a national resource to be protected as a source of essential raw materials, as a source of foreign exchange, as a means of protecting water and soil resources which are essen-

tial to irrigated agriculture, and as esthetic and recreational assets of the entire Kingdom. As we shall see in later parts of this book, swidden agriculture is normal for many people, and this implies temporary, sometimes cyclical patterns of agricultural land use, coupled with extensive use of uncultivated products in the uncultivated or fallow forest. For many upland farmers land is a communally held good, to which use-rights are granted by virtue of membership in the community (among the Lua' and Karen as described in chapters 6 and 9 by Kunstadter and Hinton, and among the Northern Thai as described in chapter 12 by Chapman); for others it is a free good, available for the taking if it is not occupied at the moment as among the Akha, described by Kickert (1969), and among the Hmong (Meo) as described by Geddes (1970, 1973, 1976), and by Keen (1966) and in chapter 11 of this volume; or it may be some combination of these extremes, where anyone within the community may use land within the communally held territory not presently claimed by anyone else, as among the Yao described by Miles (1967). Those uplanders who have treated land as a free good have assumed that the purpose of the forest was to supply fertile sites for farming, and wood for construction and fuel, with little regard to the effects of their cultivation on conservation of resources for themselves or for their downstream neighbors. They have assumed that there was sufficient unoccupied swidden land for all who might need it, if not in the immediate vicinity, then somewhere in the next range of mountains. Their villages have often been temporary assemblages of households which split and coalesced depending on the local availability of land.

Those villagers who have considered land as a community resource generally recognize the function of forest regrowth in restoring soil fertility, and have practiced conservation measures which have allowed them to maintain communities settled within the same territory for many generations. They consider that their village territory is bounded, and know they and their descendants will have to live within it in the future. The land and forest laws of Thailand recognize no difference between these types of land tenure and land use, despite the obvious difference in resource conservation.

So long as there was plenty of land there was little conflict between those who held different legal or customary concepts of land tenure and forest land use. In fact, as former Director-General Dusit (chapter 4) and the late Dean Thiem (chapter 5) indicate, the forestry laws have often been ignored or circumvented, or at best only rarely and sporadically enforced. With rapid population increase, conflicts are inevitable, both between lowland Thais and hill peoples, and between different groups of hill people who may have completely different concepts of land ownership and who have no peaceful and systematic way of resolving their differences. Judge Sophon suggests that the laws either be enforced or (as that will be difficult at best) modified to suit existing conditions, so that the obvious disparity between law and the actual behavior of farmers in the forest will not lead to contempt for the law in all contexts.

Dusit Banijbatana, formerly Director-General of the Royal Forest Department, describes two kinds of attempts to deal with the need to increase productivity in the forests: the *taungya* system of teak cultivation, in use for many years, and the pine plantation system being developed in the Baw Luang Plateau, about 100 km southwest of Chiang Mai. Both systems are land-extensive. The *taungya* system allows production of subsistence crops by the workers, but involves a 50-year or longer rotation cycle before the teak is harvested and the workers are allowed to clear and cultivate again for one or two years. Thus it seems ill adapted to areas of high population density. The pine plantation system involves the intention to supplement or replace subsistence swiddening with wage work, in cultivating pine trees for the pulp industry. It remains to be seen whether the local inhabitants who are losing their fallow swidden lands to the plantation will receive adequate compensation in the form of paying jobs to allow them to maintain or improve their level of subsistence.

Thiem Komkris, the late Dean of Faculty of Forestry at Kasetsart University, has developed a philosophy of multiple use for forested hill land, recognizing the needs of the local population to support themselves, and simultaneously recognizing the dangers in continuing uncontrolled swiddening in areas where population pressure is too great to allow adequate regeneration of the forests and protection of the watershed.

3

Legal Aspects of Land Occupation and Development

Sophon Ratanakhon

Much of land in the northern provinces of Thailand, especially that of the forests and the hills, is not permanently occupied or developed. This so-called waste-land is regarded as public domain, property of the State. Agriculture in this area is largely swidden cultivation, practiced on hills and mountains, without irrigation systems and fertilization.

Swidden cultivation in the North gives rise to many legal problems which do not occur where stabilized farming is practiced on valley land which is "properly" occupied and developed. Occupation of land on hills and mountains is not normally permitted by law. Occupation of the "waste-land" or the degradation of the condition of land without license is illegal. Occupation or destruction of forest is a crime. Felling trees in forest areas without official government permission is subject to legal punishment. The presence of the non-Thai "hill-tribe" peoples, whose legal status may be uncertain, further complicates the matter.

SOME PRINCIPLES OF LAND LAW AND LAW OF PROPERTY

Concepts of land possession and land ownership must be distinguished. The basis of Thai Land Law is that all land in the country belongs to the King, or in the modern sense, to the State. Land can be divided roughly into two types: land with document of title (*cha-node*), and land without document of title. The first type consists of plots which have been developed, and usually is found in cities, towns, or some long-settled portions of rural districts. The government surveys such plots, fixes their boundaries, and records them in the Registration Book. This kind of land can be privately owned. All legal transactions concerning this kind of land must be conducted in the form prescribed by law and must be recorded in the official Registration Book. The records also appear on the document of title which is held by the landowner. By this registration, the amount of the land, its present and former owners, and other important information about it can easily be checked. This makes the land more valuable.

In theory, these plots of land still "belong" to the King, who grants ownership to citizens. Owners of such land enjoy full rights over it—the same rights as over their other property—with the exception that the State may take it back, with appropriate compensation, for public utilities or for national security.

The other type of land is simply that for which document of title has not been issued by the government. This may be because the land has not been occupied or developed—the so-called wasteland. It may be because legally the government cannot permit it to be occupied or to be owned by anyone, as is the case with reserved land, protected forests, and hill land. It also includes land already occupied and developed, but for which the government is not ready to make a survey and issue the document of title. Generally, land without document of title cannot be privately owned; that is, no one but the State can *own* it.[1] The occupant of such land has only the right of possession, which is legally inferior to true ownership.

According to the general rule of the Law of Property, a person acquires the possessory right of anything by holding it with intention to keep it for himself.[2] By this rule a person may obtain the possessory right in land by the fact of his physical control over the land with intention to exclude other people from that land. For example, a man may gain possession of land by clearing forest for some purpose of his own, such as building a house, growing rice, or raising cattle. Once he has possession of the land, if he is disturbed or deprived of possession by unlawful interference by another individual, he can take legal action within one year to remove the disturbance or to recover the possession of the land.[3] The right of possession will remain as long as the person holds the property with the intention of keeping it, but it ceases if the possessor no longer intends to possess, or when he no longer holds the property, for example, when a farmer leaves his land permanently for a new site.

A person who maintains that he has possession of a piece of land has to prove that two conditions have been fulfilled: the occupation of the land, and the intention to hold the land for himself and not for any other person. By contrast, a person who owns a piece of land with document of title has not only the right of possession but also the ownership of the land. He is presumed by law to be the owner of the land, and it is up to any person who challenges his right to prove to the contrary.[4] The ownership is also permanent in the sense that the owner may leave the property without losing the right in it. Land without document of title can be the subject of only the possessory right, and cannot be transferred by conveyance (for example, by legal sale), except by way of inheritance.[5] However, such land may be transferred by the ordinary method of handing over the land by the transferror to the transferree, and if the latter holds the land with intention of keeping it for himself, then he acquires possession of the land by virtue of the Law of Property.[6]

One who legally occupies land without document of title is usually given a license to hold it by the land authority. The license is not a document of right, but it is prima facie evidence that the holder of such a license holds the land. If the licensee occupies the land and develops it, he will be awarded a "land certificate of development." This means that the land authority recognizes the occupant's right of possession in the land. He can thereafter transfer his land by conveyance and can register legal transactions concerning his land. Eventually, he will be given a "land document of title" when the government is ready to issue such document. Legally, a land document of title is significant in two ways. It shows that private land ownership is recognized by the government, and the person whose name appears on the document is presumed to be the legal owner of such land. On the other hand, occupation of land is illegal if it is conducted without license of land authority, or if occupation of that land is prohibited by law (as in reserved forests). Illegal occupation will never be recognized by the government; the occupant will never obtain a government document to certify his legal right in the land, and he may also be faced with eviction and criminal charges for trespassing on land of the State. However, with regard to disputes between citizens, one who holds land with intention to keep it for himself, even if it is illegal, may still have some right of possession in the land according to the Law of Property, which enables him to exclude all unlawful interference by private persons.

THE ACQUISITION OF LAND
FOR CULTIVATION

Only a small proportion of the agricultural land in the North has document of title (see page 22). Some parts have not been occupied or developed, and some are not allowed by law to be occupied. The usual purpose of occupation of such land is for swidden cultivation, and only the acqustion of land for this purpose will be discussed.

The above rules of law for acquiring possessory rights in land without document of title have been modified in the Land Code. The code recognized the possessory land rights existing at the time the code came into force[7] only if the occupant of the land had notified the district officer of his occupation of the land within the 180-day time limit prescribed by the code. Persons who

failed to do so were deemed by law to have intended to relinquish their possession of the land.[8]

By the code, a person who has neither the right of possession nor permission from a land officer is forbidden to hold or occupy forest land. Whoever violates or fails to comply with the said provision shall be fined up to 500 *baht*.[9] Under the present law a person can acquire a piece of land which is not owned or possessed by another person only if he holds the land with the intention of keeping it for himself according to the general rules of the Law of Property, and only if such holding is not forbidden by either the Land Law or any other law concerning that land, and is also authorized by the land officer according to the rules and regulations concerned. A person can legally acquire such land in one of three ways:

1. ALLOTMENT OF "LAND FOR PEOPLE"
UNDER THE LAND CODE

The Land Code gives the Director-General of the Land Department authority to grant State land, in which no one has prior right of possession, to people for dwelling and making a living according to practices, regulations, and conditions fixed by the National Committee for the Allotment of Land.[10] The committee has laid down regulations specifying conditions under which lands may be allotted which are neither lands in possession of anyone nor property held for the common use of the public. Land which has been reserved by law for any other purpose and land on hills and mountains is not available for allotment. Land to be allotted under the Land Code is usually not occupied by anyone. It may be land which has been surrendered or abandoned by the owner, or which has otherwise reverted to the State according to the Land Law. A person who is granted a piece of land will be allowed to occupy and develop it, and he will obtain a certificate of land development and document of title in due course.

2. APPLICATION FOR LAND UNDER THE LAND CODE

Having complied with rules and regulations set forth by the National Committee for the Allotment of Land, a person may apply for land which has not been possessed by any person and which has not been declared to be under prospective survey for the purpose of the type of public allotment mentioned above. A person may also apply for a small piece of leftover unoccupied land which adjoins his land.[11] Permission will not be granted for hill land unless it is well suited for cultivation and is not a stream headwater or a forest. According to the law, if permission is granted the applicant will be allowed to enter the land to occupy and develop it, and a certificate for temporary possession will be issued to him. He will then acquire his right in the land in the same way as one who obtains land by the allotment scheme mentioned above. Actually no such permission has ever been granted to an individual. The decision to do so would probably be at the discretion of the Minister of Interior.

3. ALLOTMENT UNDER THE LAND-FOR-LIVING ACT OF B.E. 2511 (A.D. 1968)

By the Act, the government may set up self-help settlements or cooperative settlements to provide land for members of settlements, so that they can make a living from the land. Having been members of the settlement for at least five years, those who have developed their land and paid back their share of expenses advanced by the government in setting up the settlement will be awarded a "land certificate of development." Thereafter, these members may ask for the "doc-ument of title" for their land under the provisions of the Land Code. However, within a period of five years from the date they obtain title to their land, they may not dispose of it except by inheritance.

The Hill Tribe Land Settlement Projects (nikhom) of the Department of Public Welfare have operated under the provisions of this Act.

LEGAL PROBLEMS OF LAND OCCUPATION AND FOREST FARMING

Much of the land of the northern provinces was once densely forested hills. Over the course of years, swidden agriculture, unregulated logging, and fires have destroyed a vast area of forest, which is one of the nation's most valuable natural resources. Swidden cultivation is therefore regarded by law as very harmful to the economy of the nation and is indirectly prohibited. It is the government's policy to keep half of its territory as forest. It is believed that the destruction of forest will cause a shortage of natural water supply during the dry season. This will result in losses to the agriculture and economy of the nation.[12] For these reasons acts of parliament have been passed to restrict such practices.

The Land Code provides that persons who have neither the right of possession nor permission from the land officer are forbidden (1) to hold or to take possession of land belonging to the State or to damage or set fire to forest, (2) to destroy or to damage State land within localities declared by the Ministry of Interior in the *Royal Gazette*, and (3) to do anything tending to destroy natural resources in State land. Whoever violates or fails to comply with such provisions commits an offense and is liable to fines up to 500 *baht*.[13] By this provision the Ministry of Interior has declared that land on hills or mountains and land within 40 meters from the foot of a hill or mountain must not be damaged or destroyed by anyone.[14]

Also, under the provisions of the Forest Act a person who destroys, damages, or sets fire to forest without license is liable to punishment of up to one year imprisonment or a fine of 4,000 *baht* or both. If more than 50 *rai* (8 hectares) of forest area is destroyed, damaged, or burned, a punishment of six months' to five years' imprisonment, or a fine of 2,000 to 20,000 *baht*, or both, may be imposed. The court, in finding a person guilty of such act, may also evict him from the land upon which the forest is destroyed, damaged, or burned.[15]

The punishment will be more severe for similar acts if done in an area declared by the government to be national reserved forest, under the National Reserved Forest Act.[16]

Thus a person who practices swidden cultivation starts his business by committing a crime as soon as he moves onto the land. When he begins to clear the ground by cutting and burning trees, he breaks another law; and he remains liable to punishment as long as he stays on the land. After a few years, if the land is exhausted and he moves to a new site, he commits a new series of crimes. As far as the government is concerned, he will never have any right whatsoever in the land. The government may compel him to leave the land without compensation at any time and can also bring a criminal charge against him. However, vis-à-vis other individuals, one who occupies the land in this fashion may have a better right in such land than a trespasser. As mentioned above, one who holds land with the intention of keeping it for himself, *even illegally*, may be considered to have possession of the land by the Law of Property. Thus a person who occupies a piece of land while practicing swidden cultivation has a right not to be disturbed or deprived of his land by unlawful interference by any other private citizen. But one who occupies land without permission of the land authority may lose his land if the government wants it or grants it to another person.

If the swidden farmer leaves for a new site, he loses possession of the land, and anyone can enter and take it. It is doubtful whether those who practice shifting cultivation by using land in rotation, coming back to the old place every few years, still retain any right in the land they left. According to the Law of Property, one who maintains no physical control over the land has no possession of it; and if he allows another person to hold his land in defiance of his right for a period of one year, he can never claim it back. By this interpretation, one who leaves his land *even with the intention of coming back* will have possession of such land only if he still has physical control over it. The physical control in this case may be shown by such acts as fencing the field, marking the boundaries, grazing cattle, frequent visits, or some other act intended to prevent others from interfering with the land without permission. If anyone interferes with his land he must be quick to stop such interference, or bring his case to the court within one year's time; otherwise he will lose his claim of possession of the land.

Swidden cultivation continues in spite of the laws, and the government has never enforced the law seriously, except in some of those cases in which reserved forest was destroyed. In the past, much swidden cultivation on hill fields was practiced by hill-tribe peoples. Now, as land in lower areas becomes less available and more crowded, more Thai people from the lowlands are moving up to the hills. The high birthrate among farmers and the rapid growth of the rural population have led to a rapid expansion of the area under swidden cultivation. It is said that these people have destroyed a great deal of forest, but at the same time it is admitted that they brought a vast area of regulated land into some productive use.

It is still a debatable question whether all kinds of forest farming are really harmful to natural resources. It has been maintained that shifting cultivation with a short cropping period and long fallow period will not cause excessive soil erosion and that upland valley floors may be turned into irrigated rice fields. It has also been argued that a great part of land used for shifting cultivation is no longer forest, that some of the forests which are used have no teak or any valuable timber to be destroyed, and that some hill fields are suitable for plantation or grazing industries. It may be that the use of such land can be managed without any destruction of the nation's natural resources.

It is time for the government to make a careful and serious study of all kinds of shifting cultivation in all areas. That which is harmful to the economy of the nation should be put to an end. If there is any good reason for not enforcing the law prohibiting it, then some other effective measures should be adopted to deter it. If it is proved that shifting cultivation of some kinds or in some areas is not harmful and could be allowed, then the occupation of the land for this kind of farming which now is illegal must be legalized. This means that such cultivation should be allowed on hill and mountain land on which shifting cultivation could be carried out without endangering natural resources. If it is the government's policy not to allow anyone to have title to land on hills and mountains, then the government should grant some kind of long lease to people who already occupy it.[17] Such a lease would make occupation of such land legal and under control of the government. This would be better than allowing people to commit a crime without punishment, which is not a good policy

from the administrative point of view. This would also encourage people to develop neglected land and turn it into cultivated fields. Under the present circumstances one cannot expect people who practice swidden cultivation to establish stabilized farms or to invest their money to develop land in which they can never have any proper right.

HILL-TRIBE PEOPLES AND THE OCCUPATION AND DEVELOPMENT OF LAND

A large number of hill-tribe peoples, such as Lahu, Hmong (Meo), Akha, Yao, Lisu, Lua', and Karen, live in the mountainous area of the North. Some of them stay on the frontier regions bordering Laos and Burma. They are different from the Thai people in ethnic, linguistic, religious, and cultural characteristics. While practicing swidden cultivation they have destroyed portions of the forest and harmed the condition of the soil without any intervention by the law. Some have moved from place to place without any kind of control, leaving behind land whose fertility has been exhausted. Some of these peoples are said to have been living in the hills in the northern part of Thailand for many hundreds of years, long before Thai people in the lowlands knew this area. There are even claims, based on some evidence, that these peoples have some right in the land because the princes who ruled the northern provinces of Thailand in the past granted it to them. Nonetheless, *legally* these peoples are in no better position than the Thai people from the lowlands who move up to occupy hill land. They are all subject to the same law. By practicing swidden cultivation on hill land they break the law, and the government never recognizes their rights in the land.

In recent years some of the hill-tribe people have moved from the hills to occupy lowlands.

But even if the lowland in which these hill-tribe people are living can be legally occupied, it is still doubtful whether their occupation is recognized by law. According to the Land Code, one can legally occupy land only with authority of the land officer. The hill-tribe people, as well as some Thai people, never bother to ask for a license to occupy land that belongs to the State, partly because of their ignorance of the law and partly because of the complicated process of applying for a license. Some may have been occupying the land long before the Land Code came into force, but, because they failed to report their occupation in due time, their rights in such land are not recognized by the Land Code.

Apart from the land ownership questions, there are many other legal, political, administrative, economic, social, and national security problems associated with the activities of the hill-tribe peoples. Such questions are closely related, and it is well to consider them together. Many hill people grow the opium poppy, which is prohibited by law. Some are recent immigrants who have crossed the border against the regulations of the Immigration Act, and many of them keep firearms and other explosive weapons without license. Many never pay taxes nor accept any of the duties or obligations of a citizen. They rule their own communities and administer their own affairs according to their own customs. They do not respect the law of the country, or, to be more precise, they are ignorant of the law. The fact that some of their communities have been infiltrated in recent years and some of them have been incited to defy the government authorities also creates a great problem of national security.

To solve these problems the government has made plans to stabilize their agriculture, to end poppy growing by promoting other means of livelihood, to develop their economic and social conditions by promoting hill-tribe settlements, and to maintain the national security by developing their sense of belonging and loyalty to the nation. Border Patrol Police forces have been dispatched to hill villages to protect them from terrorists. They have founded schools for education of the children, and distributed medicine and clothes among these peoples. Buddhist priests have made frequent visits to some villages to teach Buddhism and morality, and hundreds of young men have been ordained Buddhist priests under the auspices of the government. His Majesty the King has launched projects to improve the living conditions and welfare of these peoples. Still, many legal problems concerning these peoples are unsolved and no plan has been made to solve them.

POSSIBLE CHANGES IN THE LEGAL STATUS OF FOREST FARMERS

Theoretically, the State may exercise jurisdiction over property, persons, or acts occurring within its territory. The hill-tribe peoples are no exception. However, in practice they are ignorant of the law and law enforcement has rarely been applied to them. Further, according to the Nationality Act, their children born within the territory of Thailand automatically have Thai nationality,[18] and therefore they enjoy the same rights and benefits of citizenship as do Thai people. Again, in practice many never recognize any of these rights and never claim anything. They prefer to be left alone to lead their own lives in their own way. On the other hand, many never render any service to the country nor fulfill any duty of a citizen.

So long as these people live in isolation in the remote areas, the problems are not serious. However, as they come in more frequent contact with Thai people and as it is the government's policy to absorb them into the Thai community, the problems will become grave, and solutions should be planned in advance. It is not intended here to urge strict enforcement of law among these peoples, without discretion and sympathy. To do so would cause sudden hardship for those peace-loving peoples who have no real intention to defy the law, and such enforcement of law will only drive them back into the deeper parts of the jungle or into the hands of the communist terrorists. In the near future special laws conforming with some aspects of their customs may be necessary, including laws pertaining to land occupation and to family and inheritance. If possible, such special laws should apply for only a transition period, until the hill-tribe peoples become fully aware of the customs and law of the country, and are ready to accept them. However, a completely separate system of law, or lawlessness, for the hill-tribe peoples will be of no good to them or the nation as a whole, for it will not help to integrate them into the Thai community.

For administrative and security reasons, the system of identity cards and birth and death registration may be introduced to the hill people. Full citizenship may not be granted to them automatically until they are ready and willing to accept the full obligations of a citizen. In the meantime the government should provide schools, make them feel that they are part of the nation, and give them a chance to assimilate into the Thai community.

To implement the government's existing plans to control and improve their areas of cultivation, suitable measures must be set up which conform with the government's policy for conservation of the nation's natural resources. Some kind of right in the land they occupy should be recognized and regulated to prevent disputes and to encourage their sense of belonging to the land. Some of the hill people's customs may have to be recognized by law, such as the custom that land may belong to a family or to a community, and the custom that the one who first clears the land retains use-rights to it and can always come back to the land even if he leaves it for some years. According to the present law only a person, natural or juristic, can hold land. A family, a group of persons, or a community cannot, since they are not legal entities and therefore can have no right, unless they form themselves into a juristic person, such as a company, association, or cooperative.

The idea of bringing hill-tribe people to live in the lowlands or in cities may not be an ideal solution. Most of these people are not accustomed to the patterns and standards of life in the lowlands. To set up land settlements for them requires a great deal of land and large sums of money, and there is not much valley land left. It is too early to say whether the government's present land settlements for the hill-tribe people in the lowlands are successful. Giving too much preference to the hill people could cause frustration among the Thai people in the lowlands. To move hill people down from the hills will also create a vacuum in the areas they leave, and other hill-tribe people from neighboring countries may move in. To allow these people to remain in their traditional environment, giving them all necessary help and treating them well and fairly so that they can live happily, may be the best solution.

NOTES

1. Land Code, section 2.
2. Civil and Commercial Code, section 1367.
3. Civil and Commercial Code, sections 1374 and 1375.
4. Civil and Commercial Code, section 1373.

5. Promulgation of Land Code Act of B.E. 2497.

6. Civil and Commercial Code, sections 1377 and 1378.

7. The Land Code came into force on December 1, 1954.

8. Promulgation of Land Code Act of B.E. 2497, section 5.

9. Land Code, sections 9 and 108.

10. Land Code, section 27.

11. Land Code, section 33.

12. A note indicating reasons for enacting the National Reserved Forest Act of B.E. 2507.

13. Land Code, sections 9 and 108.

14. Declaration of the Ministry of Interior, dated March 27, 1956, issued by virtue of section 9 (2) of the Land Code.

15. Forest Act of B.E. 2484, as amended by the Act of B.E. 2503, sections 54 and 72.

16. National Reserved Forest Act of B.E. 2507, sections 14 and 31.

17. By section 10 of the Land Code, the Director-General of the Land Department may grant a lease of land which is neither in the possession of anyone nor available for the common use of the public.

18. Nationality Act of B.E. 2508, section 7 (3).

4

Forest Policy in Northern Thailand

Dusit Banijbatana

Northern Thailand is a primary source of world-renowned teak and other tropical hardwoods. It is also the catchment area of the four main tributaries, the Ping, Wang, Yom, and Nan, of the Chao Phraya River that irrigate the Central Plain.

For purposes of assessing forest resources, it is convenient to consider the eight provinces on the immediate northern margins of the Central Plain (Tak, Sukhothai, Phitsanulok, Kamphaeng Phet, Phichit, Phetchabun, Nakhon Sawan, and Uthai Thani) which go to make up administrative Region Six of the Kingdom, together with the eight provinces of Region Five (Mae Hong Son, Chiang Mai, Chiang Rai, Nan, Lamphun, Lampang, Phrae, and Uttaradit). This is an area of some 170,000 sq km, of which perhaps 70 percent were covered with forests of one type or another at the end of the 1960s (table 4.1).

The Mixed Deciduous type of forest is the primary habitat of teak *(Tectona grandis)*. Other valuable tree species in this forest association include *Xylia kerrii, X. dolabriformis, Lagerstroemia calyculata, L. balansae, Afzelia xylocarpa, Pterocarpus macrocarpus, Adina cordi-*

TABLE 4.1 Types of Forest in Northern Thailand, 1962[a]

Forest Type	Area (sq km)
Evergreen (Lower Montane)	17,497
Mixed Deciduous	41,329
Dry Dipterocarp	53,144
Tropical Pine (Coniferous)	1,340
Scrub	1,913
Teak plantations	57
Other tree plantations	10

[a] Figures given are for the combined areas of Region Five and Region Six (see text), based on interpretation of aerial photographs taken in 1962.

folia, Bombax insigne, Terminalia tomentosa, T. bellirica, T. pyrifolia, Lannea grandis, Tetrameles nudiflora, Duabanga sonneratoides, Mangifera caloneura, Anogeissus acuminata, Garuga pinnata, Chukrasia velutina, Cedrela toona, Streospermum spp., and *Bischoffia javanica.*

The outlook for the forest and natural resources in this area is poor. By the late 1960s, about two-thirds of the forested area above 1,000 meters in elevation had been cut over, both by "hill-tribe" people and by lowland Thai. Teak forests, which once flourished in rich

TABLE 4.2 Growing Forest Stock in Northern Thailand, 1966–1967

Size of Trees	Number	Cubic Meters
30–64 cm dbh [a]	419,589,087	487,417,359
Over cut limit (64 cm dbh)	314,874,810	409,270,726
Total growing stock	734,463,897	896,658,085
Teak trees over 30 cm dbh	24,869,900	–

[a] dbh = diameter at breast height.

alluvial soil in the lowlands, have largely been replaced by rice fields and other farm crops of the fast-growing agricultural settlements. Illegally and often wastefully cut teak apparently exceeds in amount the teak extracted according to government regulations.

The average annual output of teak during the years 1934 to 1938, before the Second World War, was about 184,000 cubic meters, and the annual export was 82,000 cubic meters. During the war there was a slump in production and export. After the war the annual average output increased to about 215,000 cubic meters, while export registered 65,000 cubic meters annually. An enumeration survey of growing stock undertaken in 1966–1967 showed that there were some 24,869,900 teak trees which had attained 30 cm diameter at breast height (dbh) (table 4.2).

Within the past 50 years or so, and especially since World War II, the basic soil, water, and forest resources of the North have been seriously deteriorating. This has been due mainly to the population explosion among the local inhabitants, and to a lesser extent to the influx of hill-tribe people from the neighboring countries. Interpretation of aerial photographs taken in 1953 showed that about 65 percent of the forested area above 1,000 meters altitude in Lampang, Chiang Mai, Lamphun, Chiang Rai, and Phrae provinces had been cut for use in shifting cultivation. The loss of this great quantity of

forest cover directly exposed the soil on the mountain slopes to intense sunlight and heavy rain, allowing the soil to be heavily eroded in some places. Loss of soil in a catchment area causes rapid siltation of the stream and river beds, and a sharp increase of the surface runoff, which results in destructive flooding and reduction of surface and underground water storage.

Most of the teak trees left standing in areas cleared for farms were illicitly cut, girdled, or killed through inundation of the areas when they were turned into farms. Only the teak trees standing on poorer types of soil on the hills have survived. Due to loopholes in the Forest Act of 1960, and the scarcity of forestry officers to patrol and enforce the law, teak trees fall prey to timber thieves who slip into the forests, fell the trees, saw them into smaller-dimension stock (not exceeding 0.2 cubic meters), and bring the wood out of the forest, generally by bicycles.

The stipulation in the law that an individual may keep up to 0.2 cubic meters of the lumber was intended to apply only to legally cut timber which might be left over after logs have been used for house building or other household uses. It is regrettable that this provision has been interpreted by competent authorities to cover illegally cut timber as well.

Another illegal practice that is prevalent in the teak forests of Phrae and Lampang has often evaded the intent of the Forest Act. Illegally cut teak trees are converted into huge houseposts and thick planks, right at the spot in the forest where the trees are cut. They are actually planned for sale and future conversion to veneer logs, furniture, or other commercial use. The illicit timber is carted out of the forests to prepared sites in villages and is built into improvised houses overnight. These teak houses are generally built of exceptionally big posts which number far more than is necessary for supporting such a small house. The flooring and walls are built with thick planks, quite often in two or three layers. These houses, after standing for a short period, are sold to timber traders at attractive prices. The owners claim that they have been built for more than the two years specified by the Forest Act. Without any eye witnesses to testify where and when the teak trees were cut, converted, and carried out of the forest, such serious forest offenses cannot be effectively brought to the Court of Justice or successfully prosecuted.

The stump inventory taken in 1956–1957 showed that teak trees illicitly cut in Phrae, Lampang, Lamphun, Chiang Mai, and Chiang Rai annually during the period between 1937 and 1956 amounted to 218,621 cubic meters, or about 148.6 percent of the legal annual production of 147,104 cubic meters.

FOREST POLICY AND ADMINISTRATION

Forests are of direct and indirect importance in the economy of man and nature through their produce, through the influence which they exert on climate and on the moisture content and stability of the soil, and through their environmental and esthetic effects on man.

Because the forests in Thailand are owned by the State, and because the North is not only the home of valuable teak, but also the catchment area of the Ping, Wang, Yom, and Nan rivers, the forest policy for this region should be con-

cerned with both productive and protective values. Teak and other forests are best managed on a sustained-yield basis. The annual production of teak and other commercial woods should be maintained at about 200,000 cubic meters and 500,000 cubic meters, respectively. Similarly, forests covering the catchment areas, especially on the steep mountain slopes, should be strictly conserved for their indirect utility, and the denuded areas should be reforested by the Royal Forest Department or by private concerns. In other words, the forest policy for the North, as well as for the whole Kingdom, should aim at the greatest good for the greatest possible number of people.

In order that forest policy may be translated into action, it is necessary to promulgate forest laws and organize a forest service to administer the forests. The Royal Thai government, during the reign of King Rama V, proclaimed royal decrees controlling the exploitation, sale, protection, hammer marking, and transport of teak. On September 18, 1896, the Royal Forest Department was created, with headquarters at first located at Chiang Mai (the present Chiang Mai Divisional Forest Office). Headquarters were later transferred to Bangkok. The nucleus thus formed gradually developed into the present six divisional offices, 16 provincial offices, and 120 forest districts, to take charge of 11,338,700 hectares of forests. At the same time, forest laws have been amended and enforced.

THE IMPLEMENTATION OF FOREST POLICY

Forestry problems facing the Northern Region may be classified into two main categories: (1) the encroachment on teak and other valuable timber forests for temporary or permanent cultivation, as well as the illegal cutting of teak; and (2) the denuding of forests in the catchment area, especially in the area above 1,000 meters elevation, through shifting cultivation.

Both of these problems call for prompt and effective action. The response of the Royal Forest Department to the first has been to list a large number of valuable species, all of which are claimed by the government, and to require a permit for felling trees of any listed species. The number of species is so great and the area over which they grow is so large that these laws are very difficult to enforce. Attempts have been made to control cutting by selling concessions to private companies for harvesting teak or other valuable species from a defined area.

Slash-and-burn farming of forest sites in watershed areas has been practiced partly by hill tribes and partly by the Thai villagers who live in provinces having limited valley land for their paddy farming. Several governmental departments have approached various aspects of the "hill-tribe problem." In 1959 the government appointed a committee dealing with the welfare of hill tribes, with the Minister of the Interior as Chairman, and the Director General of the Public Welfare Department as Secretary. In addition, 29 concerned departments and divisions, including Agriculture, Land Development, Forestry, Irrigation, Highway, and Border Patrol Police are active members of the committee. Four hill-tribe settlements *(nikhom)* have been established at Chiang Dao in Chiang Mai Province, Doi Musser in Tak, Mae Chan in Chiang Rai, and Pulomlo in Loei. About 8,000 people belonging to six different tribes have become members of these settlements.

Every year about 100 Buddhist monks have gone to different hill-tribe settlements to preach religious precepts and morals. As a result many hill people have become Buddhists, and some of them have joined the priesthood.

The Tribal Research Centre has been established on the campus of Chiang Mai University to study the socio-economic conditions of some of the hill people, with technical assistance especially from the government of Australia. To prevent further immigration of hill people from neighboring countries, the Department of Local Administration has started issuing identity cards to some of the hill people in more accessible areas. In the field of education, Border Patrol Police have established about 40 primary schools, offering a four-year course; some of these schools have been transferred to the Department of Education, which has also begun to build and staff schools in the hill areas.

The law prohibits the growing of opium, and hill people are encouraged to cultivate substitute crops, such as chilies, castor beans, tea, coffee, and temperate-climate fruit trees. In addition, 55 mobile units, consisting of one social worker, one agriculturist, and one nurse for each unit, have been created and assigned to aid and advise the hill people in their health, welfare, and farming practices.

Unfortunately none of these approaches has solved the economic and ecological problems outlined above.

FOREST DEVELOPMENT SCHEMES: THE *TAUNGYA* SYSTEM AND THE BAW LUANG PINE PLANTATION

The Forest Department has tried the teak *taungya* agrisilvicultivation system since 1906 in parts of Phrae, Lampang, Nan, Chiang Mai, Phitsanulok, and Sukhothai provinces, in an attempt to increase teak production in combination with shifting cultivation. Foresters are responsible for selecting areas to be planted with teak each year. After villagers have cleared and burned the fields they are allowed to grow their field crops between rows of teak stumps or seedlings, which the villagers also plant. It takes two or three years for the teak seedlings to grow taller than the farmers' field crops. The villagers remain in the area during this time to look after their own crops, and simultaneously keep down the weeds for the seedlings. The Royal Forest Department rewards the farmers on the basis of the percentage of reforested trees which survive on their respective areas. A total of about 8,000 hectares of teak had been planted in this way by the end of the 1960s.

The assumption underlying this method is that the farmers are shifting cultivators who move their villages as well as their fields. The system allows a growth and harvest cycle of 50 to 80 years for the teak trees before the farmers can return to the farm plots, and thus requires much more land per farmer than is involved in a 10-year cultivation-fallow cycle for subsistence agriculture. The advantage in the system is that it covers the ground with a useful and valuable forest species. Most of this benefit goes to the owners of the forest. The benefit to the farmers is only in allowing them access to agricultural land which they are not considered to own. The disadvantage to the farmer is that he must move his residence from time to time as new areas are opened for planting trees and old ones are closed to agriculture to allow the trees to grow (see chapter 16).

Another project of the Silviculture Division of the Royal Forest Department is the pine plantation at Baw Luang, in the hills of Hot District, about 130 km southwest of Chiang Mai. The location, on an ancient caravan route, lies on either side of a recently completed all-weather road to Chiang Mai. The plantation was established in 1963, in an area that had traditionally been used for shifting cultivation by Lua' people living in five permanently settled villages with a total population of about 4,000. Within this area about 60,000 hectares (375,000 *rai*) of old

swiddens is suitable for pine plantation. The area also contains small tracts in the narrow upland valleys which the Lua' have used for many years as irrigated fields. The people have been self-sufficient subsistence farmers producing enough food for themselves and for feeding about 3,000 cattle.

Environmental conditions in this upland area favor the growth of conifers. The altitude is about 1,000 meters, with an annual rainfall of about 1,000 mm and a temperature ranging from a mean minimum of 7°C in January to a mean maximum of 32°C in April. The soil, identified as red-yellow podzolic, is slightly acid.

The Royal Forest Department decided to convert this "waste land" (land without legal private title; see chapter 3) to commercial forest. By 1970, about 2,000 hectares (12,500 *rai*) had been planted with *Pinus kesiya*, the native three-needled pine. This species was selected for the first extensive planting, despite its relatively poor form, because of its long fiber length and rapid growth. The other native species, the two-needled *P. merkusii*, has better form and is more fire resistant, but grows very slowly during a "grass stage" in its first two or three years. Tropical pines grow quickly, with two growing seasons—the summer rainy season and the winter cool, dry season. *P. kesiya* should reach a diameter of 15 cm after 6 years, and should reach merchantable size in 10 years.

The minimum annual increment is expected to be 2 cubic meters per *rai* (12.5 cu m per hectare), with 400 trees planted at 2-by-2-meter intervals, thinned to 200 trees per *rai* on a 15–20 year rotation, or perhaps as short as a 10-year rotation. This would yield 30 cubic meters of lumber per *rai* in 15 years. At the 1970 price of 60 *baht* per cubic meter this would give 120 *baht* per *rai*, or 750 *baht* per hectare per year.[1]

In the late 1960s the planting was carried out

on about 320 hectares per year. Labor is also needed in collecting the pine cones, which must be picked before they open, and in planting and caring for the seedlings before they are transplanted. In contrast with the *taungya* system, the land in the pine plantation is not used agriculturally. Thus clearing and weeding are done by wage labor. About 200 to 300 people are hired at a daily wage of 6 to 10 *baht* per day. The monthly labor budget as of January 1970 was 65,000 *baht*. The cost for the first three years has been figured at about 500 *baht* per *rai* (3,125 *baht*, or about US $156, per hectare). The costs per *rai* are expected to decrease in future years as the older trees require less attention. On the average, annual payments to unskilled workers are estimated at 43 *baht* per *rai* over the 20-year cycle (see chapter 16 for further evaluation of this system).

Originally the Lua' villagers objected to the project, but these complaints declined in the early 1970s once wage-labor opportunities became available. There was trouble from forest fires and trampling of the seedlings by buffalo, as there was no budget for fencing. The fire danger was reduced by clearing a 6-meter firebreak around the area. Additional problems were encountered in obtaining enough seed and in pollination of the flowers.

A forest-tree planting experiment station was established near Baw Luang in 1964, under the Pulp and Paper Material Survey Project financed by the United Nations Special Fund. The main objective of this station is to select species suitable for pulpwood which should be planted at Baw Luang or other areas with similar conditions. Since 1964 the station has conducted a series of planting experiments, including arboretum trials, field trials, crop performance trials, spacing trials, and an experiment on planting seasons. Fifteen indigenous species and

seven exotics have been tried in an area of 125 hectares. Most of the species in the trials have been conifers, including *Pinus kesiya*, *P. merkusii*, *P. caribaea* varieties *hondurensis* and *cubensis*, *P. taeda*, *P. patula*, *P. elliotii*, *P. clausa*, and *Cupressus arizonica*. The station produces 200,000 seedlings annually, and collects seeds of various species for its own use and for exchange with other experiment stations.

The importance of forest-tree improvement has been recognized increasingly since the establishment of the Thai-Danish Teak Improvement Project in 1965. Cultivation of pine and other fast growing species, if properly selected, treated, and planted, should reverse the present downward trend of timber production and should improve the condition of various wood processing industries, especially pulp and paper production. This may also assist in balance of payments problems, because paper is a major import into Thailand.

A Pine Improvement Station was opened in February 1970 in the Baw Luang–Mae Sanam area with the assistance of the Danish government. The work includes surveys of pine forests throughout the country, collection of seeds of local and exotic species for experiments, and experiments on nursery techniques, vegetative propagation, controlled pollination, and the inducement of hybrid conifers. It is hoped that these experiments will solve some of the problems encountered with native species (slow early growth of *Pinus merkusii*, poor form of *P. kesiya*, limited seed sources).

Because the pine plantation project is still in its early stages, it is not yet possible to tell the overall effect on the local villagers. Land once used for swidden agriculture and grazing is now being used for tree culture. Loss of subsistence products is compensated for by wages, but the net value of this form of labor, and the effects of transformation of these people from subsistence farmers to wage workers have not yet been studied.

CONCLUSIONS

Land-use and economic and human development policies and practices are not yet adequate to cope with the complex problems of conservation and sustained use of the upland forests in northern Thailand. Some of the unresolved problems and their possible solutions are outlined as follows.

Research is needed in several areas. Because the environmental and ethnic characteristics of the upland areas are significantly different from the lowlands, a separate multidisciplinary scientific unit should be set up to study problems of the uplands. Subjects of study should include characteristics of the population (distribution, numbers, growth rates, present agricultural practices); current characteristics of the upland environment (distribution, amounts, and qualities of remaining forests; land capability; distribution of land requiring emergency treatment for protection of soil, watershed, and other valuable resources). Land-use regulations should be established on the basis of the results of such surveys.

Given the population increase in Thailand and the increased demand for products of the upland areas, combined with the destruction of upland resources already known to have taken place, it is obvious that more intensive development of these resources will be needed. Development should probably proceed along several lines: (1) *protection of essential soil and watershed resources*, through reforestation and construction of check dams on tributaries of the major northern rivers; (2) *development of plantations for commercial tree crops*, probably emphasizing teak at the lower elevations up to about 800 meters, and fast-growing species such as pines at higher elevations; (3) *development of systems combining agriculture and silviculture*, which will result in both subsistence crop production and wage labor for the upland residents; and (4) *specific agricultural development*, with the objective of producing crops best suited for the upland environment with methods that conserve soil and water.

Educational programs should be established to increase awareness on the part of the general public and appropriate government departments of the acute problems of destruction of upland forest, soil, and watershed resources. Suggestions should also be given for ways in which these problems can be solved.

Some steps have already been taken along these lines, for example, in the development of *taungya* teak forests and pine plantations, but only about 8,000 hectares of teak and 2,000 hectares of pine have been planted. Compared with the millions of deforested hectares, this is obviously only a tiny beginning, and more resources should be allocated to such projects. The Land Use Research Centre in Nan Province, which has been established by the Department of Land Development, with technical assistance from the government of Australia (see chapter 12), has demonstrated the possibility of more permanent, more intensive upland cultivation combined with conservation of land resources. Similar stations should be set up in other provinces so that more farmers can observe and imitate these techniques. Further suggestions for land-use policies under present socio-economic conditions are discussed in chapter 5.

NOTE

1. As of 1977 the newsprint company which was to be formed to process the wood had not been established due to lack of foreign investment capital, no mill had been built, and no trees had been harvested. —Eds.

5

Forestry Aspects of Land Use in Areas of Swidden Cultivation

Thiem Komkris

The problems of swidden cultivation were summarized by Dr. Tom Gill, president of the International Society of Tropical Foresters, in a paper he presented in 1967 as chairman of the First Session of the FAO Committee of Forest Development in the Tropics:

> Shifting agriculture has become the most menacing land use problem of the tropical world. Over the centuries it has destroyed and degraded millions of hectares of forests and forest soils. Today it is a major obstacle to the development of many countries and to efforts to increase the food supply of the tropics. During recent years new influences have heightened its destructiveness and diminished its ability to support dependent populations. Social and economic evolution, together with population increases, rapid means of transportation and nationalism, have disastrously altered its ancestral pattern. Governments whose people depend in large part on shifting agriculture face the need to find remedial measures before further damage is done to forests and soils and before the inability of shifting agriculture to produce sufficient food precipitates a political crisis (FAO 1967).

THE PATTERNS OF SWIDDEN CULTIVATION IN VARIOUS REGIONS OF THAILAND

Swidden cultivation is prevalent throughout all of northern Thailand, in the watershed areas which supply the Chao Phraya River and the Central Plain, as well as in the tributary valleys of the Mekong and Salween systems. In all these areas the local lowland Thai people take up swidden cultivation to supplement their permanent wet rice cultivation where the area available for wet rice is insufficient for their needs, or where, as in many parts of Nan and Mae Hong Son provinces, there is practically no irrigable land. In these cases, swiddens are cut both in Mixed Deciduous and the Tropical Evergreen forests, as well as in areas of secondary growth. Hill rice, maize, cotton, sesame, chilies, vegetables, and other crops are grown for one or two seasons, and the area is then left to fallow because of competition from weeds and impoverishment of the soil. The area may be cultivated again after lying fallow for 10 years or so, but such rotation tends to become shorter and shorter with an increase in population and the demand for more production, until the soil is too exhausted to support agricultural crops and reverts to grassland of the *Imperata* type. It then becomes virtually useless for cultivation, and many decades may elapse before pioneer species of forest trees can colonize and a secondary forest is again established in the area.

The pattern of crops cultivated by the hill swiddeners is very similar to that of the lowland shifting cultivators. The principal crops are upland rice and maize, with the addition in some areas of potatoes and opium poppies, which are not cultivated by the lowlanders. Wild peaches and other fruit crops are grown commercially in the hills only near urban centers where the fruit can be sold.

The hill fields may be farmed for subsistence crops for two or three years, but the yield is very much lower after the first year. Row-crop cultivation, as is used with maize, leads to greater erosion and soil loss. Most hill people practice some form of field rotation, but the length of fallow and cultivation periods is variable. Research described in chapters 6–8, at the Lua' village of Ban Pa Pae in Mae Sariang District, showed that a fallow period of nine years after one year of cultivation tends to restore the soil to its original condition. A shorter period, however, would impoverish the soil and might render it useless for further cultivation.

The sometimes uncontrolled fires that accompany swidden cultivation in northern Thailand have reduced thousands of hectares of magnificent forests to *Imperata* grasslands. This can be seen, for instance, at Ban Pha Mon, Doi Inthanon, in Chiang Mai Province, and in many other places.

Swidden farming in Thailand is not confined to the North. In the Central Region swidden agriculture is widely practiced. In the lowlands, however, it is only one phase in the process of turning the land to more or less permanent cultivation. This process can be seen in Saraburi, Lopburi, Cholburi, Prachinburi, Rayong, Chantaburi, and other provinces. The forests, mostly of the Tropical Evergreen type, are cleared by the local people, or by migrants from other provinces, and then planted to maize, cassava, and other field crops. Thereafter the land is gradually turned into permanent fields of sugarcane, cassava, maize, fruit trees, or other crops. These fields are usually sold to big landowners or to newcomers, and the shifting cultivators move on to fresh pieces of forested land, usually in a forest reserve, and start clearing new holdings again. This process is repeated ad infinitum until most of the forests are gone.

In the hilly parts surrounding the central region, as in Petchabun and Kanchanaburi provinces, hill people including Hmong and Karen groups practice the same types of swidden cultivation as do their kin in the North. Thus they are responsible for the destruction of thousands of *rai* of forested catchment areas annually.

In the Northeast, swidden farming involves mostly the planting of kenaf and maize as cash crops, although upland rice is also universally planted. In this region the area which was originally occupied by Tropical Evergreen forest, which usually has good soil capable of retaining moisture, is the first to be turned into permanent rainfed or irrigated rice fields and sugarcane plantations. The sites occupied originally by the Dry Deciduous Dipterocarp forest, which comprise over 60 percent of the total area of the region, are often cultivated on short rotations of three to five years. This system rapidly impoverishes the soil, and turns the area into grasslands or useless savanna forests. These are burned annually, a practice which tends to maintain this form of secondary vegetation. As a result of population pressure and land scarcity, more and more of the area under shifting cultivation is being turned into permanent use, with consequent poorer yield and soil depletion, unless scientific cultivation and fertilization are used.

In the South, shifting cultivation and tropical storms have been responsible for turning vast areas of dense Tropical Evergreen forest into grasslands, as can be seen at Huey Sak and Thung Theparaj in Prachuap Kiri Khan and Chumphon provinces, and Tung Ka Tale in Surat Thani Province. If shifting cultivation cannot be curbed in these areas it is probable that great stretches of forest will revert to grassland. It is fortunate for the South that rubber planting is very much favored by the local population and swidden areas in many cases ultimately are planted with rubber. But rubber planting on steep slopes without adequate terracing probably contributes more to soil and water loss than do areas of abandoned shifting cultivation. The danger in the South is that when all the arable lowland areas are taken up by rubber plantations and other cultivation, the people may resort to swidden farming for their food crops in the upper parts of the Tennaserim Range. This was occurring in the 1960s and early 1970s in Rayong, Krabi, and Phangnga provinces. Inevitably, this will cause havoc in the lowlands, in the form of flash floods and sedimentation, as well as losses of life and property.

LOSSES RESULTING FROM SHIFTING CULTIVATION

There are several bases for estimating the land area, original forest type, and value of the forest which has been destroyed in shifting cultivation in Thailand. In 1969 the Royal Forest Department estimated in a report of the FAO that the total area being cleared annually by shifting cultivators in Thailand was about 30,000 to 40,000 hectares (187,500–250,000 *rai*). In northern Thailand alone, they estimated on the basis of aerial photographs taken in 1956–1959 that almost 70 percent of the evergreen forests (about 3,000,000 hectares or 18,750,000 *rai*), had been cleared in the most important watershed areas of the country. By the 1970s, this figure must have increased considerably.

In 1967, in connection with a survey for the United Nations Division of Narcotics, the Department of Public Welfare estimated that there was a total population of about 275,000 or about 48,123 households of "hill-tribe" people living in the North. In a paper presented by the FAO Secretariat to the Second Session of the FAO Committee of Forest Development in the Tropics (1969), an estimate of 0.9 hectares was given as the annual average area cleared per household of shifting cultivators in nine countries in the Asia and Pacific Region. Assuming that Thai swiddeners behave in an "average" fashion, this estimate, together with the Department of Public Welfare estimate on number of households, suggested that the area cleared annually in Thailand at that time was about 43,310 hectares (370,690 *rai*).

The same FAO report estimated that on the average 0.5 percent of the total land area of countries in the Asia and Pacific Region were newly cleared each year for shifting cultivation, and that at any one time an average total of about 10 percent of the land area of each country was being used for shifting cultivation or was fallow from shifting cultivation. These figures, when applied to Thailand with a total land area of 51,800,000 hectares, suggested a total of 5,180,000 hectares at one or another stage of

TABLE 5.1   Estimates of Damage to Forests Due to Shifting Cultivation in Thailand

Basic Figures		Source
A.	Estimated area cleared annually per family	0.9 ha	FAO
B.	Estimated area cleared annually per family	1–5 ha	Forest Dept.
C.	Number of "hill tribe" families in northern Thailand	48,123	Welfare Dept.
D.	Total land area of Thailand	51,800,000 ha	
E.	Percentage of total land area cleared annually for shifting cultivation	0.5	FAO
F.	Percentage of total land area cultivated or fallow for shifting cultivation	10.0	FAO
Estimates of Land Area Used in Shifting Cultivation		
G.	Total area cleared annually	30–40,000 ha	Forest Dept.
H.	Total area cleared annually (A × C)	43,310 ha	
I.	Total area cleared annually (B × C)	48,123–240,615 ha	
J.	Total area cleared annually (D × E)	259,000 ha	
K.	Total area cultivated and fallow used in shifting cultivation (D × F)	5,180,000 ha	
L.	Total forest cleared in northern Thailand for shifting cultivation	3,000,000 ha	Forest Dept.
Estimates of Value of Forest Cleared for Shifting Cultivation		
M.	Annual value per hectare of forest cleared for cultivation	US $17.81	Burma
N.	Annual estimate for Thailand (G × M)	US $534,300–$712,400	
O.	Annual estimate for Thailand (H × M)	US $771,351.10	
P.	Annual estimate for Thailand (J × M)	US $4,612,790.00	
Q.	Total estimate for Thailand (K × M)	US $92,255,800.00	
Estimates of Types of Forest Cleared for Shifting Cultivation		
R.	Percentage of annual clearing in high forest	23	FAO
S.	Percentage of annual clearing in secondary forest	60	FAO
T.	Percentage of annual clearing in scrub or old cultivation	17	FAO
U.	Estimated annual clearing of high forest area in Thailand		
	(R × G)	5,100–6,800 ha	
	(R × H)	7,362.70 ha	
	(R × I)	8,180.91–40,904.55 ha	
	(R × J)	44,030.00 ha	

fallow or cultivation, with about 259,000 hectares cleared for cultivation each year. This contrasts markedly with the Royal Forest Department's estimate of 30–40,000 hectares cleared annually in the 1960s.

Similar problems are encountered in attempting to estimate the areas of different types of forest which are cleared, and the value of the destroyed forests. The cleared area consists of both virgin and secondary forests, as well as old cultivation sites. The FAO estimates of percentage of area of different forest types cleared for swidden cultivation in the Asia and Pacific Region are: about 23 percent high (dense, closed canopy) forest, 60 percent secondary forest, and 17 percent scrub or old cultivation.

No figure is available for the value of the forest destroyed annually by swidden cultivation in Thailand. In Burma, which has very similar forest conditions, it is reported that the annual value of forests which are cleared is about US $17.81 per hectare. Using the 1969 FAO estimates, the economic value of the forest destroyed annually by hill people in Thailand should have been about $771,351 (15,427,020 *baht*) for the estimated 43,310 hectares cleared. Using the other figures listed in table 5.1, the range in estimated loss per year would be between $534,300 and $4,612,790. This represents only the timber value. No estimate is available for the value of soil and water lost.

Using regional averages to estimate values in Thailand may not be exactly valid, but it is one way of suggesting that the country's forests have already suffered very heavily from swidden cultivation. From the *forestry* point of view, all forms of farming in the forest should therefore be stopped immediately. This, however, is more easily said than done. From the socio-economic and political angles it would be impossible to carry out such a policy at the present time, even if foresters had all the necessary means to prevent the practice, which they do not have. The foresters may therefore have to arrive at some form of compromise in handling this problem.

Swidden cultivation is not a forestry problem alone. It is a complex problem of land-use customs and age-old practices which may be unsuited for present conditions. The foresters are doomed to failure if they attempt to solve these problems by using forestry methods alone, as is shown by the results since 1896 of the Royal Forest Department's efforts to clamp down on shifting cultivation. During this long period, laws and regulations have been enacted and many measures have been introduced to combat the evil, but so far with meager success. The foresters in Thailand must, therefore, admit to themselves that though swidden cultivation is a form of land use which they want to see abolished, or at least drastically reduced, they will have to bear with it under present-day conditions, whether they like it or not. In many cases they will even have to cooperate and organize some form of forest farming themselves, in order to further some of their own purposes, especially in their afforestation projects.

FORESTRY ASPECTS OF LAND USE IN AREAS OF SWIDDEN CULTIVATION

From the forester's point of view, the areas in which swidden cultivation is carried out can be classified into three broad categories, each with different implications: the lowlands, the foothills, and the high mountains.

In this context the lowlands include all the undulating ground between the plains and the foothills. The chief land use in this area is, of course, largely agriculture.

In areas of poor soil, high salinity, or low moisture, the most economical form of land use is probably to put these areas under forests of some kind. For example, most of the areas now being farmed in the Northeast and the Central regions, which were originally covered by Dry Deciduous Dipterocarp forests, will be impossible to irrigate. These should be put back into plantations of fast-growing species, such as native pines, for the production of pulp and paper and for other industrial purposes. In such areas, agriculture can be practiced only on a subsistence level and will never be able to compete with production from irrigated areas. Even in areas with good soil and irrigation, some land should be set aside for forest plantations on a commercial basis and for esthetic reasons, as well as for windbreaks and for the protection of canal and river banks. Also, roadside plantations, if well carried out, not only should bring in a steady revenue, but will be a boon to travelers and give shelter to people and cattle living nearby.

Swidden cultivation in lowland areas may simply die out in the near future. The availability of new land will be very limited, and no one will be able to afford to move onto a new piece of land every two or three years, as is the practice in swidden cultivation. Adequate planning will still be required to solve the problem of what to do with the people who formerly made their living in this way.

Swidden cultivation and annual fires have been most destructive in the foothills, the second category of forest land, where most of the commercial forests of the country are located. Swiddening is done here both by the local Thai population, and by some of the hill-tribe people, such as the Karen. These areas include forests of high economic value, such as teak and other Mixed Deciduous forests of the North and Central regions, the Dry Deciduous Dipterocarp and Dry Evergreen forests of the Northeast and Central regions, and the Tropical Evergreen forests of the rest of the country.

Swidden farming coupled with annual forest fires has made the foothills into the largest potential source in the country of sedimentation and flash floods. The extent of the damage is suggested by research carried out by the Faculty of Forestry, Kasetsart University, at the Mae Huad Forest, Lampang Province, between 1960 and 1968. Soil loss from three plots in a teak forest with an average size of 2 by 10 meters and a 12-percent slope averaged about 179.69 mm in depth per year, during the period when the forest was burned annually. When the area was protected from fire for three years, the annual soil loss fell as low as 19.97 mm. Water loss from these plots during the first three years of the study, when they were burned annually, averaged 248.39 mm annually. After three years of fire protection, this was reduced to as low as 6.14 mm. These figures show that annual burning is a cause of major soil and water losses in these low-lying forests. It can be expected that there would be much greater loss from totally cleared areas of swidden farms.

From the standpoints of soil and moisture conservation and of forestry, land-use plans in these middle elevations should totally ban swiddening and burning wherever possible. Permanent cultivation should be allowed only on gently sloped sites with nonerodible, properly terraced soil. When these lands are classified, areas allocated as forest reserves should be adequately protected and swiddening should be allowed only for the formation of *taungya* forest plantations (see chapter 4).

At present, however, the majority of forest reserves or areas intended for reservation as permanent forest in the foothills have been heavily damaged by illegal squatters. They clear and burn large areas with uncontrolled swidden fires. They may turn to more permanent crops or, in the majority of cases, sell the lots to newcomers. The Royal Forest Department seems at present unable to evict squatters and settlers. At the same time, it may be impossible for the squatters to occupy these lands under any legal form of tenure (see chapter 3). To turn these areas again into forest by afforestation would be costly and would probably cause much political furor. In the end it may be better policy for the Royal Forest Department to give up gracefully in areas suitable for agriculture, which were formerly parts of reserved forests but which have now been denuded of trees, and to attempt to salvage what is left elsewhere.

In the meantime, measures should be introduced to parcel out unclassified land to landless and land-hungry people as speedily as possible. This may be done by accelerating the establishment of land settlement projects (see chapter 12) and the alienation of land to needy people by local administrative officers. This process should be strictly supervised to make sure that land is allotted only to deserving people, and not to land grabbers, speculators, or influential persons, or even to local officials and their families. If these measures cannot be enforced, uncontrolled swidden cultivation will continue to expand in the reserved and planned reserved forests. This will lead to continued grave financial loss to the country and accelerated impoverishment of soil and water resources, as well as continued poverty of the landless people. All of these conditions will eventually impair the nation's economic progress.

For the Karen and other hill-tribe people who make swiddens in the low hills, suitable land allotment and intensified effort in educating them to proper agricultural practices should gradually wean them away from swidden cultivation. They already know wet rice farming and terracing, but they lack the technical knowledge, tools, and most of all, the capital for carving rice fields out of the hillsides. Modern irrigation equipment, if supplied, will certainly help

them become permanent settlers. This may take some decades, but it is worthwhile to begin now rather than allowing the continued annual destruction of thousands of hectares of valuable forests. These people may also be recruited for forest labor, such as logging, road construction, and tree planting, if the money is available in the Forest Department budget. These forms of activity may divert people from expanding their subsistence swiddening. Efforts must also be made to stop the growth of the upland population, if measures to increase the productivity and stability of their farming are not to go for naught.

The government should also support the Royal Forest Department in executing a comprehensive scheme of rehabilitation in the reserved forests. Large-scale planting of valuable and fast-growing species in cleared areas, or areas poor in commercial timber, should be done by the *taungya* method (see chapters 4, 16). In this, the local population, both Thai and hill-tribe, should be employed in clearing and planting the land, and at the same time allowed to grow their food crops for the first one or two years. If a planting scheme is drawn up with the needs of the local population in mind, illegal shifting cultivation in the reserved forests can be minimized, and the country will stand to gain enormously from the increased timber stock and protection of soil and watershed thus obtained.

The third category of land, the high mountains, in this discussion is meant to include land of 600–700 meters elevation and above, on steep slopes of the principal mountain ranges of the country. In this environment are found magnificent and dense forests of Hill Evergreen (Lower Montane), Tropical Evergreen, Dry Evergreen and in some areas Dry Deciduous Dipterocarp and Pine Forest types. These forests contain valuable species (chapter 2) but are not of very high commercial value at present because of their inaccessibility. They comprise the natural vegetation cover needed to conserve and regulate the flow of water to the lowlands, and are thus of high economic importance.

An experiment carried out at Huai Kok Ma, Doi Pui, Chiang Mai Province, by the Faculty of Forestry, through the courtesy of the Royal Forest Department, shows that even with a small watershed area of only 65 hectares and with an annual rainfall of 1,938.6 mm, a yield of 481,825.5 cubic meters of water is supplied annually to the stream flowing down to the Mae Ping. This small watershed is situated at an elevation of 1,400 meters and is covered with dense vegetation of the Hill Evergreen (Lower Montane) type. This suggests the importance of preserving permanently all the forests in this land category as watershed protection in the source areas of essential water supplies. Unfortunately, this has not been the case, and, as has been mentioned above, for the Northern Region alone it is estimated that 70 percent or more of these forests have already been destroyed, and the percentage is increasing rapidly every year.

As a start toward the creation of a centrally coordinated agency for research on conservation and stabilization of land use by hill people, a Watershed Management Research Sub-Committee was created under the National Watershed Committee. A 20,000-hectare pilot watershed study area, at Huai Mae Nai, Chiang Mai Province, was selected for experimentation.

One can imagine the foresters' frustration when they wish for the power to drive most of the hill tribes out of the mountains as quickly as possible, while at the same time, for political and humanitarian reasons, the mountain people are being courted and pampered by various agencies of the government to a greater extent than ever before. It should not be concluded that

the foresters have no humanitarian feelings for these people, but most of them have the conviction that as long as these people stay in the hills it will not be possible to stop indiscriminate clearing and burning. They fear that vast areas of forests will continue to be destroyed, to the detriment of the lowland people who have to depend on the watersheds for water needed for agriculture, industry, communication, power, and household uses.

As the foresters have not, and will never have, the means and support to carry out what they think will be the best form of land use in the mountains, it would be advisable for them to join with other government agencies, notably the departments of Public Welfare, Land Development, and Local Administration, to devise the most practical form of land use for these areas. In 1970 this was being done by the National Watershed Management Committee, chaired by the under-secretary of the Ministry of National Development, but no definite policy was drawn up because of the lack of surveys giving detailed knowledge of these watersheds, and the committee was abolished in 1972.

CONCLUSIONS AND RECOMMENDATIONS

As an ex-forester, the writer offers his opinion that in mountainous areas already inhabited by the hill tribes some simple control should be placed on their methods of cultivation. The Royal Forest Department, supported by the Border Patrol Police, should see to it that no new virgin forest is cleared for cultivation, as the area already cleared is more than the country can afford. This can be done by using helicopter patrols during the dry season, and by instruction and persuasion by the Border Police of the people under their jurisdiction. Investment in more helicopters and men would be no more costly than the continuing sedimentation of rivers and streams, and the dearth of much-needed water in the dry season.

Subsequently, all the principal watersheds of the country should be surveyed by teams of competent professionals from the Royal Forest Department and the Land Development Department, with people from other departments assisting as necessary. After the survey and evaluation of these watersheds, management plans should be drawn for each watershed separately, specifying what should be done, which agency should do it, and an appropriate budget. The National Watershed Committee should budget for the appropriation and should supervise all operations prescribed in watershed management plans. There will certainly be many difficulties and delays in the execution of the plans, but the committee will have to prove itself to be strong enough to carry on its function, which is so vital to the country's welfare.

A proper watershed management plan in areas inhabited by hill tribes should incorporate the following broad principles:

1. No new clearing of virgin forest should be permitted.
2. Cultivation areas should be prescribed for each village in consultation with the villagers concerned. Some form of simple demarcation of areas should be done.
3. Whenever possible, the area allotted to a village should be large enough to allow a long enough rotation cycle to maintain soil fertility (the length of the cycle, and therefore the size of the area, will depend on local soil moisture and forest conditions).
4. During cultivation, some simple form of conservation practices should be taught to the hill people to prevent soil and water losses. These may include strip cropping,

contour trenching, or even just the piling of slash along the contour at proper intervals.
5. No clearing should be made on ridge tops and near perennial streams.
6. Fire should be prevented from spreading from swidden sites to surrounding forests or fallow fields.

In other words, the hill people should be taught to adopt systematically the conservation practices which have allowed people like the Lua' hill villagers (chapter 6) to remain in settled villages, dependent on upland cultivation of the same fields on a regular cycle, for hundreds of years.

In conjunction with the above prescriptions, research should be carried out on the proper use and conservation of mountain lands and in the stabilization of land use by hill people. This should be done by a centrally coordinated agency created for this purpose.

If the attempts succeed in stabilizing the agriculture while developing the economy of the hill people and protecting the watershed at the Mae Nai experimental area, and if these practices can be put into operation in all the swidden cultivation areas, the destruction of forest and watershed areas should be minimized. To achieve this goal, more intensive education and extension services should be provided for the hill people, children as well as adults, especially by the mobile units of the Public Welfare Department. In the meantime, more roads should be built to connect inaccessible areas. These should be constructed with caution, however, to prevent further erosion and sedimentation. Because land is limited in the watershed areas, the movement of lowlanders into the mountains should be strictly controlled. At the same time, population growth of the hill people should be curbed, and those among them who wish to migrate to the lowlands or to towns and cities should be educated and encouraged to do so. Otherwise the population growth will negate all efforts at conservation of these vital forest and watershed resources. The aim should be to keep as few people on the watershed areas as possible.

The whole watershed areas should not be given over to permanent or swidden cultivation by hill-tribe or other people. The land should be classified in the watershed management plans, according to its capabilities, into agricultural and forest areas. The forested areas should include ridge tops, steep slopes of over 20 percent gradient, and areas along streams. If they have already been denuded these types of land should be afforested and kept under some form of forest or perpetual vegetative cover, including grass. They should also be protected from fire. This may require investment of time and money, but it is the only suitable form of land use that can be prescribed for these areas. It is an investment that is truly necessary and worthwhile to conserve the country's precious soil and water supply.

PART III

SUBSISTENCE SWIDDEN SYSTEMS

Introduction

Peter Kunstadter

The subsistence swidden systems of the Lua' and Karen described in this part are probably the most widespread forest farming systems among hill people in Thailand (illustrated in photos 20–120). In the past they have been relatively conservative in that they have used fairly regular field rotations, which have allowed permanently settled villages to remain in the same location on communally held lands for several generations, or perhaps hundreds of years.

The demographic conditions within which these people maintained a land-extensive cultivation system have changed rapidly, and, as the detailed descriptions show, the people in the areas described are beginning to face land shortages and problems of inadequate subsistence production. Their responses to these problems have included the use of irrigated agriculture (strictly limited by the nature of the terrain), temporary wage work for lowland employers, and permanent migration to the lowlands. The latter two options may place these people in direct competition with the rapidly growing lowland population in areas of land shortage and oversupply of untrained labor.

Kunstadter (chapter 6) describes agricultural methods and production among Lua' and Skaw Karen villagers engaged in a subsistence economy with both swiddens and irrigated fields. The productivity of the two villages is inadequate to supply the subsistence needs of the people and to keep them out of increasing debt. Few of the villagers are able to accumulate enough capital to invest in increasing their productivity. Hinton's description (chapter 9) of a nearby Pwo Karen community confirms the impression that the farmers in these hills are finding increasing difficulty in maintaining their meager standard of living in the face of continued population growth and limited opportunities for alternate employment.

The agronomic dimensions of the problem are indicated in the papers by Zinke and Sabhasri (chapters 7 and 8), which document the necessity for an adequate fallow period for the restoration of soil fertility in this forest farming system. The people described in these chapters have already reached or surpassed the carrying capacity of their land as utilized under their technological system, and are exceeding the capacity of their socioeconomic system to cope with this problem.

6

Subsistence Agricultural Economies of Lua' and Karen Hill Farmers, Mae Sariang District, Northwestern Thailand

Peter Kunstadter

This chapter describes the subsistence economies[1] of the 233 Lua' villagers of Pa Pae and the 183 Skaw Karen at Laykawkey village in the hills of Mae Sariang District, Mae Hong Son Province, northwestern Thailand, in 1967 and 1968. They resemble the 25,600 hill villagers living in Mae Sariang District and Mae La Noi Subdistrict. The hill population is apparently doubling in size every generation despite heavy migration to the valleys and a relatively high mortality rate. The average population density in these two villages now is between 18 and 21 *rai* per person (a little under 3 hectares per person) or about 34 persons per square km, including all agricultural land, both cultivated and fallow. Population pressure is being felt in the region at the present time in terms of breakdown of traditional systems of leadership, increased conflicts between villagers, and increased migration to the lowlands.

Although the villagers are primarily subsistence rice farmers who live remote from highways and administrative offices, these hill villagers participate in lowland markets and seek wage work with lowland employers. In

their subsistence farming these hill people use simple tools and techniques to cultivate a great variety of food plants and other useful plants in both upland and irrigated fields. Their farming methods are conservative and have allowed them to protect soil, water, and forest resources while they have lived in settled villages in the same location for several generations. Population pressure is now threatening their economic system by forcing them to shorten the length of the fallow period in their upland fields.

The rice production of these farmers in their upland fields is about 13 *tang* per *rai* (equivalent to about 1,000 kg/ha), and compares favorably with yields in Thailand for nonirrigated rain-fed paddy (average 630–940 kg/ha). The yields from Lua' irrigated fields are about 32.5 *tang* per *rai* (about 2,200 kg/ha), and are about average for irrigated fields in Thailand (1,900–2,200 kg/ha), but the Karen irrigated fields average only about 22 *tang/rai* (about 1,500 kg/ha). (Thailand averages are from Asian Development Bank 1969.)

The Lua' of Pa Pae appear to produce more rice than they need for subsistence, but because of heavy interest payments on accumulated debts, they must buy or borrow about one-third of all the rice they eat. The Laykawkey Karens produce less rice than do the Pa Pae villagers, but they have fewer debts and need to borrow only about 4 percent of the rice they eat.

The economic situation in both villages appears to be worsening as population expands and demands for cash increase. Apparently neither village could subsist only on the rice it produces. Income from wage labor outside the village is also essential.

Solution of the economic problems in these hill villages must involve not only improvements of the subsistence technology, but more importantly, increased wage-labor opportunities for temporary and permanent migrants from the hills.

SOURCES OF DATA

Data for this chapter come from field research in Lua' and Karen villages in Mae Sariang District, northwestern Thailand, during the years 1963–1965 and 1966–1969.[2] I lived in the Lua' village of Ban Pa Pae from January to July 1964, December 1964 to January 1965, and November 1966 to January 1968, and in the Karen village of Laykawkey (Thai designation: Mae Umlong Noi) between February 1968 and February 1969. The fieldwork involved standard ethnographic techniques of observation, participation, and photographic recording of the behavior of the villagers, plus systematic use of questionnaires and census forms.

A census was conducted of a number of neighboring villages by research assistants specially trained for this purpose. Within the two villages in which I lived, I collected information from each family on agriculture, concentrating on production, distribution, and consumption of the main agricultural crop, rice. A question-

naire was used for this purpose, administered shortly after harvest.

Information on soils, vegetation, and climate was collected in cooperation with Dr. Sanga Sabhasri and his colleagues from the Faculty of Forestry of Kasetsart University, Dr. Tem Smitinand, Curator of the Royal Forest Herbarium, and Professor Paul Zinke of the Department of Forestry and Conservation, University of California. Methods and results of the studies of vegetation, climate, and soils are reported in appendixes 6.1 and 6.2 (pages 127 and 130), and chapters 7 and 8, and in Kunstadter, Sabhasri and Smitinand (1977). This chapter deals primarily with the human behavioral aspects of the agricultural economy of these two upland villages.

ENVIRONMENT

Ban Pa Pae and Laykawkey are two of the numerous Lua' and Karen hill villages in northwestern Thailand (see endpaper map). Most of these villages are built on or near the crests of hills, near the sources of the plentiful creeks and streams which drain the hilly plateau country. Pa Pae is an exception to the rule; it lies astride the Mae Amlan, which drains into the Mae Sariang, and in turn into the Yuam, which joins the Moei and then the Salween on its way to the Andaman Sea. The 51 houses of the 233 Lua' villagers of Pa Pae lie in a narrow valley at an elevation of about 720 meters (photo 15). A sacred forest remains uncut on the two closest hillsides, and a green belt is left around the village "to keep it cool and pleasant," while swidden fields in various stages of cultivation or regrowth cover the more distant hills (see figs. 7.2–7.5). In the valley above and below the village are irrigated fields, some of them owned by Karen from nearby villages, who obtained them by purchase or by default of mortgages from their original Lua' owners. During the dry season, between December and April, neatly fenced gardens line the river on the lower banks. These are flooded out each year when the river rises to a raging torrent fed by heavy rains early in the rainy season.

The monsoon climate of Pa Pae concentrates most of an average annual rainfall of about 1.4 meters in the months of June through September. Minimum temperatures (2°C) were recorded in January, and maximum temperatures (38°C), in April and May. During the growing season temperatures remain in the low and mid 20s C, and humidity remains above 90 percent for long periods.

The 31 houses of the 183 Karen inhabitants of Laykawkey are scattered on the hillsides at about 800 meters elevation near the source of the Mae Umlong Noi (another tributary of the Mae Sariang),about an hour-and-a-half walk (7 km) southwest of Pa Pae. Irrigated fields lie in the valleys upstream and downstream from the village. The soil here is stonier and poorer than at Pa Pae, and the forest is of a Dry Dipterocarp type, with fewer evergreen species than at Pa Pae. Some large fruit trees remain near the houses, but aside from a few hilltop spots used as cemeteries the hillsides right up to the houses have been used for swiddens in some years.

The boundaries of the lands claimed by the two villages adjoin in the area to the northeast of Laykawkey and to the southwest of Pa Pae, and when the two villages cultivate in this area they are in direct competition for land. For each village this situation is repeated by competing villages on all sides, except that the southwestern border of Laykawkey land is vaguely defined. This is an area of steep slopes and unproductive soil, cultivated only once in the past 30 years or so by Karen villagers of Mae Umlong Luang, who have no real claim to it.

POPULATION

About 1945 two closely spaced disasters—a smallpox epidemic and a fire at Pa Pae—reduced the Lua' village to about half its previous population. About 80 people died in the epidemic, and a number of households moved temporarily or permanently to the valley after all their possessions and stores of rice were burned at planting time. In the late 1960s Pa Pae's population was growing rapidly, but had not yet recovered its former size. Meanwhile the Pa Pae villagers have lost a bit of their land each year, as Karen from neighboring villages have rented, purchased, begged, or squatted on the swidden areas which the Lua' villagers could no longer fill. The Karen villages survived the smallpox epidemic with much less loss of life. Laykawkey villagers were successful in quarantining the village during the epidemic, and no cases of smallpox occurred there.

With the exception of Pa Pae, populations of all villages in the region appear to have grown rapidly in the recent past. Most of the Karen villages in the immediate area are reported to have doubled in size in each of the past four or five generations. The Karen are relative newcomers in this hill region, having begun to settle here in very small numbers only since about 1850. The hills in a rectangle 20 km to the north and 18 km to the east of the town of Mae Sariang were once the exclusive property of the three Lua' villages of Pa Pae, Ban Dong, and La'up. Now the spaces between these Lua' villages have been filled with about 30 Karen hamlets whose total population is probably three times that of the Lua' hill villages.

When the few Karen pioneers first arrived, they obtained permission from the Lua' to build their houses and to farm on the hilltops in the less favorable land. By now their descendants outnumber the Lua' in the area, and the relative economic position of Lua' and Karen has also changed. When they first arrived, the Karen were obliged to pay the Lua', who were the traditional owners of all this land, a fee of 10 percent of their annual rice crop, in return for use of the land. The right to collect this rent was recognized by the Northern Thai Princes, to whom both Lua' and Karen villagers paid tribute (Nimmanahaeminda 1965). When the Central Thai government abolished the princely prerogatives, about the turn of the century, the Lua' also lost their right to collect rent from the Karen, because the Central Thai did not recognize the Lua' claim to ownership of this land. The hills became a part of the Royal Forest, and both the Lua' and the Karen had to pay taxes directly to the representatives of the Royal Thai government.

Perhaps as a result of the equalization of the tax burden, combined with the rapid growth of Karen population, the Lua' have lost their economic predominance in the area. Pa Pae is apparently poorer than the other Lua' villages in this district, but there are few relatively rich Lua' even in the fairly prosperous villages of La'up and Ban Dong. Laykawkey is not a particularly prosperous Karen village, but eight families own shares in 10 elephants, the ultimate status symbol and prestige possession in these hills. Although several Pa Pae families used to own elephants, or have shares in them, the last of these was sold in the late 1940s. The relative dominance of the Karen is shown by the increasing amount of swidden and irrigated land they hold in territory which was once solidly Lua'.

The total "hill-tribe" population in Mae Sariang District and Mae La Noi Subdistrict was estimated at about 25,600 by the Border Patrol Police in 1969. This may have been about 10 percent of the total "tribal" population in Thai-

TABLE 6.1 Population Characteristics of Some Upland Lua' and Karen Villages in Mae Sariang District

	Lua'	Karen
Number of villages censused	3	4 (16 hamlets)
Total population	1,255	1,791
Median age (years)	17.11	16.07
Mean number of livebirths to women of completed fertility (A)	4.83	6.85
Mean number of surviving children born to women of completed fertility (B)	2.87	4.37
Mean number of liveborn children born to women of completed fertility who did not survive to time of census	1.95	2.48
Survival ratio (B)/(A)	.596	.638

land at that time, and was probably one of the highest concentrations of hill-tribe people in the kingdom.

Our census figures show that the populations of both Lua' and Karen villages in these hills are young and growing rapidly, although survival rates are low (only about 60 percent of the children born to women of completed fertility survived to the time of the census; see table 6.1).

As compared with the other villages censused in the hills of Mae Sariang District, the Pa Pae population is a bit older (about 20 years median age) and has grown at a slightly slower rate than other Lua' villages. Laykawkey's population is younger (about 12 years median age) and is growing more rapidly than most of the other Karen villages in this region.

Migration has been an important factor in the local demography. About 15–20 percent of the upland Lua' population in the district has moved to the lowlands within the past generation, a pattern of migration which has persisted

TABLE 6.2 Population Density on Land Used for Agriculture

	Population, December 1968	Estimated Total Agricultural Land Area (ha)	Agricultural Land Area per Person (ha)	Persons per Hectare of Agricultural Land
Pa Pae Lua'	233	706.38	3.03	0.330
Laykawkey Karen	182	552.60	2.87	0.349

over many years. The extent of Karen migration to the lowlands is much less but is accelerating. Until recently Karen population expansion could be accommodated by setting up new hamlets and villages in unoccupied land areas in the hills; but no vacant land remains, and it is no longer possible for the Karen villages to split up as they once did when local population pressure became too great (see Kunstadter 1969).

Despite relatively high mortality rates and extensive migration, the population in these hills continues to grow rapidly. The population is doubling every generation as a result of the surplus of births over deaths and migration. No systematic attempt has yet been made in these hills to limit the number of births by use of modern birth control methods, and birth rates and growth rates, as measured by numbers of surviving children born to women of completed fertility, have remained higher in the hill villages than in communities of the same ethnic groups surveyed in the lowlands (Kunstadter 1971).

With respect to the two villages of Pa Pae and Laykawkey, we can estimate population density by comparing population figures with the estimated amount of agricultural land traditionally claimed by each of these villages. The figures for land areas were derived by Paul Zinke from aerial photographs which we annotated in the field. We used several informants from each village to determine boundaries, which usually ran along clearly defined landmarks, such as ridges or creek beds.

The limitations of the figures in table 6.2 are acknowledged. Each village has an area within which the villagers believe they have the right to cultivate. Since there is no legal recognition of claims to swidden land, the village land claim boundary is *de facto* determined each year as the fields are cut, and is dependent on the presence or absence of conflicting claims with neighboring villages. Furthermore, the status of claims by outsiders to lands lying within the contiguous boundaries (rented, purchased, leased, etc.) is often unclear until an attempt is made to exercise use-rights. The figures given are for horizontal area of irrigated and swidden land, *not* surface area corrected for slope.

Estimated population density on land used for swidden and irrigated agriculture is about 33 per sq km, equivalent to 3 hectares per person for the Lua' villagers of Pa Pae, and about 34.9 per sq km, equivalent to 2.87 hectares per person for the Karen villagers of Laykawkey (table 6.2).

We cannot draw conclusions on the basis of these figures about the population density of all of the hill region in Mae Sariang District. The figures for Pa Pae and Laykawkey may or may not be typical, and there is no way of knowing until more extensive surveys are made. Some areas are undoubtedly overpopulated in terms of their present systems of land use, while others may not have reached their maximum carrying capacity. Anecdotal information from the area around Mae Haw', Mae Lit, and Mae La—Karen villages lying near the highway about 18 km east of Mae Sariang—suggests that the area is seriously overpopulated with respect to swidden-based agriculture, but the population has been growing and the economy changing rapidly (see also chapter 9). Between 1960 and 1969, 80 or more Karen families moved out, seeking new swidden land, some moving as far as Fang in Chiang Mai Province and to Chiang Rai Province, 250 km to the northeast. This migration was initially started and encouraged by the Catholic mission, but non-Christians have also participated. Since the highway was completed through this area in about 1965, the population concentration has increased markedly at Mae Haw', where the Hill Tribe Development Centre (under the Department of Public Welfare), a school (under the Ministry of Education), a highway checkpoint, and several stores have been established. Buses and trucks also make it possible for a number of people to go from Mae Sariang to Mae Haw' daily to collect wild vegetables or garden produce which they sell in the Mae Sariang markets.

Crowding is beginning to be felt in the Laykawkey and Pa Pae area in a number of ways, including increased internal dissension among the villagers, decline in authority of traditional leaders over land use, increased friction between villages over agricultural land on their borders, and increased price of irrigated and irrigable land. Karen can no longer form new villages in nearby vacant areas. There are no known vacant areas left, and so land and other disputes which once could be settled by village fission may now be settled by display of force, or may persist through months or years of wrangling. Ideals of family size are still determined by the desires of household heads to have large numbers of children in order to be able to cultivate large field areas and raise large crops. These motives have tended to persist despite the fact that some of the villagers now recognize the limitations of their land resources and the declining swidden yields associated with decreased length of the fallow period.

SOCIAL STRUCTURES AND LAND TENURE

The hill villages in this region are generally the swidden landholding units. Lua' village social structure is clearly organized around the holding and control of swidden lands (Kunstadter 1966). Swidden lands are held in common, but household use-rights, established by previous use, are recognized, and to some extent are heritable by descendants of the household. Village religious officials have first choice of swidden sites each year, and the *samang*, or chief priest of the village, has the first choice of all; he also has the responsibility for settling disputes between claimants to the same parcel of swidden land. The priests have the responsibility of conducting ceremonies on behalf of the village which are designed to appease the spirits of the forests in which the swiddens are cut.

Rights to use swidden land freely are inherited by descendants of the village founders, or descendants of families specifically adopted into the village. These households have first choice of the land remaining after village religious officials have chosen their land. After these families have chosen, the descendants of households without a primary claim on the land may choose their swidden sites. In practice most households return to the spot they farmed during the previous round of swidden cultivation. If two claimants to the same plot cannot reach a mutually agreeable settlement, the chief priest will allow neither to use the land. Household use-rights to swiddens are usually divided at the time a married son leaves his father's house to establish his own household. Irrigated plots, which are usually small, are not subdivided, but may be shared or worked in alternate years by two married brothers. The youngest son usually stays in his father's house and inherits the bulk of his father's property and responsibilities.

Irrigated land is owned by individuals and may be bought, sold, mortgaged, or exchanged. The initial claim to a parcel of irrigated land belongs to the person or persons who cleared the land, constructed the dams and ditches, and brought water to it. The government registers irrigated fields and recognizes individual ownership of them. Many of the irrigated fields in this area have been surveyed, and some of their owners have received preliminary titles to them. All irrigated fields were made out of what was once swidden land, but if the developer of the irrigated field happened not to own the plot, he simply obtained permission from the previous use-right holder. He was rarely obliged to pay even a nominal sum for the privilege.

The individual household, normally composed of husband, wife, children, and sometimes an unmarried brother of the husband, or perhaps the parents of the husband, is the primary land-working unit. Most agricultural work does not involve all family members, or exclusively members of a single household, but is instead organized around the sharing of labor between relatives or friends. There are formally sanctioned obligations to share labor at planting and harvest times, when a large amount of work must be completed rapidly. These obligations involve in-laws and members of the household's patrilineage. Exchanges based on friendship or kinship, in which one man-day of labor is given for every man-day received, take place at these times and also during the long weeding season when the pace of the work is much slower. Similar patterns of exchange labor are followed in working the irrigated fields. There is very little agricultural work for wages, either in cash or in kind, within the village. At the present time everyone has access to cultivable land, and only

those whose family structure makes it impossible for them to work their own swiddens (mostly widows) work for wages (in kind) as a primary means of subsistence.

Karen social structure is quite different from Lua' social structure, chiefly in that the preferred and usual pattern of post-marital residence is matrilocal rather than patrilocal, and responsibilities and powers of the village leaders (at least at Laykawkey) are not so clearly defined. In one sense swidden land is a communally held good. As at Pa Pae, an individual born outside the village has no claim on village land unless he marries or resides with a native-born villager who descended from one of the village founders. Final authority in division of land resources seems not to belong to the village religious leader, as at Pa Pae. Disputes over land claims between villagers may persist for a long time, and may be settled by the strength or threat of force of relatives if both disputants are descended from one of the founding families of the village. There is no higher authority to which disputants may appeal. Irrigated land is privately held property, as at Pa Pae. Ideally, property should be evenly divided among siblings at the death of the household head, but in practice movable property (livestock) is given to children who have moved away (especially sons), while claims to fields usually go to daughters and their husbands.

Karen labor exchange is based on kinship ties, as among the Lua', and both brothers and brothers-in-law, sons and sons-in-law are called on for mutual assistance.

THE VILLAGE AND THE OUTSIDE WORLD

Both Pa Pae and Laykawkey, like most mountain villages in this region, are remote in the sense that they are several hours' walk from the nearest road, the nearest market, and the nearest government office. Nonetheless the villagers are not isolated. Several schools have been built in Lua' and Karen hill villages since the early 1960s. Missionaries and native evangelists, peddlers and police, anthropologists and campaigners for public office find their ways to the mountain villages on a fairly regular basis. The villages have government-recognized headmen, and the villagers walk to town to license their guns, to pay their taxes, to sell their surplus crops, and to buy tools and other supplies. Most men and some women also go to the lowlands to seek wage work, and many of them have relatives who have migrated to live permanently in the lowlands.

The villagers feel there is no satisfactory way of dealing with land disputes between villages unless a compromise can be worked out between the disputing individuals, or, as is more likely, between the headmen of the respective villages. The villagers are loath to involve government officials since they are aware they have no legal claim to swidden lands; likewise, government officials are reported to have expressed the opinion that the hill people should settle their own disputes. Stubbornness and persistence seems to win disputes for Karen against Lua', threat or use of superior force wins disputes for Hmong against Lua' or Karen.

SUBSISTENCE PRODUCTION

Despite their relations with the outside world, the Lua' and Karen hill villagers in this region are primarily subsistence agriculturists, farming in ways that have been relatively unchanged for hundreds of years.

TECHNOLOGY

Lua' and Karen hill farmers depend on a small, simple set of multipurpose tools in their farming. These include a long, straight-bladed iron knife, used for chopping down trees to clear the swidden, and for any other purpose requiring heavy chopping, such as cutting wood for firewood, fencing, or field shelters. Field fires are kindled with torches made of dried split bamboo stakes, lit with a flint and steel or with a kerosene-fueled pocket lighter of European manufacture. Fields are planted with the aid of an iron-tipped planting stick with a long bamboo handle. The same iron tip may be mounted on a short handle and used to dig postholes or to plant or dig root crops. Weeding is done with a short-handled tool with an L-shaped iron blade, sharpened on the end for chopping at the base of large shoots, and on the lower part of the blade, which is used to scrape weeds off at ground level. These tools may also be used to harvest root crops. Rice is harvested with a sickle having a curved 20-cm blade. Plows, harrows, and harnesses are made of wood and locally spun rope. The plowshare and the hoe blade, made of cast iron or steel, are the only two items in the tool kit which Lua' or Karen blacksmiths cannot make for themselves out of scrap iron, but in general blanks or completed tools are purchased in town markets.

THE ANNUAL CYCLE OF CULTIVATION AND CHOICE OF SWIDDEN SITE

The cycle of shifting cultivation begins in January with a search for cultivation sites (table 6.3). In the Lua' village the search is carried out by the older men of the village, including the religious leaders and other elders. They know what the next area to be cultivated should be in the orderly round of cultivation and fallow, but they must verify that the forest has reached the proper stage of maturity, that the soil is not "tasteless" or infertile, and that there is no evidence that a recent fire has burned through the site to be cultivated this year. If these conditions are not met, they go on to the next area in the field rotation cycle. When they have found a

TABLE 6.3 The Annual Cycle of Cultivation

Month	Weather	Swidden Activities	Irrigated Field Activities
January	Cool, dry	Select swidden sites, begin clearing swiddens.	Clear and level new fields, dig new ditches. No fixed schedule.
February	Warming, dry	Cut swiddens, dry slash.	Same as January.
March	Hot, dry	Dry slash, burn fields, plant root crops and maize, pile and reburn incompletely burned slash.	Same as January.
April	Hot, dry	Pile and reburn slash, build field shelters, plant rice and minor crops, fence fields.	Same as January; also prepare and sow swidden-style nursery, if any.
May	Hot, dry, rains begin	Finish planting, fencing; begin weeding; set rat traps.	Begin clearing old fields, repair dikes. No fixed schedule. Prepare and sow irrigated nursery after rains begin.
June	Warm, intermittent rain	Continue weeding. Some vegetables ripen.	Begin plowing, harrowing, flooding of fields. Schedule depends on onset of rains.
July	Warm, humid, heavy rain	Continue weeding. Vegetables and maize ripen.	Complete plowing, harrowing, flooding of fields; transplant seedlings; fence fields; weed; repair dams, dikes, and ditches as necessary.
August	Warm, humid, heavy rain	Continue weeding. Vegetables ripen.	Weed and make repairs as necessary.
September	Warm, humid, rains decline	Final weeding. Earliest rice ripens.	Earliest rice ripens. Begin harvest.
October	Cool, rain stops	Rice ripens. Begin harvest (cutting, drying, threshing).	Rice ripens. Continue harvest.
November	Cool, dry	Complete harvest; begin carrying rice to village barns.	Complete harvest; begin carrying rice to village barns.
December	Cold, dry	Finish carrying rice to village. End-of-year ceremonies.	Complete carrying rice to village.

location where the conditions are met, they confirm the choice ceremonially; after the religious leaders make their choice of fields, the other villagers may return to the field sites which they cultivated 10 years previously. Each non-Christian household must confirm its choice of field by sacrificing a chicken to obtain an omen, and, if the omen is good, the household members may begin clearing this field; if the omen is poor, they must seek another spot, or trade with another household, and sacrifice another chicken until they obtain a favorable omen (photo 20).

Karen choice of field sites is not so formal. Each household makes its own evaluation of conditions and its own choice, and, though there is often some agreement on the general area in which fields are cut, the Karen make no concerted effort to cut fields in a single contiguous block, as do the Lua'. Nor do the Karen hesitate to cut an isolated field or to cut a field in the midst of fields of some other group, as the Lua' are loath to do.

PREPARING SWIDDEN FIELDS (photos 21–23)

The work of clearing the fields starts late in January and lasts two or three weeks. Men, women, and older children work together in the heavy labor of cutting the jungle. Small trees and brush are cut as close to the ground as possible; larger trees are cut, leaving about half-meter or meter-high stumps; the largest trees may not be felled, but their branches are trimmed close to the main trunk so that any re-growth will not shade the crops. The Lua' avoid cutting trees on the ridge tops and along water-courses in a conscious effort to preserve the watersheds and reduce erosion. Karen in Laykaw-key are not so careful to observe these niceties and even cut swiddens in areas protecting the village water supply. This is an offense punishable by stiff fines in the Lua' village of Pa Pae.

BURNING THE SWIDDENS (photos 24–29)

The fields are allowed to dry for about six weeks, until the end of March, the hottest and driest time of the year. The villagers want the brush to be as dry as possible to insure a complete burn, but they are afraid to wait too long for fear the extreme heat of late March will trigger thunderstorms which will wet the brush and cause a delay in the burn. The Lua' villagers depend on the wisdom and accumulated knowledge of the chief priest to decide the date for the burn. Now, however, his independence in the matter is limited by the fact that Karen fields may have been cut within, adjacent to, or nearby the Lua' fields; so the timing of the burn must be negotiated with the headmen of any Karen

villages whose fields lie near the Lua' fields. The Lua' feel that they are sometimes forced to burn earlier than they want to by the "irresponsibility" of Karen, who may burn their fields any time they feel like it, without attending to decisions made by headmen.

Among the Lua' the burn is preceded and accompanied by a major communal ceremony conducted by the priests and elders to placate the spirits and to insure that the fields will burn completely but not out of control. Meanwhile the younger men run from the tops of the fields down to their base touching off the fire; then they gather in stream beds and other protected areas, with their muzzle-loading muskets ready, waiting for any game that may be driven out of the flaming brush. The Lua' are very careful to construct firebreaks around the sides and tops of their fields before they burn them, by cutting a 5- or 10-meter-wide corridor and sweeping it clear of underbrush to protect future years' swidden areas (photo 23).

The Karen join in this activity where their fields adjoin Lua' land, but they are not nearly as careful as the Lua' in controlling and fighting fire which escapes from the burns, in spite of the fact that they, like the Lua', recognize that a fire burning through the forest will reduce the productivity of a swidden cut there in future years. Each Pa Pae household has the obligation to send one of its members to help fight any forest fire which threatens to burn over fallowed swidden land. This obligation is reinforced by annually assessed village taxes, in which those households which do not contribute to fighting the fires are taxed to help pay those who contributed more than their share to communal effort. The Karen of Laykawkey often seem content to sit and watch accidental forest fires burn through future swidden lands, and admit that they are not nearly as well organized as the Lua' and have no way of forcing anyone to go out to fight fires.

REBURNING, FENCING, AND EROSION CONTROL (photos 30–34)

The Lua' plant their root crops and sometimes maize and cotton as soon as the swidden fires have burned out, and after they have claimed their fields symbolically from the forest spirits by erecting a *taleo* taboo sign. Two or three weeks are spent gathering, piling, and reburning the unburned slash material which has not been consumed by the swidden fires. They gather piles of logs and orient them up and down the slope of the hills to increase the draft and produce a clean-burning fire, leaving only a pile of ash and a reddened scar on the soil surface. While they are piling unburned slash and short logs for reburning, they also collect longer unburned poles, which they lean against taller tree stumps and carry back to the village for firewood (photos 100, 101). Each household probably uses about 5 to 10 kg of firewood per day, almost all of which is gathered from swiddened areas.

Long poles are also set along the contours of the hillsides, held in place against stumps, in an attempt to control soil slippage and erosion. These are effective in forming miniature terraces when the very friable ash and loose surface soil slides against them (photo 48).

The Lua' farmers build frameworks of poles and sometimes set rocks and poles across the small creases on the hillsides, both to retard erosion and as sites on which to plant viney plants such as squash, which require a lot of water. Karen farmers are familiar with these techniques, but are not as systematic in applying them.

Either before or just after the swiddens are planted they must be fenced in order to keep out livestock, especially water buffalo, which are ordinarily turned loose to graze in the fallowed swiddens and irrigated fields, and also to keep out elephants that are turned loose to graze in the jungle. The fences are inadequate to restrain the elephants, but at least they warn the elephant owners to restrict their animals to areas which are not being farmed, and to stop using the trails that lead through the fields. Lua' farmers fence their fields with carefully spaced fence posts joined by three or four rows of fence poles, and build neat stiles or ladders for exit or entry. They use bamboo which they cut and store for this purpose in stream beds when they are clearing and burning swiddens. Karen characteristically build fences around their swiddens using forked poles to hold up a single row of horizontal bars, against which they pile branches and brush, to form an impenetrable barrier against cows and buffalos. The upper boundaries of Lua' swiddens are usually neatly squared off in a straight line of uncut trees, while the tops of Karen swiddens are generally curving.

ORGANIZATION OF WORK IN SWIDDEN PREPARATION

Swidden-cutting time is a period of concentrated work, but there is little time pressure involved. A few days more or less of drying time at the beginning of the drying period are not felt to be too important by the villagers. The start of cutting of swiddens at Pa Pae was delayed until almost mid-February in 1969 because of the parliamentary election held that year. Campaigners and election officials were in the village and walking the trails for a couple of weeks before the election. Until they left, the Lua' were unable to make their sacrifice of a cow, which was essential before they could begin cutting their swiddens in a part of the forest believed to be inhabited by particularly powerful spirits.

Cutting swiddens early in the dry season has a beneficial effect that may not be clearly understood by these farmers. This is the preservation of soil moisture which otherwise is lost through the vegetation by evapotranspiration during the hot dry months before the start of the monsoon rains. Soil moisture in the swiddens at the time of planting is actually higher than in the comparable uncut forest, and this moisture is available to assist in the germination of the seed and early growth of the crops before the monsoon rains become dependable, which may be as late as mid-July (see chapter 7).

Between December (when the harvest has been completed and the rice has been carried back to the village for storage) and the middle or end of April (when swidden planting begins) there is little urgent field work. Some family members may be hunting, fishing (photos 108–109), or gathering (photos 102–103), while others are working on the swiddens. Some young men leave the village as soon as the harvest has been completed to seek wage work in the valley (where the harvest comes a month or so later than in the hills), in the lumber industry, or in mines (photos 114, 115, 119).

This is also the time when hill villagers try to enlarge their irrigated fields (photo 68). They may do the work themselves, or exchange labor with other irrigated field owners, or hire Lua' or Karen from neighboring villages. Unlike swidden fields, irrigated fields commonly require the investment of cash or payment in kind for their development; thus only someone with surplus capital or rice (in addition to access to land) could get started in irrigated agriculture even when land was freely available for the construction of paddy fields. The development of paddy fields seems to be primarily men's work,

whereas most of the work on swidden fields can be and is done by both men and women in the Lua' and Karen villages.

After the swidden fields have been cleared and reburned, each farm family prepares a shelter in their swidden, unless it is located very close to the village. The shelter is usually built in the same place each year the swidden is cultivated. A spot is leveled on the slope, and the low-roofed shelter, covering an area perhaps 2 or 3 meters square, is erected on short piles. It has a single ridgepole, running parallel with the contour of the hillside; flooring is made of split and flattened bamboo, and the roof and ends are covered with long shingles made of dipterocarp leaves. The roof on the uphill side extends all the way to the ground, and on the downhill side projects for half a meter or more to give shelter to people who may sit below when the inside is crowded. The uphill side of the shelter is left without bamboo flooring; the earth is leveled and used as a hearth and cooking area. Firewood is chopped and stored under the downhill side of the shelter. The farmers retreat to the shelter during heavy rains or when the sun is too strong in the heat of the day, and it is here that the sacrificial meals are prepared and shrines are erected during planting, harvest, and other ceremonies. Farmers or their children may stay here overnight to guard the fields just before and during harvest. The shelter is used as a temporary barn to store rice during the harvest.

Clearing swidden fields is primarily the responsibility of individual households. The work is often done by work parties of 10 or more people, with exchange labor organized on the basis of kinship, friendship, and the happenstance alignment of fields. Field burning involves community coordination and action because of the perceived dangers to life, to the village itself, and to communal land resources. Piling, reburning, and fencing are the responsibilities of individual households, and are usually done by one or two members of the household, with little or no exchange labor. The full mobilization of exchange labor and the drawing power of the net of kinship obligations is seen in planting the swiddens.

PLANTING THE SWIDDENS (photos 35–40)

Planting begins about the tenth of April, if possible before the rains have begun and the loose ash and topsoil have been swept down the slopes. At Pa Pae the chief priest must be the first to begin planting his field. Other households follow on days of the week they choose as propitious, depending on past experience with days which have been lucky or unlucky. The Laykawkey villagers have similar feelings about lucky days, but although the religious leader of the village or the subgroup should take precedence in planting, some households may go ahead without waiting for the leaders to begin.

When the field has been cleared and the brush has been piled and burned, or, at the latest, on the first day of planting their fields, each Lua' household must make several sacrifices to spirits of the locality, the forest, and the watercourses which drain the field. Also on the day of planting, the household must make sacrifices to the ancestor spirits of the household, to the ancestors of the wife's father's household, and to the ancestors of the previous owners of the field, whoever they may have been. The households of various classes of relatives are obliged to provide liquor and labor on this occasion, which symbolizes the common interests of the relatives in the agricultural process, and clearly shows the stability of the connection between the Lua' villagers and their claims to a particular area, through their ancestors. These ceremonies are conducted on behalf of the household (and related households) by the male household head, often assisted by one of the old men or priests of the village.

Karen ceremonies at planting time are less elaborate. They are led by the *ceremonial* owner of the field. This is often a young child, boy or girl, who is selected by the family as the field owner for the year. Thus it is he (or she) who takes the omens to determine whether the field will be a good one, who plants the first and last rice seed, who cuts and threshes the first and last bundles of rice, and who makes the offerings for the spirits (with the assistance of an older man) at several points during the agricultural cycle. A similar system is used with irrigated fields, and again the ceremonial owner of the field may or may not be the actual legal, registered owner of the paddy. The Karen like to select a young field owner because of the probability that a young person has not been exposed to, nor had a chance to offend the spirits as much as an older person. If the field is bountiful, its young ritual owner will continue in this role as long as his (or her) luck holds, or until he has children of his own to take the responsibility; but if he is unlucky, he may never again assume ritual responsibility for a field for fear that his unsuccessful relationship with the spirits will be repeated.

In planting the fields, young men make small holes by thrusting the iron tips of their long-handled planting sticks 5 or 10 cm into the soil. Women, girls, boys, and older men follow behind and throw a few rice seeds in each hole. No attempt is made to cover the seeds. Soil slippage, assisted by the first light rains, helps to work the seeds into the holes and covers the seeds. The men use no spacing device to assure that the holes will be evenly or optimally spaced, nor are the seeds carefully counted by the planters before being thrown at the holes. The holes are made at fairly regular intervals, and any over-seeded or underseeded areas are corrected by pulling out the surplus rice shoots and transplanting them as necessary after the rains have started and the rice is about 15–20 cm tall, at the time of the first weeding (photo 49).

Usually a household head is able to mobilize a large labor supply only on the first day he starts to plant. If he is a skillful manager, and lucky, he will get a good portion of his field done on this day, before he must disperse his household to repay his exchange labor debts and honor the obligations to assist his relatives in planting their fields. Large supplies of labor on the first day of planting are in part insured by the promise of a meal including meat from the animals that are sacrificed to the spirits, and the liquor that the household head and his relatives must provide. Ordinarily a householder is not able to provide meat and liquor on more than one day, and on subsequent planting days the household head must rely on exchange labor obligations and friendships for assistance in planting. Thus, as the planting proceeds, the work groups become small and may be confined to immediate household members. This is one of the occasions when a man is happy to have a number of adolescent children, especially daughters,who can attract friends to help in the work.

SWIDDEN CROPS

A wide variety of crops is planted in the swiddens especially in the Lua' fields (see table 6.19), which are arranged in an orderly fashion. Rice is the primary crop. Ordinarily each swidden contains a number of different strains of rice, classified in the native terminology as glutinous or nonglutinous; as slow, medium, or fast ripening; and by color and shape of grain (short, long, red, white, yellow, black, etc.). At both Pa Pae and Laykawkey the most commonly planted va-rieties are nonglutinous, slow maturing rice with a fairly short, rounded grain. These varieties are preferred because of their taste and storage qualities. Ordinarily each household keeps its own seed separate from all other rice, and prefers its own to that of other households. Seed rice is harvested separately and may be specially selected to improve the quality of the crop (see below). Thus there are many distinct strains even within the major varieties. Most families plant one or more varieties of glutinous rice in relatively small quantities. A few families prefer to eat glutinous rice frequently, but for most it is a grain to be specially prepared on ritual occasions, and not a staple, though it may be used regularly for brewing rice liquor.

Some families plant large amounts of early ripening rice. These are usually the poorest families who cannot afford to wait the extra month or six weeks for late rice to mature. Planting early rice, which matures in late September, is somewhat risky because the weather will probably still be rainy when it ripens, and the ripe grain is more likely to be knocked down. Also, early ripening rice may have poorer storage qualities than the later ripening varieties, which mature in October or early November, perhaps because it cannot be dried as thoroughly at harvest. Nonetheless, some of the Pa Pae families are so poor that they are already borrowing rice at planting time and begin their harvest as soon as the rice is edible, in the "milk" stage, when the grain is still green. Karen informants in Laykawkey say that none of the villagers there needed to plant early ripening swidden rice in 1967 or 1968 because all of them had sufficient rice stocks to last them until the next harvest.

The planting of several different varieties of rice over a period which stretches out three weeks or so is probably beneficial when it comes to harvest time, because there might not be sufficient labor to harvest all the rice were it all to ripen at the same time. Different ripening dates also reduce the risk of total crop loss due to an unseasonal storm at the end of the rainy season.

The borders of Lua' fields, especially where they adjoin other swiddens, are marked with logs running up and down the slopes, and a row of sorghum *(Sorghum vulgare)*. The sorghum plants grow to a height of 2 or 3 meters or more, and prevent any accidental harvesting of rice from the neighboring field. This is an action which the Lua' believe would offend the soul of rice, and would lead to reduced rice yield for both the offender and the owner of the invaded field. Any such transgression must be settled by payment of a fine of a chicken to the owner of the invaded field. The chicken is sacrificed to the soul of the rice at harvest time. One variety of grain sorghum is used in brewing rice liquor; the grains of another variety may be popped and eaten on special occasions, or boiled and eaten.

Most Lua' swiddens have a small area, usually close to the field shelter, which is used as a chili pepper *(Capsicum frutescens)* garden (photo 92). Peppers are ordinarily started at home in old pots or cans and then transplanted to the swiddens early in the rainy season. Peppers may also be grown in a separate small swidden in parts of the forest not suitable for rice swiddens. Peppers are harvested throughout the year, as soon as they begin to bear. Peppers and sometimes cotton are the only crops which may be harvested in a swidden the year following the single year of rice cultivation. Produce in a fallow swidden is a "free good" and anyone who troubles himself to walk through the thick underbrush growing there may harvest the peppers. A number of varieties of peppers are grown, some of them traditional strains, and others grown from seeds purchased in the valley. They are grown primar-

ily for home consumption, very rarely in quantities large enough for sale or trade.

Most Lua' households grow cotton for their homespun clothing, either in their rice swiddens, or in small swiddens in marginal land unsuitable for rice. Cotton is one of the first crops to be planted. A few handfuls of seeds are scattered near the site of the field shelter when the swidden fire has burned out, at the time the swidden is claimed for human use. More substantial seeding of cotton is done later, when the field has been recleared. Cotton seed is scattered by flicking a small handful of seeds off the end of a flat bamboo stick about 25–50 cm long. It lies on the surface of the soil, and no attempt is made to cover it. The cotton plants grow among the rice in a rice swidden; the Lua' say they do not plant all the cotton (or all of the plants of any type, with the exceptions already noted) in one place, because they want to avoid shading the rice plants. The cotton is very slow to mature (eight or nine months) and is not picked until December or even January, so cotton picking does not interfere with the rice harvest.

At least four varieties of flowers are planted in the swiddens, scattered around the field shelter site after the swidden has been burned. These include marigolds (*Tagetes* spp.), purple "everlasting" flowers, cosmos (*Cosmos sulphureus*, which also reseed themselves), and yellow and red varieties of *Celosia argentea*. The latter is especially significant ritually, because it is believed to scare away harmful spirits when it is blooming during the harvest season. The flowers make a colorful display in the dry clear days of the harvest season when the rice plants are beginning to turn golden, and they are gathered to form an essential part of the altars and offerings of the harvest ceremonies, as well as to garland the children and the harvesters.

Maize *(Zea mays)* is planted soon after the

swidden has been burned, in scattered spots around the swidden. A few seeds are dropped in a shallow hole made by a short-handled, iron-tipped digging stick, and the hole is then closed by stepping on it. "Native" varieties of maize resemble "Indian corn," with multicolored grains on small cobs; recently larger-eared, single-colored maize has been introduced from the lowlands. Maize ripens in late June or July and is a welcome addition to the diet because rice stocks are often running low by this time. Maize and beans seem to be more important supplements to the food supply in Laykawkey than in Pa Pae.

Several varieties of beans and soya beans (*Dolichos lablab*, *Dolichos* sp., *Phaseolus* sp., *Psophocarpus tetragonolobus*, *Glycine max*) are planted in the swiddens. Many of these are trained to grow on poles or stumps. They are harvested as they ripen, late in the rainy season, and are an important supplement to the diet at harvest time (photo 93). At Pa Pae only a few are dried and stored for seed, and except for a few soya beans (which may also be grown in the dry season on fallow irrigated fields), virtually none are dried for use as food later in the year. They are more important both as fresh and dried foodstuff at Laykawkey.

Two local varieties of mustard greens (*Brassica* sp.), known respectively as Lua' and Karen varieties, are broadcast-sown in the midst of the rice in upland fields. This is the first crop available in the swiddens; it is harvested from the time of the first or second weeding, when plants as small as 2 or 3 cm are thinned out and eaten. It is an important food up until about the end of July, when the plants are tall and the leaves increasingly bitter. When they are plentiful, the leaves are dried and stored for future use. The Lua' feel this is a "real Lua' food," and that "if you do not eat mustard greens and peppers, you

cannot work like a Lua'." Although there is time left in the rainy season for a second swidden crop of mustard greens, the Lua' never plant one, for fear of offending the spirits. Mustard greens are, however, one of the most important winter garden crops. White Chinese cabbage (*Brassica petasites*) is grown in swiddens and gardens from seed purchased in the valley.

Root and tuber crops, including several varieties of taro (*Colocasia antiquorum*), sweet potatoes (*Ipomea batatas*), yams (*Dioscorea alata*), manioc (*Manihot esculenta*), and others (e.g. *Amorphophallus* sp.), are common supplemental swidden crops. Manioc is propagated by use of stem cuttings, which are planted in well-watered spots. Root crops become important in the diet by the middle of the rainy season, and most can be readily stored for use through the dry season.

Tobacco (*Nicotiana tabacum*) is sometimes grown in the swiddens but more commonly in separate patches in gardens, in irrigated fields in the dry season, or in isolated swiddens. Tobacco is one of the few agricultural products of which large quantities are purchased (on the basis of taste preferences) by upland villagers who may travel to the lowland to get it.

A great variety of viney plants—squashes, melons, cucumbers, gourds (*Luffa acutangula*, *Lagenaria leucantha*, *Cucurbita pepo*, *Trichosanthes* sp., and others)—are grown in the swidden, placed according to their growth habits and water requirements. Leaves and flowers from some of the squash vines are an important dietary supplement from the middle of the rainy season onward to harvest time, and some of these plants are grown in winter gardens as well. Several of the cucumber and squash species are stored for use in the dry season.

Many different kinds of herbs and seasoning plants are grown in the swiddens as well as in winter gardens. These include garlic and onions *(Allium sativum, A. porrum)*, coriander *(Foeniculum vulgare)*, lemon grass *(Cymbopogon citratus)*, mint *(Mentha arvensis)*, and a variety of other herbs *(Mesona* sp., *Spilanthes acmella, Heracleum burmanicum*, etc.).

Several kinds of seed or grain plants are grown in the swiddens or along their margins. Sorghum has already been mentioned. Others include Job's tears *(Coix lachryma-jobi)*, used primarily for beads, millet *(Setaria italica)* and *Eleusine coracana*, used for brewing liquor in some Lua' villages, and sesame *(Sesamum indicum)*, pounded and mixed with rice as a flavoring in special ceremonial foods.

A few other species such as eggplant *(Solanum* spp.) and tomatoes *(Lycopersicum* sp.) may be grown in swiddens but are more commonly planted in gardens. Several varieties of eggplant grow wild around the village and are gathered occasionally. Tomato seeds were first introduced at Pa Pae by a Border Patrol Police teacher in about 1960; tomatoes are now grown from seeds purchased in the valley.

This review of plants grown in swiddens indicates something of the variety of swidden crops, their relative importance, and the variety of cultivation techniques (see appendix 6.2). One of the remarkable things to a novice in this type of gardening is the ability of the Lua' and Karen farmers, even as young children, to distinguish successfully between the 84 cultivated varieties plus 16 useful uncultivated varieties that grow together with numerous weeds, even at the stage when the plants are less than a centimeter in size.

By early May the planting has been completed and there is another lull in the work as the people wait for the rains to begin. Soon the rice will sprout and the annual battle with weeds will start; and as soon as the rains have softened the ground, work can begin in earnest on the irrigated fields.

WEEDING THE SWIDDENS (photos 41–42)

Weeding is the most time consuming, most labor consuming, most uncomfortable, and most disliked portion of swidden agriculture. The weeding season starts as soon as the sprouting rice is distinguishable from other growing plants. This is shortly after the first rains have come, as early as the end of May or the beginning of June. Weeding parties are usually small, generally limited to household members or immediate relatives (brothers, sisters, brothers-in-law, sisters-in-law, sons, daughters, sons-in-law, daughters-in-law, parents, or parents-in-law) and close friends. The Lua' consider it unpleasant because often only one or two people will go out together, bending over in the hot sun or the pouring rain, scratching, pulling, and chopping at the fast-growing weeds with their short-handled, L-shaped weeding tools, tying up innumerable small bundles of weeds, and leaving them to decay on the stumps of the felled trees and bare patches in the swiddens. The task seems endless and can be abandoned only when the rice is about to ripen, sometimes in mid-September.

Three complete weedings are considered to be the minimum, but few households are able to get through four weedings of their swiddens. All farmers assert that rice production increases according to the number of times a field is weeded during the growing season. This impression is confirmed when, for some reason, the weeding cannot be completed on schedule. In August 1966 there was a measles outbreak at Pa Pae, the first in 20 years, and everyone under 20 years of age was infected with the disease. Weeding came to a halt because everyone in the village was either sick or at home nursing those who were ill. By harvest time the weeds on most fields were as high as the rice, and the harvest that year was the worst anyone in the area could remember.

Most farmers state that the reason they do not clear larger swiddens is that they recognize the limitations of their household's labor supply, and larger swiddens, though they could be cleared and planted, could not be weeded. Weed growth is also a major reason why swiddens in this area are not planted for more than one year in succession. The effect of the swidden fire in delaying and limiting weed growth and influencing the survival of species in swiddened areas has not been systematically investigated, but this may be one of the most important side effects of the use of fires in swidden agriculture. Weeding itself may influence survival of species in the secondary growth, but this has not been investigated, and it would be difficult to study in areas where swiddening has been practiced for many decades. The number of noncultivated plants used by Lua' villagers, which grow and are collected in the fallow swiddens during the period between cultivations totals about 200 varieties, as shown in table 6.19.

Lua' and Karen farmers recognize the need for a long fallow period in order to restore fertility to swidden fields. This opinion has been confirmed by the studies of Sanga Sabhasri and Paul Zinke at Pa Pae, which are reported in detail in chapters 7 and 8. Their studies show that it takes at least seven years for the trend toward leaching of soil nutrients to be reversed and for recycling of a major portion of the nutrients into the secondary growth plants. After about nine years of fallow the soil conditions have returned to approximately their state prior to cultivation. Thus the 10-year cultivation-fallow cycle appears to be a stable pattern. Grassy plants such as bamboo and *Imperata* are present in the secondary growth but do not dominate it even where this pattern of cultivation and fallow has been followed for many cycles. A decrease in the length of fallow would undoubtedly lead to a decline in soil fertility and a decline in crop yield in the cultivated area. A shortening of the cycle might also lead to a change in the succession of secondary plant growth from predominantly leafy species to grassy species, making further use of the land for swidden cultivation difficult or impossible, as has happened in some Hmong hill fields.[3]

The increase in population is already forcing the Karen in Laykawkey and elsewhere in this area to shorten their cultivation-fallow cycle, and occasionally to farm marginal land. This has had the predictable result of decreased yield and may be leading to changes in the pattern of secondary vegetation in the marginal land.

PREPARING THE IRRIGATED FIELDS
(photos 68–76)

Most of the heavy work of irrigated agriculture takes place during the weeding season, and a shortage of labor thus limits the amount of swidden cultivation that can be done by farmers with sizeable irrigated fields.

Ordinarily the irrigated fields are not double cropped; after harvest the fences are taken down and domestic animals are left to graze on the stubble. One early task in the new cultivation season is the preparation and sowing of the seed nursery. The nursery may be planted either in a small irrigated section or on a small hillside swidden. Use of a swidden nursery simplifies and speeds the work, but it is not satisfactory for some varieties of rice grown in the irrigated fields and has a lower seed/yield ratio. The irrigated nurseries are usually made on a portion of the irrigated field near the irrigation ditch, to which water can be brought easily even before the streams rise to their normal rainy-season level. The dam and ditch must be cleaned and prepared before this nursery can be sown.

Dams in this area are relatively simple constructions. At the simplest, they involve merely channeling the water of a small creek into a ditch leading to the fields. At the largest, the dams in this hill region span a distance of no more than 15 or 20 meters and serve to raise the water level in the streams no more than a meter. No attempt is made to block the flow of the stream completely. The objective is to raise the water level and divert a portion of the water into the ditches. Dams are built by thrusting or hammering sharpened stakes into the stream bed and then piling logs, brush, stones, and mud against them on the upstream side. The dams usually have to be rebuilt each year before the irrigation season, when the water in the streams is still low. They are often damaged by the occasional torrents which follow heavy rains and may raise the level of water in the streams by a meter or more in a few minutes. The speed and volume of water at these times is very great, and the water may shift large stones in the stream bed.

The owners of the fields served by the dam have the responsibility to repair and rebuild the dam and clean the ditches. Since these irrigation systems rarely encompass more than three or four fields, the work crews are rarely very large. Often one person is considered to be the head of the dam and ditch system. This is usually the person who originally organized the building of the system, or his descendant or the purchaser of his field. This man plans and organizes the work that must be done on the system, including the ritual for the spirit of the dam, in which all of the field owners participate at the time the dam and ditches have been renewed for the new agricultural season.

Irrigated agriculture has been practiced by Lua' mountain dwellers in villages such as Baw Luang at least since the 1880s, and probably earlier (see Hallett 1890). The Lua' and Karen in eastern Mae Sariang District, however, began making irrigated fields only about 40 years ago. At first they attempted to imitate the Northern Thai farmers whom they had seen in the lowlands, but these attempts were unsuccessful. Lua' from Pa Pae then employed Northern Thai from around Umeng in San Pa Tong District, Chiang Mai Province, to come and teach the techniques of irrigation. These "foreign advisers" also instructed the Lua' villagers in Northern Thai rituals associated with irrigated agriculture. The Lua' use Northern Thai prayers and rituals for the dam and ditch spirits, but use traditional Lua' rituals when harvesting these fields.

Most of the Karen in this area learned irrigation techniques from the Lua' but have transformed the rituals into Karen form. Karen have often employed Lua' workers to build the dams and ditches and level the fields, because they believe the Lua' are more skilled and do a neater job than would Karen. Karen ordinarily do their own repair and maintenance of the irrigation systems.

Irrigated agriculture involves cooperation between Lua' and Karen farmers on a much more regular basis than does shifting cultivation, since many of the irrigation systems in this area serve fields owned by both Lua' and Karen farmers. Lua' also occasionally employ Karen workers to help with the heavy work of plowing and harrowing. These are usually teenage boys from poor families in nearby villages. They work for their room and board and wages paid in cash or kind. Similar arrangements may be made within the village, so that a young boy will live for a month or two with the farmer's family or in the field shelter while he helps by leading the buffalos, plowing or harrowing, or assisting in fencing. This sort of arrangement is usually made by the owner of an irrigated field who has neither son nor younger brother to help with these tasks.

Once the dam and ditch have been repaired the farmer can prepare his irrigated nursery. The ground is usually hoed, then thoroughly irrigated to soften the soil, which then may be hoed again. When the soil has reached a smooth, muddy consistency it is carefully leveled with a long stick or pole as the irrigation water is allowed to reach a depth of about 5 cm. The water is allowed to clear, and the rice seed is broadcast onto the water, evenly distributed over the nursery. No special fertilizer is used in the nursery.

The seedlings are ready for transplanting in a month or six weeks, when they have grown to about 20–30 cm. The timing of sowing and transplanting depends on the rains, since the sun-baked fields harden to almost concrete-like consistency and must be thoroughly soaked before they can be plowed. The irrigated nurseries are usually sown in June and transplanted in July. Swidden-style nurseries are sown earlier.

Before the irrigated fields can be transplanted the dikes between the field sections must be repaired and cleaned of weeds, and the field must be plowed, harrowed, and fenced. The dikes are cleaned and weeded with a hoe. Dikes are repaired, and new gates are built in them as necessary. Short sections of bamboo are used to shunt the water from one section of the field to the next. After the fields have been flooded they can be plowed with a buffalo-drawn plow. This requires two people—one man to guide the plow, and another, often a young boy or occasionally a woman, to lead the buffalo. Plowing is hard work for man and beast, trudging through the knee-deep mud, lifting the heavy plow over each dike as the field is plowed from one end to another, and persuading the buffalo to stop, go, and turn as necessary. The farmers try to avoid plowing or harrowing in the heat of the day in order to conserve the strength of the buffalos. This is the only work the buffalos do all year, but the farmers are concerned lest the exertion cause them to lose strength, get thin, and die. After the plowing season the farmers hold a ceremony for the souls of their buffalos, so that the souls will stay with the animals and prevent their illness.

TRANSPLANTING IRRIGATED FIELDS
(photos 77–79)

Transplanting the irrigated fields requires a large concentration of labor in a short period of time. Those farmers who have no swiddens and who have gone to help plant the swiddens of their relatives and friends can call on them now to repay the debt of reciprocal labor, but they may have to hire additional workers and engage in reciprocal labor arrangements with other owners of irrigated fields.

The rice nursery (if it is irrigated) is drained and the soil allowed to dry slightly before the seedlings are pulled, usually the day before transplanting. Women usually do this work while the men are busy completing the plowing and harrowing to prepare the fields for transplanting.

The seedlings are pulled from the moist earth, a few at a time, then collected in a bundle and tied. The top 10 or 15 cm is twisted off the seedlings, and they are now ready for transplanting.

Transplanting can be done by older men or women, but is most commonly done by adolescent and young-adult boys and girls. Three or four seedlings are pushed into the mud at one time; spacing is judged by eye and is fairly regular, but no attempt is made to regulate spacing with any precision.

Once the fields are transplanted, relatively little work remains until harvest. The level of the water must be regulated; the dikes, ditches, and dam must be kept in repair; and the fields must be weeded perhaps twice before harvest, but this is a relatively easy job, compared with weeding the swiddens.

The irrigated crop is generally a nonglutinous rice which ripens slightly ahead of the upland crop. Several other varieties are grown, including different colors of glutinous rice, and several varieties which may be grown either in upland or irrigated fields. Some farmers plant tobacco, peppers, or soya beans along the dikes of their fields, but never as many varieties as are commonly planted in the swiddens.

Usually the farmers put fish traps in their fields, commonly placing them so that the water entering the field must pass through a trap; they also install traps to catch any fish as the water flows from one section of the field to the next.

WATER RIGHTS

In this area water is not scarce during the rainy season, and the people of Pa Pae and Laykawkey report no problems about allocation of water among the users of a single dam and ditch system. Conflicts between owners of different dams on the same stream are theoretically possible, but no cases have been reported. Informants suggest that two principles would be used in handling such cases: the owner of the first dam to be built should have priority, and the people above should have priority over those downstream. No formal mechanism exists for resolving water disputes between owners from different villages. During the dry season, when water is scarce, there is a greater possibility of conflicts, but dry-season irrigated crops are very rarely planted, and no conflicts are reported. Possibilities of double cropping appear to be limited by scarcity of water and perhaps by unsuitability of local varieties to temperature and sunlight conditions of the dry and early rainy season.

COSTS OF DEVELOPING IRRIGATED FIELDS

The cost of irrigated agriculture in these hills rose sharply in the late 1960s, but there was no compensating increase in rice price to finance investment or increased production. The price of rice sold in the mountains followed a relatively stable pattern, starting at about 5 *baht* (US 25 cents) per *tang* (20 liters) of unhusked rice at harvest, rising to 10 *baht* per *tang* within two or three months, and reaching 20 or even 30 or 35 *baht* in bad years, before harvest. This seasonal pattern remained in the hills through the 1960s, at which time husked hill rice sold in the valley for 20 to 35 *baht* per *tang*. Rice ripens earlier in the hills than in the valley, and there used to be a price differential favoring hill farmers at harvest time. Thus it was profitable for them to husk rice and carry it to the lowlands for sale. The price difference, which used to favor hill farmers, has diminished or vanished since the all-weather road connected Mae Sariang and the Yuam valley (traditionally a rice deficit area) with Chiang Mai and the Ping valley (a rice surplus area).

Meanwhile the costs of irrigated farming in the hills have increased. The increase in land prices has already been mentioned. The price of buffalos in the hills used to be far below that in the Chiang Mai valley, but doubled between 1964 and 1969. After the all-weather road was built to Mae Sariang, stock buyers began to come through the mountain villages regularly to buy buffalos and cows and ship them to Chiang Mai. The price for a large adult buffalo reached at least 1,200 *baht* (US $60), and most farmers could no longer afford to buy them. Rent for buffalos also increased (average cost to 11 Lua' farmers in 1968 was about 105 *baht* per season), and it became harder to find any to rent. Pa Pae farmers said that buffalo owners from other villages refused to rent them buffalos because a number of the animals died in the Pa Pae area in the past few years, and they feared that the cause of death might be contagious. These conditions have made it more difficult for new families to get started in irrigated agriculture and for some of those with smaller irrigated land holdings and no buffalo to continue irrigated farming.

Irrigated fields have been made in all the wider and flatter spots in the narrow mountain valleys. By now all of the easily irrigated spots in the area of Pa Pae and Laykawkey have been developed. The enlargement of the total area under irrigation now depends on the yearly addition of a few square meters of terraces, painstakingly carved with hoes out of the hillsides at the lower ends of existing fields. A few tiny patches of well-watered bottomland remain in the smaller valleys, and all of these have been claimed. There seems to be little possibility of further major expansion of irrigation with the limited technology and resources available to these people.

PEST CONTROL (photos 43–47)

Crops in the swiddens and irrigated fields are subject to a variety of pests, but traditional techniques are not very effective in dealing with them. Ants and other creatures begin to carry off the seed as soon as the swiddens are planted. Pests of this type are considered in the same category as epidemics, and both Lua' and Karen appeal for supernatural aid to limit these losses (Karen planting prayers specifically mention "little red ants" and ask that they stay away). Deadfall traps and snares in a variety of forms are put up in the swiddens to attempt to deal with rats, one of the major pests. Lua' farmers erect long fences of closely spaced bamboo stakes about 25 cm tall to force the rats to run through deadfalls which are baited with a few rice grains.

Bears and wild pigs are major threats to the fields, especially when maize and other crops begin to ripen. Both are believed to be smart and dangerous, and they are hunted but without regular success. Pigs were reported to be plentiful and very destructive of crops in 1968; green parrots were common in the fields and very destructive in 1967. As the fields begin to ripen, the villagers move to their field huts to spend the nights. They wake periodically to build up the fire, talk, sing, and blow on their buffalo horns, hoping the noise will scare away the animals. The Karen villagers wanted to borrow my tape recorder or radio to play at night so the bears or pigs would think there were people about, thereby letting the farmers get a good night's sleep. The farmers also have wind- and water-powered noisemakers to scare animals and birds, but the animals quickly learn to ignore them.

Many insects and diseases attack the crops, but the farmers have only prayers to fight them off. They use local plants in their households for insecticides or repellents (Desmodium pulchellum, Moghania strobilifera), and have learned of chemical insecticides from malaria control teams which periodically visit the villages to spray houses for mosquitos. These people have neither the knowledge nor the resources to apply insecticides to the crops. Other than the unintended effects of swidden fires and of moving their fields each year, their only recourse is to the supernatural—attempting to influence the action of the insect pests and diseases by prayers and offerings to the spirits. Both Lua' and Karen villagers hold major ceremonies during the growing season to enlist help from the spirits in promoting growth of the crops and protecting them from various pests.

HARVEST (photos 50–67)

Unlike the start of planting of the swiddens, the time of harvest is not subject to rules of precedence dependent on village social structure. As already mentioned, minor crops (maize, mustard greens, peppers, etc.) are harvested from time to time as they ripen; rice is harvested when it is mature, or, if the field owner has run out of rice, as soon as the grain becomes edible. The rice harvest involves a series of operations: cutting the rice, drying it, building a threshing floor, piling the dried sheaves, carrying them to the threshing platform, threshing, cleaning, winnowing, temporary storage, and transport to permanent storage. Rituals accompany most of these steps, to insure a bountiful harvest and to prevent the rice from being used up too fast through loss of its "soul."

Starting late in September, the rice plants turn yellow as they mature and the heavy rains of the monsoon begin to taper off. The rice, both in the irrigated fields and in the swiddens, grows in clumps of two to five or more plants. Unless the seed has been mixed, these usually mature simultaneously. When the rice is judged to be ripe, it is cut, one clump at a time. This work is usually done by family members, sometimes assisted by relatives and friends on an exchange labor basis. Both men and women join in the work. The curved, serrated, iron-bladed sickle is held in the right hand, while the clump of rice plants is grasped with the left hand, and the sickle is drawn across the stalks, cutting them so as to leave about 25 cm of stubble and at least 75 cm of stem attached to the ears. The cut bunch is carried in the crook of the left arm until five or more bunches have been cut. These are carefully laid to dry on top of the stubble, taking care to keep both the ears and the stem ends off the dirt. The small work crews take several days to cut the rice on a single swidden.

The cut rice is left to dry for at least one day, sometimes for several days, depending on its ripeness, the weather, the press of other work,

the amount of rice left to be cut, and the ability to organize a large enough work party for threshing.

Men build the threshing platforms in the swiddens by leveling off, excavating, and filling to make a flat area at least 2 meters wide and 3 or more meters long. They pack and smooth the soil, supporting the downhill side by stakes. Using sturdy mats made of split bamboo to line the floor, the men form a surface on which the sheaves can be piled while awaiting threshing. Mats are tied to a height of about 2 or 2.5 meters on a pole framework on the downhill side, to catch the grains as they are threshed.

If possible, a large crew must be assembled for at least the first day of threshing. Ritual activities and cooking are the duties of the older men and of the field owner, who, depending on his age, will also assist in various phases of the threshing. It is usually the task of younger men to do the threshing itself. Women and children collect the dried bunches of rice stalks into huge armloads, and other women and older children carry them to the threshing floor.

Each thresher picks up a bunch of stalks, ties them at their base with a woven threshing cloth (Lua') or a rope braided out of rice straw (Karen), lifts the bundle over his or her head and beats the heads of the stalks on the mats of the threshing floor. They hit each bundle on the floor four or five times, twisting and shaking the bundle between strokes to free the grains which have been knocked loose. Among the Lua' this is men's work, but occasionally Karen women will thresh. Usually two people will thresh in this manner, while two others, usually men, stand at either end of the platform and beat the discarded straw with bamboo beaters shaped like hockey sticks. The beaters pick up the straw with their sticks, shake it and beat it repeatedly to knock out all possible grain. Then they lift the straw on their lower leg and kick it over the side of the platform, where it piles up as the day wears on. In spite of the heavy investment in labor, the yield from beating is quite low—the beaters probably salvage no more than 5 percent of the grain, though they form 10 to 20 percent of the harvest work force. Most of the grain is actually knocked off by the first stroke of the threshers. Beating also increases the amount of broken straw, unfilled kernels, and chaff in the rice, which increases the task of winnowing. Even though they realize that beating is not very productive, the farmers feel it is necessary and that it would be wasteful not to do this task. This is another indication of the marginality and labor intensiveness of this form of agriculture.

Threshing and beating is exhausting labor and the workers usually take a break or change jobs every hour or so, while the pilers and carriers restock the supply of unthreshed rice at the platform.

The Karen use a large round woven bamboo fan with a short bamboo handle for winnowing. This is usually a job for men. After a large pile of grain has been accumulated on the threshing floor, one of the workers, often a woman, will sort through the grain with outspread fingers to remove as much straw as possible. Then one or more men fan the rice while stirring it up with their feet, blowing the straw and chaff to the ends of the threshing platform, where it can be either fanned off or picked through and sorted out by hand. The Karen winnow repeatedly between sessions of threshing, all the while urging the rice to climb higher and higher as they hit the rice stalks against the floor.

The Lua' farmers use a separate winnowing floor, which they level and line with mats. They build a short ladder by setting two heavy notched poles in the ground and lashing crossbars to them. After the rice has been threshed and partially winnowed by the same techniques as used by the Karen, young Lua' girls and maidens carry baskets of rice to the winnowing floor, climb the ladder, and pour the rice over their shoulders to the floor, while boys and young men stand below and fan the falling grain to blow away the chaff.

The farmers like to complete as much of the harvest as possible on the first day they begin threshing, because they are rarely able to organize a large work group later in the harvest. On succeeding days the turnout is much smaller at any one field, as everyone is anxious to complete his own field in case of high wind or rain, or in case bears, pigs, or birds should appear. As each area of the field is cleared, the farmers may make new threshing platforms to reduce the distance over which the unthreshed rice must be carried. In this way the harvest continues for a month or six weeks, starting with the earliest ripening strains in the irrigated fields and in wettest portions of the swiddens, and moving on to the late ripening varieties and finally to the seed rice.

Rice which will be used for seed is usually allowed to stand on the stalk until all other rice has been reaped, to insure that it is thoroughly mature. Usually a good-looking section of the crop is reserved for this purpose. Sometimes if the farmers are dissatisfied with their seed or the quality of rice, especially if they feel it has become mixed (glutinous mixed with nonglutinous varieties), they attempt to purify the seed. They do this by selecting individual heads which appear to have the desired characteristics. They sow this seed separately from the main crop the following year, and after two years they usually have enough seed to sow the entire field with the purified strain.

When all the day's grain has been winnowed, it is measured into a "standard" size basket or kerosene tin and loaded into a rice-carrying basket to be carried to a temporary barn. As each measuring basket is filled and loaded into a carrying basket, one man keeps a tally by making a sharp bend in a stick of split bamboo. The tally sticks are kept in bundles of ten, and each stick is bent in ten places to keep track of the total number of baskets harvested.

If the fields are very close to the village, the grain may be carried directly to the barn or porch of the farmer's house, but usually the farmer makes a temporary barn out of his field shelter by reinforcing the walls and lining the floor and walls with mats. Usually two or more family members sleep in the temporary barn to guard the rice against animal pests and human thieves until it can be carried to the village.

The harvest is not considered complete until the rice has been carried safely home to the village. Unless the family has immediate need for rice, this task is not begun until the threshing has been completed. If the fields are unusually far from the village, the farmers may build another temporary barn along the trail, and shuttle back and forth between field and temporary barn before carrying the rice to the village. Rice is carried on the backs of men and women, boys and girls, in rice baskets which may hold as much as 40 liters or more—a weight of 25–30 kg for upland rice. Women carry rice by supporting the load on a woven rattan forehead strap; men carry their loads by rigging a rope through a pair of carrying hooks, one of which rests on each shoulder. These hooks are made of curved sections of bamboo stems and roots through which a hole has been bored or burned for passage of the rope. If the harvest has been good and the distance to the fields is great, it may take two weeks or more after the end of the threshing to carry all the rice back to the village.

Thus the harvest period extends from late in September, when the earliest ripening rice is cut, up to the end of November or even early December. By this time the weather has become cool and dry, food is relatively plentiful, and it is time to complete the ceremonial cycle associated with cultivation. These ceremonies attempt to restore the beings of the supernatural world to their conditions prior to cultivation. The souls of the people must be called from the swiddens, where they may have lingered, back to the village to live within the bodies of their owners; the spirit owners of the fields are allowed to return to their homes, and the guardian spirits of the village are asked for assistance in protecting the village, its possessions, and its inhabitants for another year.

By mid-December these rites have been completed, the old year has ended, and a new one begins with a period of relatively limited activity. This is the time of year for weddings, for cutting roofing grass (*Imperata* sp.) and weaving grass shingles, for reroofing and repairing houses and barns, for gardening, and for visits to market. Only the cotton remains to be harvested in the swiddens, and this is picked from time to time as it ripens.

The struggle to have enough to eat throughout the year continues in the village after the harvest has been brought home. The richer villagers have rice barns—pile structures built of wood and bamboo and roofed with grass or leaf shingles. Often these villagers attempt to keep out rodents by tying smooth and shiny bamboo culm covers around each of the uprights that support the rice barn; a few of the more affluent may use the sheet metal from kerosene tins for the same purpose. In spite of these efforts, rats often find a way in, and occasionally even domestic chickens will find holes in the roof through which they can fly or climb. Poorer people keep their rice in large baskets woven of heavy bamboo, lined with mats, and packed on the outside with a mixture of mud and dung. These are loosely covered with a mat and are even less proof against rats than the storehouses.

Very few domestic cats have survived in the mountains since the malaria control teams have begun to visit the hill villages. The cats apparently die of DDT poisoning within a week or two of the time the houses have been sprayed for malaria control. The rat population, perhaps as a result, appears to have increased rapidly in the past few years, and though both Lua' and Karen have a variety of traps, the villagers say that their loss to rats has increased markedly. Children occasionally organize rat hunts in the houses or barns, catching baby rats by hand or stabbing them with sharpened bamboo stakes. This offers only temporary relief. Without better storage technology, the villagers are able to do nothing further about the rats than to appeal to the spirits to help them.

USE OF SWIDDENS AFTER HARVEST

The swiddens continue to be used after the harvest and during the fallow period. Gathering of peppers has already been mentioned, and a variety of wild products appear as the secondary growth returns to the fields. Domestic animals are allowed to graze in the fields as soon as the food crops have been harvested and the fences are taken down. Women continue to go to fallow swiddens in their daily search for firewood, and they may gather a variety of edible and otherwise useful plants while they are there. The Lua' recognize and use several hundred species of plants in the fallow swiddens (see appendix 6.2).

MINOR AGRICULTURAL ACTIVITIES: SECOND CROPPING AND GARDENING (photos 85–91)

Second cropping (use of irrigated fields in the dry season) is rarely done in this area. No farmers at Laykawkey and only one farmer at Pa Pae cultivated a second rice crop in the two years of observation at Laykawkey and the five years at Pa Pae. The farmers feel that second cropping is only marginally productive, and the experience of the one Pa Pae farmer tends to confirm this. His second rice crop was planted in February and not harvested until late June 1968. His yield was only 40 *tang*, as compared with 120 *tang* from his 1967 rainy-season crop, and the decline in his 1968 rainy-season crop to 86 *tang* was perhaps attributable to double cropping (photo 74). The exact cause of the low yield is not known. Water quantity seemed sufficient, but cool weather during the early dry season, and photoperiodicity of the rice variety probably contributed to the low yield.

A few Karen farmers in nearby villages (not Laykawkey) grow soya beans in their irrigated fields during the dry season, and some Lua' and Karen farmers raise a dry-season crop of tobacco in a small portion of their irrigated fields, but that is the extent of double cropping in this region. No dry-season crops are planted on the swiddens.

All Pa Pae households and some of the households at Laykawkey make vegetable gardens during the dry season. Many families own or share semipermanent agricultural resources such as fruit trees and sugarcane, or semidomesticated plants such as rattan and bamboo, which they plant around the village. Pa Pae villagers locate their dry-season gardens along the banks of the stream that runs through their village, and they have developed small ditches to bring water to the gardens. They begin preparing their gardens after the harvest is completed and the end-of-the-year ceremonies have been held. The gardens are abandoned late in the dry season or early in the rainy season. Gardening is the work of the household, and there is little or no exchange labor and no wage labor in this activity.

The gardens must be very carefully fenced in order to exclude pigs, chickens, and ducks, which wander freely around the village. Soil is prepared by mixing in manure from domestic animals. Chicken manure is preferred for this purpose. Human feces are not used. The Lua' plant mainly mustard greens, onions, garlic, herbs, and a few other vegetables in their gardens (see appendix 6.2), and these form an important addition to the diet during the early part of the dry season. The gardens are carefully tended and weeded. Vegetables of a single type ordinarily are grown in rows or in slightly raised groups of rows. The Lua' ordinarily irrigate early in the morning or late in the afternoon, by flicking water from the stream or from pools in the gardens over the plants. They use a curved section of bamboo 10–15 cm wide and about 50–75 cm long to scoop up the water. In the late 1960s a few of the gardeners developed irrigation systems within their gardens to lead the water directly between the rows of plants, and others began using watering cans made from kerosene tins which they purchased in the lowlands. Laykawkey Karen make relatively few dry-season vegetable gardens and occasionally buy surplus greens from Pa Pae gardeners.

Another type of garden, made by both Pa Pae and Laykawkey villagers, is more permanent and contains such plants as sugarcane, bananas, lemon grass, ginger, *kha* root, bamboo and other long-lived plants. Once these plants are established they do not require watering, and they do not have to be fenced and tended as carefully as the vegetable gardens. Many bananas are eaten by babies in the form of a gruel which is premasticated by their parents.

A large number and variety of fruit trees are planted in and around Pa Pae. Most conspicuous are the jackfruit, mango, pomelo, lime, and guava trees, and the areca (betel nut) and coconut palms. These trees are owned by the individual who planted them or by his descendants. When the fruits are plentiful they are usually shared with anyone who asks permission to pick them. The main exceptions are coconut and betel nut trees. Pa Pae seems to be located at about the upper elevation limit at which coconuts will grow, and there are no other coco palms for many kilometers; betel nut is a highly saleable product and is given away only as a matter of hospitality in the home, or at ceremonies. Few of the Karen villages in the area have been established for as long as Pa Pae, and not many Karen have troubled to plant fruit trees other than bananas. They frequently come to Pa Pae to ask for fruit of various kinds.

With the exception of jackfruit, fruit is consumed primarily by children. Of the fruits grown at Pa Pae, the jackfruit is probably the most important source of food. Jackfruits ripen early in the rainy season (June–July), but unripe fruits are picked and curried from the time they reach 10 cm in length. Mangoes are also important. Most of the wild and domesticated fruits are eaten by children before they are completely ripe. Although the total quantity eaten may not be very large, fruits are probably an important source of vitamins and minerals not plentiful elsewhere in the diet.

DOMESTIC ANIMALS

Domestic animals in these Lua' and Karen villages include dogs, cats, chickens, ducks, pigs, cows, water buffalos, and elephants (table 6.4). Most Pa Pae and Laykawkey households have one or more dogs. Dogs in the mountains resemble the typical "Thai dogs" in the north of Thailand. They are shorthaired and have a long tail that curls over the back, a relatively long pointed nose, and short ears. The dogs are used by both Lua' and Karen households as watch-

TABLE 6.4 Domestic Animals Owned by Lua' and Karen Villagers

| | Lua' of Pa Pae [a] | | Karen of Laykawkey [b] | |
| | Families Owning Animals | Total Number Owned | Families Owning Animals | Total Number Owned |
Animals	No. (%)		No. (%)	
Buffalos	15 (30)	59	23 (74)	80
Cows	0 (0)	0	3 (10)	10
Pigs	46 (92)	138	25 (81)	75
Chickens	48 (96)	703+	31 (100)	311+
Ducks	2 (4)	4	0 (0)	0
Dogs	17 (28)	20	21 (68)	29
Cats [c]	2 (4)	2	0 (0)	0
Elephants (owned)	0 (0)	0	4 (13)	5
Elephants (shared)	0 (0)	0	5 (16)	5
Elephants owned or shared [d]	0 (0)	0	8 (26)	n.a.

[a] Ownership as of June 1967, 50 households.
[b] Ownership as of June 1968, 31 households.
[c] Supplied by the author after all other cats in the village had died.
[d] Many of these are shared in several villages, and thus the shares cannot be added to represent whole animals present in a single village.

dogs and scavengers of spoiled and leftover food and human feces, and in some households as pets. They are fed leftover rice and curry. Pa Pae villagers use dogs as sacrifices to forest and other spirits and sometimes have to buy them for this purpose. Pa Pae villagers do not eat dogs, but Lua' of Chang Maw village, and several other villages farther to the north, eat dogs on ceremonial occasions. Karen in this area neither eat dogs nor sacrifice them. Dogs are penned or tied only when they are new to a household or when they are destined to be sacrificial offerings. Otherwise they are allowed to roam freely.

In the past, Lua' and Karen have kept cats as household pets, and especially to control domestic rats and mice. Cats are allowed to roam freely throughout the village. As already mentioned, almost every cat in this mountain area died following the DDT spraying by malaria control teams.

Almost every household keeps a few chickens, primarily for sacrifice or consumption, but not for eggs. Eggs are rarely eaten except on ceremonial occasions and are not felt to be appropriate food except for old people. Chicks and chickens are sacrificed in most minor agricultural and curing rituals and are used in combination with larger animals during the major agricultural and communal ceremonies. A few old widows eke out a living raising chickens and pigs and brewing liquor for local sale. Chickens are fed when released from their pens at dawn and are given a few grains of rice to encourage them to return to their pens at night. They are allowed to scavenge when rice is being pounded or winnowed (photo 82). The chickens probably get most of their food by scratching, by eating unguarded rice when it is left to dry before pounding, or on the rare occasions when they find their way into a rice barn or under a leaking rice basket. Chickens are kept in round split-bamboo baskets placed in pens under the houses at night, and are allowed to run free during the day. Karen households which follow the ancestor-worship variety of religion *(awxe)* must rear special lines of chickens and pigs for eventual sacrifice to the family spirits. These animals cannot be killed, sold, or used for any other purpose. The nuisance of seeking and keeping separate lines of animals for this purpose is one reason commonly mentioned by Karen of Laykawkey for converting to the "tattooing" *(cekosi)* form of Karen religion, or to Christianity.

Only a few families keep ducks, perhaps because they are more trouble to rear than chickens. Duck owners must dig up the dirt every day so that the ducklings can scratch for grubs, and apparently ducks are more liable to be eaten by domestic dogs and cats than are chickens. Ducklings or ducks are occasionally required for sacrifices to spirits causing illness.

Most families keep swine of the black-and-white, sparse-haired, straight-tailed, sway-backed variety. They raise pigs for food, for sacrifice on ritual occasions, and sometimes for sale either locally or in the lowland market. Pigs are usually fed twice a day on a mixture of boiled rice, bran, food scraps, banana stalks, and wild taro leaves and stems. Pigs are also scavengers and spend the day rooting around for whatever they can find. They are penned under the house at night.

Buffalos are much less widely held than pigs or chickens. They represent a much higher investment per animal, and in general are owned by those who have irrigated fields, although not all irrigated field owners have buffalos of their own. Buffalos are ordinarily turned loose to graze in the fallow swiddens (or in the fallow irrigated fields in the dry season). During the plowing season they are brought home or to the irrigated field shelter and tied up every night, but when they are not being used in the fields they are usually allowed to graze for three or four days, or a week or more at a time, before being brought home and tied up overnight. In this area buffalos are used only for plowing and harrowing, never for transport. Buffalos are not ordinarily fed, but may receive a little straw or salt in order to accustom them to their masters and to tame them. They are looked after solicitously, though without much knowledge, if they become ill, develop sores, or lose their appetite. Their owners make no real effort to control their grazing or to improve their pasture. Often they do not know exactly where the animals are, and sometimes the young boys of the families, who act as herdsmen, have to hunt for several hours before they are found. The distinct sound of each buffalo's wooden bell helps guide the owners to their animals, but occasionally the bell ropes break or the bells get clogged with mud, making them even more difficult to locate.

In addition to their use in plowing and harrowing, buffalos are sometimes used as sacrificial animals. This is a very rare event for the Karen, who would sacrifice a buffalo only in the case of a ritual to appease one of the major earth spirits; Lua' at Pa Pae may sacrifice several buffalos per year in communal agricultural ceremonies, for funerals of important people, for the guardian spirits of the village, or to appease spirits in case of a serious illness. In recent years these have all been small buffalos, although ideally they should be fully mature with well-developed horns. The increasing poverty of the people of Pa Pae, combined with the rise in the cost of buffalos, has caused them to delay or in some cases forego sacrifices which were customary in more affluent times.

Lua' entrepreneurs may butcher a young buffalo at a time when there is a great demand for meat. This might happen during either the planting or the harvest season, when a number of families are obliged to feed all the people who come to help in their fields. Often a small group of men will pool their resources to buy a buffalo and then sell shares in the meat, realizing about 10 percent profit on their investment; in the late 1960s and early 1970s, when cash has been scarce, they often sell shares before they purchase the animal for slaughter. Meat is not regularly obtainable in these mountain villages where there is no market, and anyone offering to sell meat usually can find buyers. Similar methods are used for obtaining large pigs to be butchered, and for purchasing large animals which are used in communal sacrifices, most of the meat of which is shared out in equal portions to all households in the village. The Karen of Laykawkey slaughter and eat large animals much less frequently than do the Lua' of Pa Pae.

The Lua' at Pa Pae have not owned cows for many years. Informants claim that cows they had in the past were difficult to control, required extensive fencing to keep them out of houses and gardens, and did a lot of property damage. Three households at Laykawkey have cows, and the nonowners confirm the Pa Pae opinion of the destructiveness of cattle. On rare occasions Lua' villagers need cows for ritual sacrifice, but ordinarily the cows in this region are sold to lowland buyers. In this hill area villagers use cows neither as draft animals nor for milk or meat. Mountain villagers do not use them as draft animals. The Laykawkey cows are herded by their adult owners. Every day they are turned loose or sometimes have to be driven out of the village to graze in fallow fields, and return each evening to be tied up under their owners' houses.

In the old days, three or four Pa Pae men owned elephants or shares in elephants, but the last of the animals was sold in the late 1940s. A few men in the nearby Lua' villages of La'up and Ban Dong own shares in elephants now. Lua' consider an elephant owner to be obviously wealthy, but they attach no other particular prestige to elephant ownership. They consider irrigated fields, well-built houses, and maintenance of the traditional standards of religious observances with expensive animal sacrifices to be more appropriate uses of their small surplus of capital or labor.

Many older Lua' informants recall working for European lumber company managers during a period when the Pa Pae villagers were richer than they are now. They attribute the general loss of affluence, including the loss of the elephants, to high prices for food coupled with low demand for work in the lumber industry and low prices for elephants in the days following the Second World War. The decline in the teak industry in this area after the war was a result of the closing of the Burmese border due to unsettled political conditions on the Burma side of the border and excessive taxes placed on teak logs floated down the Salween to market. The teak industry has revived in Mae Sariang District since the Phanasit Company, and later the Thai government, built a dry-season road connecting Mae Sariang with the Chiang Mai valley in the middle and late 1950s. Present-day elephant owners, especially Karen, benefit from this boom.

Several elephants are owned by Karen villagers at Laykawkey, and almost every nearby Karen village—Mae Umpok, Ban Hak Mai, Mae Umlong Luang, Ban Huai Pyng—has one or more elephant owners. There are also several elephant owners in the lowland Karen villages near Mae Sariang—Phaekho and Mae Tia. Ownership of an elephant or even sharing in elephant ownership confers great prestige upon a Karen, including even a special title. This prestige evidently is a powerful motivation for capital accumulation and investment in elephants.

Elephants have been a good investment in recent years. The demand for them has increased, and the price rose from perhaps 9,000–10,000 *baht* ($450–$500) in 1964 to 13,000–16,000 *baht* ($650–$800) or more for an adult elephant in 1969. Aside from the increase in value of elephants in recent years, the economic benefits of elephant ownership are not entirely clear. Costs of borrowing money (locally, at least 3 percent per month), wages for elephant drivers (about 150 *baht* per month, usually including food), and contract rates for use of elephants (about 20 *baht* per day, but varying widely with conditions of the contract) remained relatively constant over those five years. Under these conditions the rate of return on an elephant would seem to be relatively low, and the economic benefit appears to be from capital gains rather than from interest or earnings on the investment. One method which elephant owners in this mountain area have used to realize capital gains has been the rearing of young animals for sale or trade at markets as far away as Lampang (170 km in a straight line to the east).

Whatever the actual economic return, elephant ownership apparently enjoys the top priority in planning expenditures beyond the bare subsistence level. Most of the Karen questioned on the subject say they would prefer to invest in elephants rather than irrigated fields, and most have delayed spending money or time on building substantial houses with wooden siding (one mark of Lua' affluence) until they have acquired an elephant. Karen are almost unanimous in preferring to save money for elephants rather than spending it on expensive animal sacrifices, and they compliment themselves for having less-

demanding spirits than do their Lua' neighbors. As a result, they consume less meat and may suffer more from protein malnutrition.

Elephants are loved and pampered, especially in their youth, far more than any other domestic animal. They are grazed in the jungle and, rarely, in the fallow swiddens. Their owners visit them in the forest every few days, perhaps to move them from place to place, to insure that they are not getting into trouble and causing property damage, to bathe them, and to tend to any sores or cuts. Baby elephants are fed special balls of food to accustom them to human handling. Almost every Lua' and Karen boy from the age of 12–15 years knows how to drive an elephant, sitting on its head and guiding it by tickling or kicking it behind the ears, calling out the commands, and on occasion beating it on the head with a heavy jungle knife. Training elephants to work, however, is a highly complex, carefully protected professional skill, surrounded by a great deal of ritual. Only a few older men in the area have the proper technical and ritual knowledge, including knowledge of the proper chants, to train elephants. Their services are widely sought, even by Christian elephant owners.

Elephants are hired out mainly in the rainy season and the cooler part of the dry season. They are kept in the jungle-covered hills during the hot season and brought down to work in the valley after the rains start. Aside from a little local hauling of building materials and occasional transporting of rice from field to village (photo 66) or from village to market (a job for which they are not very well suited), elephants are employed primarily in the lumber industry, where they drag the logs to other forms of transportation, pile them, and move them from place to place in the drying and storage areas (photo 119).

Lumber companies with concessions to cut trees in specific parts of the forest usually arrange with contractors to have logs delivered to a road or track where they can be trucked to another destination. In Mae Sariang District, most of the contractors are Karen, and ownership and driving of elephants is practically a Karen monopoly. The contractors make subcontracts with elephant owners and drivers within a radius of at least 50 km to do parts of the elephant work, which need not be confined to work in Mae Sariang District. Contracts for elephant and driver may amount to 300–500 *baht* per month, but the amount is hard to calculate since it is usually based on number of logs delivered to a certain point. Because conditions vary widely, bidding on the contracts requires great skill and experience in estimating the length of time required to do the job.

The lumber industry is important to the people in the hill areas in absorbing some of the surplus labor. However, because of the timing of elephant use, this form of employment often conflicts with the requirements of the subsistence agricultural cycle. Also, because there has been very little reforestation, the lumbering industry in this area has been purely extractive, and employment cannot continue indefinitely at present levels.

The raising of domestic animals, from chickens to elephants, is usually seen as a supplement to subsistence agricultural activities. Until the early 1960s, when foreign breeding stock was introduced into this mountain area by the Border Patrol Police and missionaries, there has been no attempt to control or influence the breeding of domestic animals, nor to increase productivity by systematically improved feeding or care. The farmers are concerned about the ritual well-being of their animals (a head-washing, soul-restoring ceremony is held for each buffalo at the end of the plowing season, and for elephants when they have been worked hard or have been contaminated by contact with women), but aside from quarantine or isolation they have little practical knowledge of protection of the animals' health. They make relatively incomplete use of the products or by-products of the animals: they rarely use eggs as food except on a few ceremonial occasions, and make little attempt to see that eggs are collected or protected; they do not milk their buffalos or cows (as is true also of the goats that are reared in a few villages farther north); cows are not used as draft animals, and buffalos are used as draft animals for only about two months out of the year; neither cows nor buffalos are used as pack animals, although their use might help solve some of the transportation problems in the area; the farmers make little or no attempt to improve pasturage for grazing animals, although the burning of areas for swiddens may result in increased amounts of grass in the fallow swiddens. Unlike agriculture there is virtually no use of cooperative labor in animal husbandry, although cooperation might lead to more efficient grazing. There seems to be much room for improvement in subsistence use of domestic animals; this would require research to adapt methods to the requirements of the upland environment and the traditional socio-economic organization, knowledge, and practices of the hill villagers.

GATHERING, FISHING, AND HUNTING

Gathering, fishing, and hunting are regular supplementary subsistence activities which can be turned to when agriculture fails, or as a pleasant diversion from other routine activities.

Gathering becomes particularly important during the late dry season and especially during the early rainy season, when vegetable supplies from the swiddens and gardens are at their lowest ebb. Gathering is usually done by small groups of women. The most important food products, gathered in the largest quantities, are ferns, bamboo shoots, and mushrooms. From April (when the village gardens are almost dried up) through June (when the swiddens begin to produce) these probably are the major "vegetable" component of the diet.

Fishing yields an important but probably declining source of protein for the diet. Several methods are used to get fish from the small mountain streams (photos 108, 109). Trapping fish in the irrigated fields with conical or basket-shaped traps woven of bamboo has already been mentioned. Similar traps may also be set in the streams, especially where water overflows through holes in the dam. Another method, requiring cooperation of a number of people, is to dam off a portion of the creek bed when the water is low, and then bail the water out of the dammed off portion; the fish are then easily found on the dry creek bed. Lua' and Karen women use large dip nets, suspended from two crossed pieces of bamboo, which they lower into the river with a long bamboo pole. They also use small home-woven conical nets tied on a bent-bamboo hoop. Men sometimes use large casting nets, purchased or locally woven, weighted with pieces of chain. Another technique is simply to work along the stream bottom, behind and under rocks where the fish hide, feeling for fish and grabbing them by hand.

The yield from these operations is not great. Five people working for a day using several of these techniques may get as much as 10 liters of small fish, pollywogs, crayfish, and edible water insects. These are equally divided among all participants and taken home to enhance the daily curry. Fish are never caught in large enough quantity to be preserved or sold. These days,

anything longer than 7 or 8 cm is considered a large fish, but the older village residents tell of catching fish 50 cm long and larger "in the old days." They say the decline in abundance of fish is due to the use of chemical fish poisons and explosives, possibly by Thai living in the valley. Other possible explanations include the increased density of human population in the hills, the dumping of surplus DDT in creeks by malaria spray teams and possibly the damming of rivers downstream (if these dams affect the spawning habits of fish species formerly caught at higher elevations).

The Lua' are familiar with several plant species which can be used as fish poisons (*Acacia* sp., *Derris* sp.), but they claim they do not use them, and I have never observed them being used.

Beginning in the late 1960s, several attempts were made in these hill villages to introduce exotic, fast-growing fish species *(Tilapia)* into man-made fish ponds. The first attempt at Pa Pae, sponsored by the Border Patrol Police, failed when high water washed out the pond which had been built alongside the stream. A second attempt was successful in rearing fairly sizeable (20-cm or more) fish, but it was troubled by fish-eating snakes. Several individuals or groups of villagers at Pa Pae, inspired by this example, built ponds of their own, with varying success. A similar attempt by several families at Laykawkey was unsuccessful and abandoned because, they said, people stole the fish and it was difficult to keep the ponds from silting up or washing away. One farmer at Ban Huai Pyng, a nearby Karen hill village, had great success in developing a pond and rearing large (40-cm) fish; within 18 months he had given away fish to almost 100 farmers from 15 or more nearby villages so that they could stock their own ponds.

Undoubtedly, domesticated fish could be an important source of protein in this hill area, but the successful diffusion of fish culture depends on more extensive spread of technical knowledge and follow-up assistance after the ponds are constructed and the fish fry distributed.

Hunting, these days, provides a relatively minor source of protein. Many large animal species (wild cattle, tigers, etc.) are said to have vanished from this area within the past generation or two, probably as a result of increased population density and hunting pressure. Hunting techniques and weapons are primitive, which probably accounts for the survival of some species. Caplock, or even flintlock, guns are the principal weapons. No one in these hills except the police and the Hmong can afford to own and operate guns that use manufactured cartridges. Local blacksmiths in the hill villages can repair the muzzle-loading guns, and some of the blacksmiths are clever enough to be able to make new caplock guns out of scrap metal. The cost of guns is related to their quality and condition, and, in recent years, to their legality. They can be purchased for under 100 *baht* (US $5.00) up to 300 *baht* or more. Late in 1967, Thai officials attempted to register all guns. In Mae Sariang District the nominal fee for registration was about 75 *baht*, to which was added, in some cases, a special tax of about 25 *baht* to raise money for a bridge to be built near Mae Sariang. The fee was felt to be excessive by many of the villagers, some of whom could not raise the required cash. Many of the villagers paid the registration fee, but some simply gave up their weapons or attempted to sell them at much depressed prices; others made sure to keep them well concealed when government officials or strangers were around the village.

Many farmers take their guns with them when they go to burn the swiddens, hoping that the heat and flames will drive animals out of the burning fields. These hopes are rarely realized.

Hunters also go in large groups to beat through the woods and fallow swiddens in the hope of flushing a barking deer or a wild pig, but most of these expeditions are unsuccessful. Some men now are beginning to use flashlights for hunting at night. When a large animal is killed, it is shared among those who participated in the hunt, with the largest share belonging to the person or persons who actually shot the animal. Lua' villagers are obliged to give one leg of any large animal they shoot to the chief priest *(samang)* of the village. Karen villagers have no such obligation. Hunters also go out singly or in small groups, hoping to track down large game animals. On the rare occasions when a large animal is shot by a small party of hunters, there will be enough meat to sell in the village or even in nearby villages, but this seems to happen no more than three or four times a year. Game is sold at roughly the same local price as pork, between 5 and 10 *baht* per kilo in 1967. No one in this area makes his living by hunting. Bird hunters occasionally use guns, but they are not very successful at hitting the birds because they use relatively large, home-made shot, and are unable to control the scatter pattern very well. Successful small-animal and bird hunters usually use traps, snares, deadfalls, or trained cock decoys.

Lua' and Karen villagers gather a few products in the jungle to sell in the Mae Sariang market. These include orchids and the stems of a viney plant which is used for shampoo. They also may sell a few wild animals (monkeys, lorises) which they catch, as well as the hides and horns of deer and barking deer. They make little specific effort to obtain these items for sale and derive from them only a small amount of cash.

WAGE LABOR

As soon as the harvest is completed at Pa Pae, some of the young men leave to seek work in the lowlands, helping with the harvest there for several weeks, or taking jobs in the mines. All of the adult men at Pa Pae and many of the women have worked for wages in the lowlands at one time or another. Some of the young men leave the village on a regular schedule whenever they can afford to be away from subsistence agricultural tasks; other men have lived away from the village for a year or more, up to 20 years, working for a variety of lowland employers. In the event of a poor harvest some individuals or families have moved to the valley for a year or more, and, as already noted, a number of families moved permanently to the lowlands after a fire in Pa Pae in the late 1940s.

Karen men from Laykawkey also work for wages, but most of them shun the mines as too dangerous, perferring to work for the lumber industry. Most of their work is associated with elephants, and they find their jobs through contacts with Karen relatives and friends in the valley. A few of them also seek agricultural work in the valley during the dry season. A number of families have moved out of Laykawkey in search of better economic opportunities: some have moved to the valley, and some to other mountain villages; a few have been forced to return to Laykawkey because of shortage of land in other mountain areas.

Despite rapid economic and administrative development in Mae Sariang during the 1960s, there was little improvement in wage-work opportunities for hill people in the district. In fact, the opposite seems to have occurred. Some traditional jobs (porterage) were lost, and hill people are not trained to take the new jobs (truck driving, clerical work, etc.). Meanwhile the flow of hill dwellers seeking work increased noticeably, and the average wage for a day's unskilled work declined from the customary 10 *baht* to a reported 5 or 6. Some people attribute the decline in wages to the increasing number of opium addicts who are willing to work for whatever small wages they can get to support their habit. In fact, it was probably due simply to the oversupply of unskilled labor resulting from the general population increase in rural areas.

PRODUCTIVITY OF AGRICULTURAL SYSTEMS IN THE HILLS

Following this description of Lua' and Karen production systems, we may ask how productive these methods are, and how they compare with productivity elsewhere.

MEASURES OF PRODUCTIVITY

In order to determine quantities of rice produced, we asked each household head how much rice of each type his household had harvested (early, late, glutinous, and that reserved for seed), and also what he used to measure the yield. Both Lua' and Karen keep a tally of their rice production by counting the basketfuls of rice after it is threshed and winnowed, at the time it is loaded into the temporary rice barns, before it is carried to the village (photos 62, 63). The measures they use are variable. The Lua' of Pa Pae use two standard-size baskets, one roughly equivalent to the standard Thai measure of one *tang* (20 liters), and another twice this size. Most of the measuring baskets are made by a few craftsmen; they are used in the harvest rituals, and are kept for many years by the same household. All the baskets measured at Pa Pae (using an officially certified Thai standard *tang*) were within one-half liter (2.5%) of the stated size. This appears to be well within the accuracy obtainable when measuring volume of rice in the field, because of differences in packing. The standard *tang* used in measuring these quantities contained 20.25 loosely packed liters, as measured with a standard liter; an empty kerosene tin, which is usually accepted as the equivalent of a *tang*, contained 20.75 liters of loosely packed rice. Tight packing increased these amounts by 10–12 percent. Because Lua' measures proved to be quite accurate, we relied on the statements of informants regarding the size of their baskets (or their use of kerosene tins) in deriving our figures of productivity.

Karen baskets at Laykawkey were not uniform in size, and we measured each one in order to standardize figures for yields. For statistical summaries we adjusted the farmers' figures for variations in sizes of baskets and kerosene tins.

In many households there was a strong tendency to round off yield figures to the closest five baskets, and in general this probably resulted in a slight underestimate of yield. When pressed for exact figures some household heads would give them to the nearest basket, while others would say that the "leftovers" were not counted and that anything less than an even basket which was left over was supposed to be used for brewing liquor and was not counted in the tally of yield.

International figures on rice production are sometimes quoted in metric tons (1 metric ton = 2,204.6 pounds) rather than in volume. In order to convert the volumetric figures to weight, we can use weight figures for an "average" *tang* of rice. The weight of rice varies significantly with its moisture content and with the variety of rice in question. Our estimate of the relationship of rice volume to weight is from rice measured and weighed in January and February, early in the dry season, and is probably lower than for rice weighed at harvest time. The average weight of a *tang* of Lua' or Karen upland rice, removed

from storage and before sun drying for milling, is about 12.4 kg; the average weight of a *tang* of irrigated rice from the villages is about 10.8 kg.

Lua' and Karen farmers are familiar with the differences in weight of rice and relate them to the fact that most upland varieties of grain are shorter and plumper than the irrigated varieties. Although the farmers know that a *tang* of irrigated paddy rice yields less milled or pounded rice than a *tang* of upland rice, there is no difference in price.

PRODUCTIVITY OF LUA' AND KAREN AGRICULTURE

Using production figures derived in this way, combined with information on areas cultivated, we can compare productivity of Lua' and Karen swiddening (tables 6.5, 6.6). The average annual yield over the two-year period, about 13 *tang/rai* or about 1,000 kg/ha, compared favorably with nonirrigated, rain-fed paddy fields in Thailand (630–940 kg/ha), but unfavorably with average yields for lowland irrigated rice in Thailand (1,900–2,200 kg/ha) (Asian Development Bank 1969:160). There is no evidence in our figures for a significant difference in productivity per unit area between Lua' and Karen upland farmers.

Yields in the Lua' irrigated fields averaged about 32.5 *tang/rai*, or about 2,200 kg/ha, which is about average for irrigated rice in Thailand; Karen yields from irrigated fields are lower on the average, about 22 *tang/rai*, or 1,500 kg/ha, about 600 kg below average for irrigated fields in Thailand.

These figures indicate that the irrigated fields are almost three times as productive per unit area as swidden fields for the Lua', and about twice as productive per unit area as swidden fields for Karen. We can speculate on the reasons for the difference between Lua' and Karen

TABLE 6.5   Basic Rice Production Figures for Lua' and Karen Agriculture, 1967 and 1968

	Lua'			Karen		
	1967	1968	1969	1967	1968	1969
Total population	224	233	247	192	182	195
Total households	50	51	51	34	31	33
Total working population [a]	128	124		105	96	
Households with swiddens						
Number	42	44		31	28	
Population	200	215		189	177	
Working population	116	117		103	94	
Area of swiddens (ha)	65.05	72.5		51.27	48.75	
Seed in swiddens (liters)	9,365	12,097		7,522	7,276	
Yield from swiddens (liters)	107,000	122,060	103,060	93,560	60,440	57,420
Households with irrigated fields [b]						
Number	27	26		24	24	
Population	145	144		159	160	
Working population	80	77		84	82	
Area of irrigated fields (ha)	18.24	18.91		20.57 [c]	24.42 [d]	
Seed in irrigated fields (liters)	2,731	2,708		2,910	3,414	
Yield from irrigated fields (liters)	74,660	76,180	79,250	60,720	62,860	66,020

[a] Includes all those individuals regularly engaged in agricultural labor on their own fields or in exchange labor.
[b] Includes all those households actually working irrigated fields, whether wholly owned, shared, leased, or mortgaged.
[c] Includes estimated 1.90 ha not measured in village area + estimated 0.42 ha owned and worked outside the village.
[d] Includes estimated 3.00 ha not measured in village area + estimated 0.86 ha owned and worked outside the village.

irrigated fields, but our data from these two villages are too limited to be conclusive. Karen irrigated fields are on the average smaller than Lua' fields and more scattered; also Karen farmers at Laykawkey almost always cultivate both irrigated and swidden fields, whereas Lua' farmers at Pa Pae tend to specialize in one or the other form of agriculture.[4] The Karen admit that the Lua' are neater and more careful with their irrigated fields in building, weeding, and repairing the bunds, in transplanting in a more systematic manner, and so forth. Another possible explanation is that the Lua' fields are slightly lower in the drainage systems, and may have larger and more dependable water supply, greater deposition of alluvium, and better water retention, and the soil may be more fertile as a result. Karen fields also suffered badly from the depredations of wild pigs before the 1968 harvest, which may have caused a further drop in their average yield.

USE OF AGRICULTURAL LAND

The annual use of agricultural land is shown in table 6.7. The average annual amount of land used for agriculture by the Lua' of Pa Pae in 1967–1968 was about 87.35 hectares, including about 68.78 hectares of swidden land and 18.58 hectares of irrigated land. The Karen of Laykawkey used about 72.51 hectares of land for agriculture in the same period, including about 50.01 hectares for swidden and 22.50 hectares for irrigated fields. Since the swidden land is actually used on a cycle of about 10 years, in

TABLE 6.6 Productivity of Lua' and Karen Swidden and Irrigated Fields

	Swidden		Irrigated	
	Pa Pae Lua'	Laykawkey Karen	Pa Pae Lua'	Lakawkey Karen
1967				
Yield (kg)	66,340	58,007	40,316	32,789
Area (ha)	65.05	51.27	18.24	20.57
Average kg/ha	1,019	1,131	2,210	1,594
kg/ha per field	1,053	1,232	2,734	1,615
Range	359–2,630	76–5,456	487–5,535	245–3,226
Standard deviation	505	572	1,641	830
No. of fields	40	34	29	26
1968				
Yield (kg)	75,677	37,472	41,137	33,944
Area (ha)	72.50	48.75	18.91	24.42
Average kg/ha	1,044	769	2,175	1,390
kg/ha per field	1,050	1,024	2,670	1,637
Range	200–2,971	198–2,748	152–7,714	171–4,984
Standard deviation	495	1,038	1,794	1,171
No. of fields	47	30	30	30
1967–1968 Pooled average				
kg/ha	1,032	955	2,193	1,483

NOTE: Units are defined as follows: 1 *tang* = 20 liters; 1 *rai* = 1,600 sq meters; 1 hectare = 10,000 sq meters. Rice production was measured by volume and converted to weight using 12.4 kilograms/*tang* as the average field weight of upland rice, and 10.8 kilograms/*tang* as the average field weight of irrigated rice. "Average" figures are based on the aggregate totals from all fields; "per field" figures are based on the unweighted observations from each field regardless of field size. Differences in yield per unit area result from the different bases of compilation.

which one year of cultivation is followed by nine years fallow, the amounts of land used by the Lua' of Pa Pae in the entire cultivation system, *including fallow*, are about 706.38 hectares, with about 687.80 hectares in swiddens. The Karen of Laykawkey use about 522.6 hectares in their entire cultivation system, *including fallow*, with about 500.1 hectares used in swidden. These figures assume that the amounts of irrigated land under cultivation for the entire 10-year swidden cycle remain constant at the 1967–1968 average. The figures do not include the uncleared forest on ridge tops, along

streams, and between blocks of swiddens. These uncultivated areas are considered to be community property and are essential for control of erosion and as sources of seed for reforestation.

As has already been mentioned, the fallow land is not completely unproductive. It is used extensively for the grazing of domestic animals, and for gathering firewood and useful uncultivated plants.

The amounts of land used per family, per person, and per worker are shown in table 6.8. The Karen of Laykawkey used more land per family than the Lua' of Pa Pae, but the amount of land

TABLE 6.7 Agricultural Land Used by Lua' and Karen (Including Fallow)

	Land Used in Swidden Fields (ha)		Land Used in Irrigated Fields (ha)		Total Land Used (ha)	
	Pa Pae Lua'	Laykawkey Karen	Pa Pae Lua'	Laykawkey Karen	Pa Pae Lua'	Laykawkey Karen
1967	65.05	51.27	18.24	20.57	83.29	71.84
1968	72.50	48.75	18.91	24.42	91.41	73.17
1967–1968 Pooled average	68.78	50.01	18.58	22.50	87.35	72.51
Total land used in average 10–year swidden cycle (est.) [a]	687.80	500.10	18.58	22.50	706.38	522.60

[a] Assuming that swidden land is cultivated on the average of once every 10 years and fallowed for nine years, and that the amount of swidden and irrigated land under cultivation remains constant at the 1967–1968 average.

TABLE 6.8 Annual Land Use per Family, per Capita, and per Worker

	Land Used by Total Population		Land Used by Agriculturally Active Population			
			Swidden		Irrigated	
	Pa Pae Lua'	Laykawkey Karen	Pa Pae Lua'	Laykawkey Karen	Pa Pae Lua'	Laykawkey Karen
1967						
Hectares per family	1.67	2.11	1.55	1.65	0.68	0.86
Hectares per person	0.37	0.37	0.33	0.27	0.13	0.13
Hectares per worker	0.65	0.68	0.56	0.50	0.23	0.24
1968						
Hectares per family	1.79	2.36	1.65	1.74	0.73	1.02
Hectares per person	0.39	0.40	0.34	0.28	0.13	0.17
Hectares per worker	0.74	0.76	0.62	0.52	0.25	0.30
1967–1968 Pooled average						
Hectares per family	1.73	2.23	1.60	1.92	0.70	0.94
Hectares per person	0.38	0.39	0.33	0.27	0.13	0.15
Hectares per worker	0.69	0.72	0.59	0.51	0.24	0.27
Annual land use estimated on basis of 10-year fallow cycle [a]						
Hectares per family	13.99	16.08	16.00	19.20	0.70	0.94
Hectares per person	3.09	2.79	3.30	2.70	0.13	0.15
Hectares per worker	5.61	5.20	5.90	5.10	0.24	0.27

[a] Assuming that swidden land is cultivated on the average of once every 10 years and fallowed for nine years, that population composition remains constant at the 1967–1968 average, and that the amount of swidden and irrigated land under cultivation remains constant at the 1967–1968 average.

TABLE 6.9 Production per Unit of Seed of Lua' and Karen Swidden and Irrigated
Fields

	Swidden		Irrigated	
	Pa Pae Lua'	Laykawkey Karen	Pa Pae Lua'	Laykawkey Karen
1967				
Total seed (liters)	9,365	7,522	2,731	2,910
Average liters of seed sown per *rai*	23.03	23.47	23.96	22.64
Average liters of seed sown per ha	143.97	146.71	149.73	141.47
Average yield per unit of seed	11.425	12.438	27.34	21.55
Yield per unit of seed per field	11.55	12.79	31.86	21.06
Range	6.06–32.92	5.66–20.0	1.85–59.0	5.13–42.44
Standard deviation	4.44	3.87	11.54	9.99
No. of fields	42	34	30	33
1968				
Total seed (liters)	12,097	7,276	2,708	3,414
Average liters of seed sown per *rai*	26.70	23.88	22.91	22.37
Average liters of seed sown per ha	166.86	149.25	143.20	139.80
Average yield per unit of seed	9.411	8.307	28.13	17.89
Yield per unit of seed per field	9.63	8.74	28.97	19.51
Range	3.36–16.12	0.0–39.5	6.67–53.33	3.0–36.67
Standard deviation	3.37	6.90	11.90	8.29
No. of fields	47	32	32	40
1967–1968 Pooled average				
Yield per unit of seed	10.26	10.41	27.73	20.23
Liters seed sown per *rai*	24.96	23.67	23.42	22.49
Liters seed sown per ha	156.03	147.95	146.41	140.56

NOTE: "Average" figures are based on the aggregate totals from all fields; "per field" figures are based on the unweighted observations from each field regardless of size. Differences in yield per unit of seed result from the different bases of compilation.

used per person in the years 1967–1968 was about equal for both groups (about 0.4 ha per person). Considering the 10-year cultivation and fallow cycle, the Lua' used a slightly larger amount of land per person (3.09 ha) than the Karen (2.79 ha). The higher figure for amount of land used per person by the Lua', when fallow land is included in the calculations, is accounted for by the higher proportion of swidden to irri-gated land used by the Pa Pae villagers. Other than this, there is little difference in the per capita use of land in these two villages.

YIELD PER UNIT OF SEED

In addition to considering the amounts of land used, productivity may also be measured in terms of yield per unit of seed and yield per unit of population. The results of our study indicated that the Lua' of Pa Pae used slightly more seed than the Karen of Laykawkey, both in their swiddens and in their irrigated fields (table 6.9).

The yields are quite different in the two types of fields; both groups obtained only slightly over 10 times their seed in the upland fields, while the Lua' got almost 28 times their seed, and the Karen about 20 times their seed from irrigated fields. These average yield figures may reflect the fact that the Karen use swidden-like seed beds more frequently than do the Lua', who usually use irrigated seed beds. The swidden-like seed beds are said to require about two-thirds more seed than do the irrigated seed beds for a given area of paddy. The amount of seed used by the Lua' in the swiddens is about 156 liters/ha, and by the Karen, about 148 liters/ha. The Lua' sow about 146.5 liters/ha in the irrigated fields, and the Karen sow about 140.5 liters/ha.

VARIABILITY OF YIELD

Farmers must contend with variability as well as quantity of yield. We have suggested (chapter 1) that irrigated farming may be inherently less variable than swiddening because of the greater degree of environmental control in irrigation. The field studies of swidden cultivation (see table 1.2) indicate the large range in reported productivity from different sites, but yields have been reported in terms of averages, sample sizes have almost always been small, and there have been few reported measurements of variation within a given environment.

Tables 6.6 and 6.9 give ranges and standard deviations as measures of the variability of the yields per unit area and per unit of seed from the individual Lua' and Karen fields. The variability is high for both swidden and irrigated fields, for both Lua' and Karen, and for both years. The maximum range in swiddens is from 76 to 5,456 kg/ha (122 to 8,800 liters/ha) in the 34 Karen swiddens measured in 1967, and surprisingly the range is even larger, from 152 to 7,714 kg/ha (282 to 14,286 liters/ha) in 30 Lua' irrigated fields in 1968. Standard deviations of the yields per unit area are also high; for the 30 Karen swiddens in 1968 it is larger than the

mean yield (ratio of s.d. to mean yield per ha = 1.01).

Because of the problems of surveying in rough terrain and the numbers of fields to be covered, we measured field areas on 1:50,000 maps, using field-annotated aerial photographs as guides to the field boundaries (chapter 7). Because fields were relatively small, measurement errors may account for some of the apparent variation in yields. The yields per unit of seed generally parallel the results of yield per unit area, but the ratios of the standard deviations of the yields per unit of seed to the mean of yield per unit seed are lower than the ratios for yield per unit area. Because the farmers adjust the amounts of seed to the areas planted, amount of seed may be a quick and reasonably accurate measure of individual field areas, provided the ratio of seed to area is known from a measurement of the entire area which is being farmed.

We believe the high standard deviations show clearly the importance of high variability as a characteristic of upland farming with traditional technology. Determination of the reasons for variability would require sampling and analysing soil fertility, water supply, labor force, seed varieties, cultivation techniques, field site characteristics, insects and other plant pests, etc., on an individual field basis. In this chapter we can only suggest the importance of future studies directed at describing and understanding the field by field and annual variability as well as the averages in upland farming.

PRODUCTION PER FAMILY, PER CAPITA, AND PER WORKER

Rice yields per family in the two villages reflect the differences in family size, but there are also consistent differences between the villages in production per capita or per worker (table 6.10). The Lua' of Pa Pae, with an average

TABLE 6.10 Rice Production by Lua' and Karen, per Family, per Capita, and per Worker

| | Total Population | | Agricultural Population | | | |
| | | | Swidden | | Irrigated | |
	Pa Pae Lua'	Laykawkey Karen	Pa Pae Lua'	Laykawkey Karen	Pa Pae Lua'	Laykawkey Karen
1967						
Number of families	50	34	42	31	27	24
Number of people	224	192	200	189	145	159
Number of workers	128	105	116	103	80	84
Rice production *(tang)*						
Total	9,083	7,714	5,350	4,678	3,733	3,036
Per family	181.66	226.76	127.38	150.90	138.26	126.50
Per person	40.55	40.18	26.75	24.75	25.74	19.09
Per worker	70.96	73.47	46.12	45.42	46.66	36.14
1968						
Number of Families	51	31	44	28	26	24
Number of people	233	182	215	177	144	160
Number of workers	124	96	117	94	77	82
Rice production *(tang)*						
Total	9,912	6,165	6,103	3,022	3,809	3,143
Per family	194.31	196.93	138.70	107.93	146.50	130.96
Per person	42.54	33.87	28.39	17.07	26.45	19.66
Per worker	88.00	64.22	52.16	32.14	49.47	38.33
1967–1968 Pooled average						
Rice production *(tang)*						
Per family	188.07	213.37	133.14	130.51	142.30	128.73
Per person	41.57	37.11	27.59	21.04	26.09	19.34
Per worker	75.34	69.05	49.15	39.08	48.04	37.22

NOTE: *Total population* includes all persons and families resident in the village during the agricultural year in question. *Agricultural population* consists of those families and individuals living within households which worked a swidden or an irrigated field or both in the year in question. Families and individuals with both types of fields are listed in both swidden and irrigated columns. *Workers* are those persons who regularly worked in their own fields or in exchange labor. Two widows living in separate houses at Laykawkey, but working with and eating with their children are included in the agricultural population and workers figures, but not counted as separate agricultural households. One family at Pa Pae, with two workers, made no fields in 1967 but worked for cash or rice, and was not included in the agricultural population figures but was included in the total population and total number of workers for that year. One man living by himself at Pa Pae worked for his relatives and neighbors on a share or cash basis and did not make a field of his own in 1968. He was not included in the agricultural population figures for that year, although he was included in the total working population figures.

family size of about 4.5 persons, had an average annual rice production in 1967 and 1968 of about 3,760 liters per family, or 830 liters per person; the Karen families of Laykawkey, averaging about 6 persons, had an average yield of about 4,260 liters per family, or 742 liters per person. Lua' production per worker (1,506 liters) was higher than Karen (1,380 liters).

The production figures indicate a consistently higher rate of production per worker among the Lua', in both swidden and irrigated agriculture. Production per worker was more variable in the swidden fields than in the irrigated fields, which probably reflects the variability of conditions in the swiddens. An explanation of Lua'-Karen differences may be that the Lua' farmers of Pa Pae tended to specialize in either irrigated or swidden agriculture; their fields were larger and less scattered than those of the Karen farmers of Laykawkey. Also the Lua' fields appeared to be more neatly tended, and this may have had some effect on productivity, although the effect may also have reflected environmental conditions at the two villages.

DISTRIBUTION AND CONSUMPTION IN THE AGRICULTURAL ECONOMY: CREDIT AND INTEREST

Agriculture in these upland villages in the 1970s is still based on a minimum of capital investment and a maximum of labor. Most agricultural operations are "financed" by the farmer and his family with their own inputs of labor. This is particularly true of swidden cropping, in which there is no use of monetary credit to finance the farming. Swidden fields are not mortgaged, but by the 1960s (in contrast with traditional practice) they were sometimes rented or sold. Each household provides all or most of its own labor by doing its own work, or by using reciprocal labor exchanges. "Rent," equipment,

and supply costs are very low compared with the labor input, since there is usually no cost for the land, unless communal religious obligations and fire-fighting duties are considered rent.

Lua' and Karen swidden farmers occasionally use credit for subsistence. Rice for home consumption may be borrowed with the expectation that the debt, or at least interest, will be paid from the next harvest, but the lender does not have an explicit claim or mortgage on the crop or on the swidden land.

Interest rates vary depending on supply and demand conditions and on the kinship or other relationship between borrower and lender. Sometimes relatives and close friends take no interest; unrelated people or creditors from distant villages get 50–100 percent interest. The stated rate of interest is based on a debt to be repaid after the next harvest. A loan at 50-percent interest is to be repaid with that much interest after the next harvest, whether the loan was made 2 months or 10 months previously. Thus the true time rate of interest might vary from 5 percent per month to 25 percent per month, depending on when in the agricultural year the loan was made. These differences may accurately reflect conditions influencing the costs of credit, rather than profit. Borrowing early will result in more loss through shrinkage before the rice is actually consumed; and rice is almost always scarce during the rainy season in the three or four months before harvest.

Frequently interest rates are not firmly fixed. There are no written contracts. Both borrower and lender may say they do not know what interest will be charged, or paid, until the debt is settled. Repeated questioning failed to reveal how these questions are actually resolved when the debts are paid.

Irrigated agriculture involves much more use of cash and credit than does swidden farming.

TABLE 6.11   Mortgages on Lua' and Karen Irrigated Fields, 1967 and 1968

	Fields Mortgaged		Fields Not Mortgaged		Total No. Fields	Total Amount of Mortgages (baht)
	No.	(%)	No.	(%)		
Lua',						
Pa Pae (June 1967)	8	(31)	18	(69)	26	15,500
Karen,						
Laykawkey (June 1968)	1	(4)	24	(96)	25	4,000

The construction of irrigated fields requires a much higher input of labor than does the clearing of swidden fields. Although some of this may be done through exchange of labor between the farmers who share a dam and a ditch, other workers are usually hired for cash or rice. Another way of spreading out the investment costs is to enlarge the irrigated fields little by little each year, as cash or labor is available, thus allowing continual investment in increasing productivity. This is not possible with swidden fields because the size of a family's swidden field is not limited by the amount that can be cleared or planted, but by the amount of labor available for weeding. Timing of activities in irrigated fields is not nearly as crucial as in swiddens; thus labor may be used more efficiently than in swiddens.

Costs of land for irrigated fields are becoming much more important than in the past, when land suitable for irrigation was essentially free for the taking. The prices paid for irrigated land in the Pa Pae–Laykawkey area are much higher than for swiddens. It is difficult to give an exact price because most transfers of irrigated land were the result of mortgage foreclosures, and the mortgages have generally been for small fractions of the recognized value of the land.

Irrigated fields are sometimes mortgaged. Interest rates on money or on mortgages are at least 3 percent per month, and sometimes higher. Money is sometimes loaned in exchange for the right to cultivate the field in alternate years as payment of interest. Such debts are virtually impossible to repay and are contracted only by poor farmers in order to raise money to buy subsistence rice, or by addicts to purchase opium. Often monetary debts are negotiated to be repaid in rice rather than cash, with the interest also to be paid in rice, at rice rates of interest (50 percent or more). Eight of 26 Pa Pae field owners (31 percent) reported in June 1967 that their irrigated fields were mortgaged for amounts ranging from 1,200 to 4,200 *baht*. Only one Karen (4 percent) at Laykawkey reported that his field was mortgaged in 1968, for 4,000 *baht* (table 6.11).

SUBSISTENCE INDEBTEDNESS

Subsistence indebtedness may be defined as the need to borrow rice or money for subsistence, and the inability to repay the entire debt after harvest. This, as well as mortgages on irrigated fields, was a major problem for the Lua' villagers at Pa Pae, but was not as much of a problem for the Karen of Laykawkey (table 6.12).

Despite their lower productivity, the Karen of Laykawkey have in general been able to stay out of debt, while the Lua' of Pa Pae seem unable to escape debt, despite the fact that they produce more than enough for their subsistence. It is

TABLE 6.12   Rice and Cash Borrowed by Lua' and Karen Households after 1967 Harvest and Remaining Unpaid after 1968 Harvest[a]

	Total Households	Households with More than 10–tang or 50–baht Unpaid Debts		Total Unpaid Rice Debts (tang)	Total Unpaid Money Debts (baht)	Mean Debt per Family (baht)[b]
		No.	(%)			
Lua', Pa Pae	51	26	(51)	734	9,730+	263
Karen, Laykawkey	29	11	(38)	137	2,950	125

[a] Does not include unpaid mortgage debts.
[b] Rice debts converted to baht at 5 baht per tang.

clear that interest payments on debts are sufficient to reduce many of the families at Pa Pae to the bare subsistence level, or below. These problems are discussed in more detail below, when we consider distribution and consumption of the rice crops.

SOURCES OF AGRICULTURAL CREDIT

When these mountain villagers want to borrow money they turn first to their relatives, then to other friends and neighbors, and finally to acquaintances in more distant villages, wherever they think money may be available. If large amounts are involved, they may send a representative to seek the loan for them, and may use a third party as a guarantor of the loan. This is usually the case in mortgages. The person who represents the borrower is not a broker, in the sense that he does not do this as his regular occupation, and does not receive any payment for his service; he may in fact assume some moral liability to see that the loan is repaid. When a man needs to borrow rice for subsistence, he almost always goes to look for the rice himself, following the same route as if he were seeking to borrow money.

An additional source of rice credit became available to some Karen villages in about 1967 when the Baptist missionaries in Mae Sariang began to develop a "rice bank" program in a few Christian Karen communities. The first banks were started with nonrenewable gifts of rice purchased by the mission. The rice was kept in a barn built by the villagers, and the loans were administered by a committee chosen by them. At first no interest was charged, but by 1968 interest was being charged at the annual rate of 50 percent in order to make up for defaulted loans and for shrinkage, and to allow the program to be expanded to other villages. Some Laykawkey villagers, especially those who were already Christian or who converted to Christianity during 1968 and 1969, expressed an interest in the rice bank idea, and one family secured a loan from the Christian rice bank in Mae Sariang. Until 1970 no similar arrangements were available for the non-Christian Karen, or for the Lua' villagers (see below).

Few of the hill villagers in this area believe they can get credit from lowland merchants for purchases of tools, clothes, and the like, and fewer still have ever used credit from merchants. Those who say they have credit claim it on the basis of their good name and long-time friend-

TABLE 6.13   Distribution by Lua' and Karen of the 1967 Rice Crop (Unmilled Rice)

	Rice Paid Out *(tang)*			Rice Received *(tang)*	
	Lua'	Karen		Lua'	Karen
Sold	200.5	632	Bought	450	223
Traded	264	173.5	Traded	181	0
Repaid	1,729	131.5	Repaid	305	16.5
Wage	250	74	Rent, wages	250	685 [a]
Field rent	88	0			
Animal rent	64	95			
Other	2	75	Other	16	22
Loaned	220	179.5	Borrowed	1,255	176
Total	2,806.5	1,360.5	Total rec'd	2,502	1,122
			Total harvest	9,083	7,714

[a]Includes 625 *tang* of rice received for rent of distant fields, and sold for cash.

ship with the merchants. In this immediate area no merchants have shown an interest in taking mortgages on irrigated fields, although evidently they have done so in some of the closer hill villages farther to the north in Mae La Noi Subdistrict.

DISTRIBUTION AND CONSUMPTION OF THE RICE CROP: FAILURE AND SUCCESS OF THE SUBSISTENCE ECONOMY

The hill families consume most of the rice they grow. Some of the rice is used to repay debts; some is used to make loans; some is sold or traded, either locally or elsewhere (table 6.13). Although the Lua' of Pa Pae appear to produce more rice than do the Karen in Laykawkey, figures on distribution and consumption show that the Pa Pae villagers are in worse economic condition than the Karen of Laykawkey as a result of accumulated indebtedness.

SALES AND TRADE OF AGRICULTURAL PRODUCTS

The farmers of Pa Pae sell and trade only about 5 percent of their rice crop; the Laykawkey Karen sell and trade about 10 percent of their crop. There are no shops or markets in either village. Neither the Lua' nor the Karen mountain villagers have current market information when they take their agricultural products to the lowlands for sale. They are at a disadvantage because the purchasers know they will not carry the rice or drive the pigs back up to the hill villages. Most agricultural products are sold seasonally, at times determined by the condition of trails and the subsistence agricultural work load, rather than being held for highest market prices. The hill villagers sell most of the rice shortly after harvest and may enjoy a slight price advantage at that time because the lowland crops have not yet been harvested, but this advantage is less now than it was before the highway was completed from Hot District to Mae Sariang in about 1965. The Mae Sariang valley has been a rice-deficit area, but the highway now makes it possible to bring rice in from Chiang Mai. Most hill village households have to sell some of their rice, even though they may not have enough for home consumption, in order to buy a few manufactured necessities, such as hoe blades or salt, and perhaps a few luxuries, such as matches, tobacco, and flashlight batteries.

Some of the rice is sold to merchants, but much of it is sold to friends and relatives who have migrated to the valley but still prefer the taste of mountain rice (photo 112). Most of the rice sold from Laykawkey after the 1967 and 1968 harvests was sold to a former Laykawkey resident who has moved to the valley. She brought up goods to trade in the village and returned to the valley with several elephant loads of rice, which she used to feed Karen lumber workers and other employees of her husband. A few traders move about through these hill villages, bringing beads, medicines, fermented tea, and a few other products from the valley. If possible, they try to sell their goods for money rather than rice because of transportation problems. A few livestock buyers come through these villages, usually looking for buffalos and cows which they will drive to the road and then ship by truck to the Chiang Mai valley. Since highway transportation has become available, the price of buffalos and cows has approximately doubled, to reach the level of the current market in the Chiang Mai area.

Hill villagers usually bring pigs, another important hill product, down to market in the cool season after harvest, or early in the rainy season before the rivers rise. Pigs cannot be brought at other times because of high water, or because the heat of the dry season may kill the pigs on the trail before they reach market. The most favorable time to sell pigs would probably be just before the major holidays, such as the Northern Thai New Year (mid-April) or the beginning and end of Buddhist Lent (July and November), but these times are ruled out by weather or work conditions.

Most trade and sale is on a very small scale. The usual amount of rice which a farmer takes to market is the amount he can carry on his back, about 20 liters of husked rice. In the hills housewives may exchange a few liters of rice for some cotton, vegetables, or fruit, or for a kilo or two of meat. This petty trade is carried out almost exclusively in the mountain villages. Usually the person obtaining the rice is someone who has not been able to produce enough for his or her own consumption, or who has a small surplus of something perishable. Usually a person with something to sell will let it be known around the village, or will take it to another nearby village. A few widows at Pa Pae eke out a living in this way, carrying vegetables, liquor, or yeast cakes for brewing liquor to nearby Karen villages to exchange for small quantities of rice, or perhaps for chicks.

During the 1968 agricultural year one man supported himself and his family at Pa Pae by blacksmithing in exchange for rice or sometimes for money. He had to supplement his earnings with a small swidden field and by working for wages in cash or kind in other people's fields. There was no other local nonagricultural specialist in either Pa Pae or Laykawkey, although there are a few silver- and ironsmiths at La'up who support themselves largely through their crafts. Thus trade contributes relatively little to the mountain economy except in helping to distribute a few local surpluses, variety goods, and services. Most of the mountain villagers produce most of what they themselves consume. Any profit from surplus production usually ends up in the lowlands where the merchants and manufactured goods are to be found. Almost all of the money in circulation in the hills comes ultimately from the lowlands, primarily from wage labor, and secondarily from sale of small amounts of agricultural produce.

RICE CONSUMPTION

Figures on rice consumption were gathered in two ways: (1) each household head in both vil-

TABLE 6.14 Estimated Domestic Consumption of Rice by Lua' and Karen Villagers

	Number of Households	Number of Persons	Village Total Daily Rice Consumption (liters of milled rice) [a]	Daily Mean Consumption per Household (liters of milled rice)	Daily Mean Consumption per Person (liters of milled rice)	Daily Mean Consumption per Person (kg of milled rice)	Total Annual Village Consumption (*tang* of unmilled rice) [b]
Lua', Pa Pae	51	233	202.5	3.97	0.87	0.71	7,391
Karen, Laykawkey	31	182	121.0	3.90	0.67	0.55	4,417

[a] Includes rice consumed by family members, as estimated by household head; rice consumed by domestic animals is not included in this figure, and would add 20–30 percent to the total.

[b] Calculated by multiplying daily estimated rice consumption by 365, at 20 liters per *tang*, and assuming one *tang* of husked rice equals approximately two *tang* of unhusked rice. This figure does not allow for "shrinkage," but represents the total amount of rice required annually to meet estimated daily requirements.

lages was asked to state the amount of rice used by that household per day and per year, and (2) in each of three households in both villages, the amount of rice eaten by every member of each household for each meal during a 48-hour period was weighed. Informants in both villages normally stated that an adult eats about one liter of uncooked, husked rice per day. In a series of weighings, husked upland rice averaged about 826.5 gm/liter and irrigated rice about 809 gm/liter. The household survey figures indicate that the per person consumption of husked rice at Pa Pae was approximately 0.87 liters (0.72 kg) per day, and about 0.67 liters (0.55 kg) per day at Laykawkey (table 6.14). The calculation of annual consumption rates did not include an estimate of shrinkage due to spoilage, loss to vermin, and so on. The lower figures for Laykawkey probably reflect the lower median age of the population at Laykawkey (about 12 years), as compared with the median age at Pa Pae (about 20 years). Hinton (chapter 9) estimates rice consumption for the "average" 4.8-person Pwo Karen family to be 1,552 kg per year. This amounts to 0.886 kg of rice per person per day, higher than the figures from Pa Pae and Laykawkey. Izikowitz (1951:228) estimates

0.55 kg of unhusked rice or, according to our calculation, 0.205 kg of husked rice eaten per person per day by the Lamet, swidden cultivators in northern Laos. These figures seem considerably lower than ours, but they were gathered by different methods.

A study of the relationship between weight of rice consumed and body weight of Pa Pae villagers indicated a significant correlation ($r = 0.8533$) between the two. As their weight increases, children tend to eat more rice per unit of body weight than do adults. Adolescents and young adults are the heaviest members of the population and are the heaviest eaters.

Analysis of 13 samples of rice from Pa Pae and Laykawkey under the direction of Dr. Krisna Chutima (of the Department of Chemistry, Kasetsart University, Bangkhen, Bangkok) gave a range of 6.55–10.59 percent protein for field-dried rice, with a mean of about 7.8 percent (table 6.15). This figure is about the same as the average for 1,800 samples from all parts of Thailand analyzed by Dr. Chutima.[5] This suggests that the average intake of protein from rice is about 55 gm per person per day for the Lua' villagers at Pa Pae, and about 43 gm per person per day for the Karen at Laykawkey. Their rice

TABLE 6.15   Protein Content of Varieties of Rice Grown by Lua' and Karen

Source	Where Grown	Type	Ripening Time	Protein (% field wt.)
Lua', Pa Pae	upland	nonglutinous	late	7.03
Lua'	upland	nonglutinous	late	7.68
Lua'	upland	nonglutinous	medium	7.32
Lua'	upland	nonglutinous	early	7.63
Lua'	upland	nonglutinous		7.72
Karen, Laykawkey	upland	nonglutinous	med.–late	6.91
Lua'	upland	glutinous	late	8.46
Lua'	upland	glutinous	early	7.25
Lua'	irrig.	nonglutinous	early	6.58
Lua'	irrig.	nonglutinous		6.55
Lua'	irrig.	nonglutinous		7.57
Karen	irrig.	nonglutinous	med.–late	10.59
Karen	irrig.	nonglutinous	med.–late	9.99
Mean for all varieties				7.84

SOURCE: Analysed under the direction of Dr. Krisna Chutima, Chemistry Department, Kasetsart University, Bangkok.

TABLE 6.16   Chemical Content of Two Samples of Lua' Rice

Type of Rice	Moisture	Protein	Carbohydrate	Fat	Crude Fiber	Ash	P	K	C	Mg
Upland, nonglutinous, late ripening	7.50	7.72	80.55	1.97	0.57	1.68	0.60	0.37	0.30	0.27
Irrigated, nonglutinous	7.55	6.55	80.93	2.18	0.83	1.96	0.45	0.37	0.63	0.23

SOURCE: Analysed under the direction of Dr. Krisna Chutima, Chemistry Department, Kasetsart University, Bangkok.

is about 80 percent carbohydrate (table 6.16), and so the average daily intake of rice carbohydrate would be about 576 gm at Pa Pae, and about 443 gm at Laykawkey. These figures suggest that the people get a significant amount of their protein, as well as calories, from rice.

THE PROBLEMS OF INCREASING DEBT

The Laykawkey villagers repaid debts totaling only 131.5 *tang*, or less than 2 percent of their 1967 crop. The Pa Pae villagers paid back a total of 1,729 *tang*, more than 19 percent of their crop, and were still unable to escape in-

debtedness which has accumulated over many years. Although the Lua' are more deeply in debt than the Karen, they appear to feel the social pressure more strongly to make loans to their friends and relatives, and to try to repay their debts promptly.

In addition to the information on indebtedness, another indication of the success or failure of the subsistence agricultural operation is whether or not these villagers had sufficient rice to last from one harvest to the next. A survey of all household heads of Pa Pae and Laykawkey after the 1968 harvest indicated that a much

TABLE 6.17   Success of Subsistence Farming

| | No. Families | Families Whose 1967 Rice Crop Lasted to 1 Nov. 1968 | | Families Whose 1967 Rice Crop Did Not Last to 1 Nov. 1968 | | Net Deficit[a] | |
		No.	Liters Remaining[b]	No.	Liters Short[b]	Liters	%
Lua', Pa Pae	48	4	328	44	24,860	24,532	33.2
Karen, Laykawkey	29	15	2,816	14	4,645	1,829	4.1

NOTE: Success is defined as having sufficient rice from one harvest to last until 1 Nov. of the following year, approximately midway through harvest.

[a] Percentage of total annual estimated consumption (table 6.14) for which rice had to be borrowed or purchased. These figures are based on estimated consumption per family, but agree well with figures derived from distribution of the 1967 rice crop (table 6.13).

[b] Number of days remaining or short as of 1 Nov. 1968 multiplied by estimated daily consumption of rice per family.

lower percentage of Pa Pae villagers (29%) than of Laykawkey villagers (59%) had enough rice from their own 1967 harvest to last until they could start eating the 1968 crop. As indicated in the figures on distribution of the rice from the 1967 harvest, in large part this deficiency is due to accumulated debts from the past, rather than failure of the production system. Some Lua' families at Pa Pae produced enough or nearly enough rice for their own subsistence, but after paying their debts or interest on their debts they had only enough rice for two or three months after the harvest. Two Pa Pae families had no rice left to eat after repaying their debts at the conclusion of the 1967 harvest.

Thus it is clear that average production and consumption figures alone do not give a true picture of the success of the subsistence farming system. We have seen that the total production by the Lua' of Pa Pae in 1967 was 181,660 liters (9,083 tang) of unhusked rice, while their estimated total subsistence consumption for that crop was 147,820 liters (7,391 tang). During the same period the Karen of Laykawkey produced 154,820 liters (7,741 tang) and consumed an estimated 88,340 liters (4,417 tang). This would

indicate that both villages produced more than enough rice for their own consumption, with a substantial amount left over for the feeding of domestic animals, or for trade. But the Pa Pae villagers had to pay out 56,120 liters (2,806 tang), including 34,580 liters (1,729 tang) in repayment of debts, leaving the village below its subsistence needs.

Another measure of the success of the subsistence farming system—one which has more meaning for the people and shows the effect of indebtedness—is the number of days per year when rice had to be purchased or borrowed. These figures are shown in table 6.17. They indicate that over 33 percent of the rice needed for subsistence by Pa Pae villagers had to be purchased or borrowed, in spite of the fact that the village produced more than enough to eat. At Laykawkey there was a net deficit of only about 4 percent of the rice consumed which had to be purchased or borrowed. These figures suggest that problems of the subsistence economy in this area are not ones of production alone, but are also problems of distribution and particularly the high interest rates.

Rice distribution within these villages, and

distribution between the villages is uneven. One indication of the relative success of some of the Laykawkey villagers is that six household heads (almost 20%) own eight irrigated fields away from the village territory, mostly in the valley near Mae Sariang, and receive a total of 12,500 liters (625 *tang*) of rice from the rent of these fields. Residents of other Karen mountain villages also own land in the valley, which is one of the two preferred forms of capital investment, the other being elephants.

One relatively rich man at Laykawkey owns one elephant and a half share of another; he has seven buffalos and two irrigated fields, including one in the valley, from which he receives 1,600 liters (80 *tang*) in rent. His chief economic complaints are that it is difficult to sell his surplus rice in the mountains, and sometimes he finds himself eating two-year-old rice. Also his sons are too young to help him with his elephants, and so he cannot realize the maximum profit from that investment. Another prosperous Laykawkey villager has a half share in one elephant and more than a half share in another; he has two buffalos and three irrigated fields, two of which he rents for 6,000 liters (300 *tang*) per year. By contrast, no one at Pa Pae has a share in an elephant, nor do any Pa Pae villagers own fields outside their village area. No Pa Pae villager receives rent for his irrigated field. The richest people at Pa Pae are those who are out of debt, own two or three buffalos, and have clear titles to their irrigated fields. Both villages have some very poor people, but there are more poor people and more families unable to escape debt at Pa Pae.

By February of 1970, after the 1969 harvest, total unpaid debts at Pa Pae reached almost 32,000 liters (1,600 *tang*) of rice, and over 27,000 *baht*. The people estimated they would require a total of about 73,120 liters (3,656 *tang*) of rice, in addition to what they had

stored, in order to last through the time of the 1970 harvest. At Laykawkey total unpaid debts in rice rose to 3,900 liters (195 *tang*), with cash debts of over 7,000 *baht* outstanding. Laykawkey villagers estimated they would require 68,760 liters (3,438 *tang*) of rice beyond that in their storehouses to last through harvest.[6]

HOUSEHOLD REGULATION OF POPULATION SIZE AND MOTIVATION FOR ECONOMIC DEVELOPMENT IN THE HILLS

Lua' and Karen hill villagers are hardworking farmers who struggle to provide their families with enough to eat. Their ideals concerning the proper use of resources are different. Lua' villagers of Pa Pae believe it is important to have a well-built house, a plentiful supply of dry firewood, well-made homespun clothes, and if possible, silver jewelry as a means of storing their accumulated wealth. They value irrigated fields highly, and most field owners try to enlarge their fields each year, but in recent years only two households have saved enough capital to buy fields, while 10 or more fields have been sold or lost through mortgages to Karen. The Lua' ideal that property should be accumulated primarily for consumption is supported by their requirement that a man should pay a sizeable brideprice when he marries, and that weddings should include elaborate and expensive feasts. Lua' newlyweds should be able to build their own house as soon as possible after their marriage if more than one married sibling lives in the same household.

The requirement for a brideprice delays the age of marriage for poor Pa Pae men to age 22 or 25, or even later. It forces unmarried men into the wage-labor market, and probably results in lowering the net reproduction rate for women, whose marriage is usually delayed beyond age 21, by forcing them to wait while their boy friends accumulate the brideprice. Lua' marriages may also be delayed by the proscription on a younger sibling marrying before his or her elder sibling marries. Once married, however, almost all Lua' want to have large families, and most say they desire "as many children as possible" to help with the farm work.

The Karen villagers of Laykawkey have a different prestige and value system. Elephants are the ultimate prestige symbol, and a Karen household head will keep his family minimally supplied with food, clothing, and shelter in order to accumulate enough money to buy an elephant or an irrigated field. Young Karen men seek wage work to save money for similar goals. In recent years the Karen in Laykawkey have been much more successful than their Pa Pae neighbors in acquiring and building new irrigated fields and in retaining and expanding their elephant herd.

In the attempt to accumulate wealth for these purposes, a Karen man tries to enlarge his household's work force to a much greater extent than does a Lua' man, both by having as many children as possible and by encouraging the early marriage of his daughters, thus bringing other able-bodied young men into the household. In spite of the usual Karen pattern of matrilocal marriage, household heads are happy when they can persuade a son to marry within his own village, or to return to his home village with his bride after a short period of matrilocal residence. Karen may dress themselves and their children in rags, may build only the minimum bamboo house, and may honor their spirits with the minimum of cheap sacrifices, but they are happy if they can accumulate the money for an elephant in this way.

The Lua' strategy of delayed marriage has made for a slower-growing, older population, with less burden of child dependency. This may

help to account for the relatively higher productivity per person and per worker as compared with the Karen (table 6.10). Lua' traditions for honoring their ancestral and other spirits with expensive animal sacrifices may have increased their intake of animal protein, but may also have increased their indebtedness.

The Karen strategy of having as many children as early as possible may have increased the burden of child dependency and decreased per-worker productivity, but the population pressure they have more or less consciously generated has allowed them to take over increasing amounts of land by sheer weight of numbers in their competition with the Lua' for upland resources (Kunstadter 1969, 1970). The Karen willingness to satisfy their spirits with minimal sacrifices and to delay gratification of consumer needs for long-term investments in elephants and fields has helped them to take over these productive resources from the Lua', perhaps at the expense of protein malnutrition.

Lua' and Karen hill villagers seem quite willing to accept some innovations in order to improve their economic position. Some have changed their traditional religion to forms which demand fewer expensive sacrifices. Many have accepted the idea of planting new kinds of crops and raising new kinds of animals. Almost all adults accept the idea of wage work, and many have worked for lowland employers. Despite the people's flexibility and willingness to work, the upland economy is threatened by the high birthrate as well as by the failure to develop new kinds of economic resources.

The existence of different sets of values and motivations among Lua' and Karen suggests that different strategies might be appropriate in dealing with the problems of population control and economic development. Both groups are already familiar with wage labor as a means of accumulating capital. The motivations for individual accumulation are perhaps best not emphasized among these people for fear of increasing the malnutrition problem among the Karen, and weakening the family and community ties of the Lua'.

An appeal to the Lua' to limit family size could perhaps be phrased in terms of conserving resources (a concept they already understand), as well as increasing their ability to care properly for the children they have. The appeal to the Karen might be phrased in terms of increasing their ability to accumulate capital for purchasing productive resources such as fields and elephants. The goal of limiting family size among the Karen will probably be more difficult to attain because of the complexity of their motivations for large families, and their use of large families for economic advantage.

If either of these appeals is to be successful, some security must be given to titles to upland farming areas; otherwise, the Karen strategy of increasing population in order to increase claims to land will prove to be more advantageous. At the same time there must be increased opportunities for employment, or the mounting pressure to produce subsistence goods will further increase the strains on limited hill land resources.

SUMMARY

The data presented in this chapter describe the swidden and irrigated agricultural systems of two upland villages in Mae Sariang District, Mae Hong Son Province, northwestern Thailand —Pa Pae, a Lua' village, and Laykawkey, a Karen village. Despite the fact that these villages are remote, located in the hills away from roads, administrative centers, and markets, the economic systems discussed here are not isolated. The people have participated in the general population growth of Thailand and have contributed substantially to the growth of the lowland population. The people also participate directly in the lowland labor market in order to supplement their income from subsistence agriculture.

The agricultural systems can produce enough for the subsistence needs of these villagers, but two conditions have threatened the success of these systems. These are population increase and problems of credit and indebtedness. It is clear from demographic data analysed elsewhere (Kunstadter 1971) that migration out of this hill area has for a long time siphoned off surplus population. In spite of migration and the relatively high death rates, the population in the hills continues to grow rapidly, doubling every generation.

The agricultural systems of the Lua' and Karen, as described in this paper, have been conservative and have allowed permanent settlement of sizeable populations and the rapid growth of these populations. In the 1970s there is little or no room to absorb further population growth in the upland environment without some basic change in the economic system. This can be either a change in the system of production (such as increased yield from improved seed, increased amount of irrigated land, or increased reliance on wage labor), or a change in the environment and the pattern of use of the environment (decreased fallow time leading to degradation of soil, vegetation, and moisture conditions, leading quickly to a decline in productivity). Because virtually no research has been done on the development of more productive upland crops, and because there is no capital available for developing more elaborate irrigation systems in these hills, increase in wage-labor opportunities appears to be the most immediately feasible solution to the increasing economic problems in these hills.

The Lua' villagers of Pa Pae produce enough to feed themselves, but they appear to be below the subsistence level as a result of indebtedness and high rates of interest. This is one sign of the inadequacy of the upland economic system to provide subsistence for the upland villagers, despite their ability to produce enough rice for subsistence needs. Until now the Karen people of Laykawkey have produced enough to feed themselves, and have managed to stay fairly clear of debt. The people of Pa Pae and Laykawkey appear to be getting poorer, both relative to their past condition, and relative to the growing affluence of the lowland population. This situation is changing for the worse, as the Laykawkey population grows rapidly, and no more land is available in this area. Migration out of the area is one possible solution which has been followed by some Pa Pae and Laykawkey villagers. Assuming that the upland area is overpopulated for an economy based on subsistence agriculture with minimal technology, continued migration

implies a need for economic development in the lowlands to support these migrants, as well as to care for the expanding lowland populations.

These villagers participate extensively in the lowland economy as wage earners. The data presented in this paper suggest that the upland agricultural system by itself is not sufficient to provide subsistence for the upland population without the supplement of lowland wage earnings. This situation will probably get worse for two reasons. First, the population pressure in the hills will make it even more difficult to raise enough food for the hill population; and second, as a result of economic expansion in the lowland, expectations are rising among the hill people for goods which must be bought with cash. Thus cash needs are increasing, and there is increasing pressure to sell subsistence crops for cash at the same time as the need for subsistence crops is increasing due to population increases.

Appendix 6.1
The Climate of Pa Pae

Data on temperature, humidity, and rainfall were collected in order to compare the climate of Pa Pae with that of lowland areas of Thailand, and to determine the microclimatic conditions associated with different stages in the forest cultivation and fallow cycle.

WEATHER MEASUREMENT

Three weather stations were established at Pa Pae: (1) in the village schoolyard, with equipment including a Belfort hygrothermograph installed in a standard Thai weather instrument shelter and a Western Weather Systems rain gage; (2) in an upland field which had been cut in 1967 about 2 km southwest of the village, the

station equipped with a hygrothermograph in a weather instrument shelter; and (3) in the uncut forest about 0.5 km east southeast of the village, containing a hygrothermograph and instrument shelter.

Rainfall data were collected from 1967 through 30 June 1969. Nai Saman Khamhyang of Pa Pae assisted in collecting the rainfall and hygrothermograph data from February 1967 through June 1969.

Professor Charles F. Keyes collected hygrothermograph data from an instrument set up in his house at 27 Mae Sariang Road, in Mae Sariang town, between December 1967 and October 1968. This instrument was placed on a

TABLE 6.18 Weather Observation at Pa Pae

Observation Site	Elev. in meters	Temperature (°C)									Rel. Humidity (%)	
		Min. (date)[e]	Max. (date)[e]	Minimum Range (date)[e]			Maximum Range (date)[e]			Min. (date)[e]	Max. Range (date)[e]
				Min.	Max.	Dif.	Min.	Max.	Dif.		
Swidden[a]	700	2.2 (20/1/68)	37.2 (25/4/69)	21.1	24.4 (6/6/67)	3.3	12.2	34.1 (10/4/68)	21.9	15 (20/3/68)	15–100 (20/3/68)
Ban Pa Pae[b]	720	3.3 (20/1/68) (4/1/69) (19/1/69)	37.8 (24/4/69) (5/5/69)	20.6	22.8 (11/8/68)	2.2	13.3	34.5 (10/4/68)	21.1	15 (20/3/68)	15–100 (20/3/68)
Old Forest[c]	ca. 800	5.6 (4/1/69)	34.1 (25/4/69)	20	21.3 (13/8/68)	1.3	20.0	32.8 (10/4/68)	12.8	27 (20/3/68)	27–100 (20/3/68)
Mae Sariang Town[d]	ca. 280	10.5 (25/1/68)	38.9 (18/4/68)	23.3	26.1 (5/6/68)	2.8	13.9	32.2 (28/2/68)	183	20 (16/3/68)	26–100 (19/4/68)

[a]Swidden field cut in 1967, 2 km SW of Ban Pa Pae.
[b]Ban Pa Pae village schoolyard.
[c]Old forest, 450 meters ESE of Ban Pa Pae.
[d]27 Mae Sariang Road, Mae Sariang Town.
[e]Day/month/year.

covered, open-sided porch, freely exposed to air movements, and the records are probably roughly comparable to the results from the instruments in the standard shelters.

Temperature and humidity observations at the four sites are presented in table 6.18.

CHARACTERISTICS OF THE CLIMATE AT PA PAE

The climate at Pa Pae is monsoonal. Rainfall is concentrated in the six months of April through October, with the heaviest rainfall recorded in June, July, and August. Little or no rain falls between December and March. Average annual rainfall for 1967 and 1968 was about 1.43 meters. The heaviest daily rainfall was 11 cm, recorded 24 July 1968. There were 148 days with recorded rainfall in 1968.

Temperature and humidity regimes are close-ly related to the pattern of the monsoon, reflecting three major seasons: the cold season (December through mid-February), the hot season (late February through early May), and the rainy season (mid-May through early November). The lowest temperatures were recorded during the crystal clear nights of January, with the minimum of 2°C recorded on 20 January 1968 at the upland field site. The highest recorded temperature was 38°C recorded in the village on 24 April and 5 May 1969, after a few showers had cleared the air of smoke and haze from the field fires. The greatest diurnal temperature range (22°C) was recorded at the upland field site on 10 April 1968, and the smallest diurnal range (1°C) was recorded in the forest in mid-rainy season, on 13 August 1968.

The lowest relative humidity (15%) was recorded both in the upland field and the village on 20 March 1968, which was also the date of the greatest range in humidity (15%–100%) at both sites.

Violent thunderstorms, with cloud-to-ground lightning and gusty high winds, occur at the beginning and end of the rainy season, on days which start out clear and hot. Early thunderstorms may start forest fires in the tinder-dry woods at the end of the dry season. Such storms are often destructive to the newly planted upland fields in April, because the heavy downpour washes away seeds and topsoil before the rice has had a chance to take root. Large field fires, set late in March at the hottest time of the day, usually result in cumulus cloud buildups above the site of the fire and sometimes result in local rain showers, but the air is usually too dry at this time of year to allow much rain to reach ground level.

The onset of steady monsoon rains may be delayed until June or even July, which may result in desiccation of the upland crops before their roots are well established. Early onset of the rains results in heavy weed growth before the crop plants are well established. Rains continuing into late October and early November, especially if accompanied by wind and thunderstorms, may damage the ripening crops and reduce the harvest.

EFFECTS OF CLEARING ON MICRO-CLIMATE

Clearing the forest, either for a village site or for an upland field, modifies the microclimate. The uncut forest shows a higher minimum and lower maximum temperature, a smaller maximum daily range of temperature, a higher minimum humidity, and a smaller maximum range of humidity than do either of the cleared sites.

The humidity tends to be higher in the forest than in the cleared sites during daytime. High nighttime humidity (approaching or reaching 100%) is characteristic of both open and forest-covered sites in the Pa Pae area at all times of the year. Heavy dew was observed in the morning at the schoolyard site, especially in the cold season. The period of minimum daytime humidity (mid- to late March) coincides with the time the Pa Pae villagers burn their upland fields, which they cut late in January and early February. The highest temperatures are reached in the open sites late in April and early in May, and the high temperatures trigger thunderstorms which mark the end of the hot season.

During the cloudy, rainy days of the rainy season, both temperature and humidity show little variation; the temperature hovers around 21°C, and humidity stays close to 100 percent, even at midday in the open sites. The forest cover helps to retain moisture in the surface soil, which dries out rapidly in the open sites, but the soil under forest cover is drier at the end of the dry season than that in a newly cleared site. Apparently this is because the trees are cut early in the dry season before they have transpired much of the soil moisture.

Compared with the valley town of Mae Sariang, Pa Pae has lower maximum and minimum temperatures, greater temperature ranges, lower minimum humidity, and lower daytime humidity during the hot season. The maximum temperatures in the valley during the hot season were observed to be only 1°C higher than in the mountains, but the relative humidity is higher and there is less cooling at night in the valley, which probably accounts for the complaints of hill people regarding the lowland climate.

Appendix 6.2 Plants in the Pa Pae Environment

In order to document the botanical environment, as well as to learn of the pattern of use of the environment by the people of Pa Pae, we collected and identified more than 2,000 plant specimens. The species names, locations from which they came, and the uses to which they are put by upland people have been reported in detail (Kunstadter, Sabhasri, and Smitinand 1978). The information is summarized in table 6.19.

METHODS

Systematic collections of plants were made at different seasons during the work at Pa Pae, by Dr. Sanga Sabhasri, Dr. Tem Smitinand, and the authors, with the help of village research assistants. Specimens were identified by Dr. Tem Smitinand in the field and at the Royal Forest Herbarium in Bangkok.

The tabulation that follows is the result of the collaborative work described above.

CONCLUSION

The people of Pa Pae recognize and use a wide variety of plants from several parts of their environment. The variety is demonstrated in table 6.19, which shows that 70 food species are cultivated in the swiddens, 48 food species are cultivated in village gardens, and more than 20 species in other areas. There are at least 13 cultivated medicinal plants, and at least 16 plants cultivated for decoration and for ceremonial and other uses. Relatively few species are purchased—only 3 food species and 11 medicinal species. Uncultivated areas around the village contribute the major number of species for all uses, including 110 varieties of food plants from fallow swiddens, 48 food plants from the uncut

forest, 27 that grow wild in the village, and many collected from other parts of the village environment. Uncultivated varieties also dominate for animal fodder, medicine, weaving and dying, and decorative and other uses. All varieties used for fuel and most of those used for construction are uncultivated. These data reinforce the view that the Lua' derive most of their livelihood from their own environment, that swidden agriculture is a far more complex and diverse system of production than is irrigated agriculture, that fallow swiddens make important contributions to the economy of Pa Pae in addition to their role in restoring soil fertility for the next cycle of cultivation, and that the uncultivated portions of the environment are of major economic importance.

NOTES

1. Use of the term "subsistence economies" implies that the people subsist largely on what they produce, and that they organize their lives largely around production for their own subsistence. As noted below, wage work for employers outside the village community is an essential feature of their economies. See Wharton's discussion of definitions of subsistence agriculture (1969:12ff.). Since most of these people produce little more than they consume (and sometimes produce less than they need), they are subsistence agriculturists in terms of Wharton's definitions, both in their production and consumption.

2. Research during the initial period of fieldwork was supported by grants from the National Institute of General Medical Sciences and the National Geographic Society; support was also received from Princeton University. During the second period of fieldwork, the research was supported primarily by the National Science Foundation, supplemented by the grant from the National Institute of General Medical Sciences. All research was carried out under the sponsorship of the Social Science Division of the National Research Council of Thailand.

3. Hmong villagers have a complex agricultural economy involving opium and other cash crops, and corn as a subsistence crop. The Hmong village of Mae Tho, founded in about 1960, is located on the eastern boundary of Mae Sariang District. Some of the Mae Tho fields lie astride the headwaters of the Mae Amlan, which runs through Pa Pae. Hmong of Mae Tho regularly employ Lua' and Karen villagers to work in their fields for wages paid in cash or opium, and regularly purchase Lua' and Karen rice to supplement their subsistence. Succession to grassy species after removal of the forest cover has been observed in Mae Tho fields. The Hmong cultivate opium, corn, and potatoes for several years before abandoning their swiddens to the grass. See Keen (chapter 11) for further details of the Hmong system and Geddes (1970, 1973, 1976) for a more complete description of the Hmong at Mae Tho.

4. Six of the Karen farmers living at Laykawkey also own fields in the lowlands. Some of these fields are only a walk of an hour or two from the village, and these are regularly worked by the villagers. Other fields, located near Mae Sariang, 15 or 20 km distant, are regularly rented out,

and the owners ordinarily sell their share of the harvest in the lowlands. Figures for land area and productivity of these rented fields are not included in the table of productivity for Laykawkey fields; only those fields regularly worked by residents of Laykawkey are included in these productivity tabulations.

5. Personal communications of 28 February, 22 April, 8 May, and 18 June 1969.

6. In an attempt to deal with the problem of increasing indebtedness as related to high interest rates, His Majesty, the King of Thailand, sponsored the formation of rice banks in each of these villages. The banks were organized by village members who formed committees to oversee their operation. They built a rice barn in each village, purchased rice from nearby villages where surpluses were available, and established their own rules for loans and interest repayments. The banks continued in operation as of early 1977. The bank at Laykawkey is maintaining its capital, but at Pa Pae the bank has not been successful in breaking the cycle of high interest payments and increasing indebtedness.

TABLE 6.19   Locations and Uses of Plants at Pa Pae (Nos. of Varieties)

Location	Food	Animal Food	Med- icine	Weav- ing, Dying	Con- struc- tion	Deco- ration
Cultivated						
Swidden	70	3	13	2	2	16
Irrigated	5	2	3			5
Village garden	48		13	1	3	6
Hill garden				1		1
In village	19	1	12	6	6	14
Stream bed			1	3		1
Field margin	6		2			3
Purchased	3		11			
Fish pond	1					
Unspecified	6					
Uncultivated						
Swidden	4	1	2		3	1
Fallow swidden	110	27	42	14	45	16
Uncut forest	48	8	19	7	23	11
Old forest	45	4	11	7	12	10
Stream bed	22	3	6	3	3	2
Field margin	5		1		1	1
Along trail	9	1	1	1	1	1
Hillsides	6	2	4		2	2
Dry Dipterocarp	1		2		2	
In village	27	2	23	6	5	21
Burned areas					1	1
Unknown	23	7	19	5	11	5
Total number of different varieties[a]	295	44	123	33	79	75

NOTE: Plants were collected during the work described in this chapter and in chapters 7 and 8. Plants were identified by Dr. Tem Smitinand and Dr. Sanga Sabhasri. A more complete discussion of methods and results, including botanical species identifications and Lua' names for the varieties, is contained in Kunstadter, Sabhasri, and Smitinand (1978). The number of varieties is not equivalent to the number of botanically distinct species because some of the varieties were defined in terms of Lua' designations and local statements concerning place of occurrence and

TABLE 6.19 (continued)

| | | | Insect | | | | Total No. |
| | Poi- | Fenc- | Repel- | Mis-cella- | Not | Un- | Varieties |
Fuel	son	ing	lent	neous	Used	known	per Location[a]
							84
							10
							60
							1
				3	3		43
							5
		1					7
							13
							1
							6
				2	10	5	21
22	4	24	3	15	157	122	482
6	2	8		5	59	19	164
5	4			4	23	10	101
				1	7	1	39
					3		9
						2	13
					6	7	23
					6		9
	1			2	29	4	84
					1	1	3
7	2	7	2	1	75	13	147
27	8	29	5	23	280	162	967

other characteristics. The total number of locally recognized cultivated varieties is understated in this tabulation. For example, with regard to rice, almost every household has one or more distinctive varieties, seed for which they have carefully selected for taste or other desirable features, in addition to the glutinous, nonglutinous, early, late and color variations.

[a] Row and column totals do not equal the sums of figures in each row and column because any given plant variety may be found in more than one location and may have more than one use.

7

Soil Fertility Aspects of the Lua' Forest Fallow System of Shifting Cultivation

Paul J. Zinke
Sanga Sabhasri
Peter Kunstadter

The long-term success of a shifting cultivation system depends on the maintenance of soil fertility. If the nutrients lost or displaced during the cultivation phase of the cycle are approximately balanced by those replaced during fallow, the system may continue in practice indefinitely. The length of time the system has been followed in one place or the number of cycles completed on one field indicate whether or not the balance has been approached. The Lua' people of Ban Pa Pae in Mae Hong Son Province have used their soils (latosols developed on granodiorite) in a short cultivation–long fallow cycle in the same location for over 100 years.[1] This time span is indicated by historical records of relationships with Northern Thai principalities, traditional stories of land ownership and settlement histories, and by remnants of old Lua' villages within the territory of presently occupied villages. Because of this evidence of success of their agricultural system, it is of interest to trace the changes in nutrient contents of soil and vegetation through various phases of the forest fallow cultivation cycle.[2]

THE LUA' FOREST FALLOW SYSTEM
BURNING THE FIELDS

The Lua' forest fallow system can be considered as a cycle lasting approximately ten years, beginning and ending in the early part of a dry season when the forest cover is cut in a previously cultivated field (figure 7.1). The trees and other vegetation are felled to lie uniformly; they form a fuel bed which is allowed to dry for six or more weeks. Farmers fell smaller trees, leaving a one-half-meter or one-meter stump from which sprouts may later grow. These stumps show evidence of repeated cutting and coppice growth, confirming the fact that the fields have been used repeatedly. Lua' farmers leave most of the larger trees standing, but trim their branches to reduce shading of the crops.

The fields are burned a few weeks before the end of the dry season. Too late a burn may result in a fuel bed wet by thunderstorms that occur several weeks before the start of the monsoon, while too early a date may find fuel incompletely dried. The approximate date of burning is

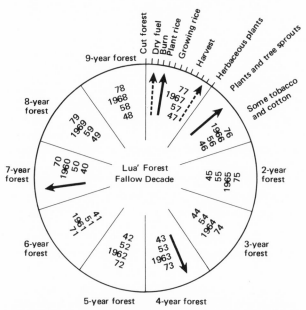

FIGURE 7.1 Lua' forest fallow cultivation cycle of 10 years; chronology as of end of March 1967, when fields were burned. Solid arrows indicate soil and vegetation sample times relative to phases of the cycle. Dashed arrows point to additional sample times relative to the chronology, taken before the burn and after the 1967 rainy season.

known several months in advance, and in 1968 the fields were burned on the preselected date of March 25, in coordination with the burning of fields of an adjacent village. Lua' avoid burning during a time of waning moon for fear there will be too many weeds. A leeway of several days is possible if the headman thinks the weather is unfavorable or if a neighboring village plans to burn their fields at an earlier date.

Fuel breaks are prepared around the area to be burned to prevent the escape of fire into the adjacent uncut forest. At sunrise on the day of burning, the oldest women go to the edge of the village and sacrifice a little rice and other foodstuffs, liquor, yarn, and cowrie shells to the an-

cestral spirits. Later in the morning older men who are religious leaders construct an altar of branches and leaves in the forest along the trail to the year's fields. They sacrifice a dog and pig and several chicks to the field spirits, calling for their assistance in achieving a good burn. The old men continue the ceremony until youths and young men light the fuel bed, offering small amounts of rice liquor to the spirits, and drinking the remainder from the sacrificial bottles. The fire-setters maintain strict sobriety for their dangerous task.

The fields have a considerable range of elevation, with some steep slopes (1967 range from 680 to 820 meters above sea level; 1968 range from 740 to 1,040 meters, with slopes up to 70 percent) creating the potential for strong updrafts. The torch-bearers are fully aware of the danger of being caught in the rapid spread of flames sweeping up the slopes. At about midday, when conditions are hottest and driest (32°C and 10–20 percent relative humidity at the time of the 1968 fire), they begin to light the fuel bed, starting on the ridges.

After lighting the highest points on the fields, the men run down along the field edges, and the fire begins to burn down the slope. As the fuel begins to burn, it causes an indraft, and by the time the fire reaches the lower edges of the fields, a strong wind is blowing into the fire. In 1968 there was between 5 and 6 km of periphery to be lit. The firing of the lower periphery was accompanied by indraft winds of 40 to 65 km per hour. Small, intense firestorm whirlwinds developed in the fuel bed area as it burned. These were spiral masses of flame up to 100 meters tall, developing intense winds at their centers. They were strong enough to tear out temperature measuring templates partially buried under some of the slash.

In the 1968 burn, approximately 54,636 metric tons (oven dried weight) of fuel was burned on 94.2 hectares in less than an hour. One effect was a 10–20,000-foot column of smoke and ash, topped by a cumulus cloud with precipitation downwind. Flocks of swallows flew through the edges of the smoke cloud, hunting insects in the updrafts.

The burn left a fairly uniform ash bed laid over the fields. Most leaves, branches, and smaller stems were burned. In the next few weeks, the villagers laid charred logs horizontally on the slopes behind stumps, to form revetments which are effective in controlling soil creep. They placed as many as 100 logs per hectare, and collected the rest of the larger logs and stems for field border markers, fencing, and firewood. The remainder of unburned slash they piled and reburned in small hot fires. The ash is black over most of the burned area, with whiter ash where fire temperatures were higher, and small regions of white ash and reddened earth where the reburn piles had been.

Villagers plant rice in the ash-covered fields after cleaning up the unburned slash. Men jab the soil with long metal-tipped bamboo poles, making about 14 holes per square meter. Women, children and older men follow, casting a few seeds at each hole.

The rice begins to grow with the onset of the monsoon rains, and is harvested toward the end of the rainy season. Even before the rains begin, soil is moist below about 5 cm, because the early cutting of the forest conserves soil moisture which would otherwise be lost by evapotranspiration in the dry season.

Despite continuous weeding throughout the rice-growing season, herbaceous species, dominated by *Eupatorium odoratum*, cover the swiddens soon after harvest. Most of the trees are not killed by cutting or the fire. They begin sprouting from stumps soon after the fire, and eventually form a coppice of sprout growth shading out most of the herbaceous plants. Thus the fallow fields are eventually dominated by tree species, with some bamboo (see appendix, chapter 8). A high proportion of presumably nitrogen-fixing leguminous trees occur in the forest fallow vegetation, which grows for about nine years before the cycle is repeated (figure 7.1).

AREA AND TIME RELATIONSHIPS

Various stages of the Lua' forest fallow cultivation cycle can easily be identified on aerial photograhs taken in the dry season (figure 7.2). The land from which the rice crop has just been harvested appears as a uniform light-tone zone with white dots representing the rice threshing areas. The stages of forest fallow regrowth on fields cut in earlier years are indicated by the density of tree crowns and their height, which increase through the cycle, as observed stereoscopically on aerial photographs. Maps of the cultivation stages were prepared of the field areas around Pa Pae using these features (figures 7.3, 7.4).

The cultivation sites for each year of a decade were identified by their appearance on aerial photographs made in 1964–1965. Boundaries were verified by ground checks with informants from the village, and transcribed to a planimetric map. The map shows the land dimensions of the cultivation and fallow cycle. Thus with the time scale of the cycle as shown in figure 7.1, the area identified on the map as "1968" had previously been cultivated in 1958, and had a nine-year-old forest when cut and burned in 1968.

The areas included in cultivation sites for each year averaged 100 hectares but may range up to 300 hectares, including interior unburned

FIGURE 7.2   The Pa Pae–Laykawkey area after the 1965 harvest. Solid line outlines the area shown in figure 7.5. Swiddens to the north of Laykawkey *(lower left)* were farmed in 1965; area to the west of Pa Pae *(upper right)* was cut in 1962.

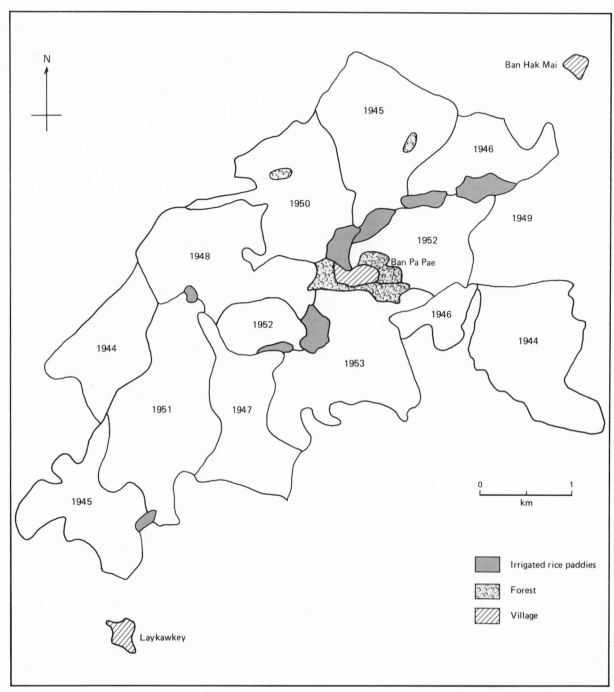

FIGURE 7.3 Pa Pae swidden land use for the decade 1944–1953, as determined from 1954 aerial photograph.

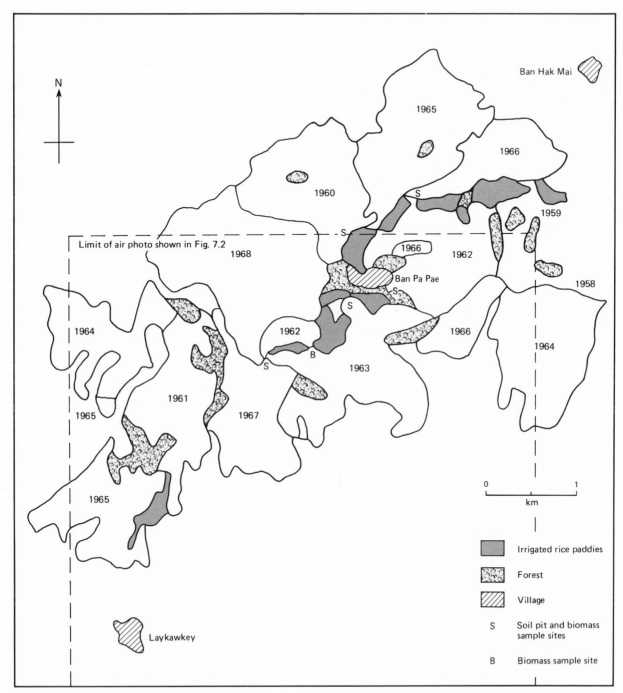

FIGURE 7.4   Pa Pae land use as determined from aerial photographs taken after the 1965 harvest, annotated in the field.

forest areas. Ridge tops, narrow gullies, boundaries between cultivation zones, and edges of watercourses are not cut or burned. In some years of the cycle, the cultivated land is located in two separate areas. Total land used including interior unburned areas) through the 1959–1968 cycle was 1,553 hectares for a village population that averaged about 200 people. Of the total, about 706 hectares were cultivated, including about 688 hectares of swidden and about 18 of irrigated fields (for details of agricultural land use see table 6.5). The unburned areas serve vital functions in this system. They maintain seed sources for reforestation, protect against erosion, and are important sources of useful plants (see appendix 6.2, pp. 130–132).

The cultivation site dimensions of an earlier rotation of the cycle were determined by examining another set of aerial photographs taken in 1954. It was possible to identify in these photographs the forest fallow stages of swiddens cut, burned, and cropped as long ago as 1947 (figure 7.3). Comparison of figures 7.3 and 7.4 confirms that approximately the same field areas are cultivated cyclically, each decade.

In a given year the swiddened area is further subdivided into individual family plots. These were mapped for the year 1967, as shown in figure 7.5. The size of each family holding depends on the number of working people in the family. Field use ownership and boundaries were verified at harvest time (figure 7.6).

METHODS OF STUDY

SAMPLING PROCEDURES

The cultivation sites for different years of the Lua' forest fallow cycle were used as a basis for studying changes in soil fertility. Study plots were established early in 1967 in several fields, representing stages in the land-use cycle: (1) an

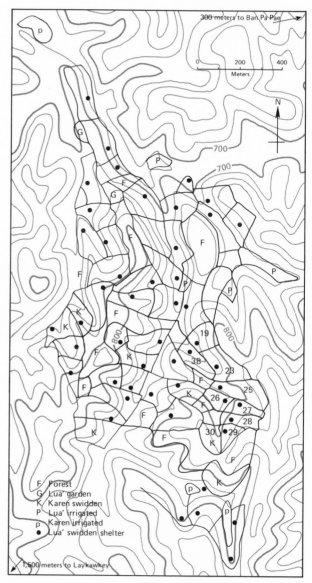

FIGURE 7.5 Pa Pae and some Karen individual swidden and irrigated field holdings cultivated in 1967, originally annotated on aerial photograph (see figure 7.2), projected onto contour map to determine field sizes. Base map is Sheet 4665 IV, Series L 708, edition 1-AMS.

FIGURE 7.6 Photograph taken in Lua' swidden November 1967, annotated with identification of farm holdings to verify ownership and boundaries. Numerals correspond to those shown in figure 7.5. Rows of sorghum mark field boundaries between 3B and half-harvested 23, and between 27 and 28. Field 3B, planted to early rice, was harvested about one month previously. Field 30, cleared by a Lua' farmer from Pa Pae, was used by Karen from Laykawkey because the Lua' farmer felt too isolated.

area to be burned and cultivated in 1967; (2) an area with herbaceous regrowth, one year after cultivation; (3) an area of fourth-year forest regrowth; and (4) an area of seven-year-old forest regrowth. A fifth study plot located in old-growth forest served as a control representing the condition of forest and soil in the absence of cyclical cultivation. In selecting specific sites within the fields, care was taken to assure that conditions of slope, exposure, and soil type would be similar in all plots. The locations chosen are shown in figure 7.4; their relation to the cultivation cycle is shown by the solid arrows in figure 7.1.

Standard samples of soil, leaf litter, and vegetation were taken at each location, and biomass was determined for each site. All vegetation was cut on a 10-by-20-meter area of each swidden

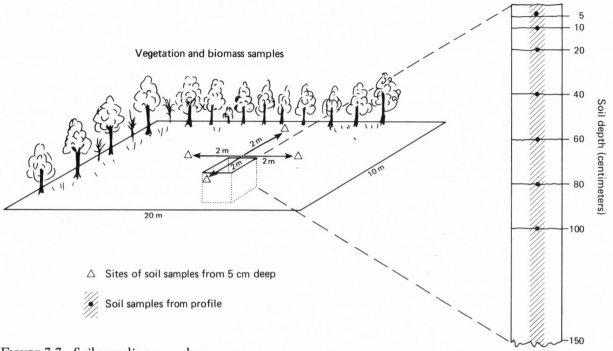

Vegetation and biomass samples

△ Sites of soil samples from 5 cm deep

● Soil samples from profile

FIGURE 7.7 Soil sampling procedure.

cycle study plot. The vegetation was divided into leguminous trees, nonleguminous trees, bamboo, and herbaceous understory, and the tree samples were further subdivided into foliage and small branches, and stem portions before weighing. Biomass of the old forest was estimated using a formula based on height, girth, and crown size, derived from measurements in similar forests elsewhere in Thailand (see chapter 8). Subsamples by species and plant part were also taken for determination of moisture content and chemical analysis for nitrogen, phosphorus, calcium, magnesium, potassium, and pH. All biomass and subsequent fertility element weights are reported on an oven-dry basis.

Soil and leaf litter samples were obtained from a sampling area within the biomass plot after it had been cleared. Five surface soil samples were taken: one from the top of the soil profile test pit, and one from each of four points located 2 meters away in the cardinal directions. All surface soil samples were taken from 0–5 cm depth. Samples of the soil profile were taken at depths of 0–5 cm, 5–10 cm, 10–20 cm, 20–40 cm, 40–60 cm, 60–80 cm, 80–100 cm, and 100–150 cm, to determine soil properties as a function of depth (figure 7.7). Bulk density samples of approximately 220 cc were taken corresponding to each soil sample taken for analysis. The soil bulk density was used for subsequent conversion of analytical data to field weight per unit area. Soil density samples were obtained by driving a tube sampler into the soil. Roots were later sieved from the bulk density samples so that root weights could be deducted from total soil mass.

Soil samples were taken three times during the first year of the study to represent soil conditions (1) after cutting but before burning (February), (2) after burning (April), and (3) after rice harvest at the end of the monsoon rains (November). The sampling times are indicated by dashed arrows on figure 7.2.

Leaf litter samples consisted of litter collected from 0.1 m² circular plots located at each surface soil sampling location. The leaf litter weights were adjusted to an oven-dry basis, after moisture content was determined.

Ash samples in the current burned field were collected along a line transect at 10-meter intervals. Ten such samples were collected, each containing ash from a 0.1 m² area.

SOIL TEMPERATURE AND EROSION

Soil and surface temperatures under the swidden fire were measured by partially burying mica sheets, coated with temperature-indicating lacquers, under fuel accumulations judged to be medium and heavy, and under a reburn pile. The temperature of bare ash and soil surfaces after the fire were measured under midday sun with hand-held chemical thermometers.

Erosion was studied by measuring changes in soil surface level as indicated on marked stakes driven into a swidden field and an adjacent uncut wooded patch, by collecting eroded soil in a ditch running across a swidden, and by examining the deposit fan below swidden fields (see also chapter 8).

CHEMICAL ANALYSES

The soil properties considered to be of greatest importance to fertility were quantity of nitrogen, carbon, and phosphorus; the cation ex-

change capacity (c.e.c.) and composition, including exchangeable calcium, magnesium, potassium, and sodium; and the soil reaction or pH. These laboratory analyses were performed under Zinke's direction at the School of Forestry and Conservation, University of California, Berkeley. Independent analyses done in Thailand are reported in chapter 8.

Soil carbon content was determined by dry combustion, total nitrogen by the Kjehldahl method, and the exchangeable cations by leaching with 1 N ammonium acetate. Phosphorus in the soil was determined as that amount soluble in a bicarbonate solution. All analyses were run on the less than 2-mm fraction of soil particles. Gravel and stone particles larger than 2 mm and roots were screened out and weighed to allow subsequent calculations of weight per unit area to be made for each element.

Leaf litter and vegetation samples were chemically analyzed to allow a comparison with the corresponding soil properties. The samples were subjected to wet digestion with perchloric-nitric acid. The digestate was analyzed by absorption spectrophotometry for calcium, magnesium, potassium, and sodium. Phosphorus in the same solution was determined colorimetrically. Nitrogen was determined by the Kjehldahl method.

The results were converted to weights of each element per unit area. In the case of the exchangeable cations, values were expressed in gram equivalent weights or gram equivalents per square meter for each soil depth. Carbon, nitrogen, and phosphorus content were calculated as weights per square meter at the specified depth.

The removal of rice from the swiddens during harvest is a normal part of the cultivation cycle. The effects of harvest on the fertility balance of soil and vegetation were estimated by combin-

TABLE 7.1   Soil and Surface Temperatures at Time of Burning

Elevation (+) and Depth (−) from Soil Surface (cm)	Heavy fuel [a]	Moderate fuel [a]	Reburn pile
+2	650	450	600
+1	510–590	420	600
0 (surface)	427–590	205	430–570
−1	205–480	150	375–450
−2	150	70	325–375
−3	70	(soil moist)	150–300
−5	n.a.	n.a.	less than 150 [b]

[a] Heavy fuel included large logs; light fuel consisted mainly of smaller branches and leaves. All values in °C.

[b] Soil below 5 cm was warmed only slightly above ambient soil temperature.

ing rice harvest data (chapter 6) with chemical analyses of rice samples.

Logs are also removed from the fields for firewood and for a limited amount of construction. We have no measurement of the quantities of fertility elements removed from the swidden fields in this way, but an estimated 5 to 10 kg of firewood per household per day is suggested by casual observations of amounts of firewood carried into the village and used for cooking two meals per day, brewing, cooking pig food, and heating the houses during cold winter nights.

RESULTS

SOIL TEMPERATURE

Temperatures induced by the swidden fire reached 650°C 2 cm above the soil surface, and nearly 600°C at the surface. Temperatures sufficient to sterilize the soil (75°) occurred at least to a depth of 2 cm at the time of the fire (table 7.1). The depth to which the high temperature penetrated the soil was limited partly by soil moisture. At the time the temperature-sensitive mica sheets were inserted in the soil, the soil was seen to be moist below the 2 cm depth. The lacquered mica sheets were steamed in this moist layer, confirming the presence of this damp zone. The swidden fire lasted for only about an hour, not long enough, apparently, to dry out the soil moisture. Several days after the main field fire, piles of unburned fuel are stacked and burned. Under these reburn piles, temperatures of 150°C reached 5 cm, and some heating was measured at 10 cm. Reburning occurs only on a small portion of the total swidden area.

Following the fire, the ash bed lying on the slopes under intense sunlight also developed relatively high temperatures. The black ash surface exposed to midday sun measured up to 53°C; at the same time shaded surfaces measured 33°C. Presumably temperatures of the sunlit ash bed would be high enough to kill small insects.

CARBON

Carbon contents for each sampling plot are compared in terms of grams per square meter of field surface soil.[3] Results from the 0–5-cm level at each stage of the cultivation–fallow cycle are presented in table 7.2. The lowest amount of carbon in the surface soil (1.8 kg/m²) is found immediately following the swidden fire, and the

TABLE 7.2   Carbon and Nitrogen in the Top 5 cm of Soils at Various Stages
of the Lua' Forest Fallow Cycle (g/m² to 5 cm depth)

| | Portion of Cycle | | | | |
	Burned Field	1-Year Regrowth	4-Year Regrowth	7-Year Regrowth	Old Unburned Forest
Carbon	1770	2013	1963	2101	1734
Nitrogen	97	103	85	100	95
C/N	18	20	23	21	18

NOTE: All values are means of five replicate surface samples.

TABLE 7.3   Cumulative Weight of Carbon and Nitrogen as Functions of
Soil Depth Expressed as Linear Logarithmic Functions [a]
[Log Cumulative Weight of Element = Log Intercept + (Slope) (Log Soil Depth)]

| | Carbon | | Nitrogen | |
Stage of Cycle	Slope	Log Intercept	Slope	Log Intercept
Burned field	.609	2.80072	.693	1.52070
1-Year regrowth	.671	2.81501	.773	1.50981
4-Year regrowth	.481	2.95345	.606	1.55702
7-Year regrowth	.448	3.02501	.599	1.65297
Unburned old forest	.527	2.93252	.712	1.45477

NOTE: Correlation coefficients range from .990 to .998.
[a] Weight as grams per square meter, depth as centimeters.

highest (2.1 kg/m²) in the older portion of the forest fallow. Figure 7.8 A, which shows the carbon contents for the entire soil profile, indicates that carbon accumulation at increasing depths is highest in the portions of the fallow cycle immediately following burning (current burned field, and one year after), decreases toward the middle of the cycle (four years after burn), and increases toward the end of the cycle. The carbon content toward the end of the fallow cycle approaches that of the old unburned forests. The apparent anomaly of an increase in amount of carbon with increasing depths in the field which has just been burned is probably the result of the presence in the lower portion of this soil profile of root materials from the cut trees,

and removal of organic matter at the surface by combustion.

The cumulative carbon contents as a function of soil depth plotted in figure 7.8 A indicate that a curvilinear function could be used to describe these distributions. These data are so represented in table 7.3. It is seen that the slope of the function is greatest in the early portions of the cycle and decreases with time, whereas the intercept (the logarithm of the carbon content in the top centimeter of the soil) is highest toward the end of the cycle.

Thus, through the Lua' swidden cycle the soil organic matter, as represented by carbon content to a depth of one meter, ranges from 12.0 to 7.8 kg/m²; it is highest during the year of culti-

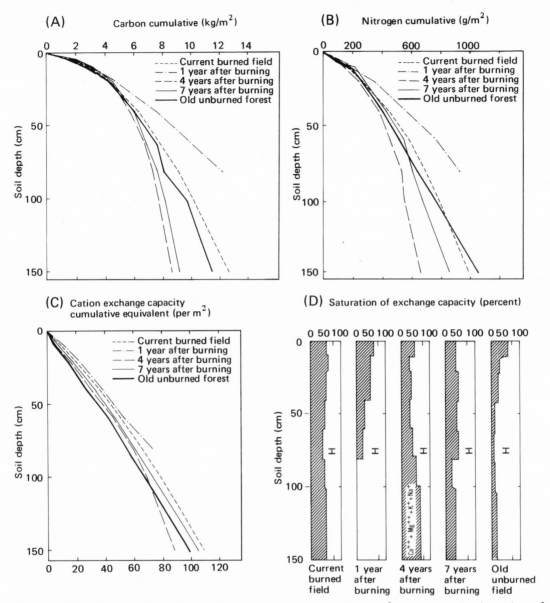

FIGURE 7.8 Changes in carbon and nitrogen content, cation exchange capacity (c.e.c.), and saturation of c.e.c. at various phases of Pa Pae cultivation–fallow cycle, and at various soil depths.

vation and lowest in the middle of the forest fallow. This carbon is probably most important as an energy source for soil chemical processes associated with microorganisms. The change in carbon content during fallow represents a replenishment of soil organic matter which would be rapidly depleted were the soil depth in continuous production under these tropical conditions.

NITROGEN

The nitrogen content of the soil follows a pattern similar to that of carbon during the Lua' forest fallow cycle. The surface soil nitrogen content varied 18 g/m² through the cycle. Lowest amounts occured in the mid-period of the forest fallow (table 7.2). Taking into account the entire soil depth studied, the cumulative nitrogen content is highest in the period of the cycle immediately after the cutting and burning of the forest fallow. This is seen in figure 7.8 B. In contrast to the old unburned forest, the tendency during the forest fallow cycle is a shift of the soil nitrogen to the layers of the soil in the upper half meter. This is illustrated by the values for intercept and slope of equations describing the cumulative nitrogen content as a function of soil depth. Slopes of the regression are highest in the early parts of the cycle beginning with the cutting and burning of the forest fallow, with increasing intercepts (surface nitrogen contents) through the fallow cycle. This illustrates the increase in nitrogen content of the surface soil during regrowth of the forest.

The ratio of carbon to nitrogen (C/N) is an important aspect of the interpretation of organic content of the soil, since it indicates the availability of nitrogen for plant growth. The C/N ratio reaches its lowest point (18) in the surface soils immediately after the swidden is burned. A similar level is found under the old uncut forest.

The ratio decreases with depth, to 9 or 10, at all stages of the cycle. The low ratio after burning means that there is a greater excess of nitrogen available for crops, over the needs of soil organisms involved in organic matter decomposition. Soil carbon in such lateritic soils is important in supplying cation exchange capacity to the soil.

SOIL CATION EXCHANGE COMPLEX

Under tropical conditions of heat and moisture, fertility elements tend to leach out of the upper levels of the soil. The cation exchange capacity of a soil is a measure of the potential of that soil to retain fertility elements against leaching. Table 7.4 indicates a range in surface soil exchange capacities at the four stages of the fallow cycle, of from 5.7 to 7.1 gram equivalents per square meter. This variation generally followed the changes in carbon content in these soils as seen in table 7.5. The association of changes in cations with changes in carbon averages three equivalents of exchange capacity per kg of carbon in the soil, ranging from 2.7 to 3.6 in these soils. Thus one outcome of the Lua' swidden cycle is maintenance of an adequate supply of organic matter, which in turn maintains ion storage capacity. In addition, the cutting, burning, ash deposition, and forest fallow regrowth affect the amounts and relative proportions of the cations absorbed on this exchange capacity.

EXCHANGEABLE CATIONS:
CALCIUM, MAGNESIUM, POTASSIUM

There are four sources of basic cations in the upper levels of the soil: weathering of soil parent material, decay of subsurface organic matter, decay of surface litter, and ash from the burning of forest slash. The importance of fire in this

TABLE 7.4 Cation Exchange Properties of Surface Soils at Various Stages of Lua' Forest Fallow Cycle

Stage of Cycle	Cation Exchange Capacity*	Cation Composition				
		Ca^{++}	Mg^{++}	K$^+$	Na$^+$	H$^+$
Burned field	6.4	2.4 (37.5%)	1.2 (18.7%)	0.2 (3.1%)	0.0 (0)	2.6 (40.7%)
1-Year regrowth	7.1	3.1 (43.6%)	1.0 (14.2%)	0.4 (5.6%)	0.0 (0)	2.6 (36.6%)
4-Year regrowth	5.7	1.9 (33.3%)	0.6 (10.5%)	0.2 (3.5%)	0.0 (0)	3.0 (52.7%)
7-Year regrowth	6.2	1.6 (25.7%)	0.6 (9.8%)	0.2 (3.2%)	0.0 (0)	3.8 (61.3%)
Old unburned forest	4.6	1.8 (39.1%)	0.8 (17.4%)	0.3 (6.5%)	0.0 (0)	1.7 (37.0%)

NOTE: Cation exchange properties expressed as gram equivalent weights per square meter to a depth of 5 cm. Means of five surface-to-5-cm soil samples at each stage of cycle. Conversion to weights is made by multiplying by equivalent weight of element. Percent compositions are listed in parentheses.

TABLE 7.5 Cation Exchange Capacity and Carbon Contents of Surface Soils to 5 cm Depth

	Burned Field	1-Year Regrowth	4-Year Regrowth	7-Year Regrowth	Old Unburned Forest
Equivalents of exchange capacity per square meter	6.4	7.1	5.7	6.2	4.6
Kg of carbon per square meter	1.8	2.0	2.0	2.1	1.7
Equivalents per kg carbon	2.8	3.6	2.8	3.0	2.7

system is seen from the fact that the exchangeable calcium content is definitely higher in the surface soils following the burn and during first-year regrowth of the cycle, and less in amount as the forest regrows. The same is true of magnesium and potassium. This can be seen from the data of table 7.4. Thus the sum of these basic cations is highest at the beginning of the cycle at the time of cutting and burning as the forest

fallow regrows. One effect of the cutting and burning of the forest cover crop is to recharge the soil cation exchange capacity with these basic cations.

The sum of the basic cations subtracted from the cation exchange capacity gives an estimate of presumably exchangeable hydrogen. This base unsaturation or exchangeable hydrogen content increases as the forest fallow regrows.

These changes are apparent from table 7.4 if one considers the range in percentage composition of the exchange complex from a low of 36.6 percent exchangeable hydrogen immediately after burning and rice harvest to 61 percent in the soil samples from the seven-year regrowth sample. The old unburned forest maintains a high base-element status on the exchange complex of the top level of the soil, probably associated with the amount of litter normally decomposing there.

Cutting and burning the forest has the effect of taking these basic elements from the vegetation and adding them to the surface soil where they can be used by the crops. The amounts which are added (or, more properly, returned) to the soil are implied by table 7.4. Calcium varies by 0.8 gram equivalents per square meter, magnesium by 0.6, and potassium by 0.2. By converting gram equivalent weights to total weights we can calculate the total variation in calcium, magnesium, and potassium in the top 5 cm of soil through the forest fallow cycle. Calcium varies 30 g/m^2; potassium 8 g/m^2; and magnesium 7.2 g/m^2. Presumably if there was continuous cropping, without allowing the forest to regenerate, comparable weights would have to be applied as fertilizer to the top 5 cm of the soil. This is equivalent to about 450 kg per hectare, assuming these elements could be purchased in pure form. This would obviously impose an impossible financial and transportation burden on these relatively isolated subsistence farmers.

Similar changes are observed in the soil cation exchange properties examined to 150-cm depth in these soils during the cycle. The cumulative cation exchange capacity to this depth amounts to from 80 to 100 equivalents per square meter as shown in figure 7.8 C. The exchange capacity is higher for all phases of the forest fallow cycle than for the soil of the unburned old forest. Also,

all phases of the cycle maintain a soil that is charged to a greater degree with basic cations, as is seen in figure 7.8 D. The recharge of the soil cation exchange column by the early processes in the cycle is clearly seen. Gradually these elements are depleted from the top of the soil column as the forest fallow progresses, by leaching of cations to lower portions of the soil profile. The soil in the old unburned forest is maintained nearly base-discharged except at the surface. Any accumulation of basic cations is confined to a small portion of the top of the soil column. Presumably this comes from leaching of leaf litter and foliage, which recharges the top of the column.

The effect of the long-time growth of this Hill Evergreen Forest is a striking depletion of soil calcium, as is seen in figure 7.9 A. Most of the phases of the forest fallow cycle maintain a total of 15 more equivalents of exchangeable calcium per square meter of the soil down to 150 cm than does the old-forest soil. The general result of recharging the soil by burning is to make the calcium content (especially at the soil surface) highest in the years immediately following the burning phase. Then, as the forest fallow regrows, there is a gradual discharge of the calcium in the soil column as it is taken up by the regrowing forest. If the fallow period were to continue longer, the degree of discharge shown in the soil column under the old forest would eventually be reached. These data indicate that a major influence of the Lua' forest fallow cycle is the recharge and maintenance of calcium on the soil exchange column.

Table 7.6 compares the amount of calcium contained at different stages in the forest fallow with equivalent cation exchange capacity depths for 25 and 50 equivalents of exchange capacity per square meter.

Assuming that the maximum difference in

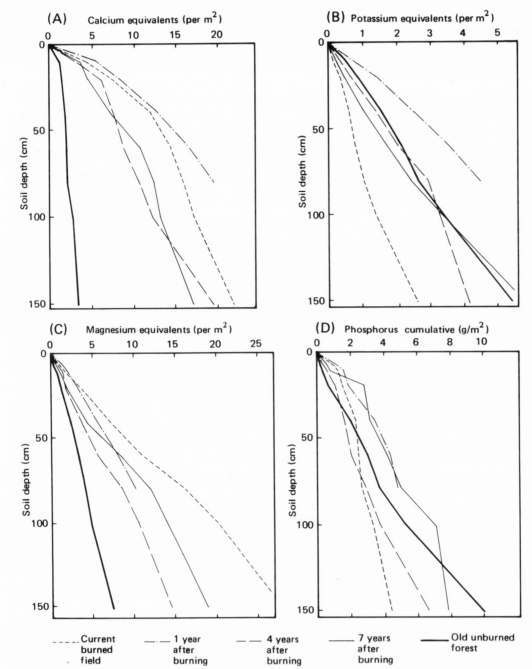

FIGURE 7.9 Cumulative amounts of (A) calcium, (B) potassium, (C) magnesium, and (D) phosphorus at various stages of Pa Pae cultivation–fallow cycle, and at various soil depths.

TABLE 7.6 Storage of Exchangeable Calcium in Soils of the Lua' Forest Fallow Cycle (expressed in equivalent depths of exchange column capacity on a square meter area)

Uniform Depths of Exchange Capacity in Soil	Burned Field	1-Year Regrowth	4-Year Regrowth	7-Year Regrowth	Old Unburned Forest
25	8.6	8.8	6.6	6.0	1.8
50	14.4	15.7	9.4	11.0	2.2

amount of calcium during the fallow cycle is the recharge amount involved, the recharge to a soil column equivalent depth of 25 is 2.8 equivalents of calcium (56 g/sq m), and to 50 equivalents depth of soil column it is 6.3 equivalents of calcium (126 g/sq m). This maximum difference occurs between the first and fourth years following cultivation.

Potassium and magnesium in the exchange capacity of soils in the Lua' forest fallow cycle do not show as pronounced a variation as does calcium. Potassium content is highest the year after burning and drops, as the forest regrows, to a minimum in the current burned field (figure 7.9 B). A high potassium content is maintained under the old forest. The range in potassium to a 60-cm soil depth is from 0.8 equivalents immediately after burning (before any leaching has occurred from the ash) to a high of 3.6 equivalents a year later. If the fallow cycle were to be replaced by equivalent fertilization, 2.8 equivalents of potassium or 110 g/m^2 might be required.

The magnesium content of the soils tends to be higher during all stages of the fallow cycle than in comparable unburned forest. The magnesium contents to 60 cm of soil depth for various phases of the cycle are 11.5 in the current burn year, 8.3 at one year, 5.9 at four years, and 8.5 in the seventh year contrasted with 3.6 in the old forest. During the cycle the amount of magnesium varies within a range of 5.6 equivalents per square meter to 60-cm depth (67.2 g/m^2). See figure 7.9 C.

PHOSPHORUS

Phosphorus is a very important and frequently limiting soil fertility element. Bicarbonate soluble phosphorus was the form analyzed in this study. The soils in all phases of the forest fallow cycle show higher amounts of phosphorus than the soil under unburned forest (figure 7.9 D). The amounts involved are small, as is seen in table 7.7. During the cycle, the range in surface soil phosphorus content is 0.7 g/m^2 in the top 5 cm, and 2.3 g/m^2 to 60-cm depth (phosphorus as phosphate; approximately one-third of these amounts are elemental phosphorus). In soil under old-growth unburned forest most of the the phosphorus is in the lower soil depths, in contrast with the soils of the forest fallow cycle where greater amounts of phosphorus are maintained in the upper portions of the soil. In this cycle, maximum phosphorus contents are reached during and immediately following the rice harvest, and a major effect of the Lua' system is the concentrate available phosphorus in the surface soil layers during the cultivation period (figure 7.9 D).

Since the soils are latosols and probably an

TABLE 7.7   Phosphorus[a] Contents of Soils at Various Stages of Lua' Forest Fallow Cycle (g/m²)

Portion of Soil	Burned Field	1-Year Regrowth	4-Year Regrowth	7-Year Regrowth	Old Unburned Forest
Surface to 5-cm depth (means of 5 samples)	1.1	1.1	0.4	0.5	0.2
Cumulative to 60 cm	2.4	4.3	2.0	4.1	2.6
Cumulative to 150 cm	4.2	–	6.6	7.6	9.6

[a] Bicarbonate soluble phosphorus.

TABLE 7.8   pH of Surface Soils at Various Stages of the Lua' Forest Fallow Cycle

	Burned Field	1-Year Regrowth	4-Year Regrowth	7-Year Regrowth	Old Unburned Forest
Mean of 5 samples	6.7	6.6	6.1	6.2	6.0
Range	6.3–7.0	6.4–6.9	6.0–6.3	6.0–6.5	5.7–6.3

TABLE 7.9   pH and Phosphorus and Potassium Content of Surface Soil at Various Stages of Cultivation

	Before Burn (February)	After Burn (April)	After Monsoon and Harvest (November)
pH	6.2	6.7	6.4
Phosphorus (ppm)	4.0	32.5	18.5
Potassium (ppm)	208.0	296.0	177.0

NOTE: All values given are means of four samples.

iron phosphate solubility system is involved, the availability of phosphorus will be strongly influenced by pH, with more acid conditions resulting in lower available phosphorus.

SOIL REACTION (pH)

The reaction of the soil (pH) found during various phases of the forest fallow cycle will be of importance particularly in respect to solubility of phosphorus, and also as an indicator of base status of the soil. Table 7.8 shows that the surface soils are least acid in the period immediately after burning, becoming more acid with years of fallow, and are most acid under the old unburned forest. The same holds true for pH of the entire soil profile of each area studied (figure 7.10). Thus another major result of the Lua' forest fallow system is the maintenance of less acid conditions in the soils on which it is practiced.

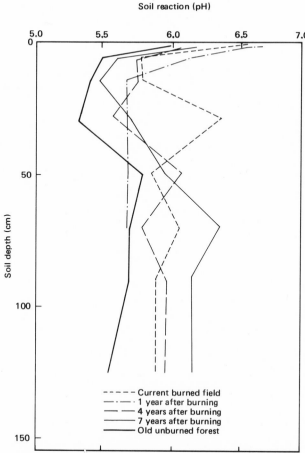

Soil reaction (pH)

FIGURE 7.10   Soil pH under Pa Pae cultivation cycle at various depths. Note decline in surface pH in the year following swidden burn and cultivation.

SURFACE SOIL VARIATION DURING YEAR OF BURNING AND HARVEST

The most rapid and important changes in soil properties occur in the Lua' forest fallow cycle during the year of cutting the forest, burning the cut forest, and growing and harvesting the rice. The data presented in table 7.9 indicate that there is a rise in soil pH immediately after the burn. Phosphorus content is very low just before the fire but is very high just after. Potassium content is also highest immediately after burn but drops rapidly after growth of the rice crop and leaching by monsoon rains. The effect of cutting and burning at the end of the forest fallow cycle is to bring the surface soil to peak fertility for the six months of rice crop growth out of the 120 months of the cycle.

EROSION AND SOIL DEPOSITION BELOW FIELDS

The erosion process gives a graphic history of the use of a forest area for past shifting cultivation cycles. The deposition fan at the base of a small watershed subjected to shifting cultivation in 1968 had distinct layers, presumably dating from each time the forest was burned on that watershed (see figure 7.11). The soil profile of the fan in the 1968 field had distinct layers, each representing a deposition from a time when the field above was subject to cutting, burning, and rice harvest. This is physical evidence of the repetition of the Lua' forest fallow cycle. The size of the fan was about 100 square meters, with an average deposition of 20 cm over the fan for the most recent cycle, from a watershed area estimated to be about 20,000 square meters. The deposited soil is slightly more dense (1.33) than the soil on the recently burned fields (density 1.16). Therefore, an approximation of the depth of erosion may be 1.15 mm per 10 years, or 11.5 cm per millennium, assuming that all the eroded soil has remained on the fan and is not carried any lower. In the situation at Pa Pae, this erosion and redeposition contribute directly to settled agriculture since the fans at the base of many small watersheds have been turned into irrigated fields. Higher erosion rates, calculated by a different method, are reported in chapter 8.

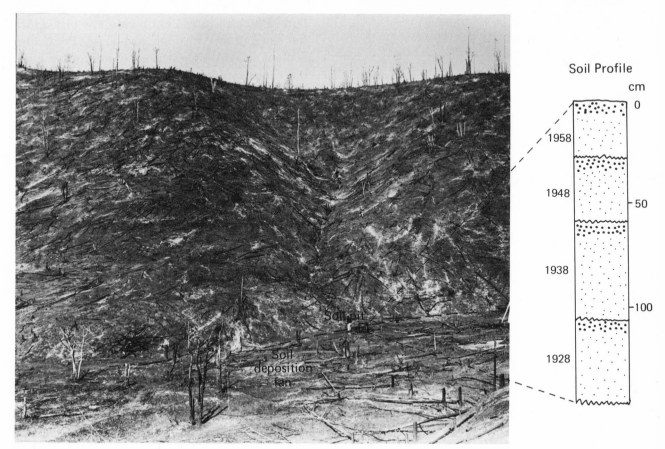

FIGURE 7.11   Soil deposition fan below Pa Pae swidden in which soil profile showed evidence of successive cultivation periods. Estimates of soil erosion were made by measuring changes in surface level at stakes driven into this swidden during the 1968 cultivation year; estimates of deposition were made by measuring the size and depth of the fan below the swidden. See also chapter 8.

VEGETATION PROPERTIES RELATIVE TO SOIL FERTILITY

BALANCE OF ELEMENTS BETWEEN VEGETATION AND SOIL

We must appraise the role of the forest fallow in maintaining soil fertility in order to understand the Lua' system of shifting cultivation. The regrowing forest takes up fertility elements from the soil, and subsequently returns some of these elements to the soil surface in the form of leaf litter and eventually in ash at the time of burning. These processes must be related to the rice crop and its composition, in order to close the cycle of fertility which parallels the forest fallow cultivation cycle. Studies of the development of biomass are reported in detail in chapter 8 of this volume. Data showing the content of

TABLE 7.10 Distribution of Fertility Elements in Vegetation, Leaf Litter, Ash, and Soil in Various Phases of Lua' Forest Fallow Cycle

	Burned Field	1-Year Regrowth	4-Year Regrowth	7-Year Regrowth	Old Unburned Forest
Nitrogen (g/m²)					
Vegetation	0.0	2.1	14.2	14.3	180.0
Leaf litter	0.0	1.7	5.8	5.0	16.0
Ash	1.0	0.0	0.0	0.0	0.0
Soil (top 20 cm)	176.0	212.0	158.0	203.0	248.0
Phosphorus (g/m²)					
Vegetation	0.0	0.2	1.6	1.6	23.6
Leaf litter	0.0	0.3	0.6	0.7	0.8
Ash	–	0.0	0.0	0.0	0.0
Soil (top 20 cm)	0.5	0.6	0.6	0.9	0.2
Calcium (equivs/m²) [a]					
Vegetation	0.00	0.04	0.67	0.71	14.08
Leaf litter	0.00	0.09	0.43	0.39	0.74
Ash	0.28	0.00	0.00	0.00	0.00
Soil (top 20 cm)	7.57	9.08	6.29	4.54	1.44
Magnesium (equivs/m²) [a]					
Vegetation	0.00	0.07	0.28	0.29	6.52
Leaf litter	0.00	0.05	0.22	0.27	0.33
Ash	0.06	0.00	0.00	0.00	0.00
Soil (top 20 cm)	3.90	3.59	2.26	2.05	1.74
Potassium (equivs/m²) [a]					
Vegetation	0.00	0.06	0.46	0.46	6.27
Leaf litter	0.00	0.05	0.08	0.09	0.16
Ash	0.06	0.00	0.00	0.00	0.00
Soil (top 20 cm)	0.38	1.49	0.61	0.51	0.84

[a] To transform equivalents per square meter to grams per square meter multiply by the gram equivalent weights of the elements: calcium 20; magnesium 12.2; and potassium 39.1.

these elements in the vegetation are presented in table 7.10.

The nitrogen content of the surface soil is highest in the burn and rice growth part of the cycle. However, a surprisingly small amount of nitrogen is added to the soil by the ash: only 1 g/m². This indicates that nitrogen must be built up in the surface soil by some other process, such as nitrogen fixation by leguminous plants or from leaching of nitrogen-rich litter and foliage as the forest cover-crop grows. The high proportion of legumes in the cover indicates that their nitrogen-fixing activities may be the important process. Note the high quantity of nitrogen in the surface soil of old unburned forest.

Phosphorus mobilized in the Lua' forest fallow cycle is small in quantity, but provides a large proportion of available phosphorus on the site. As the forest cover crop grows, there is a notable accumulation of phosphorus in the vege-

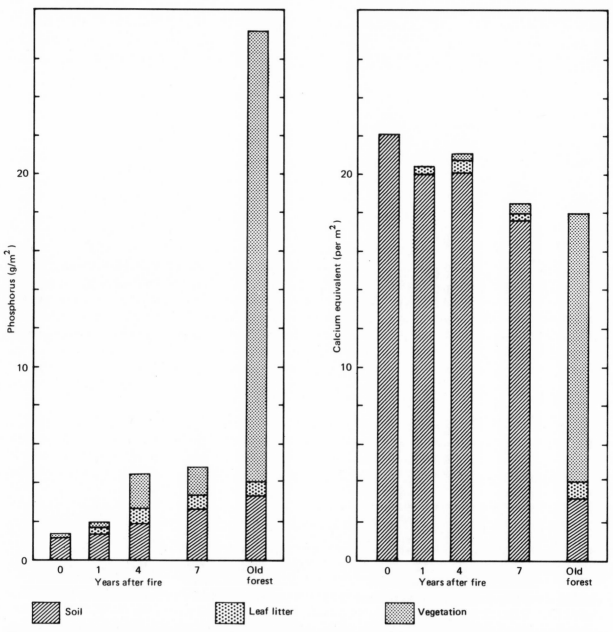

FIGURE 7.12 Available phosphorus *(left)* and calcium *(right)* in soil to depths of 150 cm, and total phosphorus and calcium in vegetation and leaf litter at various stages of Pa Pae cultivation cycle.

tation relative to available phosphorus (analyzed as bicarbonate soluble) in the soil. Presumably, there is a considerable return of phosphorus in the ash at the time of burning. The total phosphorus at each stage of the forest fallow is about 2.0 g/m². Eventually, if the forest grows into an old-growth stage, there is a strikingly large amount (24 g/m²) of phosphorus in the above-ground portion of the forest as shown in figure 7.12.

Amounts of calcium, magnesium, and potassium change in a similar manner. As the cycle progresses, the amounts of these elements in the soil decrease from the high quantities of the first years of the cycle, while there is considerable accumulation in the vegetation. These elements finally appear in the ash, but with some loss. The old-growth forest shows that a high proportion of these elements is maintained in the vegetation. In the fallow cycle, potassium and calcium are the basic elements cycled in greatest amount by the vegetation.

REMOVAL OF FERTILITY ELEMENTS ASSOCIATED WITH SHIFTING CULTIVATION

THE RICE CROP

The Lua' operate their forest fallow cultivation system in order to harvest a rice crop. Yield data, as related to the local economic system, are presented in detail in chapter 6. For purposes of the ecological analysis, a rough yield figure for the fields at the time of rice harvest is 0.1 liter of unmilled rice per square meter of field. This is what is actually removed from the field in harvest; straw is left in the fields. Samples of the rice from the 1967 harvest were analyzed, with results shown in table 7.11 (means of two subsamples). Assuming that the

unmilled rice has a field weight of 620 g/l, with 7.5-percent water content, these data indicate that each liter of the rice crop is extracting the quantities indicated in the bottom row of table 7.11. Assuming a yield of approximately 0.1 liter per square meter, the rice crop extracts the following amounts from each square meter of upland field area: phosphorus, 0.2 g; calcium, 0.03 g; potassium, 0.08 g; and nitrogen, 0.72 g. Comparing these quantities with the amounts contained in ash from burned forest (table 7.10) shows that the amounts of phosphorus, magnesium, potassium, and nitrogen returned to the soil in ash, and those harvested in the rice are about the same. The ash contains about 10 times more calcium per unit area than is extracted by the rice crop. Presumably, the requirements in terms of fertility management in the Lua' system are to maintain an input of fertility elements of this order of magnitude into the rice crop while maintaining the herbaceous portions of the rice plants in good vigor.

FIREWOOD

Assuming there was an average of about 44 households at Pa Pae in the 1959–1968 decade, and using the estimate of 5–10 kg per household per day of firewood and construction materials removed from swidden areas, the village consumption would be between 220 and 440 kg per day, or 80,300–16,600 kg per year removed from the 1,553 hectares of village lands, or 51.7–103.4 kg/ha/year (5.17–10.34 g/m²/year). This is the same order of magnitude, on an annual basis, as the amount of plant material removed in the form of rice (62 g/m² once every 10 years). Thus the total amount of fertility elements to be restored in the fields in the course of the fallow process is about twice as much as is removed in the form of rice.

TABLE 7.11   Composition of Upland Rice from Lua' Fields

	Phosphorus	Calcium	Magnesium	Potassium	Sodium	Nitrogen
Percent (of weight)	0.434	0.074	0.082	0.296	0.032	1.255
m.eq./100g [a]	–	3.68	6.68	7.58	1.39	–
m.eq./liter [a]	–	14.72	26.72	–	–	–
grams/liter	1.7	0.3	0.33	0.78	0.13	7.18

[a]m.eq. = equivalents × 0.001.

DISCUSSION

The results presented in this chapter should be regarded as preliminary. Much more study is needed of fallow cycles. Different cycle patterns are used in different situations depending on geology, climate, type of soil, and cultural patterns of the farmers. In nearby limestone areas, for example, Hmong villagers are able to extend the crop period several years, but at the cost of extremely long fallow periods. This may be due to the high calcium content of soils derived from limestone, and also perhaps to the deep cultivation and clean weeding practices of the Hmong. Presumably, cycles would have to be longer in cooler climates or on less fertile soils. There is a tendency in areas near Pa Pae to shorten the cycle because of increasing population. With these shorter cycles the people report that fertility is not adequately restored and their crop yields are declining. The Lua' cycle described apparently achieves a balance with the conditions of soil, vegetation, geology, and climate characteristic of the area.

Too short a cycle period could eventually result in fertility depletion to the point where it would be necessary to abandon the land. Regrowth of forest would occur, and ultimately fertility sufficient to restore the soil would be contained in the vegetation. This process may take a hundred years or more. This may be the reason that one finds traces of abandoned settlements in the middle of the old forests, as in Central America, around Angkor Wat in Cambodia, and in northern Thailand. The vagaries of human social and demographic history, coupled with the lack of social discipline needed to maintain a system based upon adequate periodic fallow, might bring failure.

SUMMARY

This study indicates that in the forest fallow cycle calcium, phosphorus, and potassium are returned to the soil mainly in the ash from burned cover-crop forests, and that nitrogen is added to the soil mainly during the growth phase of the forest cover crop. Soil temperatures at the time of burning are sufficient to sterilize soil to 2-cm depth. Soil moisture conservation is achieved in the Lua' forest fallow system by cutting the forest early in the dry season, with the result that soil moisture is available to crop plants before the monsoon rains have soaked the ground. In old-growth forest in the area of the study the vegetation has removed a large proportion of the fertility elements from the soil. As a result the soil will be less fertile until and unless the materials are returned by burning or by decay of the vegetation. A serious drain on site fertility would occur if the forest were completely removed without return of the stored nutrients. The successful operation of a forest fallow system involves a careful adjustment of the period of the cycle to the time required by forest growth to store sufficient nutrients in the form of vegetation above the soil surface, in order to replace the amounts removed or displaced as firewood and rice. If the system is to be sustained, these amounts must be available in the form of trees (for firewood) or returned to the soil surface in the ash, at the time of the burn, for use by the growing rice crop. The system may vary in design depending on climate, geology, vegetation, and soil. The Lua' system represents a solution appropriate to the area where it is practiced.

The general trend of restoration of soil fertility over the 10-year cultivation–fallow cycle is clear from our results, but we have too few samples to make quantitative statements regarding the *rate* of recovery over short time periods within the 10-year cycle. An ideal research design would include a longitudinal study with observations made over a 10-year or longer period in the same sample plots. Because of limitations of time and space we used a cross-sectional approach, with a limited (two-year) follow-up in selected sample sites at different points in the cycle. Our data appear to indicate that the recovery is slow between three and seven years after cutting for cultivation, and then accelerates. This may have resulted from a change in vegetation type, as described in the following chapter. An alternative explanation is that there were important differences in the environments of the third- and seventh-year sites independent of the changes associated with the cultivation–fallow cycle.

NOTES

1. See chapter 6 for a detailed description of the cultivation cycle and its products; see chapter 13 for a discussion of soil fertility problems under shorter fallow cycles in another part of northern Thailand.

2. This research on soil fertility was conducted as a part of a study of human and ecological aspects of shifting cultivation supported by grants from the National Science Foundation, National Institutes of Health, and the National Geographic Society. Cultural, demographic, and economic results of this study are reported in chapter 6. Zinke studied fertility properties of the soil associated with different stages of vegetation, while Sabhasri (chapter 8) studied the patterns of vegetational succession, forest biomass productivity, and soil erosion processes in the same system.

3. To convert these figures to pounds per acre, multiply g/m^2 by 8.9.

8

Effects of Forest Fallow Cultivation on Forest Production and Soil

Sanga Sabhasri

Results of the limited number of studies of botanical and soil effects of shifting cultivation cannot be applied to all areas where forest fallow cultivation takes place because conditions vary widely from place to place. This chapter deals with the forest fallow system practiced by the Lua' people of Pa Pae, and documents the extent to which soil fertility is restored and forest biomass is produced under the conditions which pertain at Pa Pae. In particular, this series of studies was planned to determine the ecological succession of the fallow field plant community toward climax types. The relationship between regeneration of plant species and length of time since previous cultivation was studied by examining the natural succession of plant species in fallow fields of different ages. We also investigated the effects of cultivation on soil fertility and on the production of vegetation. One approach to this question was the comparison of biological production (biomass) in the primary (uncut) forest and in the secondary succession (forest fallow) communities after repeated cultivation–fallow cycles. Erosion, a phenomenon which accompanies all disturbance of the upland forest, was also studied by observing soil

loss and soil deposition. Finally, an attempt was made to assess the extent to which forest fallow farming, as practiced by the Lua' people of Pa Pae (chapters 6 and 7) was detrimental to the forest trees and to the soil.

THE FOREST FALLOW

The forest types now found in the region of Pa Pae are transitional between the Hill Evergreen (Lower Montane) forest and Dry Evergreen forest. The climax type of forest in uncultivated areas is believed to have been Moist Evergreen, with Dry Evergreen as the subclimax. Where cultivation and burning has taken place there is a tendency for fire-resistant species to predominate (see chapter 2).

Although the fields are cleared and burned during the course of cultivation, a number of stumps are left from which coppices grow, and the soil is not disturbed in planting or weeding to a depth of more than a few centimeters. The villagers deliberately protect the forest at the ridge tops and in rills, gulleys, and creek beds from the field fires; so there is relatively undisturbed forest in the immediate vicinity of the fields to provide seed for regeneration. The land use of the Lua' interferes minimally with the natural pattern of forest and soil regeneration during the nine-year fallow. Villagers collect some firewood (often incompletely burned logs from earlier field fires), and allow buffalos to graze freely in the fallow fields. They may harvest a few peppers from old plants in the second year after clearing, and they may gather wild fruits and plants including *Imperata* grass for roof thatching in the fallow fields from time to time. By the time the farmers return for a new period of cultivation, trees reaching 7 meters in height and 10 cm or more in diameter are common, and the soil has returned to approximately the same condition as prior to the last cultivation.

Climate in this region is of the monsoon type, with rains beginning in May and generally continuing into November. Average annual rainfall is in excess of 1.4 meters. Maximum daily temperature ranges from a high of over 38°C in early April to a low of about 25°C in January. Minimum temperature during January nights may fall to 2°C (36°F), with frost very rarely reported. Relative humidity which is as low as 15 percent during the hottest days of April, remains over 90 percent for long periods during rainy seasons (see appendix A to chapter 6 for further details).

FOREST PRODUCTION
RESEARCH METHODS: DETERMINATION OF BIOMASS AND VEGETATION

The plots selected for investigation of forest production were the same as those sampled for soil (see chapter 7): old growth forest (not cut for cultivation for at least 80 to 100 years) and secondary successional forested areas where forest fallow farming was taking place. Four forested sites were selected early in 1967, and observed for a period of two years. The sites were selected to be similar in aspect, slope, and

soil series and as closely matched in altitude as possible, in order to reduce variations due to these environmental factors and climate.

Plots of 10 × 20 meters were selected on each site, situated in the middle of northeast-facing slopes (N 35°E to N 70° E) ranging in elevation from 700 to 770 meters above sea level. Slopes were between 30 and 40 percent.

The four sites were as follows: (a) old-growth stand of transitional Hill Evergreen forest, uncut for at least 80 to 100 years, just to the southeast of the village; (b) a forest fallow stand 10 years after cutting, previously farmed in 1957, to be cultivated again in 1967; (c) a forest stand 7 years after cutting, previously cut in 1960; (d) a forest fallow stand 4 years after cutting, cultivated in 1963.

All species of herbaceous plants, shrubs, and trees were recorded in each of the plots. In each stand, except for the old-growth forest, two plots were cut in February 1967 to determine the biomass. This was divided into the weights of tree stems, branches, and leaves, undergrowth below 1 meter, bamboo, and climbers. Cutting was repeated in the upper half of one of the two plots in March 1968, and the remaining half was cut in February 1969, to determine production during those periods. Species compositions were recorded on both cut and uncut portions of the plots. Plant height was recorded in 1968 and 1969, one and two years after the sites were cultivated or cut. Biomass in the uncut forest was estimated by a method described by Sabhasri and Wood (1967) and Sabhasri, Khemnark, et al. (1968).

RESULTS: FOREST PRODUCTION

Estimates of forest production are shown in tables 8.1a, b, c, 8.2, and 8.3. Oven dry weights of trees with dbh (diameter at breast height) greater than 5 cm were estimated by a method

TABLE 8.1a   Weights of Understory Vegetation in the 10 × 20-Meter Sample Plots in Old Growth Stand ("Uncut Forest"), 1969

	Green Weight (kg)	Estimated Oven Dry Weight [a] (kg)
Branches and stems	44	23.1
Leaves	14	6.7
Grass, herbs	136	49.7
Climbers	25	9.0
Total	219	88.5

[a] Samples were oven dried at 105°C for 24 hours to determine moisture content. These values were used to correct the green weights to estimated total oven dry weights.

TABLE 8.1c   Total Biomass in 10 × 20-Meter Sample Plot of Old Growth Stand, 1969

Vegetation	Green Weight (kg)	Estimated Oven Dry Weight [a] (kg)
Overstory	13,014.6 (estimated)	7,738.4
Understory	219.0 (weighed)	88.5
Total	13,233.6	7,826.9

[a] Samples were oven dried at 105°C for 24 hours to determine moisture content. These values were used to correct the green weights to estimated oven dry weights.

described in Sabhasri, Khemnark, et al. (1968). Table 2 of that report presents empirically determined weights of samples of trees of comparable species and various size classes, which were collected at Sakaerat, Korat Province.

Biomass of the old growth stand ("uncut forest") understory vegetation is shown in table 8.1a, in which dry weight totaled 88.5 kg for the 200 m² plot, or 708 kg per *rai* (1,600 m²). An estimate shown in table 8.1c indicates that total

biomass of the old growth stand of full stock, as judged by crown closure, consists of about 7.8 metric tons dry weight in the plot, or 62.6 tons per *rai*. Table 8.1b shows the species composition, size, and weight of the larger trees on this plot.

Production studies of the secondary successional stages show that the 4-year-old stand has an average of 526.85 kg oven dry weight per plot, or 4.21 metric tons per *rai*, while the 7-year-old stand has 554.3 kg per plot, or 4.43 metric tons per *rai* (table 8.2). Thus, assuming our sample plots were representative of the selected points in the fallow cycle, there is little increment of biomass per unit area for the period from the fourth to the seventh year. The final year of fallow cycle shows the production has reached 1,262.2 kg per plot, or 10.1 metric tons per *rai*.

The follow-up studies on plots farmed in 1967 show that revegetation on the area planted to rice produced approximately 0.42 kg per *rai* in the first year after clearing, and 1.46 metric tons per *rai* after two years. This indicates a high production rate of revegetation during the early portion of the fallow cycle. It should be noted that the first "year" of regrowth actually consists only of the four or five dry-season months between the end of weeding and harvest in November 1967 (when most of the vegetation is clear-cut from the field) and the cutting and weighing of the biomass sample in March 1968 (see figures in table 8.3, area cleared 1967). This confirms the visual impression that vegetative regrowth on the abandoned swiddens is rapid during the dry seasons following cultivation.

SUCCESSIONAL TRENDS

The numbers of plant species recorded in 1969 in the sample plots established in 1967 are presented in table 8.4. The number of species is

TABLE 8.1b Height and Weight of Trees with dbh over 5 cm in the 10 × 20-Meter Sample Plot of Old Growth Stand (dbh = diameter at breast height)

Species	dbh (cm)	Height (m)	Estimated Green Weight (kg)	Estimated Oven Dry Weight (kg)
Abarema montana	7.5	7.1	32.0	23.0
Aporosa sp.	3.8	5.1	8.3	4.3
Aporosa sp.	12.25	8.0	110.0	66.0
Aporosa wallichii	9.1	9.2	64.0	43.0
Castanopsis tribuloides	3.5	5.1	6.3	3.8
Castanopsis sp.	5.2	7.5	19.0	11.6
Celtis sp.	7.0	7.3	32.0	21.0
Celtis sp.	6.0	5.0	16.0	10.5
Celtis sp.	3.8	5.5	9.1	5.4
Diospryos sp.	11.2	8.1	89.0	58.0
Dracontomelon mangiferum	4.8	5.6	7.4	4.9
Elaeocarpus robustus	18.0	16.1	46.0	29.1
Engelhardia sp.	3.1	4.5	4.1	2.6
Engelhardia sp.	5.5	6.1	18.0	10.5
Eurya japonica	6.0	8.1	26.0	16.7
Glociddea sp.	7.0	6.3	28.0	18.2
Gymnacranthera sp.	7.8	6.0	34.0	20.4
Gymnacranthera mericigaceae	6.2	5.8	19.0	12.5
Gymnacranthera mericigaceae	6.5	4.5	17.0	11.0
Macropanax oreophilum	2.5	4.0	3.1	1.6
Mangifera caloneura	4.0	5.6	10.5	6.1
Manura sp.	4.5	5.0	9.4	5.3
Memecylon ovatum	3.2	3.5	3.7	1.6
Memecylon ovatum	2.4	3.0	2.0	1.1
Memecylon ovatum	3.1	3.5	3.0	1.7
Memecylon sp.	6.8	5.6	24.0	14.5
Phoebe sp.	3.7	4.25	5.9	3.5
Prunus arborea	4.5	8.0	15.0	9.2
Rhus sp.	10.1	5.7	48.0	31.4
Sapium sp.	109	27.8	12,000.	7,100.
Scleropyrum wallichianum	12.5	6.8	125.0	62.0
Shorea talura	14.0	12.1	175.0	125.0
Unidentified	3.2	4.5	4.8	2.9
Total Weight of Vegetation			13,014.6	7,738.4

TABLE 8.2 Weight of Biomass in Secondary Successional Woodland, 1967 (plot size 10 × 20 meters)

Years Since Cutting	Station Desig-nation		Stem	Branches, Leaves	Grass, Herbs	Bamboo	Climbers	Total
4	4.1	G.W.[a]	458.0	370.5	53.0	–	–	881.5
		D.W.[b]	320.6	244.5	32.3	–	–	597.4
	4.3	G.W.	293.5	400.0	66.0	34.0	21.0	814.5
		D.W.	205.5	264.0	43.3	20.7	12.8	456.3
7	7.1	G.W.	456.6	367.5	49.5	13.5	–	893.0
		D.W.	319.6	223.1	30.2	9.5	–	582.4
	7.3	G.W.	418.0	335.0	49.0	–	4.5	806.5
		D.W.	292.6	201.0	29.9	–	2.7	526.2
10	10.1	G.W.	956.5	746.0	24.5	–	16.5	1,743.5
		D.W.	669.5	447.6	14.7	–	10.1	1,141.9
	10.2	G.W.	485.0	350.0	34.0	791.5	18.5	1,679.0
		D.W.	339.5	210.0	18.4	544.1	11.3	1,123.3
	10.3	G.W.	1,445.0	594.0	39.5	75.0	18.0	2,171.5
		D.W.	1,011.5	356.4	23.7	52.5	10.9	1,455.0
	10.4	G.W.	1,172.5	638.0	144.0	33.0	15.5	2,003.0
		D.W.	820.8	328.8	86.4	29.1	9.5	1,328.6

[a]G.W. = Green weight in kg.
[b]D.W. = Oven dry weight in kg.

generally greater in the 6-year-old stand than earlier or later in the fallow cycle. During the early years of revegetation there are few pioneer species. Additional species come in as a favorable environment is created for them. As time passes, several species are crowded out due to competition for light and space; this leads to the smaller number of species in the 9-year-old stands. The relationship of species changes to biomass productivity and soil fertility is discussed below. The species identifications of plants found at different points in the fallow cycle are presented in appendix 8.1 (table 8.10).

Among the plants that occur in rotation farming areas are species that grow commonly in several different forest types. Examples are given in table 8.5.

The climax vegetation in this area was probably of the Hill Evergreen Forest type and subclimax was probably Deciduous Dipterocarp. Upland farming on a 10-year-cycle has apparently interfered with the appearance of the normal subclimax and climax.

Observation on height of growth was made in January–February 1969 on the 1967 cultivated plots when the plants were two years old; complete data are included in appendix 8.2 of this chapter (table 8.11). To investigate the capacity for rapid growth, plots 10.2 and 10.4 were selected for observation. During this period 20 to

TABLE 8.3   Production of Secondary Successional Woodland after Different Fallow Periods
(area of cutting 10 × 20 meters)

Station and History		One–year Regrowth (Cut 1968)				Two–year Regrowth (Cut 1969)			
		Branches and Stems	Leaves	Grass, Herbs	Total	Branches and Stems	Leaves	Grass, Herbs	Total
Cultivated 1963 Area Cleared 1967									
4.1	G.W.[a]	49.5	53.5	16.5	119.5	114.5	70.0	31.0	215.5
	D.W.[b]	23.01	19.95	9.74	52.70	52.2	33.4	12.1	97.7
4.3	G.W.	19.00	9.5	4.0	32.5	139.5	88.0	15.3	242.8
	D.W.	8.42	4.42	1.78	14.62	71.9	31.6	6.6	110.1
Cultivated 1960 Area Cleared 1967									
7.1	G.W.	32.5	38.5	1.5	72.5	79.5	65.6	13.0	158.0
	D.W.	12.9	13.88	0.7	27.48	34.7	21.7	6.6	63.0
7.3	G.W.	18.0	32.5	5.2	55.7	119.0	50.5	28.0	197.5
	D.W.	5.57	10.12	2.02	17.71	66.8	15.9	12.8	95.5
Cultivated 1967 Area Cleared 1967									
10.2	G.W.	5.0	14.0	34.0	53.0[c]	53.0	18.0	179.0	250.0
	D.W.	2.37	7.81	15.55	25.73	25.1	6.8	61.8	93.7
10.4	G.W.	13.5	9.5	12.5	35.5[c]	59.0	39.5	141.0	239.5
	D.W.	9.89	3.65	4.43	17.97	29.0	16.9	46.0	91.9

[a]G.W. = Green weight in kg.
[b]D.W. = Dry weight in kg.
[c]Does not include the portion of biomass removed from the field in harvest or weeding.

TABLE 8.4   Number of Species Present at Different Times in Fallow Cycle

	2 Years After Cutting for Cultivation in 1967		6 Years after Cutting for Cultivation in 1963				9 Years after Cutting for Cultivation in 1960			
	Plot 10.2	Plot 10.4	Plot 4.1	Plot 4.2	Plot 4.3	Plot 4.4	Plot 7.1	Plot 7.2	Plot 7.3	Plot 7.4
No. Species Observed in 1969	53	59	92	79	65	73	75	54	61	50
Averages	56		77				60			

NOTE: See appendix 8.1 for species identifications.

TABLE 8.5   Plant Species Found in Fallow Fields Characteristic of Different Climax Forest Types

Plant Species Found in the Fallow Stages	Climax Forest Type in which These Species are Common	Normal Environment
Castanopsis tribuloides Lithocarpus polystachya	Hill Evergreen forest (Lower Montane)	Moist, high humus content soils Higher altitudes Dense vegetation
Garuga pinnata Gmelina arborea Vitex pinnata	Mixed Deciduous forest	Medium soil moisture Sandy loam, alluvial soils Middle altitude Sparse vegetation
Phyllanthus emblica Shorea talura Shorea obtusa Cratoxylon prunifolium	Deciduous Dipterocarp forest	Dry lateritic soil Lower altitude Moderately dense vegetation

24 species had attained a height of between 1 and 2 meters and 5 to 10 species grew higher than 2 meters.

DISCUSSION: FOREST PRODUCTION

The quantity of production in terms of biomass per unit area in the old growth forest at Pa Pae is greater than that in Dry Evergreen forest on the Korat sandstone area. "Project Trend," using the same methods, found a biomass of Dry Evergreen forest at Sakaerat, Pak Thong Chai District, Nakorn Ratchasima (Korat), of only 38 tons per *rai* (Sabhasri et al. 1968), whereas that of the Pa Pae Evergreen forest is 62 tons per *rai*. However, the production as measured by weight of vegetation is far less in these semitropical forests than in temperate forests.

The lack of difference in total biomass between forests cultivated four and seven years previously suggests that the soil does not rejuvenate in less than seven years' time: The greater biomass amount when the successional stand has reached the tenth year can be interpreted as a result of soil regeneration largely due to trees (rather than grasses and herbs), by the addition of nutrients produced by accumulation of litter and greater activity of forest floor organisms, and by root activity at the depths to which nutrients have been leached. This explanation is supported by data obtained from the nutrient cycle study, assuming that the observed differences resulted from processes that took place during the time since cutting, rather than from pre-existing differences in site quality of the sample locations (see chapter 7).

The biomass of herbaceous plants and grasses in the study area does not predominate in any of the study plots after four years of regrowth. In contrast with Keen's observations of Hmong fields in western Tak (chapter 11), there is no evidence at Pa Pae of succession to grassland rather than forest cover. Grasses appear to be

suppressed by seedlings and woody growth sprouting from old stumps which have not been killed during the year of cultivation. Woody growth is common even before the harvest has been completed. The data from studies of plants at different times in the cycle suggest that the seedlings of tree species in the secondary succession are fast growing, that the soil fertility is maintained due to the long fallow period before cultivation, and that the soil does not become acidic during the single year of cultivation under these conditions. Zinke's soil studies (chapter 7) confirm these suggestions. Weeding the field three times during the growing season is another factor that retards development of grasses. Weeding stops in September, at a time when many of the grass species are in the seed stage and have stopped growing. Woody plants continue to grow for at least three more months, using soil moisture which has accumulated in the rainy season. By two or three months after harvest most fields are well covered with vegetation. Potential problems in regrowth of fields can be spotted as early as January or February.

After the first few months of regeneration, the plant cover reduces the amount of direct light on the ground and may reduce loss of soil moisture by evaporation. This probably results in accelerated biomass production in the second year after cultivation. At this stage, the 2-year-old tree seedlings are still too small to create much competition.

Table 8.3 shows the importance of length of fallow in determining the balance between woody plants and herbaceous plants in the early years of succession following cutting. Three years of regrowth prior to cutting is sufficient to allow the woody plants to become reestablished and to keep grasses from forming even 20 percent of the biomass in the next year's regrowth. At this stage the nutrient balance has not yet

been restored, however, as is shown by the biomass quantities, which are no higher than those for recently cultivated plots (compare tables 8.2 and 8.3).

During the fallow cycle the number of different species is greatest after six years of regrowth. By the ninth year of regrowth the number of different species has been reduced, and the number of plants of each remaining species has increased (table 8.4). The total biomass increases rapidly during the first two years of regrowth, then slows, and takes another spurt after seven years of fallow, as soil fertility is restored and the individuals of the later stages of the secondary succession become predominant in size and number.

Even though many different plant species grow in the area after cultivation, few of them are of major agricultural value, although they contribute to the local economy. Villagers gather fruit from a few wild trees in the fallow fields, and collect some plants whose leaves or shoots are used for food. Many species of medicinal plants gathered from the fallow swiddens have been identified by Smitinand and Kunstadter; other species are used for construction, and still others are important as browse (see table 6.19 in chapter 6, and Kunstadter, Sabhasri, and Smitinand 1977).

The vegetation stages discussed above show that the possibility of a grass community dominating the area is minimal if the Lua' system continues. The woodland ecosystem will carry on in the area after the land is abandoned for agricultural purposes. This is the result of the careful Lua' farming practices such as weeding and contour lining with logs to conserve soil.

Under the traditional system, the land's capacity for producing rice, as observed by Kunstadter, is about 13 *tang* per *rai* every tenth year. If sold, the rice would give the cultivator about

130 *baht* per *rai* every 10 years of rotation. If the land were left untouched, forest would regrow and provide firewood in the area. One intermediate cutting for weeding and clearing would stimulate the growth of forest trees big enough for firewood, or even for saw logs, in 10 years' time. At least 200 trees growing from coppice stems and from seed could be expected per *rai*. Then, if we assume that stumpage value is 9 *baht* per tree, the second-growth forest would produce firewood worth more than 400 *baht* in a 10-year period, based on a price for firewood of 50 *baht* per m³, delivered at tobacco barns (the price paid in the Mae Ping valley as of March 1970). The economic return would be better if the land in these hills were restricted to forest uses, *provided transportation and markets were available* and there were adequate alternative sources of food. At present these conditions are not fulfilled.

SOIL EROSION

RESEARCH METHODS

Four methods were used to study soil erosion: visual observation, staking, measurement of soil deposition, and examination of cross sections of a natural deposition fan.

Visual inspection was made of the cultivated and forest fallow areas, village sites, and trails. Streamlets where the water concentrates and flows rapidly were examined in order to determine whether rill or gully erosion occurred. Gully erosion was looked for on steep slopes throughout the area. Evidence of sheet erosion and landslides was also sought.

In April 1968, before the hill fields were planted, one complete watershed area of about 20,000 m² was staked with wooden poles. A nail was pounded into each stake to mark the soil surface level. In this way the depth of eroded soil could be determined by measuring distance from the nail to the new ground level after the harvest. The post-harvest measurement was made in February 1969.

Also in April 1968, a hillside which was being cultivated in 1968 was selected for study. An abandoned irrigation ditch running horizontally across the hillside was used as a catchment area for eroding soil. Ditch segments 10 meters long were used as sample collecting units. The segments were cleared in April so that all material dropped in the trench could be considered as soil eroded from the slope above the ditch during the 1968 rainy season. The deposited soil was collected and measured in February 1969.

A deposition fan of about 100 m² located at the base of the small watershed was studied by the staking method. This was an area which had been subject to repeated cycles of shifting cultivation. A soil pit was dug at one corner of the fan and the soil profile was recorded. Bands of charcoal fragments across the soil profile apparently represented deposition layers from times when the field above had been subjected to cutting, burning, and rice harvest. These data are reported in detail in chapter 7.

VISUAL OBSERVATIONS

Gully erosion was not evident in the forest fallow cultivated area, even on steep slopes. Where velocity and volume of water are high in streamlets, a few signs of rill erosion were noticed. Lua' farmers make deliberate attempts to spread and reduce the speed of water flow, by positioning logs across the slopes in fields and by constructing log frameworks in small hillside drainage paths. Viney plants, such as cucumbers and squash, are planted in these areas. The small amount of rill erosion that was noted appears to have occurred naturally; damage from rill erosion is relatively insignificant in this upland farming area.

TABLE 8.6 Soil Erosion Measured by Change in Surface Level during a One-Year Period, 1968–1969

Station	Slope (%)	Exposure	Stake Number and Change in Surface Level (cm)										Average
			1	2	3	4	5	6	7	8	9	10	
Cultivated sites													
1	29	NE	–	9.2	11.7	9.8	–	10.8	10.1	–	10.4	–	10.33
2	44	E	–	–	11.8	–	–	–	–	12.1	11.8	12.4	12.02
3	42	SE	–	13.9	–	13.1	12.2	–	12.8	–	–	–	13.00
4	33	S	11.5	–	13.8	–	–	–	–	–	–	–	12.65
5	39	SW	–	–	–	12.4	11.8	13.8	–	12.4	12.7	–	12.62
6	40	NW	–	–	–	–	–	12.1	–	–	10.3	–	11.2
Forest-covered site													
7	44	N	8.0	8.3	8.2	8.3	9.2	8.6	8.1	8.8	9.2	9.7	8.64

Evidence of serious sheet erosion, as indicated by denuded soil with exposed rocks, was observed in only a few places on swidden fields. Visual evidence of more serious erosion was noted along trails which are continually trampled clear of vegetation, and in the village area, where surface soil has been eroded away and gullies replace trails in well-traveled areas. Village sites which have been abandoned for 80 to 100 years or more are still detectable on the ground and in aerial photographs as grass-covered areas with only a few large domesticated trees (jackfruit, mango, etc.).

Hillsides, especially those near the village, are corrugated with tracks trampled by domestic animals. These are easily seen when the fields are cleared and burned.

Irrigation ditches which must be cut into steep slopes are sites for erosion and occasional landslides.

RESULTS FROM STAKING METHOD

The results obtained using the staking method of investigation of soil erosion in forest fallow farming are summarized in table 8.6.

Stations 1–6 were located in cultivated areas on different exposures in one watershed area. Station 7 was located on an adjacent second-growth forest-covered slope. Dashes in the "Stake No." columns indicate that the investigators believe that stakes were moved or disturbed. Generally, there is evidence of a higher rate of erosion on the cultivated slopes than under the forest cover.

The data from Stations 1–6 suggest that similar rates of erosion occurred on cultivated land with slope steepness ranging from 29 to 44 percent.

These data must be interpreted with caution, as the change in surface level indicated in this method may not be a direct measure of soil removed from the surface by erosion. It may also represent compaction, and change in soil moisture may cause the stakes to change position relative to the ground level. Whatever the cause, the change in surface level of cultivated areas was from 20 to 50 percent greater than the change under second-growth forest cover.

RESULTS FROM DEPOSIT SURVEY

It was difficult to collect data in the deposit survey study because portions of the trenches

TABLE 8.7 Measurement of Soil Erosion by
Volume of Deposit in Ditch

Trench width	0.3 m
Length of trench	10 m
Slope	57 %
Uncultivated slope area above cultivated area	275 m²
Cultivated area above the ditch	54 m²
Total area	329 m²
Average depth of deposit in ditch	0.15 m
Eroded volume = 0.15 m × 0.30 m × 10 m	0.45 m³

were washed away during the monsoon season. The partial results of this phase of the study are presented below, but again these must be interpreted with caution. Table 8.7 gives the data from the deposit survey (figure 8.1).

If all the deposited soil were assumed to have come from the cultivated area above the ditch (54 m²) an average of 8.3 mm depth of soil was removed from the surface of the cultivated area. If the soil deposited in the ditch came from both uncultivated and cultivated surfaces (329 m²), the average depth removed above the ditch would be about 1 mm.

FAN DEPOSITION RESULTS

The soil pit at the base of the watershed showed successive depositions as a series of distinct strata, each indicated by a scattering of charcoal fragments (see figure 7.11). The heavy horizontal lines in the wall of the pit are believed to be the mixed charcoal and soil deposited each time the field was burned for cultivation. The estimated average deposition over the 100 m² fan is about 20 cm, equivalent to an erosion rate of 20 m³ from the entire 20,000-m² watershed area. This is an erosion rate of about 1 mm per decade cycle. See chapter 7 for further discussion of this method of study.

DISCUSSION: SOIL EROSION

In general, mountain soils are subject to erosion; however, any disturbance of the area, whether by logging, cultivation, human or animal trails, or construction, will result in a greater amount of erosion. Major trails are often conspicuously eroded, as are some village sites. Compaction of soil and erosion are noticeable in frequently grazed areas.

Results from the two measures of deposition were in close agreement, but differed sharply from the results of the staking method. The staking method gave what seems to be a very high estimate of erosion. As already stated, this method may not be an accurate measure of soil removed from the surface by erosion, since the pounding force on stakes and nails breaks the ground, which may result in a higher erosion rate. The estimated rates of deposition in the ditch and on the fan are not exactly the same. The deposition fan presumably accumulated during 10-year rotation periods, while the soil in the ditch was deposited in only one year. Also, some of the deposited materials were washed away by water and blown away by wind. Thus the deposition methods of measurement probably yield an underestimate of erosion, while the staking method may represent an overestimate.

Erosion occurs every year no matter whether the forest is disturbed or undisturbed. This is a natural phenomenon in any forest community. The forest fallow cultivation system apparently increases the rate of erosion to a major extent only during the year of cultivation (as is shown by the deposit in the ditch) when the soil is exposed to direct rainfall, light, and wind, and to weeding and tramping. When the ground is fully revegetated in the second year, erosion is reduced (Sabhasri and Ruengpanit 1969).

FIGURE 8.1 Measurement of erosion by deposit of soil in abandoned Pa Pae irrigation ditch. Ditch was measured and cleaned early in April 1968, just after swidden fire, and deposit was measured after harvest. See also chapter 7.

SOIL FERTILITY

STUDY METHODS

To study the changes in soil fertility associated with clearing, burning, and planting, and with forest fallow regrowth, soil samples were collected from the same plots used in the studies of biomass and vegetation. Samples from the surface, from 15 cm depth, and from 30.5 cm were collected for physical and chemical analyses.

The times of collections were: (a) February 1967 (after cutting, before burning); (b) April 1967 (after burning and before rain); (c) November 1967 (near the end of growing season); (d) January 1968 (after harvest); and (e) January 1969.

RESULTS: SOIL FERTILITY

Results of analysis of the soil samples for properties associated with some aspects of fertility are presented in tables 8.8 and 8.9. The results show that burning the forest contributes to the agricultural system by making phosphorus and potassium available, and adjusting the pH at the soil surface.

Burning the forest vegetation reduces some of the organic matter on the soil surface. Release of bases, which are important nutrients, is shown by the increase in soil pH after the fire. At ground level the fire is hot enough to burn the litter, duff, leafmold, and other plant materials that go to make up humus. The fire changes phosphorus and potassium compounds to soluble forms which are subject to erosion and leaching during the monsoon season. After one growing season most of the phosphorus still remains at the soil surface. Some nitrogen may be volatilized and lost as a result of the high temperature of the fire.

Mature forests in this area have relatively acid soils. Most of the available base nutrients are bound up in the above-ground vegetation. After the forest is cut and burned, the soil pH rises markedly, and then falls gradually during the fallow period as leaf litter accumulates and decays in the regenerating forest. In places where there are annual fires, pH may be maintained at high levels. Forest vegetation is replaced by grasses, there is relatively little shade on the soil surface, and relatively little acid production from leaf decay.

From table 8.9 it can be seen that by 1967 the organic matter had increased to 5.4 percent during the seven years since the field was cut. Organic matter was at its minimum (4.95 percent) in a field cut four years previously. Amounts of phosphorus and potassium in the upper 15 cm of the soil also seem to drop after the forest has been cultivated and left for four years. In the later stage of fallow they increase, as shown in the field sampled seven and one-half years after cutting. This means that in the upper level of forest soil, nutrients have returned to their origi-

TABLE 8.8 Comparison of Certain Properties of a Forest Soil before and after One Growing Season in Forest Fallow Cultivation Area

Properties	Horizon	Before Burning	After Burning	After Harvest
Organic matter (percent)	surface	6.95	6.74	6.05
	15 cm	2.10	2.34	2.42
	30.5 cm	1.64	1.35	1.61
Phosphorus (ppm)	surface	3.97	32.5	18.5
	15 cm	1.35	3.65	4.72
	30.5 cm	1.35	2.55	3.42
Potassium (ppm)	surface	208.0	296.0	177.0
	15 cm	121.5	115.4	114.0
	30.5 cm	199.0	183.0	107.0
pH	surface	6.2	6.35	6.40
	15 cm	5.98	5.85	5.52
	30.5 cm	5.67	5.70	5.52

NOTE: Analyses were performed by the Laboratory of the Division of Agricultural Chemistry, Department of Agriculture, located on the Campus of Kasetsart University, Bangkhen, Bangkok.

nal (precultivation) values after one season of cultivation and six years of revegetation. The soil pH does not change much between the period of four and seven years after cutting the forest, and drops slightly at the lower horizons as the regrowing forest becomes older. Additional data on the effects of fire, cultivation, and regrowth on soils are presented in chapter 7. Although some values obtained in the independent laboratory analyses differ slightly, the pattern of relationship between soil properties and the cultivation–fallow cycle is the same. The independent laboratory analyses support our conclusion that soil fertility is restored to approximately the pre-clearing level during the nine-year regrowth period.

DISCUSSION: SOIL FERTILITY

The practice of cutting and burning the forest before cultivation increases the available nutri-

TABLE 8.9 Comparison of Certain Soil Properties at Different Stages in Forest Fallow Cycle (soil samples collected November 1967)

Property	Horizon	Year of Cutting (No. Rainy Seasons Since Cutting)		
		1967 (1)	1963 (4)	1960 (7)
Organic matter	surface	6.05	4.95	5.40
(percent)	15 cm	2.42	1.46	2.40
	30.5 cm	1.61	1.01	1.72
Phosphorus	surface	18.5	3.7	4.55
(ppm)	15 cm	4.72	3.7	5.80
	30.5 cm	3.42	3.05	4.22
Potassium	surface	177.0	127.0	151.5
(ppm)	15 cm	114.0	105.0	132.0
	30.5 cm	107.0	102.0	127.0
pH	surface	6.4	5.72	5.80
	15 cm	5.52	5.68	5.47
	30.5 cm	5.52	5.82	5.47

NOTE: Analyses were performed by the Laboratory of the Division of Agricultural Chemistry, Department of Agriculture, located on the campus of Kasetsart University, Bangkhen, Bangkok.

ents in the cultivation season, but fertility at the upper soil levels is reduced in the first few years of forest regrowth. The nutrients have been used by plants, eroded, or leached. After the land has lain fallow for a period of seven years, the surface fertility of the soil has recovered. Fertility builds up as the litter, duff, and leafmold accumulate. The precipitation, bright sun, and high temperature of the tropics help accelerate the decomposition. As the humus is mineralized, the nutrients are returned to the soil. It takes at least eight to ten years for the supply of nutrients to return to the pre-cultivation level for this forest type.

Burning in this region is an essential part of the cultivation system. The most apparent effects of the fire are quick clearing of debris, temporary reduction in growth of weeds, and release of nutrients which become available for crop growth. Several facts indicate that burning of these plant parts, rather than simply allowing them to decay, is essential in promoting the rapid turnover of nutrients in this cultivation system. The unburned plant material is low in ash; if it were allowed to decay slowly, percolating waters would leach the bases released in the humificating process, thus resulting in higher acidity of the soil. Because of the large volume of the unburned slash, the ground would be fairly well protected from the sun and would stay relatively cool, and it would take more than three years for the debris cover to decay. In addition, the upper part of the debris cover would be subjected to the parching effect of the sun and would become so leathery and tough that microbial activity would be greatly reduced. The more important factor is that the land available for farming is rather limited; the Lua' farmer cannot wait until the decomposition is completed. Burning therefore is their only choice in their system of farming. The corridor system tried in Africa is therefore of questionable value in this region. It might be practicable only if the ground is to be used for planting fruit trees.

The burning practice of the Lua' is closely adapted to the climatic conditions. For burning, they select the time of day and time of year with lowest humidity; thus the fire burns completely in a rather short time (approximately 1–2 hours). Rapid burning does not produce extreme heat deeper than 2 or 3 cm beneath the surface and allows some termites to survive and to loosen the compact soil structure caused by burning. Termite activity seems relatively unaffected in the area a few months after burning. Old, large, and active termite mounds are characteristic of cultivated, fallow, and uncut forested plots in this region. Many trees survive the fire, as indicated by heavy coppice growth in the fallow fields (Sabhasri et al. 1971; Bhodhacharoen et al. 1970).

One reason for the relatively shallow effect of the fire is probably the high soil moisture content in the burned-over area. This has resulted from cutting the forest, thus reducing loss by transpiration early in the dry season.

CONCLUSIONS

The study of secondary succession suggests that rejuvenation of the site is completed in eight to ten years after each period of cultivation under the Lua' forest fallow system.

It is obvious that time is an important factor in the forest fallow cycle in this type of shifting cultivation. Shortening of the cycle would lead to deterioration of site quality, as judged by lower productivity, decreased fertility, and a greater amount of grasses in the early stages of regrowth.

This study lends support to Kellogg's statement that in the tropical forest, trees are the soil builders, not the grasses, as are the latter in the temperate regions (Kellogg 1963). Therefore, if forest fallow cultivation cannot be avoided in the foreseeable future, weeding and thinning as practiced in forestry could stimulate tree growth and in turn accelerate the site rejuvenation. Additional benefits of weeding and thinning would be the economic return from cutting logs of high calorie species for fuel, and leaving undesirable species for slash-and-burn clearing. By this means forestry and upland farming might become essentially one system in forest fallow agriculture.

Even though the Lua' farmers are very cautious in trying to conserve the soil, their rice production as described in chapter 6 is very poor (as low as 8 *tang* per *rai* for some upland fields). If woody species in the study area are good for charcoal and saw logs, the economic return might be better if land use in these hills were restricted to forestry. This would require adequate transportation and marketing and alternate sources of substitute foods for the villagers. None of these conditions are met at the present time.

Appendix 8.1

TABLE 8.10   Succession of Species in Study Plots

Species	\multicolumn{14}{c}{Plot Number and Year Since Cleared For Cultivation}
	4.1	4.2	4.3	4.4	4th yr.	7.1	7.2	7.3	7.4	7th yr.	10.2	10.4	10th yr.	Old Forest
Abarema montana			x		x									x
Acacia concinna	x				x						x		x	
Adiantum philippense								x	x					
Aerva scandens											x		x	
Aganosma sp.	x	x			x									
Ageratum conyzoides		x			x						x	x	x	
Aglaia		x			x									
Albizzia procera												x	x	
Allophylus cobbe											x		x	
Amoora sp.								x		x				x
Andropogon sp.						x				x				
Anneslea fragrans							x			x				
Antidesma sp.			x	x	x			x		x				
Antidesma ghesaembilla		x	x	x	x									
Aporosa sp.						x				x				x
A. villosa	x	x	x	x	x	x	x	x	x	x	x	x	x	
A. wallichii														x
Ardisia sp.	x		x		x	x	x			x		x	x	
A. crenata	x			x	x									
A. crispa						x				x				
Aristida cumingiana						x		x	x	x				
Artocarpus gomeziana			x	x	x									
Asparagus filicifolius						x				x				

TABLE 8.10   *(continued)*

Species	4.1	4.2	4.3	4.4	4th yr.	7.1	7.2	7.3	7.4	7th yr.	10.2	10.4	10th yr.	Old Forest
Bambusa tulda	x		x	x	x				x	x	x	x	x	
Barleria cristata	x				x									
B. siamensis	x				x									
Berria mollis											x	x		
Blumea sp.		x	x		x			x		x				
B. balsamifera											x	x		
B. balsamifolia											x		x	
B. fistulosa	x	x	x	x	x	x	x	x	x	x		x	x	
Boehmeria sp.		x			x									
Bombax albridum						x				x				
Bridelia sp.	x	x			x	x				x		x	x	
Buddleia asiatica			x		x						x	x	x	
Butea sp.		x			x									
Cajanus cajans	x				x									
Callicarpa arborea	x		x	x	x			x	x	x	x	x	x	
Camellia chinensis	x	x	x	x	x						x	x	x	
Canarium subulatum									x	x				
Capillipedium assimile	x	x		x	x									
Carex indica			x	x										
Casearia sp.	x				x									
Cassytha filiformis	x				x	x	x	x		x				
Castanopsis tribuloides	x	x			x	x	x		x	x		x	x	x
Cayratia sp.	x				x									
Celastrus paniculata		x			x									
Celtis sp.														x
Centotheca sp.						x		x		x				
C. lappacea	x	x		x	x	x				x				
Cissampelos pareira	x	x	x	x	x		x	x		x	x	x	x	
Cissus sp.						x				x				
Clausena excavata											x		x	
Clematis smilacina	x				x									
Colquhounia elegans								x		x				
Combretum sp.	x				x									
Connarus sp.		x	x		x							x	x	

TABLE 8.10 *(continued)*

Species	4.1	4.2	4.3	4.4	4th yr.	7.1	7.2	7.3	7.4	7th yr.	10.2	10.4	10th yr.	Old Forest
Cosmos sp.						x		x		x				
C. sulphureus			x	x	x									
Costus speciosus							x			x				
Craibiodendron stellatum							x			x				
Crassocephalum crepidioides						x				x				
Cratoxylon polyanthum		x			x	x	x			x				
C. pruniflorum							x		x	x				
C. prunifolium	x			x	x									
Crotalaria sp.	x		x		x	x		x		x		x	x	
C. linifolia	x	x			x			x		x				
Croton sp.								x	x	x		x	x	
Cyperus sp.								x		x				
C. cyperoides											x	x		
Dalbergia sp.	x				x	x	x			x	x	x		
D. dongnaiensis		x		x	x						x	x		
D. fusca			x	x	x	x				x				
D. glomeriflora									x	x				
D. rimosa	x				x						x		x	
Derris sp.			x		x									
Desmodium sp.			x		x	x				x	x		x	
D. gangeticum									x	x				
D. gyroides	x	x		x	x					•				
D. oblatum	x				x				x	x				
D. triquetrum	x	x	x	x	x						x	x		
Digitaria sp.	x				x									
Dillenia aurea									x	x	x	x	x	
Dioscorea sp.	x				x									
D. glabra		x			x									
D. pentaphylla		x			x									
Diospyros sp.				x	x	x	x	x	x	x				x
D. bracheata	x	x	x	x	x						x	x		
D. ehretioides	x	x			x		x			x	x	x		
D. glandulosa		x	x	x	x	x	x	x		x	x	x		
Dracontromelon mangiferum														x

TABLE 8.10 *(continued)*

Species	4.1	4.2	4.3	4.4	4th yr.	7.1	7.2	7.3	7.4	7th yr.	10.2	10.4	10th yr.	Old Forest
Dryopteris sp.	x	x			x									
Dumasia sp.	x		x		x		x			x				
Dunbaria sp.						x			x	x		x	x	
D. longeracemosa						x				x				
Dyschoriste sp.		x	x	x	x						x		x	
Elaeocarpus robustus														x
Elephantopus scaber	x				x		x			x				
Elscholtzia winitiana	x	x		x	x	x		x		x		x	x	
Embelia furfuracea	x	x			x									
E. ribes		x			x			x		x	x		x	
Engelhardia sp.														x
E. spicata	x	x		x	x	x	x		x	x	x		x	
Eragrostis sp.			x		x				x	x				
E. unioloides			x		x	x		x	x	x				
Eupatorium odoratum	x	x	x	x	x	x	x	x	x	x	x	x	x	
Eurya acuminata	x	x	x	x	x		x			x				
E. japonica														x
Evodia sp.						x		x	x	x				
E. glomerata							x			x				
E. roxburghiana	x	x	x	x	x							x	x	
Ficus hirta		x			x	x				x				
F. hispida			x		x						x		x	
Fimbristylis sp.		x	x	x	x									
Flacourtia cataphracta	x	x			x	x				x				
Garuga pinnata						x				x	x		x	
Glociddea sp.														x
Glochidion sp.						x				x				
G. lanceolarium	x	x		x	x		x	x	x	x				x
Gmelina arborea	x				x									
Gnetum montanum	x	x		x	x				x	x	x	x	x	
Grewia sp.											x		x	
Gymnacranthera mericigaceae														x
Gymnacranthera sp.												x		x
Habenaria sp.		x			x									

TABLE 8.10   *(continued)*

Species	4.1	4.2	4.3	4.4	4th yr.	7.1	7.2	7.3	7.4	7th yr.	10.2	10.4	10th yr.	Old Forest
H. malintana				x	x									
Hedyotis sp.	x				x	x		x	x	x				
Helicia terminalis									x	x		x	x	
Helicteres sp.						x	x	x	x	x				
H. hirsuta	x	x	x	x	x							x	x	
Holarrhena antidysenterica			x		x			x		x				
Horsfieldia sp.	x		x		x							x	x	
Ilex sp.						x		x		x				
Imperata cylindrica	x	x			x	x		x	x	x	x		x	
Indigofera sp.						x				x				
Inula cappa						x				x				
Isachne sp.						x		x		x				
Ischaemum sp.									x	x				
Ixora sp.		x	x	x	x	x	x		x	x				
Jasminum sp.							x	x		x				
J. pubescens	x	x	x		x									
Lagerstroemia venusta											x		x	
Laggera aurita		x			x	x				x				
Leea sp.	x	x			x	x	x		x	x				
Lepisanthes siamensis	x	x	x		x									
Lithocarpus dealbatus											x		x	
L. lindleyanus							x			x				
L. polystachyus		x	x	x	x	x	x		x	x	x	x	x	
L. spicatus						x				x				
Litsea chinensis		x			x			x		x	x		x	
L. polyantha											x	x	x	
Lygodium flexuosum	x	x	x	x	x	x	x	x	x	x	x	x	x	
Macaranga sp.		x	x		x									
M. indica	x			x	x						x	x	x	
Macropanax oreophilum														x
Maesa montana											x	x	x	
M. ramentacea	x	x	x	x	x	x	x	x		x	x	x	x	
Mallotus philippinensis								x		x	x		x	
Mangifera caloneura														x

TABLE 8.10   (continued)

Species	4.1	4.2	4.3	4.4	4th yr.	7.1	7.2	7.3	7.4	7th yr.	10.2	10.4	10th yr.	Old Forest
Manura sp.														x
Markhamia stipulata		x			x						x	x		
Mayodendron igneum	x				x									
Melanorrhoea usitata	x	x	x	x	x		x			x				
Melastoma malabathricum	x	x	x	x	x	x		x	x	x		x	x	
Memecylon ovatum														x
M. plebejum								x		x				
Micromelum falcatum						x	x	x	x	x				
M. minutum	x	x	x	x	x						x		x	
Microstegium vagans	x				x	x			x	x	x		x	
Mitragyna brunonis						x				x				
Moghania sp.	x		x		x			x		x	x		x	
M. congesta			x		x									
Mussaenda sanderiana	x	x	x	x	x									
Myrica farquhariana			x		x									
Neyraudia reynaudiana	x	x		x	x	x			x	x	x	x	x	
Ochna integerrima	x				x		x		x	x				
Odina coromandelica			x		x									
Olea maritima	x	x	x		x	x		x		x				
Onoclea sp.											x	x		
Oroxylon indicum	x				x									
Osbeckia sp.							x			x				
Paederia sp.								x		x				
P. foetida		x			x			x		x				
Panicum montanum	x	x	x	x	x	x	x	x	x	x	x	x	x	
Paspalum sp.	x			x	x	x				x				
Passiflora sp.							x		x	x				
Pavetta indica		x			x	x	x			x				
Phoebe sp.														x
P. lanceolata	x	x	x	x	x		x		x	x				
Phyllanthus emblica	x	x	x	x	x	x	x	x	x	x		x	x	
Polygala sp.						x	x			x				
Premna tomentosa		x			x									
Prismatomeris sp.		x			x		x	x	x	x				

TABLE 8.10 *(continued)*

Species	Plot Number and Year Since Cleared For Cultivation													Old Forest
	4.1	4.2	4.3	4.4	4th yr.	7.1	7.2	7.3	7.4	7th yr.	10.2	10.4	10th yr.	
Prunus arborea														x
Pteridium aquilinum		x	x	x										
Pteris longifolia		x			x							x	x	
Pterospermum sagittatum											x		x	
P. semisagittatum											x	x	x	
Pueraria sp.								x		x				
P. candollei		x			x						x	x	x	
Quercus mespilifolioides						x	x			x				
Randia tomentosa									x	x				
Rhus sp.														x
R. chinensis	x	x	x		x	x		x		x	x		x	
Rourea santaloides			x	x										
Rungia sp.	x		x	x										
Saccharum procerum			x	x					x	x		x	x	
S. spontaneum											x		x	
Sacciolepis indica	x	x	x	x	x	x				x				
Sapium sp.														x
Schima wallichii	x	x			x		x			x				
Scleria levis											x	x	x	
S. terrestris							x			x				
Scleropyrum wallichianum						x				x				x
Selaginella sp.	x	x	x		x									
Setaria lutescens		x		x	x	x			x	x		x	x	
S. palmifolia			x		x									
Shorea obtusa							x			x				
S. talura	x				x	x	x		x	x				x
Sida acuta	x			x	x						x	x	x	
S. rhombifolia						x		x		x				
Smilax sp.	x	x		x	x						x		x	
Sporobolus diander	x	x	x	x	x									
S. indicus						x		x		x				
Stereospermum sp.	x				x									
Streblus kurzii			x		x			x		x				
Strobilanthes sp.	x	x			x						x	x		

TABLE 8.10   *(continued)*

Species	4.1	4.2	4.3	4.4	4th yr.	7.1	7.2	7.3	7.4	7th yr.	10.2	10.4	10th yr.	Old Forest
Styrax benzoides									x	x				
Syzygium sp.						x				x				
S. cumini	x	x		x	x		x	x		x				
Terminalia bellerica								x		x				
Ternstroemia japonica						x	x			x	x	x	x	
Themeda triandra								x		x				
Thysanolaena maxima	x	x	x	x	x		x		x	x	x	x	x	
Trema angustifolia											x			x
Triumfetta bartramia		x		x	x	x		x		x	x			x
T. pilosa	x			x	x		x			x	x	x	x	x
Turpinia pomifera		x		x	x							x		x
Uraria sp.		x	x		x						x			x
U. lagopodiodes				x	x				x	x				
Urena lobata	x	x	x	x	x						x			x
Vernonia sp.	x				x									
V. cinerea				x	x									
V. volkameriaefolia			x	x	x				x	x				
Vitex pinnata	x				x		x			x				
Wendlandia paniculata				x	x		x		x	x				
Wothaphoebe sp.							x			x				
Xanthophyllum sp.	x				x									
Zizyphus brunoniana	x	x	x	x	x									
Z. incurva						x	x	x	x	x	x		x	

Appendix 8.2

TABLE 8.11 Height of Plant Growth in Fallow Swiddens Two Years After Cutting (One Year Following Harvest)

	Plot 10.2		Plot 10.4	
Species	Between 1 and 2 Meters	More than 2 Meters	Between 1 and 2 Meters	More than 2 Meters
Albizzia procera			x	
Aporosa villosa	x		x	
Ardisia sp.			x	
Bambusa tulda		x	x	
Berria mollis			x	
Blumea balsamifera	x		x	
Buddleia asiatica	x		x	
Callicarpa arborea		x		x
Camellia chinensis			x	
Castanopsis tribuloides				x
Croton sp.			x	
Dalbergia sp.			x	
D. dongnaiensis				x
D. rimosa		x		
Dillenia aurea		x	x	
Diospyros ehretioides			x	
D. glandulosa	x		x	
Engelhardia spicata	x			
Eupatorium odoratum	x			
Evodia roxburghiana			x	
Ficus hispida		x		
Garuga pinnata	x			
Gymnacranthera			x	
Helicia terminalis			x	
Lagerstroemia venusta	x			
Lithocarpus dealbatus		x		
L. polystachyus	x		x	

TABLE 8.11 *(continued)*

Species	Plot 10.2		Plot 10.4	
	Between 1 and 2 Meters	More than 2 Meters	Between 1 and 2 Meters	More than 2 Meters
Litsea chinensis		x		
L. polyantha		x		x
Macaranga indica	x		x	
Maesa ramentacea	x			
Mallotus philippinensis	x			
Markhamia stipulata			x	
Melastoma malabathricum	x			
Neyraudia reynaudiana	x			
Phyllanthus emblica			x	
Pterospermum saggitatum		x		
P. semisaggitatum			x	
Rhus chinensis	x			
Saccharum procerum			x	
S. spontaneum	x			
Ternstroemia japonica		x		x
Thysanolaena maxima	x		x	
Trema angustifolia	x			
Triumfetta pilosa	x			
Turpinia pomifera			x	
Zizyphus incurva	x			
Total species	20	10	24	5

9

Declining Production Among Sedentary Swidden Cultivators: The Case of the Pwo Karen

Peter Hinton

Swidden agriculture techniques of the Karen are of interest for two compelling reasons. First, about one of every two persons living in Thailand above an altitude of 450 meters is a Karen. It is thus reasonable to suppose that their agricultural methods are the most broadly characteristic of any used in the northern uplands. Second, in adapting to land shortage, the Karen have developed measures of land conservation which run contrary to the conventional notion that swidden cultivators regard land as an expendable resource.

The field investigation on which this chapter is based was conducted during 1968 and 1969 in the Pwo Karen village of Dong Luang and several neighboring villages, which were situated in the southern portion of Mae Sariang District, about 50 km south of Pa Pae and Laykawkey, described in chapter 6 (see figure 9.1). Dong Luang is at an altitude of 1,050 meters above sea level. This is near the upper limit of Pwo Karen habitation; most of them appear to live in the zone between 500 meters (160 meters above the Ping valley floor) and 1,000 meters.

The people I studied were sedentary residents, who carefully husbanded the land available to them in village territories strictly delineated by customary law, using a more or less regular pattern of fallow rotation. They saw no possibility of fresh land being available elsewhere and maintained that they had no intention of migrating unless the extremes of economic hardship or political disturbance left them with no other alternative. It will be possible, through a discussion of the success or failure of Karen agricultural technology, to assess the potential of technologically simple swidden agriculture in this region.

I shall first describe the general features of Karen agriculture in the study area, then draw conclusions from an analysis of the statistics of production and consumption gathered during my field investigation.

SOCIAL FEATURES OF PWO KAREN SWIDDEN AGRICULTURE

Altogether there are about two and a quarter million Karen. Most live in the high country on

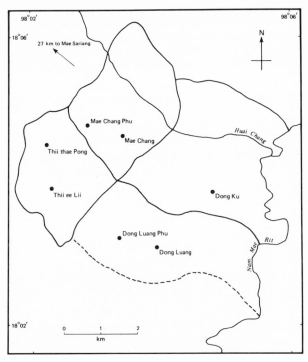

FIGURE 9.1   Map of the Dong Luang area.

the eastern and western watersheds of the Salween River, with about two million on the Burmese side of the Salween and about 250,000 on the eastern or Thai side. The heaviest concentration of Karen in Thailand is in the southwest part of Chiang Mai Province, and in Mae Sariang District of Mae Hong Son Province. Although they have settled as far north as Chiang Rai, few Karen are found farther north than Mae La Noi District in Mae Hong Son Province. There are some settlements as far south as Petchburi Province, that is, south of the latitude of Bangkok. There are only a handful of villages east of the Ping River.[1]

The Pwo are one of four major Karen subcultural groups, each speaking a distinct dialect. The other three are generally referred to as Skaw, Thongsu, and Kayah. There are about 40,000 Pwo in Thailand.

The Karen live according to a cultural tradition that distinguishes them from Northern Thai, Lua', Shan, and Burmese—the four ethnic groups they most frequently encounter. Although customary behavior varies within broad limits from one region to another, and despite the absence of any political cohesion of groups larger than the village community, all Karen have a sense of belonging to the one cultural category. Marriage with other peoples, always an index of lack of cultural exclusiveness, is rare in most areas. Karen are united in their distrust of dominant lowland-based societies, whether these be Thai or Burmese. In many senses they regard themselves as a deprived people who have suffered severely at the hands of the more powerful and wealthy lowlanders. There is a long history of oppression of Karen in Burma.

Although most Karen in Thailand live in the uplands (e.g., Jørgensen 1976), some have established lowland villages. Typical settlements of the latter type may be seen near the towns of Hot (Hamilton 1965, 1976), Mae Sariang (Iijima 1970), and Chom Thong (David Marlowe, personal communication). Residents of these settlements cultivate rice in irrigated paddies and supplementary swiddens. However, only a small proportion of Karen enjoy this means of livelihood; most grow the bulk of their rice in hill swiddens, building irrigated paddies where the rough terrain of the hills allows. The Pwo Karen of Dong Luang say that swidden cultivation is the method they have always used. They say that they learned to grow irrigated rice from the Thai, and they use a technical vocabulary in connection with irrigated rice which is adapted from the Northern dialect of the Thai language. Few communities earn cash from agricultural produce; most have rice-based subsistence economies. With the exception of a very few settlements, Karen do not grow opium, partly because they are situated at unsuitable altitudes and partly because they are unfamiliar with the relevant technique.

At the time of this investigation, the population of the immediate area studied was entirely Pwo Karen who had little contact with Thai, Lua', Shan, or Hmong. Economically they were almost completely independent of the outside world. Salt and iron for the manufacture of tools were among the few indispensable commodities which had to be purchased. These were usually procured at the small market of Mae Haw' five hours' walk away, while Mae Sariang, half an hour's travel by bus from Mae Haw' was the most important market focus and the administrative center in the region. Dong Luang people visited Mae Sariang from time to time. They had little contact with Thai government officials and did not pay taxes on their swidden or terrace land (cf. Kunstadter 1969, referring to an area about 50 km north of Dong Luang), although they went to considerable pains to obtain licenses for firearms and whiskey stills.

In 1969 there were distinct signs that the economic independence of the Dong Luang Karen was breaking down, partly through increasing preference for simple manufactured goods, but most importantly because many were unable to produce enough rice to meet their subsistence needs and were forced to seek temporary employment in the lowlands.

The first Pwo Karen to settle in the area investigated arrived about 150 to 200 years ago (Hinton 1973). They appear to have migrated east, across the present frontier of Burma, in response to intense pressure exerted by Burmese forces. They filled a vacuum which had been left by the withdrawal of the Lua' from the Dong Luang area about 30 years previously.[2] There were no Lua' in the immediate area when they arrived, but there has been some intermarriage with Lua' since then.

The first villages were established close to domestic water sources in zones of particularly promising soil. Thii ee Lii and Mae Chang were, according to informants, the oldest villages in the area. Over a period of time, these became so large that some swiddens were located several hours' walk away. Rather than tolerate this inconvenience, members with distant swiddens moved their homes. Thii Thae Pong, an offshoot from Mae Chang, was established about 70 years ago. Both Dong Luang Phu and Mae Chang Phu were founded within the last 20 years, following factional disputes within existing villages.

At the time of my investigation, all suitable land in the area was in use. Neighboring villages were never more than half an hour's walk from one another, and so the question of founding new settlements for the sake of easy access to fields did not arise. At the same time, the possibility of major disputes within large villages was always present, and a faction which was dissatisfied with the leadership of the community could, at any time, form the nucleus of a separate residential group. In such an event, the breakaway group continued to cut swiddens in the same area as before, sharing the territory of the parent village.

When Pwo Karen pioneered the area, land was plentiful and there was no need to formalize village boundaries. But as population increased and the number of villages grew, disputes over rights to fallow land became more frequent, and location of territorial boundaries was decided by negotiation between representatives of the villages concerned. Now that the area is densely populated, few boundaries remain indefinite.

Village communities, which average about 40 households and 200 individuals, are the largest land-owning groups. From my observation of perhaps 30 Pwo Karen villages surrounding the study area, I conclude that, although a large village and one or two satellite settlements sometimes share a territory, the principle of one village per territory is more prevalent at the present time. The village territory always has boundaries marked by prominent topographical features, such as creeks, ridges, or valleys, and only members of the community may cut swiddens within these boundaries.

The right of a village to use land within its territory is vested in the person of the *sjae cheng khu*, who has both ritual and secular authority. He is the main officiant in the most important agricultural rites, mediates in disputes over the use of land, and has to give permission before any outsider can become a resident of his settlement. He usually works in consultation with a council consisting of all adult male members of the community. Ideally, no individual may alienate swidden land without his consent, but in practice, in regions where Karen and other ethnic groups, particularly Thai and Hmong, are in competition for land, individuals do sell land without first approaching the *sjae cheng khu*. Since the Dong Luang area is isolated and inhabited entirely by Pwo Karen, such circumstances have not arisen.

Each household of a village cuts and works its own swidden unless exceptional circumstances, such as the death of the household head, force it to merge temporarily with a similar unit. Households consist most commonly of nuclear family groups, with a mean of 4.5 persons per household according to a 1969 survey of 166 households. Marriage is strictly monogamous. Of 161 marriages covered in a survey of Dong Luang and surrounding villages, 53 (33%) were between a man and woman of the same territory, and were followed by residence in that territory. Of the 108 marriages occurring between people from different territories, 53 (49%) were followed by permanent residence in the wife's natal territory. Neolocal residence and couples

who changed their territory of residence several times after marriage accounted for the rest.[3]

A couple lives with either the wife's or husband's parents until the conclusion of the agricultural cycle during which the wedding takes place, but almost invariably establishes its own household and cuts a separate swidden in the following year. Custom does not dictate which parental household should be the site of residence during the initial period, nor does the decision made bind the couple to permanent residence in that territory. In theory, a couple could reside in any village where either man or wife could trace cognatic links with the *sjae cheng khu*. The ability to establish such connections does not, however, give them an automatic right to live and farm in the village of their choice; permission might be refused if, for example, the *sjae cheng khu* considered that the available swidden land was pressed by the existing population. In practice, couples usually live in the village in which one or the other was born, both for reasons of sentiment and because in such villages close kin can exert pressure on the *sjae cheng khu* to permit their residence, even if land is scarce. Nonetheless there are cases in which permission to marry is withheld because the village in which the two live does not have enough land. In effect they are told that if they marry they will have to live and farm elsewhere, where their claims on land would be even more tenuous.

When the time for planting their first swidden draws near, a newly married couple may choose to cut their field on virgin land, or on a bush fallow. Since the only untouched land remaining is very poor, the former choice is made with reluctance. A more common strategy is to approach the head of an established household unit who holds residual rights over a number of fallow swiddens. This person is in some cases a close kinsman of either the bride or the groom, but almost as frequently belongs to a more distant kin category.

Rights over fallow swiddens are fairly clearly defined. Having once cleared a field, a household establishes its residual right to use that area when it is next ready for cultivation. Any other person wishing to use the field is obliged to approach the last user, who, if he holds residual rights over sufficient land for his own long-term use, usually grants his permission. If he does so, he relinquishes all rights he had over the land, full residual rights passing to the second household. Residual rights over fallow land are sometimes inherited bilaterally but could expire if the inheriting households do not use the land soon after the death of the former user. I did not record any disputes over rights to such land, but informants said that heirs could have a strong case up to five years after the death. In sum, an individual or household must have the permission of the *sjae cheng khu* to live in the village and use the land within its territory, and must have permission of the person, if any, holding residual rights for cultivation of any particular parcel of land. Mechanisms thus exist both to regulate the rights of households to particular areas of arable land, and to reallocate fallow swiddens as necessitated by the death of some users and by the demand of newly established households.

With respect to irrigated land, only terraces can be bought and sold. The purchaser of a terrace buys, not the land itself, but the right to use the improvements that the vendor may have made to the land by constructing dikes, diversion canals, dams, and so forth. Once a terrace owner allows the improvements to deteriorate beyond repair, he loses the right to sell the land. Any other man may then use the land on which the terrace is sited without asking permission from the previous owner. No Karen may cut a swidden in the territory of another village, but it is possible to buy a terrace belonging to a man from another community.

Any man can cut a swidden in forest land where many years have passed since previous use, provided that the land is within the community territory, and provided that the forest does not surround the abode of a spirit.

In the years 1968 and 1969 a mean of 55.7 percent of all households used their own fallow fields, 27.1 percent used fallow land with the permission of other households, and 12.9 percent used land which either had not been used before, or where no one could recall the last user.

TECHNICAL FEATURES OF PWO KAREN SWIDDEN AGRICULTURE

With few exceptions, the general pattern of Pwo Karen swidden cultivation is similar to that reported in chapter 6 for Lua' and Skaw Karen. The timing of the Karen agricultural cycle is determined primarily by the coming and going of the monsoon (see table 9.1). Only the most important features and differences will be mentioned here.

Karen clear their swiddens in late February. The majority clear young secondary growth, consisting mainly of saplings mixed with a dense cover of undergrowth. Those who clear forest spend longer on this task, for heavy trees have to be felled.

The fallen vegetation dries through March, the hottest month of the year, and the Karen must be vigilant lest accidental brush fires burn the vegetation before it is properly dried out. The Karen recognize that an even layer of ash is an essential contribution to the fertility of a swidden. Fire-fighting parties are hurriedly organized to control forest fires at that time of the

Table 9.1 Upland Pwo Karen Agricultural Cycle

Month	Rainfall	Process	
		Swiddens	Terraces
January	Nil	No work	No work [a]
February	Nil	Cut vegetation (late Feb.)	No work
March	Nil	No work	No work
April	Some storms	Burn (first week); second burning; build fences, huts, etc.	Repair dikes, canals, etc.
May	Some storms	Plant crops (finished by about May 10)	Plant nursery beds; plow terraces
June	Monsoon	Weed	Flood terraces and transplant seedlings from nursery beds
July	Monsoon	Weed	General attention [b]
August	Monsoon	Weed	General attention
September	Monsoon	Weed	General attention
October	Occasional showers	Harvest glutinous rice (main harvest begins late Oct.)	General attention
November	Nil	Complete harvest; carry crop to village	Begin harvest
December	Nil	No work	Complete harvest; carry crop to village

[a] No work is carried out in established terraces, but new irrigable land may be prepared. See text.
[b] Involves repair of washaways and controlling flow of water to and from fields.

year. Usually they manage to extinguish forest fires before much damage has been caused, for the vegetation in the region is such that forests are not highly inflammable, even in the dry season.

All swiddens of a village are burned on a single day in the first or second week of April, when conditions of wind and heat are judged to be suitable. Fires are usually started when the sun is high, after all the dew from the previous night has evaporated, on a day when winds are favorable. The fires usually burn intensely through the swiddens but extinguish themselves on reaching the breaks which are methodically cleared around the perimeters of all fields.[4]

The Karen aim to clear the ground of all but the heaviest trunks. They heap all unburned vegetation together setting it alight. This task, occupying the hottest weeks of the year, may not be finished until immediately before the time of planting.

Immediately after secondary burning is complete, each family constructs a shelter hut in its swidden. Ritual requires that all farmers build a field hut, even if their swiddens are adjacent to the village. At the harvest it is converted into a temporary granary.

Fencing is also an important task which has to be completed before the planting. Livestock, particularly oxen, buffalos, and elephants, are allowed to graze without continuous supervision in the village territory, and so there is always danger of damage to swiddens. Where a number of swiddens are contiguous, households combine their efforts to construct sturdy fences from large fallen trees, interwoven with cut scrub. Otherwise each household builds its own fences. More elaborate fences are necessary where swiddens are very close to settlements.

Planting begins when all preliminary work is complete, but before regular rain begins. Only two or three swiddens are planted on any one day, for large parties of people, sometimes as many as 50, cooperate. The planting of an entire swidden is usually accomplished in five or six hours. Men wield long metal-tipped bamboo dibbling poles, with which they rapidly pick holes in the soil. Women follow the men, dropping rice seeds into each of the holes.

By mid-May the rice is several inches high. By June, weeds as well as rice flourish. Growth is so prolific that constant attention is necessary to prevent the weeds from engulfing the rice, particularly where swiddens have been in fallow for only three to five years before planting. Weeding parties work through all but the heaviest rain, tending fields virtually every day from June to October. Weeders use an L-shaped tool similar to that described in chapter 6, with a scraping motion which disturbs only the surface of the soil while uprooting or cutting small weeds.

By October the main period of rain is over. Subsequently only isolated showers fall. The fruiting rice plants are anxiously watched for signs of disease or insect infestation. Efforts to trap rodents and shoot invading monkeys or bears are increased. Members of households with isolated swiddens keep an almost constant watch on their ripening crop.

In late October the harvest starts with small patches of glutinous rice, planted mainly for cer-emonial use, which mature before the bulk of the crop. At first, rice is reaped selectively, the ripe heads being cut and the unripe ones left for longer exposure to the sunlight. The people in this region do not plant any early ripening varieties.

Once the main harvest begins, small groups of workers cut systematically through the fields. Sheaves of rice are bound together with pieces of straw, then laid at an angle against the stubble of the stalks, which keeps them about 15 cm above ground level. When reaping is complete, sheaves are piled onto neat beehive-shaped stooks. A deep, 1.5-meter-diameter basket is brought to the field, and the field hut is converted into a temporary granary. Sheaves are beaten vigorously against the sides of the basket, so that the grain falls into the bottom. After rough winnowing, the grain is carried from the fields to the village. Households fortunate enough to own trained beasts of burden achieve this in a matter of one or two days, but others have to transport the crop on their own backs. Although most swiddens are a maximum of only one hour's walk from villages, this journey can entail several climbs and at least two weeks may elapse before some households complete the many trips to bring their entire crops back to the village.

The season for growing irrigated rice overlaps the swidden cycle; so people who have both terraces and swiddens need to plan carefully (see table 9.1). Most terrace construction takes place in the dry months between November and March. Repairs to dikes and canals, usually necessary after the heavy early storms of the monsoon, are effected in late April and early May. The laborious process of preparation—hoeing or plowing the surface, flooding, and breaking the clods to convert the topsoil to mud of even consistency—is completed in time for planting in mid to late June. Seedlings are raised in nursery beds and transplanted to the terraces, where the roots are pressed firmly into the mud.

Harvest of the irrigated rice commences in November, about a month after the first reaping of the swiddens. Strict coincidence with the conclusion of the monsoon season is not necessary since sufficient water remains in the streams to provide irrigation for several weeks after the rains cease. The man who has both a terrace and a swidden faces the greatest difficulty in June, when his labor force is required both to prepare and to plant terraces while keeping swidden weeds in check. Unless he is head of a particularly large household, he has to limit the size of either his swidden or his terrace, or, alternatively, engage wage laborers. Few are wealthy enough to employ others for cash. Because of topographical limitations, no terrace field is large enough to provide the entire rice requirement of a household.

Although rice is the main crop grown by the Karen, other produce is also important. Except for tobacco and fruit, which are grown in village gardens, all subsidiary crops are planted in the rice swiddens. Most important of these is maize, which is a source of food at a time of the year when the rice in most families' granaries is low. Maize is planted at the same time as the swidden rice and is harvested in June. Mustard greens, chilies, various kinds of melons, assorted herbs, cotton, yams, cassava, sesame, millet, and sorghum are also planted with the rice. Some fortunate families have surplus rice for sale, but sesame, millet, and sorghum are the only cash crops the Pwo Karen grow. The other crops mentioned provide the contents of the vegetable stews which they eat with rice. The different times of maturation provide a neat sequence: first, mustard greens from May to June, then maize (which can be smoked, preserving it

for some months), and finally, melons and tubers, which mature at about rice harvest time. Tubers do not deteriorate quickly and can be eaten up to six months after they are picked. Chilies, which the Karen eat lavishly with their meals, continue to flourish for some months after the harvest.

The feature that distinguishes Pwo Karen agricultural techniques from those of many other swidden cultivators recorded in the literature on Southeast Asia, is that these people regard land as a scarce resource and do all they can to preserve its long-term productivity. Some of the salient features of this approach are worthy of mention. Like the Lua' and Skaw Karen, the Pwo Karen never use a swidden for more than one year between fallow periods. In this respect they are in striking contrast to the Hmong (chapter 11). They take vigorous steps to control escaped fires or accidentally ignited outbreaks, recognizing that excessive burning of undergrowth encourages weed growth.

When the swiddens are cleared, the Karen usually leave belts of trees intact on the slope above each swidden. Also, they avoid felling some of the larger trees that stand in the area of the swidden itself. Although these trees are lopped so that their foliage will not shade the crop, their recovery is usually rapid. By leaving some trees intact, the Karen, as they say themselves, "help many small trees to spring up," causing satisfactory regeneration. In the late stages of weeding they take special care not to disturb these tree seedlings. It is remarkable, considering the short fallow cycle used, how few species of noxious weeds appear.

The Karen do not break the ground on steep swiddens any more than they have to. They avoid hoeing, which would loosen the topsoil and accelerate loss through erosion. The only time the soil is broken is in the process of dib-

TABLE 9.2 Population Density of Area Studied

Village	Population	Area of Territory (ha)	Hectares per Person	Hectares per Household	Population Density (persons per sq. km.)
Dong Luang	118 ⎤				
		890	5.0	22.2	20.1
Dong Luang Phu	61 ⎦				
Dong Ku	129	1080	8.4	40.0	11.9
Mae Chang	144 ⎤				
		700	3.1	14.2	31.8
Mae Chang Phu	79 ⎦				
Thii ee Lii	232 ⎤				
		670	2.5	13.4	39.8
Thii Thae Pong	35 ⎦				
Means			4.7	22.4	22.9

NOTE: Brackets denote communities sharing single territories.

bling, but this causes only superficial loosening.[5] Weeds are extracted by scraping the surface of the soil and pulling, rather than digging.

Wherever possible, fields are rotated on an adequate fallow cycle. The Karen prefer to leave swiddens for at least 10 years between successive uses. In the study area, land is scarce and an extended fallow period is not practicable; informants are concerned that degeneration will, in the long term, affect their land.

When judging whether a fallow swidden is ready for use, the Karen make very little use of indicator plants. There is very little climax vegetation remaining, and the farmers rely primarily on their knowledge of the past history of the swidden. They also have an extensive knowledge of soil types, and have a set of terms referring to consistency, structure, and rock content.

PRODUCTION AND CONSUMPTION

Even without analysing the figures relating to production and consumption, working solely on the above description of Karen agriculture, one could conclude that this swidden system is under severe stress. Such features as complex intercropping, heavy labor expenditure on weeding and conservation measures, and fairly close specification of land rights of communities and individuals all indicate that these people can ill afford to be prodigal with their land. Examination of the pertinent statistical data confirms this impression.

As the Karen live and work within strict territorial bounds, it is relatively easy to calculate the gross density of population in the area I studied. Table 9.2 shows the actual population densities for the territories of the five villages covered in my survey. These figures concern the *total area* inhabited by the Karen in the study area, including land which is arable, land which is unsuited for cultivation, and land which is not used because it is believed to be the abode of spirits. The physiological density (i.e., number of persons per square kilometer of land used for cultivation) of the area used would thus be much higher than the figures appearing in the last column of table 9.2.

A further complication is the fact that different swidden plots require different fallow periods. Some are used every four or five years, while others need 15–20 years of regeneration.

The physiological densities for Thii ee Lii on the one hand, and for Dong Luang and Dong Khu on the other, are more closely comparable than the figures in the last column of table 9.2 indicate. Virtually all of the territory of Thii ee Lii is suitable for swiddens, while large proportions of Dong Luang and Dong Khu are not. Further, there is more land lending itself to terrace construction in Thii ee Lii than in either Dong Luang or Dong Khu.

Figures of population density do not, by themselves, mean very much. It is necessary to take into consideration three important factors before they can become significant: How productive is the land? How much produce do the people consume annually? What are the long-term land requirements of the people, considering the need for a reservoir of fallow swiddens?

The 1968 harvest provides a good basis for assessing current land productivity, since informants asserted that it was an average crop. Seed requirements are about 56 kg per hectare. The mean yield from Dong Luang swiddens in 1968 was 1,464 kg per hectare of threshed, unhusked rice. The Karen thus achieved a yield return of 26 units of rice for each unit planted. Comparison with table 1.2 shows that this is a relatively high yield per unit of area by Southeast Asian standards. The high yield may be a result of favorable soil conditions at Dong Luang as compared with nearby villages. The range of yields per hectare for different household swiddens was from 907 to 2,323 kg. The mean total yield per household swidden was 1,417 kg, ranging from 373 to 3,484 kg per holding.

Terrace yields are much higher than swidden yields. The total of 0.97 hectares under terrace cultivation (divided among four households)

yielded 2,810 kg. Thus, although terraces constituted only 3.5 percent of the total area under cultivation (swiddens plus terraces) at Dong Luang in 1968, they contributed 9 percent of the total harvest from the village territory. No terrace is second-cropped.

The annual consumption of rice is in excess of the amount produced. Calculations based on a sample of 300 routine meals showed that a mean of 1,234 kg of unhusked rice is required per household per year. An adult man needs 318 kg per annum, and a family of five persons (assuming parents with three children ranging from 11 to 18 years) requires 1,327 kg per annum.

However, these figures include only rice consumed by the household in routine meals. Other requirements would increase this amount by about 25 percent. Among these must be counted rice kept for seed and rice used for feeding livestock, brewing whiskey, ceremonies, and providing hospitality for visitors. Only small quantities of rice are given to livestock, but large amounts are used for ceremonies, whiskey brewing, and hospitality.

My estimate of the annual rice requirement for an average household is thus about 1,552 kg of unhusked grain. This must be compared with the mean household harvest of 1,417 kg of unhusked grain, which is about 135 kg below requirements. Some households, of course, produced an excess above their requirements, but Karen custom did not demand that they share their surplus with those less fortunate or less industrious. Surpluses are usually sold to others at prices ranging from 10 to 15 *baht* per *tang* (20 liters), depending on the time of the year and current demand. Sometimes households with surpluses employ people who have not enough, giving payment with a quantity of rice, usually about 10 liters for a day's work (worth about

5–7.5 *baht*, locally). Many who have a rice deficit are compelled to seek cash employment in the lowlands. Such employment is invariably sought as a supplement to rice cropping, and wages are used to buy rice. It is noteworthy that none of the Karen I knew were in debt to any significant extent. Rice was either paid for in cash, or given by an employer to an employee in return for services rendered. There was one man in a village some distance from Dong Luang who was notorious for lending rice at high rates of interest. His practice was deplored, and few patronized him. Since the 1968 harvest returned an average crop with quite high yields per unit area, but which was still below subsistence requirements, it is reasonable to wonder why the Karen did not plant larger areas of land. The explanation seems to lie in the scarcity of arable land and in conditions arising from the short rotational cycle which this scarcity forced the Karen to adopt. In 1968, 32 swiddens were cut by 36 households in Dong Luang's territory. The total area under cultivation was 25.5 hectares, and the mean size of swiddens was 0.80 hectares (4.9 *rai*). Swiddens ranged in size from 0.28 to 1.53 hectares. Thirty-eight swiddens were cut by 40 households in 1969, covering a total area of 32.0 hectares. The mean size was 0.84 hectare per swidden (5.2 *rai*), with a range from 0.17 to 1.80 hectares.

Dong Luang's territory is 890 hectares in area. If we assume from these figures that the annual yearly requirement of land for the community is about 30 hectares, and if all land in the village territory were of uniformly good quality, then the Karen should be able to rotate their swiddens on a cycle longer than 20 years. In fact, this is far from the case, as table 9.3 shows. In 1968, 78 percent of swiddens cleared had been fallow for less than 10 years. The mean fallow period for these fields was only 4.5 years.

TABLE 9.3 Length of Prior Fallow Period for Swiddens Cut 1968 and 1969; Dong Luang Village Territory

Years of Fallow	No. of Cases 1968	No. of Cases 1969
10+ years or well-developed forest	7	6
10	1	9
9	–	–
8	–	–
7	–	–
6	3	3
5	2	6
4	6	1
3	8	5
2	–	–
1	–	–
Less than 10 years, period uncertain	5	8
Total	32	38

(78% for 1968; 84% for 1969)

Mean period of fallow for swiddens used less than 10 years previously, 1968 season: 4.5 years
Mean period of fallow for swiddens used less than 10 years previously, 1969 season: 6.4 years
Mean period of fallow for swiddens used less than 10 years previously, 1968–1969: 5.5 years

In 1969, the mean fallow period for the 84 percent of swiddens which had been used less than 10 years previously was 6.4 years, giving a mean fallow of 5.5 years for 81 percent of the swiddens cleared in 1968–1969. The remaining swiddens (22 percent in 1968 and 16 percent in 1969) were cleared in well-developed forests, or in bush fallows older than 10 years.

These figures reflect the fact that only a small proportion of the soil in the territory is of excellent quality for swidden farming. The higher part of the plateau on which the village is located is a zone of well-structured red earth soil type. This is less than 40 percent of the area of the territory. The first settlers who moved from Mae Chang to Dong Luang came to use this soil. As population increased over the years, more and more people used the poorer soils east of the village. Some of this area was completely unsuited for cultivation, and the rest would stand being planted once every 10 to 15 years. The dominance of the poorer podzolic soils in this part of the communal territory drastically restricts the overall land resources of the Dong Luang villagers. If the Karen tried to solve their problem of having a rice deficit by planting larger fields, they would cut into the reservoir of fallow land and further abbreviate an already short rotational cycle.

As has been indicated in chapter 6, labor is a further limiting factor for swidden size. The household, which is the typical farming unit, is almost invariably a nuclear family group, that is, a man, his wife, and their children. The average household size for villages surveyed was only 4.8 persons. A young married man, whose wife is occupied with infant children and successive pregnancies, often has to work his field virtually single-handed. A longer established household of, for instance, a man and wife of about 45 years, with several unmarried children between the ages of 12 and 20, can manage a much larger field.

The greatest demands on the household labor force occur during the monsoon, when all workers are mobilized to keep the weed growth in check. Other tasks, such as clearing and harvesting, require concentrated effort for about two weeks each, but weeding demands sustained effort nearly every day for about four months. Thus a household may be capable of clearing or harvesting quite a large swidden, but since the task of weeding it adequately is beyond their capacity, their harvest would probably be no larger than from a small field.

In 1968 there were 114 workers in Dong Luang. This figure excludes the very old, the very young, and the disabled.[6] Opium addicts comprised the greater proportion of the disabled. The workers farmed a total of 25.5 hectares of swidden land, or, in other words, there were 4.44 workers for each hectare cultivated. The yield per worker was about 333 kg. So far as I know, other than in this book, there are no comparative figures for upland northern Thailand, but I suspect that this is a fairly low figure per labor unit for swidden farmers.

CONCLUSIONS

In conclusion, I see the salient features of upland Pwo Karen agriculture to be as follows: First, it is a system of subsistence rice cultivation based on swiddens, with supplementary terraces which are much more productive than swiddens. The area of terrace development is limited by the availability of high valleys which lend themselves to this method of cultivation.

Second, it is a stable system based on sedentary residence and the use of strictly defined territories, within which all swidden cultivation of the community must take place. To gain maximum long-term productivity from the land, careful conservation measures are practiced.

As for the future, once the delicate point of equilibrium between population and land has been passed, as it has been at Dong Luang, the Karen can hope to gain reasonable yields only by using more workers in their swiddens. At their primitive level of technology, these workers can be only marginally productive. They are used to control weeds during the growing season, *not* to contribute capital improvements to land which could raise levels of productivity.

If population continues to increase while dependence on primitive methods of swidden cultivation remains, productivity can only fall off as the people are forced to a shorter and shorter fallow cycle. Capital improvements to irrigated land within the capability of the primitive farmer, such as extension of holdings and improvement of dikes and drainage systems, do increase harvests. But swiddens depend largely on the nutrients that are made available by forest regrowth during the fallow period. Thus the shorter the fallow period becomes, the smaller are the quantities of nutrients replaced. So the Karen of Dong Luang, operating on a diminishing fallow cycle, are fighting a losing battle in their attempts to sustain reasonable yields, irrespective of the amount of labor available to check the encroaching weeds.

It is difficult to see a way out of this impasse. Application of fertilizer would undoubtedly improve yields, but even if the Karen could afford to buy it, consistent use combined with tilling of the soil could break down the soil structure and result in rapid erosion. Conversion to a cash economy does not seem practicable. At present, the small quantities of cash crops they do grow are planted in the rice swiddens, because of land scarcity. The people certainly do not have enough land to grow rice *and* another crop, and they are unlikely to consider a total shift from subsistence to cash crop production. Expansion of terrace holdings will undoubtedly take place in the immediate future. All present terraces at Dong Luang village have been developed in the last decade as a response to falling swidden productivity. I do not think, however, that irrigated terraces will ever support large numbers of people in areas like Dong Luang, for neither rainfall patterns nor topographical factors favor any significant terrace expansion.

Many Pwo Karen from the hills of Mae Sariang District seek temporary employment in Mae Sariang town, to earn money to buy rice. It is safe to predict that this will become an in-creasing trend. Unfortunately, Mae Sariang is a small frontier town offering only limited opportunities for employment, and the labor market is already virtually saturated. Before long, many Karen will not be able to earn the income vital for their subsistence. The possibility of seeking employment in more distant centers, like Chiang Mai and Lamphun, was not considered by the Dong Luang villagers at the time of my field study, but may be seriously discussed in the near future.

At the beginning of this chapter I noted that the area I investigated was populated entirely by Pwo Karen. Although land is scarce and disputes over rights do arise between individuals and communities, there are ways by which these difficulties can be settled amicably, according to customary Karen law. Where Karen swiddens are contiguous with Hmong, Lua', or Thai holdings, however, land disputes are bitter and sometimes violent, as there is no system of legal norms and sanctions accepted by all. In these areas particularly, there seems to be strong need for constructive intervention by government authorities.

My findings leave scant ground for thinking that Karen agriculture will be able to provide adequate subsistence in the years to come. It is my earnest hope that the skills of legislators, agricultural scientists, and administrators will be employed to prevent the fate suggested by my gloomy prognosis.

NOTES

1. There has been no systematic census of Karen population in Thailand. In 1931 the British authorities conducted a census in Burma which indicated that there were approximately 1,228,000 Karen in that country (quoted by Lebar, Hickey, and Musgrave 1954:59). Tadaw (1961:496) estimated that by 1958 the Karen population of Burma had increased to a total of between 1,750,000 and 2,000,000.

My estimate of the Karen population of Thailand is based on analysis of the records of the malaria control teams of the Thai government's Department of Health which, during routine DDT spraying operations, reach most Karen villages about once each year.

2. This account of former Lua' residential patterns is derived from Kunstadter (1967:641). Karen traditions do not give any account of the era during which the contraction of the area under Lua' settlement occurred.

3. My discussion of postmarital residential patterns relates to community territories rather than village sites. It should be noted that most villages are reconstructed on new sites every 10 years or so, usually for religious reasons. In a sense, then, all of these Pwo Karen are residentially mobile. However, all rebuilding, whether for religious or political reasons, has ordinarily taken place within a strictly bounded territory of no more than 10 sq km. Thus, although the actual location of dwellings changes over a period, such location has a stable basis, in that it occurs within the bounds of defined territories.

4. At Dong Luang most household swiddens usually adjoin one another, forming one large block. This arrangement facilitates burning. In 1968 there were 32 swiddens at Dong Luang, arranged in two blocks, one of 24 fields and one of 8 fields. In 1969 there was a much wider dispersal of individual holdings around the village territory.

5. Kunstadter (chapter 6) has observed that the Lua' of Pa Pae place logs along the contour of steep slopes in order to retard water erosion of soil. I did not note this practice at Dong Luang.

6. Young Pwo Karen do not make any significant contribution to the agricultural labor force until they reach the age of 8 to 10 years, although they help with household tasks from the age of about five. Women with young children generally remain in the village; so throughout their child-bearing years (from marriage at about age 22 to menopause) they tend to work only spasmodically in the fields. Often old people continue to work in the fields until they are completely decrepit.

The figure recorded of 114 workers includes nursing mothers; thus it is probably an inflated calculation, although I have worked on the assumption that mothers of young children, while remaining in the village carrying out domestic chores, allow others to concentrate on agricultural work.

PART IV

COMMERCIALLY ORIENTED FOREST FARMING SYSTEMS

Introduction

Peter Kunstadter

The following chapters deal with upland agricultural systems which are largely oriented toward the production of cash crops, and which often require more intensive concentration of labor and capital than the predominantly subsistence-oriented farming systems of Lua' and Pwo and Skaw Karen villagers described in part III. The Lua' and Karen have depended on farming to supply themselves with subsistence products, while supplementing their income with wage work and occasional sale of agricultural surpluses. We have indicated that the agricultural systems of Lua' and Karen villagers are getting out of balance as population pressure makes it impossible to allow land to remain fallow long enough to restore full fertility through forest regrowth.

In the chapters that follow, as well as in the literature we have searched there are no reports of cash-cropping swiddeners in northern Thailand whose demography, ecology, and economy are balanced. Sabhasri outlines the dimension of the "opium problem" and the steps being taken to solve it in the face of deteriorating environment and growing populations (chapter 10).

Keen's description of the Hmong of Tak Province (chapter 11) suggests that their population is above the carrying capacity of the land available to them. Keen shows the tensions inherent in their economic system as they try to balance needs for subsistence against needs for cash. Their mixed economy includes rice (their major subsistence crop), maize (primarily as animal food), vegetables (for subsistence and sale), opium (the primary cash crop), and livestock (for local consumption and sale). They are committed to a cash economy but dependent on subsistence production, and they are unable to maintain both cash and subsistence production without progressive destruction of the forest environment upon which they depend for their livelihood.

A number of researchers have compiled reports on the economic systems of opium producers, including communities of Akha (Kickert, Scholz), Lahu (Jones, Spielman, Walker), Lisu (Dessaint, Durrenberger), Hmong (Geddes, Keen 1966 and chapter 11), and Yao (Kandre, Miles). There is considerable local variation in the environments of the studied communities, as well as in their social structures. Nonetheless these reports tend to reinforce the general conclusion inherent in Keen's description of the Hmong that population pressure in the hills is increasing, with consequent destruction of the forests, and that any increase or perhaps even stabilization of the standards of living of such people will require basic technological and social structural innovations. There are suggestions in several of these reports that the suppression of opium production (which is labor-intensive, and, if fallow requirements are disregarded, temporarily land-intensive) may complicate matters by forcing these people into more land-extensive cultivation of subsistence crops in areas where there are already land shortages.

Were we to stop with a description of the non-Thai subsistence swiddeners and opium growers, we might accurately reflect the amount of research and administrative attention which has been paid to upland minority people, but to do so would badly distort the demographic and economic realities of northern Thailand. The largest group of swiddeners in northern Thailand consists of people who are ethnically Northern Thai, who cut their swiddens in relatively low-lying terrace and foothill environs, and occasionally in hill fields reaching almost as high as the highest of the upland minority peoples. Chapman's description of Northern Thai swiddeners in Nan Province (chapter 12), and Charley and McGarity's description (chapter 13) of soil problems inherent in stabilizing this form of agriculture indicate that Northern Thai swiddeners are unable to avoid a decline in soil fertility while maintaining a mixed upland cash-subsistence economy in the face of population increase. They suggest changes in technology and land tenure arrangements which may be necessary to cope with the decline in soil fertility under increasing intensity of land use.

The Northern Thai swiddeners, described by Judd (1964) and Chapman, farm both for subsistence and for cash crops. They may use their upland fields for either or both purposes, but in general, at least until recently, they have viewed their swiddens as supplemental to irrigated fields and wage labor, rather than as a primary source of income.

As land shortages develop in the northern Thai lowlands, another form of upland agriculture has been created in which the entire livelihood of the practitioners is produced in the hills. Keen (chapter 14), Van Roy (1971), LeBar (1967), and Oughton and Imong (1970, 1971) describe the *miang* (fermented tea) producers. Originally some of the people who are involved may have been Khmu' immigrants from Laos (LeBar 1967), but now most identify themselves as Northern Thai. Van Roy suggests that many of these people moved into the hills temporarily to accumulate cash in order to buy irrigated fields in the lowlands, but suggests that this process might take a generation or more. Keen (chapter 14) and Oughton and Imong (1970) show that Northern Thai hill villages in the Chiang Dao area are up to 50 years old, and that new Northern Thai migrants to the hills are still arriving. It is apparent from age and sex distribution among the 1,637 residents of *miang*-producing villages (Oughton and Imong 1971:4) that these villages are growing both from natural increase and from migration.

Some Northern Thai in the hills have become swidden rice cultivators, but many have gone into a predominantly cash economy, rather than into subsistence agriculture. The chief occupation has been the production of *miang*, fermented tea leaves grown in the hills on the same species of bush *(Camellia sinensis)* which produces leaves for brewing tea. *Miang* is sold in local and regional markets, and is consumed in

TABLE IV.1   Villages in the Doi Chiang Dao Hilltribe Settlement (*Nikhom*)

| Ethnic Group | No. of Villages | Altitude (meters) | | Village Size | | | | | | Main Cash Economy (No. of Villages) | Age of Villages | |
| | | | | Households | | | Persons | | | | | |
		Range	Mean	Total Village No.	Village Range	Mean per Village	Total Village No.	Village Range	Mean per Village		Range	Mean
Northern Thai	30	400–1,200	807	490	3–61	16.3	2,416	16–303	80.5	*miang* (24) wet rice (4) labor (2)	1–50	26.7
Blue Meo (Hmong Njua)	3	900–1,400	1,200	61	6–35	20.3	462	43–303	120.7	opium (3)	2–20	11.7
Lahu Nyi	3	800–1,200	1,000	28	5–13	9.3	163	29–68	54.3	opium (3)	4–9	7
Northern Thai/ Lahu Nyi	1		900	5		5	29		29	*miang*		15
Lahu Na	1		900	30		30	200		200	plantation		15
Lahu Sheleh	1		1,100	14		14	81		81	opium		5
Skaw Karen	1		700	6		6	26		26	wet rice		8
Totals	40			634			3,377					

SOURCE: G. A. Oughton, and Niwat Imong, "Nikhom Doi Chiang Dao: Resources and Development-Potential Survey Report 2: Village Location, Ethnic Composition, and Economy," Chiang Mai, Tribal Research Centre, June 1970.

TABLE IV.2   Individuals Supported by Various Occupations at Nikhom Doi Chiang Dao

Main Occupation	Upland Thai No.	Upland Thai %	Lowland Thai No.	Lowland Thai %	Tribal No.	Tribal %	Total No.	Total %
Miang growing	1,382	75.9	–	–	–	–	1,382	40.9
Opium growing	–	–	–	–	596	63.6	596	17.6
Wage labor	379	20.8	104	16.8	19	2.0	502	14.9
Swiddening (other than opium growing)	34	1.9	158	25.5	263	28.1	455	13.5
Irrigated cropping	–	–	332	53.6	8	0.9	340	10.1
Plantation culture[a]	19	1.9	10	1.6	46	4.9	75	2.2
Government employment[b]	6	0.3	13	2.1	–	–	19	0.6
Trading[c]	1	0.05	2	0.3	5	0.3	8	0.2
Totals	1,821		619		937		3,377	100.0

SOURCE: Oughton and Imong 1970, table II (b). Main occupation was determined for each household and multiplied by number of household members.

[a] Mixed garden and tree crops, supplemented by livestock and swiddening.
[b] Includes households of three Royal Irrigation employees, five school teachers, and one tobacco curing plant foreman.
[c] Traders in tribal villages are usually Haw (Yunnanese) Chinese who often marry into the village community.

large quantities in northern Thailand. As the numbers of people involved in producing *miang* increase, there are suggestions that the demand for it, and the profitability of producing it are declining, at the same time as the economic well-being of the producers is decreasing (Keen, chapter 14; Oughton and Imong 1971:6).

There is no adequate estimate of the total number of people now living at elevations above 400 meters who identify themselves as Northern Thai, but the number is known to be substantial. In 1964 Van Roy estimated that there were 75,000 people, almost all of them Northern Thai, in *miang* producing villages in Chiang Mai Province. Thus the stereotype that the hills are occupied exclusively by "tribal" nomadic, subsistence or opium-producing farmers is untenable. The Chiang Dao Hilltribe Settlement was originally established as a development area for "hill tribes." In 1969, when the Settlement territory was surveyed, it was found that 30 of

the 40 villages, and 72 percent of the total population were Northern Thai (Oughton and Imong 1970). The Northern Thai villages within the Settlement range in altitude from about 400 to about 1,200 meters, as high as some Hmong villages in the Settlement (table IV.1). (For further details on forest and soils characteristics in this area see Khemnark et al. 1972.)

These surveys reinforce the conclusion that land shortage is acute in some lowland areas of northern Thailand, that in the face of land shortages Northern Thai people will move to as high an altitude as do hill tribes and may compete for land with them there, and that they will abandon traditional irrigated agriculture for other occupations (table IV.2). Lowland Thai are also moving into the hills to seek land and employment in "forest village" settlements as described in chapter 16. Likewise we have seen Hmong villagers in the lowlands of Sayaboury Province, Laos, growing irrigated rice, and in the hills of

Mae Sariang District, Thailand, growing fruits and vegetables for lowland markets. Keen (chapter 11) also reports Hmong working for wages in Chiang Dao District, cutting logs for Northern Thai *miang* growers, regardless of the oft-repeated cultural characteristic that "Hmong will never work for anyone but themselves."

The clear indication of land shortages in the northern region of Thailand is a cause for concern, but the evidence of flexibility of people in this area when faced with economic necessity or economic opportunity is reason for optimism. In the final chapter of this section (chapter 15) Pelzer suggests, through the use of Indonesian examples, that under some circumstances upland agriculture may be extremely productive for both subsistence and cash crops of major importance for foreign exchange. The environment in northern Thailand is quite different from that in the outer islands of Indonesia, as Professor Pelzer is careful to point out. Nonetheless, the northern Thai hills enjoy some environmental benefits, especially a cooler climate, which may make it possible to produce commodities that cannot be grown successfully in the tropical lowlands. The successful introduction of such products is a major task. Beyond this, it seems evident that expansion of wage-labor opportunities will form an essential part of the solution of economic problems in the already over-populated marginal agricultural area.

10

Opium Culture in Northern Thailand: Social and Ecological Dilemmas

Sanga Sabhasri

Thailand is considered to be one of the principal opium growing countries in Southeast Asia, and this is the major reason for international interest in upland development in the North. In 1970, the year of the latest national census, the total non-Thai population living at elevations above 600 meters was estimated at more than 275,000. The main upland groups are Hmong, Yao, Lahu, Lisu, Akha, Karen, Haw, Lua', Khmu, and Htin. The first five of these, representing well under half the upland population, are heavily engaged in opium growing, and the Haw (Yunnanese Chinese) are often engaged in purchase, transport, and sale of opium.

Estimates of total annual opium production in Thailand range from 30 to 177 tons (table 10.1). The UN Narcotics Commission estimated annual production to be about 150 tons, which would constitute 12.5 percent of the world production. This amount is sufficient to make 1.5 billion therapeutic doses of medical morphine, or 3 billion doses of heroin.

Opium growing has never been legal in Thailand. Use of opium as a narcotic was first introduced in Central Thailand by Chinese, but its history as a crop for local consumption or cash

TABLE 10.1 Estimates of Annual Opium Production in Thailand

Source	Date	Amount (tons/year)
Young (1962)	early 1960s	30
Nat'l Statistics Office	1968	38
Dept. Public Welfare	1969	75
UN Narcotics Commission	1970	113–177

in the northern hills has not yet been written. Though it has long been known in northern Thailand as a pain-relieving drug, it appears that large-scale growing and trade is a relatively recent phenomenon. From the time the Chinese brought opium into Thailand they were allowed by the Thai officials to smoke in opium dens, from which Thai were excluded. But in 1957 the Thai government established an absolute ban on production, transport, sale, and consumption of opium. Up to that point heroin had not been known in Thailand; since then it has apparently been locally manufactured and also imported from Laos. In recent years heroin addiction has become an increasing problem, especially among the Thai youth in Bangkok, the upswing of its use perhaps being associated with the presence of large numbers of U.S. military personnel in Thailand during the Viet Nam war.

As has already been noted in chapter 1, opium farming, using a long cultivation, very long fallow system, represents only a fraction of the land use in the hills, though its ecological destructive power may be great. In general, cultivation of the opium poppy as a subsistence crop has been combined with maize and sometimes rice cultivation, and in some areas where transport and marketing are available, opium is being supplemented or replaced by potatoes as a cash crop (chapter 11).

CURRENT PROBLEMS

The rapid increase in the population of northern Thailand, both in the lowlands and the hills, combined with the rising expectations of rural people, who increasingly require a source of cash income, insure that there will be increased pressure on swidden land in the forseeable future. Opium, as a labor-intensive, high-value, easily transportable, and readily marketable crop, seems ideally suited to upland economic conditions. Unfortunately, it also carries with it a string of detrimental social and ecological consequences. Regrettably, opium farming is a way of life and vital source of income for many hill people. Eliminating it will require consideration of the economic needs of these people who often have inadequate land for subsistence farming. The high value and illegality of opium have become the focus of corruption, with profits to the middlemen far higher than to the cultivators. This makes control of sale and transport extremely difficult. The physical and moral degradation of its consumers has led to tragedy for the addicts' families.

In addition to these social and moral effects, it is clear that large-scale opium production has led to widespread destruction of forests, replace-

ment of forest lands with grasses, and substantial harm to watershed and catchment areas.

CURRENT APPROACHES TO THE PROBLEM

Several policies and developmental approaches have been taken by Thai and foreign agencies and institutions. There are three major official Thai agencies concerned with economic and social development among hill people: (1) the Border Patrol Police, (2) the Department of Public Welfare of the Ministry of Interior, and (3) The King's Project.

The Border Patrol Police was established under the Police Department in 1953. It was the first official group to begin development programs in the hills, including schools, medical care, and the introduction of farm crop seeds, agricultural equipment, and livestock. These programs have reached large numbers of "hill tribes" in remote areas.

The Department of Public Welfare was assigned to carry out research and development activities in the remote mountain areas beginning in 1959. Major problems which the government faced at that time included: (1) replacing opium cultivation without striking a death blow to the economy of the hill people; (2) preventing further destruction of forests by assisting hill people to develop a more conservative system of swidden cultivation, and if possible promoting stabilized farming in the hills; (3) rendering health, educational, and other welfare services to the hill population; and (4) extending administration and control to remote hill and frontier regions (Ruenyote 1969).

In 1959 the Land Settlement Projects (nikhom) for hill people were implemented in several northern provinces by the Department of Public Welfare. The primary purpose was to settle tribes in locations suitable for them, by establishing settlement areas on ridges and high plateaus. Farmland settlement pilot projects were established between 1960 and 1963 in Tak, Chiang Mai, Chiang Rai, and Loei provinces. The settlements are felt to be overly confining among groups which traditionally move from place to place as the soil becomes exhausted, and some *nikhom* hill people find themselves competing directly with lowlanders for land (see above pp. 202–204).

In 1969 the King initiated his own program. The King's project adviser, Prince Bhisadej, listed objectives of these projects: (1) to give help to fellow men; (2) to prevent and combat subversion by raising the standard of living of these people; (3) to preserve national wealth and reputation by preventing forest destruction and halting the traffic in narcotics which has disastrous consequences for the country; (4) to promote the national economy, because the income of the hill people is a part of the national income. Two ways of achieving these objectives were outlined: first, by establishing *nikhom* settlements, and second, by giving specific on-the-spot help. The settlement scheme had been demonstrated as impracticable, because it is difficult to find an ideal location where all requirements are met, including sufficient water, good soil, good communications, security, and a suitable climate. Moreover, as already indicated, some hill people feel they are prisoners in a camp because of the regulations and occasional bad management. On-the-spot help is intended to bring assistance to the people in their own villages, and gradually introduce new farming and marketing methods.

INTERNATIONAL ASSISTANCE

The United Nations, having recognized the urgent need to solve the narcotics problem, and acknowledging the economic and social conditions involved in eliminating opium production, agreed to a program which supplemented existing projects. The Narcotic Control Project, entitled "Replacement of Opium by Other Crops and the Development of Hill Tribes in Northern Thailand," was approved by the United Nations in an agreement with the government of Thailand dated December 7, 1971. The initial period of the project was to be five years, at a cost of approximately $2 million. The project includes: (1) agricultural extension service and the training of extension agents; (2) promotion of agricultural experimentation and research; (3) land-use development; (4) trade, credit, and cooperative development (UNFDAC 1974).

The agricultural extension service aims to replace opium cultivation with other crops and economic activities yielding equivalent income, in the following ways: (a) farming and vegetable growing on high-elevation land; (b) fruit tree and nut cultivation; (c) growing other crops (tea, coffee, essential oil and drug plants, medicinal plants, hops), bee culture, mulberry cultivation, and silkworm raising; (d) development of forests and water resources; (e) animal, fowl, and fish raising; (f) applied research. Five main villages, each with five satellite villages, have been selected as experimental sites, and groups of agricultural extension agents have been assigned to stay in these villages. Existing village locations have been used. No attempt has been made to relocate populations for the convenience of these projects.

Agricultural experimentation and research stations are being set up or supported in three locations: Kasetsart University's experiment centre at Doi Pui, where a variety of basic research studies are being carried out on the hill environment, as well as studies on upland fruit crops; the experiment station at Doi Ang Khang which is being used in one of the King's projects for growing winter crops; and Doi Luang, where vegetable-seed production experiments are carried out by the Department of Agriculture.

Land-use development aims at ending "nomadic" shifting cultivation by teaching hill people about land use, land development, and conservation of water sources, and by use of new agricultural methods and equipment. It also considers recommendations for offering land tenure to hill people in order to give them pride of ownership so that they will stop burning and destroying the forests, and to prevent disputes over land claims between different groups of people in the hills.

Encouragement of trade, credit, and cooperative development aims at improving production processes, and the preservation and marketing of agricultural products. It also attempts to teach hill people the techniques of joint undertakings for commercial production, the handling of capital, and the use of local credit systems.

THE FUTURE OF HILL PROGRAMS

It seems likely that some hill people will continue to follow established patterns of assimilation into the Thai community, as has happened for many years, for example, among some Lua' people. There has been little evidence that those groups heavily engaged in opium cultivation, especially Hmong, Lahu, and Akha, will take this course. To date they have shown a strong attachment to the hill areas and to their present way of life. The development programs have thus far had little or no impact on their daily life, and it seems unlikely that poppy cultivation can be eradicated for many years to come, as long as it remains economically attractive.

Dilemmas remain among the officials who work on these problems. Questions have been raised concerning the future of economic and social development even if the immediate problem of opium production seems solved. Some might state, "Suppose all hill people stopped growing opium in the next five years—then the UN would pull out their aid, and so would Thai agencies. The hill people would be left with an unstable economy." At present those who have abandoned opium cultivation are dependent on various forms of aid. An alternative plan would be to legalize opium cultivation under the supervision of the government, and this option is still an active topic for discussion among Thai scholars working in this field. One thing appears clear: as long as there remains a world market for opium products it will be very difficult to control production in any part of the world.

11

Ecological Relationships in a Hmong (Meo) Economy

F. G. B. Keen

This chapter discusses a study of man-land relationships in two Hmong (Meo) villages, carried out by the writer in western Tak Province, Thailand, from November 1963 to March 1964 (photos 121–122). The descriptive portion applies specifically to the people of these two villages. While the Hmong are readily distinguishable as an ethnic group in many matters of dress, custom, and the like, there is considerable diversity in their way of life and economic practices in different areas. Variations in physical and human environments call for different responses from the same people, and though these responses are made on the basis of previous experience stored in a collective culture, they result in diverse patterns of choices from place to place and from time to time.

In western Tak in 1963 there were 25 villages of Hmong Njua (Blue Meo).[1] Department of Welfare records indicate they had a total population of 10,000 people, or an average of 400 per village. The village said to be the largest had a population of 600, while the two in which research was carried out contained, respectively, 400 and 280 persons.

All of these Hmong villages were in the up-lands, at altitudes of between about 800 and 1,050 meters.

The people were growing hill rice, maize, and opium poppies in swiddens, and other crops in association, including vegetables, tobacco, and some papaya. The swiddens at this time were cleared in primary forests containing large trees, commonly up to one meter or more in diameter, and the size of the trees was frequently pointed out by the Hmong as an indicator of fertile soil. None of the villages had attempted irrigated rice cultivation, though water is plentiful and there are areas of valley land where this would have been possible.

The great majority of Hmong in this area live in large houses in extended family groups (figure 11.1, photo 121). For example, the village of 400 people referred to above contained 28 houses, and averaged 14 persons per household. Only 5 of the houses contained simple nuclear families, while the largest group under one roof numbered 22.[2] Though it is difficult to estimate with accuracy, questioning indicated that new village sites are chosen at intervals of between 6 and 15 years.

The physical environment is relatively benign

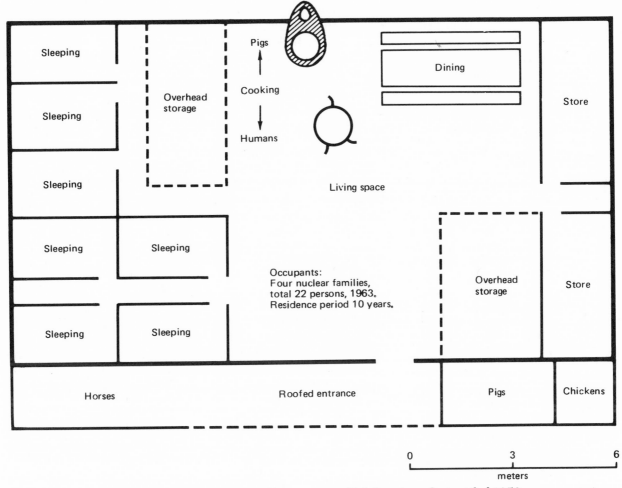

FIGURE 11.1   Hmong house plan, Meo Mai village, western Tak Province, first settled 1950.

by comparison with other upland areas of northern Thailand. Measured slopes of the fields are not too steep. A 15 to 20 degree slope from the horizontal is typical. There is a dry season of from five to six months, but the frequent clouds, occasional showers, heavy dews, and early morning mist keep the soil moist and the vegetation markedly green even in March, about six weeks before the rain could be expected. The relatively large amount of soil moisture present in the dry season is suggested by the fact that burned-off *Imperata* grass sprouted to a height of 18 cm in 14 days during late February.

Moorman et al. (1964) described the soils of this region in some detail; it need be mentioned here only that about 70 to 80 percent of the area consists of red-brown latosols (pH 5–5.5), weathered from metamorphic gneisses and mica schists. The remainder, apart from small pockets of alluvium in stream valleys, is a red-brown earth (pH up to 7), weathered from limestones in basins which appear high on the sides of the main ridges. Attention is drawn to these limestone basins because they are significant to the Hmong for opium poppy cultivation.

As suggested above, climax vegetation was heavy forest containing many large trees, which had been a factor in attracting the Hmong to the locality, but by 1963 not much more than half of this forest remained. The rest had been transformed into well-established savanna, on which there was little or no sign of regenerating forest.

In western Tak at that time, the Hmong were under no particular pressure from other ethnic groups. There were two other villages, one Lahu and one Lisu, about 7 km away from the nearest Hmong village. The Royal Thai government, through the Public Welfare Department, had recently established a very small land settlement station for hill tribes (*nikhom*) which included two Hmong villages on the fringes of its area, but at that stage had made only minor contact with them. There was an agricultural experiment station run by the Agriculture Department alongside the *nikhom*, but it was not engaged in any extension work. Apart from these groups there was no one else in the vicinity of the Hmong people. There was no competition for land resources, and the people did not feel themselves to be under any strong external influence.

A major part of the research program was a detailed examination of the Hmong economy for the purpose of measuring the effectiveness of the man-land relationship. Two fundamental questions were asked at the outset: Had the people achieved a balanced harmonious and rhythmic subsistence pattern within a given area? This could be the case, for instance, if a bush fallowing and cultivation system of land use was being practiced. Did the system contain within itself

elements that could lead to economic growth which might satisfy a population increase or a higher expectation of income?

Study of the economic pattern made it apparent that numerous organizational disadvantages were present in the economy. These appeared as opposing, or nearly opposing, elements causing one activity to be severely restricted or hindered by another. In spite of the industry and acquisitiveness of the people, real opportunities for economic growth were very limited. Of special importance was the effect of subsistence crop swiddening methods on the forest.

The forest plays a vital part in the economy of the Hmong people. It is the essential factor in the supply of land for subsistence cropping. Burning the forest is the means of preparing land for planting. The forest trees bring up the necessary minerals from the subsoil and deposit them on the surface in the form of decayed matter, and also bring them above the surface in the leaves and stems of the trees. After burning, the residual ash is available for nutrition of cultivated plants.

The forest is also the natural habitat of animals and birds, plants and fruit, which are all, in their seasons, significant as diet supplements for the Hmong.

Timber is the main construction material of the Hmong, and also the fuel supply. All kinds of buildings and many essential objects are made solely from forest products.

Obviously, the forest is vital to the continuation of the way of life of the Hmong as shifting cultivators. It is thus of the greatest significance that their key asset is steadily destroyed by their system of land use, which rapidly causes the vegetation to change from forest to grassland, and in that way takes the land out of production. A variety of Hmong actions, all closely connected with getting a living, create the situation in which significant regrowth of trees does not occur on the old clearings as long as the people remain nearby. In fact, there were certainly fewer tree seedlings on fields abandoned for 10 years or more than on those more recently in use. This suggests that the forest was not regenerating, and there are quite simple reasons for this state of affairs.

As common practice, the farmers locate their new rice or maize fields contiguously with the old ones, probably because of the relatively gentle slopes and the uniformity of soil and forest types. Fires frequently spread from newly cleared fields into the abandoned fields alongside, and so to the uncut forest edge. The people also deliberately set fire to the savanna which fails to burn by itself, in order to produce young grass regrowth for pasture for horses and cattle, and to attract game animals. In the burning season the sky is often obscured by smoke. As total clearing increases on a "soap-bubble" pattern, the oldest fields, farthest from the growing forest, receive less seed; hence the older the field, the fewer the trees and the better the grass growth for carrying fire.

Sauer (1956:55) has described the replacement of forest by grass as "a secondary fire association, or sub-climax." Sauer was referring specifically to a situation where savanna is induced through too-frequent cultivation, causing soil depletion in a land-use pattern of cyclical reoccupance of the same fields. In the Hmong case the grassland succession is caused by deliberate acts (burning for pasture) carried out in connection with some other part of the economy, as well as through overly long and intensive use of individual fields (compare Lua' and Karen forest conservation practices, chapters 6 and 9).

Another major area of conflict within the economy is that which exists between cropping and livestock keeping. Virtually all families in 1963 had pigs and chickens, most had horses, and a few owned cattle. Livestock, especially cattle, had ritual significance, and were important as a source of protein for subsistence. Horses were used regularly as beasts of burden in transporting crops.

Pigs and chickens in particular were kept in large numbers. For example, a village of 400 people had about 800 pigs and 1,000 chickens. The technological level of animal husbandry was very low; inbreeding and unsuitable diet resulted in the poorest types of animals while high losses from disease could be offset only by unrestricted reproduction. Because of these factors, domestic animals were of only limited value but were nonetheless essential as suppliers of protein and transport, as well as having ceremonial use. Essential as they were, domestic animals undoubtedly introduced difficulties, which otherwise would not have been present, in the production of food crops.

Watters (1960:70) has shown that shifting cultivators usually try to minimize the time spent in traveling from village to field, even to the extent of using less fertile land if it is closer to the village. The Hmong of western Tak did not cultivate land closer than about 15 minutes' walk from their villages, because they thought it too difficult to keep their domestic fowls and pigs from destroying plants. This had the effect of increasing the time spent in walking to the fields, and also must have decreased the time before it was necessary to move the village again.

An example can be given of a family from a hamlet about 2 km away from one of the two villages studied. These folk returned to live in the main village during the survey period and immediately began to clear the land around their old hamlet site for cultivation. They de-

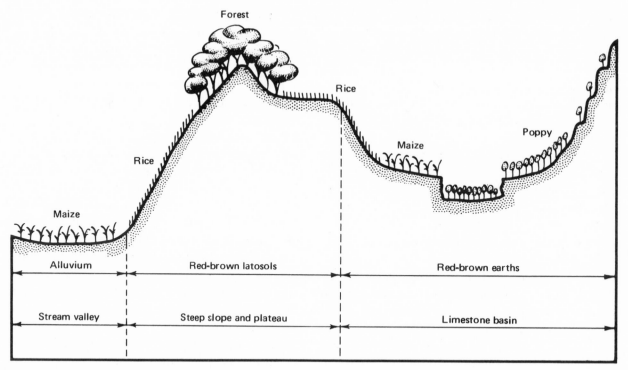

FIGURE 11.2   Schematic diagram of soils, forest, and Hmong swiddens.

scribed the area as very desirable land, which they could exploit only after the domestic animals were safely away.

No vegetable gardens were seen in any village, the Hmong explanation invariably being that it is difficult or impossible to control the pigs and chickens. Vegetables, which were used daily when available, had always to be carried from the major crop fields.

Thus the people paid a high price for their beasts of burden, for the protein in their diet, and for the satisfaction to be gained from sacrificial rites. They had only an uneasy truce with the livestock sector of their economy, which posed a threat to, and hampered growth in, other sectors (compare Lua' and Karen fencing practices, chapters 6 and 9).

In western Tak there was a close relationship between soil types and the selection of fields for specific crops, and the Hmong people had not been able to resolve this situation to their advantage. For poppy fields the people invariably favored the limestone basins, especially the bottoms of sinkholes and the pockets of earth among limestone outcrops, where pH levels were highest. Rice was believed to grow best in the more acid red-brown latosols, on steeper sunny slopes, while for maize the depth of topsoil was considered to be the important factor. Patches of alluvium in valley bottoms and other fairly flat areas were therefore preferred for this crop (figure 11.2).

The practice of planting maize in the poppy fields instead of separately is very common among the poppy-growing peoples in Thailand. The author has observed it in many villages, some Hmong included. The maize in western Tak is planted in May and harvested late in September or in October while the poppy plants are still very small. However, in this group of Hmong villages in Tak Province, a strong belief that the limestone outcrop areas contain the best soils for the poppy had resulted in grouping the poppy fields of a particular village in adjacent limestone basins, often fairly close to the village, while the rice and maize swiddens were scattered, and up to three or four hours' walk away.

The system of locating the poppy fields in limited areas of a specific type promotes a strong interest in maintaining them in production for as long a period as possible. Peas and beans are planted in association with the poppies, as this is believed to improve the soil,[3] and the fields are painstakingly weeded to keep out the tropical grasses. In some instances, where the family has enough labor, two poppy crops are harvested in the same year (but not in the same field). The first crop is planted in August and harvested from late January to March, while the second is planted in November and harvested in late April and May. Some people claimed to have cultivated the same poppy field for as long as 15 years, and use of the same field for 10 years is said to be common. By contrast, the rice swiddens are rarely cultivated for more than 2 years, and the maize for 3. The efficiency of weeding the poppy fields is shown by the almost complete absence of any burned remains of trees and stumps in the poppy fields, while stumps and charred logs are common among the subsistence crops (compare Lua' and Karen weeding practices and secondary succession in fallow swiddens, chapters 6 and 9).

When we examine the relationship between subsistence and cash-crop swidden methods, we find an inherent conflict in two land-use systems practiced by the same people. The cash crop (opium) is cultivated on a single site for as long as the soil will withstand annual cultivation. As the soil becomes exhausted, the farmers clear and use new sites in virgin jungle. Because some sites in western Tak Province will support poppy cultivation for 15 years or more, it might appear that the Hmong could become permanently settled cash croppers, perhaps by some slightly less intensive poppy cultivation method which would allow the perpetual renewal of soil fertility. This is not a realistic possibility because of subsistence requirements. Maize and rice can be grown for no more than two or three years in a single location under the Hmong system, thus Hmong subsistence cropping is very land-extensive. Because of political pressure, it is unlikely that any technological improvement in opium cultivation will be allowed; thus conversion of the Hmong to a pure cash-cropping system on the basis of a more or less permanent, settled land-use system seems unlikely. Likewise, the subsistence cultivation system seems to require movement of Hmong settlements, even if cash cropping could be stabilized. Neither alternative seems a likely possibility, and the needs of the two sectors of Hmong economy, subsistence crops and cash crops, remain unreconciled to one another.

Aside from the problem of field locations, which is in itself a source of lost time and organizational difficulties, the conflict between the food and the cash sectors is felt directly as one of individual choice and relative emphasis. While in absolute terms the Hmong could provide themselves with the essentials of food, shelter, and clothing independently of the cash sector, the availability of both consumer goods and money is developing a desire for an increasing range of items such as shotguns, electric torches, beauty aids, textiles, and confections which the subsistence sector could not provide. With no surplus unused labor, neither sector can advance except at the expense of the other. It is quite true that elasticity of demand for food is very limited once subsistence levels have been reached, but the food crops demand a high labor input to reach these levels, and the time when much of this work must be done coincides with the time that could have been spent producing the cash crop (see figure 11.3). Consequently, individual families are always involved in deciding how much time and labor are to be invested in each sector.

All families of the villages studied in Tak were fully dependent on their own food crops for subsistence. During studies in Chiang Mai and Mae Hong Son provinces in 1969, the author found a few instances of Hmong people trying to solve the problem by purchasing most of their rice while concentrating their own efforts on their opium swiddens. The shortcomings of this solution were obvious. The only families that could attempt it were those having control of particularly desirable poppy land of sufficient size. The advantage of extra cash income was offset by having to expend it on rice. In the absence of technological means to control the environment, such as artificial fertilizers and pesticides, and with uncertainties of the opium market, the risks connected with this solution were quite high. Nonetheless, this is an example of the flexibility of the Hmong economic system and the willingness of Hmong farmers to take risks for cash profits.

Other examples of Hmong entrepreneurship are given by Kunstadter (personal communication), who reports that Hmong in the Mae Tho area of Mae Hong Son Province use workers from nearby Lua' and Karen villages to clear their opium swiddens, and also attempt to raise money from the Lua' and Karen villagers to finance their opium crops. In this area the Hmong depend heavily on their neighbors for staple crops. He also reports that Hmong in some parts of Mae Chaem District, Chiang Mai Province, are said by local Karen to choose new village locations on the basis of both soil quality and availability of labor. Thus the Hmong economic system may have profound effects on non-Hmong villages in the vicinity of their settlements in addition to their ecological effects. Geddes (1973; 1976), who made an extensive study of Mae Tho reports that four-fifths of the cultivated land at Mae Tho was devoted to opium, and one-third of the families there had no rice fields.

The swiddener is often referred to as a man in harmony with nature. Watters (1960:95) describes him as "still part of the total ecosystem," and Conklin's studies (1954:458–462) of the Hanunoo show that these folk had won a "permanent" place within the natural scheme of growth and decay. My own studies indicate that the above references describe more nearly what Conklin (1957:2–3) calls an "integral-established" swiddening pattern, where, by definition, there is no cash crop to disrupt priorities and expectations, and where care is taken that forest regrowth occurs. This viewpoint is supported by several writers, notably Kunstadter and Hinton (chapters 6 and 9 in this volume) who give a figure of over 100 years for the continued residence of Lua' and Karen groups in one part of northwestern Thailand. These groups are organized and disciplined in their systems of field rotation, allowing for uninterrupted forest growth in fallow swiddens.

The Hmong of western Tak are rapidly destroying the forest on which their economy depends and are compelled to move their villages every few years. They could certainly not

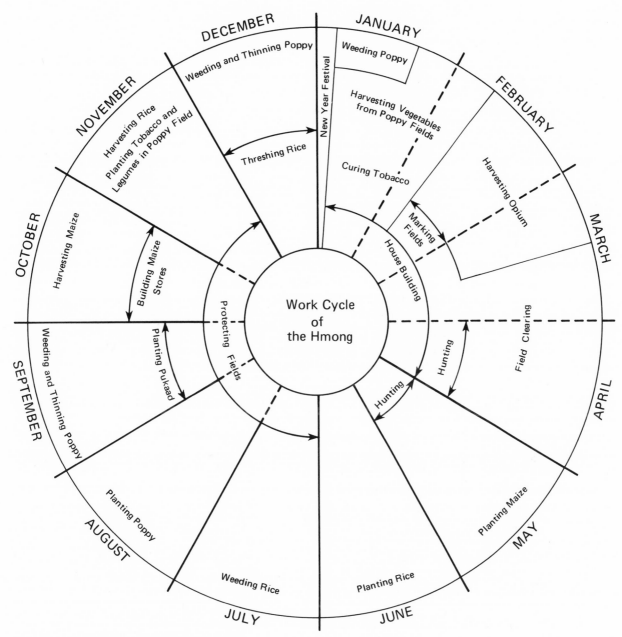

FIGURE 11.3   Hmong annual work cycle.

be described as being in harmony with their environment. Of equal significance to this study, their economic organization is not comprised of mutually supporting sectors making up a balanced whole and capable of expansion according to need. This analysis has demonstrated the way in which the major sectors—cash and subsistence crops and livestock—oppose each other so that each can expand only at the other's expense. It has also been established that the economy is quite rapidly self-destructive in that fertile, forest-covered land, as the principal form of capital is continually being taken out of production, not for a period of planned fallow, but for many years after the Hmong and their system of clearing and burning leave the locality. Put in another way, the economic organization, in spite of its being of an agricultural nature, is based on *people*, not *land*. Implicit in the attitudes of the Hmong is the idea that land is an expendable commodity in the production process, not a focal point around which both living and life are to be conducted.

Swiddening, or shifting cultivation, is commonly classified as a distinct type of agricultural economy as compared with, for example, commercial tree-crop farming, but the growing number of case studies, including some reported in the present volume, have indicated such a diversity and range of swiddening types as to greatly reduce the definitive value of the term. We cannot identify a common series of actions, expectations, or results under the term "swidden economy" and use this as a basis for comparison with other types of economy. In Thailand at least, it is not even valid to describe swiddening as an agricultural system in which fields are prepared for planting by chopping and burning woody plants. Field studies in February to March 1970 disclosed areas of grass, with few if any trees, which had been chopped ready for

burning and planting by Yao, Akha, Hmong, and Lisu people in parts of Chiang Mai, Chiang Rai, and Mae Hong Son. The terms "swiddening" or "shifting cultivation" thus have only the most general application and no longer serve as terms for any specific pattern of land use. This is not to say that when we see a certain type of farming operation we will not recognize it as swidden cultivation, but simply that, having applied this label to it, we will not have said much of predictive value.

Some common indices of measurement are needed as tools of analysis for comparing different kinds of swidden economies with each other and with other types of economic organization. It is logical to compare economies by measuring, as they are concerned mainly with quantities; but merely to measure goods is not of great significance. If we measure goods (units of production), we must ascribe to them common values in some arbitrary manner, which in the context of different economies they may not have. A good may be of marginal value in one economy and a necessity in another. The problem is compounded when we attempt to equate the products of a *mainly* cash economy with those of a *mainly* subsistence economy (Bhagwati 1966:13). It is therefore advisable to consider factors other than goods in attempting to measure and compare economic efficiency, as has been done here.

The results of the Hmong village studies have shown the value of the questions asked at the outset. Is the economic organization such that it ensures environmental stability, and does it contain the capacity for economic growth? Negative answers to both questions were found by examination of those forces which interacted between the individual sectors.

It is clear that the lack of intersectoral harmony (the capacity of several sectors of an economy to stimulate, or at least not to impede, each other) in the Hmong economy is due to faulty technology and organization. If the Hmong, for example, were to use some system of confinement or herding of livestock on the savannas they have already created, they could make use of land close to their villages. If their system of cultivation were such that cash and subsistence crops could follow each other in the same swidden, any expansion of area would favor both sectors simultaneously. Again, if their system of clearing and burning allowed for the regrowth of forest on swiddened land, they would not have to move their villages periodically, nor would they have the extra burden of clearing primary forest for every new swidden.

The criteria on which the foregoing analysis is based would seem to have general application to the study of agricultural economies. I believe that environmental stability and economic growth potential are the factors requiring the closest scrutiny in assessing economic viability. This study, in exposing the impasse between cash and subsistence sectors of the Hmong economy, demonstrates that the economy is unlikely to make significant growth unless fundamental changes occur in its technology and organization. On this basis, valid comparisons can be made with other economies by measuring the relative *capacity for growth* (in terms of underused land or labor, or underdeveloped markets, etc.), without the need to compare the relative *values of production*. The latter comparison, as has been pointed out, is much more difficult to do with accuracy.

Similarly, the failure of forest to regrow under the Hmong burning system steadily reduces the amount of forested land (capital) which is available for production, a highly unstable environmental situation which also has its parallels and can be measured. From this point of view it is possible and *meaningful* to draw comparisons between the rate at which the Hmong system takes land out of production by destroying forest,[4] and that at which, say, overgrazing of alpine grasses or the repeated planting of a single crop forces the abandonment of an area. Many other examples could be cited. The important characteristic common to all is the destruction of the basic captial asset, usable land. It is of no consequence whether we are discussing worn-out coffee lands of Brazil, or eroded tussock-meadows of New Zealand highlands, or the man-made savannas of Thailand; what makes them distinctive and comparable is the environmental instability linked to their land-use techniques.

The problem of choice, whether to opt for more cash or more food (for security of subsistence), faced by the Hmong cultivators is presumably familiar in many economies where cash and subsistence *both* contribute a large proportion of total income. The desire for money and consumer goods must surely increase as contact with more sophisticated and materialistic societies grows, and this desire is likely to outstrip the ability to earn cash in an economy which is in a transitional stage between subsistence and commercial organization. The "partial" swiddener, dependent both on subsistence and on cash crops, may well be the classic example of this type of economic conflict. He has reached the stage of desiring growth in his cash sector, but through a variety of organizational problems such as distance from markets or lack of technical skills, he is unable to reduce his dependence on his own subsistence crops without taking unjustifiable risks with the security of his subsistence.

The examples given in the preceding paragraphs show that similar characteristics can and do exist in economies which may be completely different from each other in all practical matters such as technology and products. The essential reason for this is to be found in the basis of the inquiry which has been concerned with *qualities*, especially those related to organization, rather than with more *tangible*, and therefore *infinitely varied*, features. It is suggested that this approach may help to achieve greater coherence in comparing rural economic systems without being compelled to over-simplify or to ignore differences.

In conclusion it must be reiterated that this report, in all its references to the Hmong, limits discussion to a specific group belonging to a particular time and place. There is no suggestion that the economy described here is "typical" of Hmong people as a whole, because I am convinced that an *economic generalization based on ethnic distinctiveness is not possible*. The Hmong, numbering in millions, are distributed throughout much of southern China and Southeast Asia, living in a wide range of geographical conditions and cultivating a great variety of crops. Even if the discussion is confined to Thailand and to the author's own experience, significant variations in economic organization have been noted. At the same time, without reference to other published material, the breadth of papers presented in this volume alone, have shown that terms such as "swiddening" do not serve to describe any one pattern of activity. The differences are profound.

The generalization which has been formulated is that studies of rural economies are more likely to be fruitful if based on comparative analysis of their dynamics, rather than on attempts to classify them on grounds of agricultural types or ethnic divisions. Studies of this type have practical as well as theoretical uses, especially in formulating development plans.

For the planner concerned with economic development, studies that concentrate on the dynamics of economic systems—that is, on the forces which control and shape them—can give him the foreknowledge necessary in order to base development on the conscious needs of the people concerned. For example, if people growing crops in forest clearings recognize that what prevents them from increasing production is their inability to guard any additional fields from wild animals, they will not in the first instance see any value in a more rapid forest-clearing technique. The change for which the basic motivation exists is most likely to be either a method of increasing yield from the same sized fields, or a method of excluding wild animals.

In the case of the Tak Hmong in 1963–1964, they clearly understood that it was an overall shortage of labor which prevented them from expanding the cash sector of their economy as they desired to do. They had not seen that there was any limit to the amount of forest for swiddening. Consequently, while the men were invariably eager to discuss alternative methods of earning cash which would require less labor than poppy growing, they showed no interest in developing paddy terraces. They were well aware that the additional labor required for this more intensive method of rice production would only serve to reduce their ability to produce opium. For this reason more than any other, official efforts to encourage the Hmong in Tak to adopt irrigated terraces for paddy were firmly rejected (Keen 1966:121–122). Quite simply, people do not adopt new, more labor-intensive techniques of production in the subsistence sector when *they* recognize labor shortage as being a major factor restricting a strongly desired growth in the cash sector.

A corollary to this conclusion is that the kinds of innovations most likely to be accepted (by the Hmong of this case study) would be those which saved labor, rather than those which destroyed less forest. This is a useful conclusion for rural planners in Thailand, where the dangerous significance of forest destruction has been acknowledged for some years (Central Hill Tribe Welfare Committee 1963:4). The implication is that, while a considerable part of the planners' aim is to halt the destruction of the forest, the Hmong seek solely to earn a higher cash income from the same or a reduced amount of work. Any single or progressive change to the land-use pattern perceived as serving both of these objectives would have a high chance of success.

The implication is clear. Planning organizations, when they desire to make important changes in rural economies, especially those of entrenched conservative traditions, must make them from within. Such changes must be based on a thorough empirical study of the interacting economic forces which are present. Both nega-tive and positive qualities must be exploited to achieve new economic relationships, while striving always to keep to the barest minimum the number and scale of the new skills and ideas which must be grasped.

NOTES

1. "Blue Meo" is the translation of a Thai name, taken from the clothing style of the group. The Blue Meo refer to themselves as Hmong Njua.

2. Gordon Young (1962:85) gives an average of 35 houses per village, and eight persons per house. This last figure appears too low for houses observed in western Tak, though it may well be more accurate for Thailand overall.

3. As far as could be determined, the Hmong were not in this case aware of the ability of legumes to fix nitrogen, but simply believed that they were "good for the soil."

4. Unlike Hmong farmers farther north, referred to above, many of whom are compelled through scarcity of forest to clear swiddens in savanna grasses, these Tak folk had not yet (1963) been forced to compromise with their preference for swiddening in primary forest.

12

Shifting Cultivation and Economic Development in the Lowlands of Northern Thailand

E. C. Chapman

My concern in this chapter is to focus attention on the needs and opportunities for economic advancement of the largest ethnic group of shifting cultivators in northern Thailand—Northern Thai farmers in the lowlands. It is probable that today more than one-quarter million Northern Thai villagers depend to some extent on shifting cultivation, mainly in the provinces of Nan, Phrae, Lampang, and Chiang Rai (and parts of Chiang Mai), and yet they are largely overlooked. They live at the low-altitude end of the "swidden spectrum" and it is the high-altitude end (above 1,000 meters and the "opium line") which, understandably, has captured almost all the concern about shifting cultivation in northern Thailand in recent years. Furthermore, the overwhelming majority of the "Khon Muang" who practice shifting cultivation are undoubtedly reluctant swiddeners, forced by population pressure to move in increasing numbers away from their traditional base in wet-rice cultivation. Very largely they continue a "supplementary" slash-and-burn system, where production from swiddens contributes a critical, but minor, part of total household income.

The critical issue that concerns us here, however, is not the rather academic question of differentiating the Thai supplementary, or "partial," swidden system from the more "integral" systems of "hill-tribe" groups living upslope from Thai villages (Conklin 1957; Spencer 1966; Uhlig 1969), but the fact that the Thai, Lua', Karen, and many other shifting cultivators now share an urgent need for the productivity of their swidden systems to be upgraded. Their needs are the same, stemming from the same root cause in rapid population increase, and it is surely of secondary importance whether we are concerned with Karen and Lua' who are swiddeners by long tradition, or with Northern Thai farmers compelled by economic necessity to move regressively into a less advanced cultivation system.

In this discussion I will concentrate on three matters: first, the fundamental deterioration in the man-land relationship in the northern lowlands which has led to an expansion of shifting cultivation by Thai farmers; second, the characteristics of Thai supplementary swidden cultivation and evidence of its productivity in relation to land and labor; and third, the initial small-scale efforts which have been made to upgrade one area of swidden cultivation into more productive permanent-field agriculture, in the Thai-Australian Land Development Project at Amphur Sa in Nan Province.

POPULATION CHANGE, LAND RESOURCES, AND SWIDDEN EXPANSION

If the distribution and importance of swidden cultivation in the lowlands is to be understood, it must be viewed against the background of almost static land resources, increasing slowly in recent years with the expansion of second-crop irrigation, and an immense upsurge in the rural population in the northern lowlands.

The 1947 census indicated that the seven northernmost *changwat* (provinces) had a population of about 2.02 million. By 1960 this had increased to 2.95 million, an increase of about 2.9 percent per year compared with an annual increase of about 0.4 percent in the intercensal period from 1937 to 1947. By 1970 the population of these provinces reached 3.8 million suggesting an annual growth since 1960 of over 2.5 percent (see table 2.1).

It is clear that the northern provinces, like Thailand as a whole, are in the midst of a massive population expansion, probably associated with both the virtual elimination of malaria from the valleys during the 1950s and the increasing accessibility of hospitals and other health services. It is equally clear from the evidence of the 1963 Census of Agriculture, and in the field, that the northern provinces have been hard-pressed to accommodate the rapidly growing numbers who must support themselves from farming. In 1963, of the 71 provinces in Thailand, eight provinces had a physiologic density (or "nutritional density") for the rural

population exceeding 500 per sq km of cultivated land. These included six of the seven northernmost provinces. Changwat Chiang Rai, which absorbed more than one third (36 percent) of the regional increase in population between 1947 and 1960, had a density of 397 per sq km. On the other hand, Changwat Nan, with 724 per sq km, had by far the highest physiologic density in all Thailand in 1963.

Evidence for the very diverse situation in agriculture, varying markedly from province to province, is set out in table 12.1, based on the 1963 Census of Agriculture. Nan is clearly a "poverty corner" of northern Thailand, with more than 50 percent of farm holdings under 6.0 *rai* (just under 1 hectare) and mean rice production per farm holding of 1,715 kg, which was the lowest for all 23 provinces in northern and northeastern Thailand, despite rice yields per *rai* much above the average for the kingdom. That the situation has certainly deteriorated considerably since 1963 is reflected in the steady expansion of swiddening, as farmers endeavor to compensate for the relatively static situation in wet-rice cultivation. More hill swiddens have been opened up near main roads, the fallow period between crop years on swiddens is progressively shortening, and on the sandy terrace soils of the Nan valley (for example, southeast Muang Nan), swidden land has been subdivided and allocated to villagers by *amphur* (district) officials in areas classified for farming purposes. In an extensive sample survey of villages in Nan in B.E. 2509 (1966) made by the Department of Land Development, it was found that four-fifths of rural households had swiddens, usually to supplement their rice production from irrigated fields.

It is clear that the situation is very different now from that of the first 50 years of this century, when population expanded slowly and the

TABLE 12.1   Agricultural Holdings by Size Group, and Rice Production per Holding in the Northern Provinces, 1962–1963

Changwat (Province)	Population in Agricultural Households (1960)	Size of Holdings			Productivity of Holdings (means)		
		Under 6.0 *rai* (%)	6.0–14.9 *rai* (%)	15 *rai* and Over (%)	Paddy Area Planted (*rai*)	Yield per *rai* (kg)	Total Produced (kg)
Chiang Mai	556,613	43.6	46.3	10.1	7.29	428	3,120
Chiang Rai	630,109	30.6	45.0	24.5	14.40	386	3,911
Lamphun	194,782	43.1	44.8	12.2	7.4	357	2,625
Lampang	356,760	45.5	46.5	9.1	5.7	363	2,008
Phrae	235,456	40.9	46.0	13.0	6.2	394	2,433
Nan	220,423	55.4	40.0	4.4	4.7	365	1,715
Mae Hong Son	59,930	46.3	45.4	8.3	6.1	367	2,223
Whole Kingdom		18.6	29.3	52.1	16.4	213	3,490

SOURCE: Changwat series, *Census of Agriculture 1963* and *Thailand Population Census, 1960* (National Statistical Office, Bangkok). From E. C. Chapman, "An appraisal of recent agricultural changes in the northern valleys of Thailand," Division of Land Policy, Department of Land Development, Bangkok, 1967. One *rai* = 1,600 m²; one hectare = 6.25 *rai*. Thus the average yield for the Kingdom of 213 kg/*rai* = 1,331.25 kg/ha.

northern provinces accommodated their increasing numbers adequately. Pioneer settlement was undertaken in sparsely settled areas, and throughout the lowlands there was progressive improvement of water control and the subdivision (but seldom fragmentation) of farm holdings on the wet-rice lands which occupy the floodplain and low terraces of the valley bottoms. Since about 1950 it has not been so easy for the increasing rural population to be accommodated in the time-honored ways, and farmers in the northern provinces have resorted to new methods to increase income. The chief ways have been three: second-cropping, or multiple-cropping with dry season irrigation; increasing seasonal movements of part of the farm work-force in the dry season when men often move to off-farm employment (notably timber cutting and charcoal production) either locally or in another province; and increasing cultivated area through swiddening during the rainy season. All three comprise safety valves, providing relief as the pressure of population on the lowland farmland has mounted so rapidly.

Unfortunately, economic development is usually spatially concentrated rather than diffused, and in northern Thailand the areas which most needed increased income (particularly Nan) have lagged behind. An outstanding instance is the expansion of multiple-cropping on previously one-crop riceland, strongly developed so far only in the Ping valley around Chiang Mai and in the central parts of Changwat Lampang and Changwat Phrae. The reasons are complex, but they center on such factors as the depth of stream incision within the floodplain and lower terraces (sometimes preventing gravity irrigation from bamboo weirs built by villagers), the priorities of the Royal Irrigation Department in dam construction, and the slow diffusion from Chiang Mai and Lampang of information on irrigation from field wells. A basic factor has been the varying depth of the river channel and the width of the floodplain and low terrace belt from valley to valley. In the Nan valley and many tributary valleys of the Ping (northern Chiang Mai), Wang, and Yom river systems, the limited amount of irrigable lowland has compelled villagers to look to swiddening on the higher terraces and hills, for relief from shortages of food and cash income. Except for steeply sloped portions, the middle terraces have received special attention. Although geomorphologically complex, they contain extensive areas of red and grey, sandy podzolic soils and stand in close proximity to many lowland villages situated around the margins of the irrigable bottomland.

The central part of Nan Province, shown on figure 12.1, provides a good example of the setting in which Thai supplementary swidden cultivation has expanded. The valley floor, between sharp breaks of slope to east and west, is approximately 23 km wide; of this extent about one-sixth is in the median strip of floodplain and low terrace "bottomland," flanked by complex middle-terrace terrain on either side. In the narrow bottomland along the Nan River about 100,000 people were living at the time of the 1960 census, about one-fourth of them in the towns of Nan and Sa, and the remainder in villages. It can be seen from the map, based on 1954 air photographs, that the "built-up area" of villages spread over nearly a quarter of the bottomland. Beyond the villages the low terrace areas of the floodplain are closely subdivided into bunded rice fields, with a few small citrus (tangerine) orchards on river levees and low terrace areas.

Population pressure on the bottomland in this central part of Changwat Nan is now so intense that the average household of six persons has between 3.0 and 5.0 *rai* for wet-rice cultivation, the amount varying from village to village. Yields in the area are generally about 35 *tang* (ca. 350 kg) per *rai*, indicating that a cultivated area of about 6.0 *rai* or about 1 hectare is needed to meet a household's subsistence requirements. Because the amount of irrigable lowland available is inadequate, the villages overall have

moved into a rice-deficit situation in which many households need to purchase rice for part of each year and few have rice for sale. Under these circumstances there is a strong incentive for farmers to use available labor and land (middle terrace and hill slopes) for supplementary swidden cultivation.

The local situation in central Nan is made considerably more difficult by the inability of farmers to extend their resources of cultivated land by irrigation from the Nan River. In the dry season (November–April) the Nan River flows strongly, often 50 meters wide and 3 to 4 meters deep in its channel, with high banks rising 6 to 7 meters above low-water level. The main river is too deeply incised to allow "native dams" to be effective, and waterwheels as used on the Ping near Chiang Mai have failed at Nan in the past. The small eastern streams are also incised, but here surface flow usually ceases by the middle of the dry season. The situation clearly calls for large-scale pumping from the river, from the Nam Wa, and from oxbows, and also for the use of field wells for irrigation. Pumping has been established to only a limited extent, mainly by orchardists, tobacco merchants, and (intermittently) one or two Farmers' Groups.

With irrigation limited mainly to the margins of the dry-season river channel, most men in villages are unemployed in the dry season, except where there is regular local employment or temporary out-of-province employment. And so many farmers turn their backs on the river in December and January, and head with swidden knife, rice basket, and drinking water for the scrub forest of *hiang* (*Dipterocarpus obtusifolius*) on the middle terraces. This area provides the opportunity for extending farm resources, and most of the swiddens are probably used quite legally, as the land has been classified for farming. Evidence suggests that within the past 20 years most of the increased population pres-

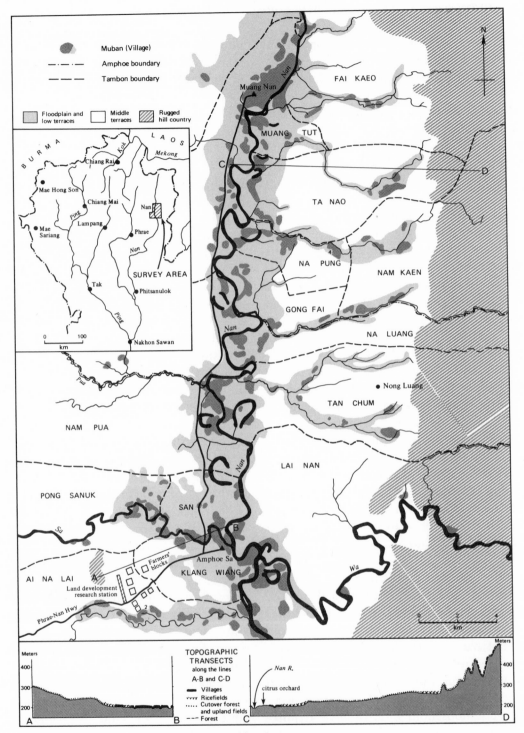

FIGURE 12.1   Nan valley settlement and land use.

sure has been absorbed in the middle-terrace areas, leading to a rapid shortening of the swidden cycle to one cropping season in two or three years, and to gradual changes from usufruct (use-right) occupation to formal land subdivision and title documentation, as the demand for swiddens has increased. For the same reason, the distance to swiddens has also tended to increase. Most villagers in the central area of Nan appear to live less than 4 km from their upland fields, but as closer areas have been filled up, the relative late-comers have needed to travel farther; in 1968, for example, a group of 60 farmers from Ban Tan Chum living near the Nan River (see figure 12.1) began swidden cultivation near Nong Luang, almost 7 km distant.

THE PRODUCTIVITY OF THAI SWIDDEN CULTIVATION

The critical features of most swidden agriculture are its low returns from the land and labor invested, both in absolute terms and relative to the productivity of permanent-field farming in the same vicinity. This is certainly true of the lowlands in northern Thailand. The data in tables 12.2 through 12.5 demonstrate the generally low level of swidden productivity in the Thai supplementary system, and hence the need for substantial improvement if the continuing increase in the rural population is to be supported within the near future.

Judd (1964) has described the hill swidden situation at Tambon Baw, about 25 km north of Nan Town, in an area where farmers have no wet-rice fields and derive supplementary income from orcharding and off-farm work. Probably the most common form of the Thai system, however, in Nan and other northern provinces, is that in which the village is essentially wet-rice oriented but has many households with swiddens, so that upland and lowland farming are integrated and may even compete for farm la-

bor, particularly for weeding during the rainy season. This is the situation in central Nan, shown in figures 12.1 and 12.2. Investigations in this area (undertaken in 1967–1968 by the Department of Land Development) provide some substantial evidence on the low productivity of Thai swiddening under population pressure.

A number of main points may be made from the tables:

(a) Table 12.2, based on interviews with 635 households with swiddens in Areas 1 and 2, indicates that 76 percent of the households cultivated lowland fields supplemented by swiddens, and the remaining 24 percent were otherwise landless. This highlights the fact that swidden cultivation has played a significant role as a safety valve, providing land for villagers who would otherwise now have no land of their own. As table 12.2 also shows, the majority of swidden households (having both lowland fields and swiddens) use their upland fields to bring the total household cultivated area up to a level of 6.0–9.0 *rai*. Surprisingly, the "swidden only" group averaged 3.0–5.0 *rai*, despite the fact that the second group could be expected to have more labor available for swidden cultivation in the rainy season. Part of the answer is certainly demographic, in that many of the "swiddens only" households are smaller or have young children who are not yet effectively part of that farm work-force; but probably more important overall, certainly in Area 2, is the fact that demand for swidden land has caused holdings to be reduced in size, in order that many households may share what little land is available. For example, in Village No. 4 of Tambon Na Pung (Ban Kot), a part of Area 2 that lies south of the village has recently been subdivided officially into blocks of 3 *rai*, so that more households may share the land available.

(b) Table 12.3 demonstrates the dependence

TABLE 12.2 Areas Cultivated by Households with Swiddens in Areas 1 and 2 of Changwat Nan (figure 12.1) (1 *rai* = 0.16 hectare)

Administrative Village (*Tambon* Name and Village No.)		Total Population			Households with Lowland Fields of 1 or More *Rai*				Households with Swiddens Only	
		No.	H/h	No. H/h	Areas cultivated (means)				No. H/h	Mean Swidden Size (*rai*)
					Lowland Fields (*rai*)	Swid-dens (*rai*)	Total (*rai*)			
AREA 1										
T. Ai Na Lai	1	1,184	205	11	4.4	8.5[a]	12.4[a]		9	19.0[a]
	2	619	106	44	4.5	3.2	7.7		19	3.9
	3	376	65	4	4.5	1.8	6.3		1	4.0
T. San	7	297	50	8	4.5	3.3	7.8		2	5.0
T. Klang Wiang	3	1,487	247	35	1.6	3.7	5.3		27	5.2
	4	1,815	334	26	4.8	2.0	6.8		11	2.3
	5	441	71	42	3.8	2.3	6.1		8	3.2
	6	482	79	19	4.5	1.7	6.2		13	4.0
T. Pong Sanuk	4	202	34	33	4.9	2.2	7.1		1	5.0
AREA 2										
T. Na Pung	1	582	96	39	4.3	4.6	8.9		9	3.3
	2	510	106	65	3.5	4.2	7.7		8	4.0
	3	1,017	176	75	4.0	4.8	8.8		24	3.2
	4	340	61	46	3.0	4.0	7.0		10	4.0
	5	470	71	35	4.3	4.2	8.5		9	6.0

NOTE: Data were obtained from householders by questionnaire interviews in February, March, and April 1967. They relate to the 1966 cropping year, except for a few supplementary interviews carried out in the early months of 1968. The data are estimates and only a small proportion of swiddens would have been measured by tape, but farmers are accustomed to the assessment of area for purposes such as taxation. Experience suggests that their assessments are often reasonably accurate for areas of 3 to 5 *rai*. Smaller holdings are often understated, and larger holdings overstated. The table should be taken as a general guide to the land situation.

It should be emphasized that the data in the last six columns refer only to households with swiddens in Areas 1 and 2. In most of the villages some households cultivated swiddens outside Areas 1 and 2. For example, in village No. 1 of Tambon Ai Na Lai, about 195 households had swiddens, including only 20 with swiddens in Area 1.

[a] Means were affected by two farmers with a relatively large area under maize; one farmer having lowland fields and 34 *rai* of maize swiddens, and a second farmer with only 134 *rai* of maize swiddens.

of swidden households on rice purchases despite the fact that rice is the chief upland crop, generally planted on about 60 percent of the swidden area each year. Peanuts, for sale, are the second most important swidden crop in central Nan, followed by small and fluctuating crops of maize, cotton, and mung beans.

(c) Table 12.4 shows the drastically low pro-ductivity of the swidden system, taking into account the land and labor resources employed. It is clear that yields from rice swiddens are generally 30–40 percent of the yields obtained from the same villages' wet-rice fields, despite considerably greater labor inputs as a consequence of the need for slash-and-burn before each crop; and the returns to the cultivator on

TABLE 12.3 Rice Purchases and Sales by Households with Swiddens, Changwat Nan (figure 12.1), in 1966

Administrative Village (*Tambon* Name and Village No.)		Total H/h with Swiddens	H/h that Bought Rice	H/h that Neither Bought nor Sold Rice	H/h that Sold Rice	H/h that Bought and Sold Rice
AREA 1						
T. Ai Na Lai	1	20	16	3	1	–
	2	63	54	8	–	1
	3	5	3	2	–	–
T. San	7	11	11	–	–	–
T. Klang Wiang	3	62	46	14	1	1
	4	38	31	6	1	–
	5	50	33	14	3	–
	6	32	24	7	1	–
T. Pong Sanuk	4	34	25	7	2	–
AREA 2						
T. Na Pung	1	49	85	13	1	–
	2	73	30[a]	38	2	–
	3	99	49[a]	39	6	1
	4	56	41	15	–	–
	5	44	28[a]	14	1	–
Total		636	476	180	19	3

NOTE: The data are for the full year 1966 and were obtained in the questionnaire survey, April 1967.

[a] In addition to the households which needed to buy rice, several households in Tambon Na Pung reported receiving rice from the *amphur* office: Three households in village 3, one household in village 5. Many other households also received free rice from the *amphur* office in all five villages of Tambon Na Pung, as famine relief measures in August and October–November 1966. In village 4, for example, 43 households from the total 61 swiddening and nonswiddening households received 3.5 liters of rice per person at both distributions.

the labor invested per *rai* are pitifully small (last two columns), mostly 4–6 *baht* per day—very much lower than for wet-rice production.

Why should so many bother to work in upland fields, an inconvenient distance from their homes, for meager returns? Yields of upland rice and other crops in these intensively cultivated swidden areas appear seldom to exceed 150 *baht* per *rai* in value of the subsistence or commerical crop at harvest; and gross returns per man-day worked are only 4–5 *baht* per day for rice swiddens, compared with daily wage rates of 7–8 *baht* for men in unskilled work. One may ask,

Why swidden? The answer stems, it seems, from the low opportunity cost of swidden labor. For much of the rainy season there is no large-scale alternative local employment available (see figure 12.2), and swidden cultivation is smoothly integrated with wet-rice cultivation in the lowland fields, except in wet years when the rains begin early and rice transplanting can begin in June. Another highly important consideration is that upland rice is usually the first rice to be planted and harvested, at a time when most household granaries are nearly empty. "Hill" rice is also welcome for its taste.

TABLE 12.4   Approximate Mean Gross Returns on Land and Labor Inputs for Main Swidden Crops in Areas 1 and 2, Changwat Nan (figure 12.1), 1966

(L.R. = lowland rice fields; U.R. = upland rice fields (swidden); P. = peanut swiddens)

Administrative Village (*Tambon* Name and Village No.)		Swidden House-holds No.	Yields (kg/*rai*)			Days Worked per *rai*			Value of Product (*baht* per day worked)		
			L.R.	U.R.	P.	L.R.	U.R.	P.	L.R.	U.R.	P.
AREA 1											
T. Ai Na Lai	1	20	320	160	147	19	23	21	17	6	9
	2	63	229	74	128	21	26	28	16	2	7
	3	5	250	63	?	26(?)	26	?	10	2	?
T. San	7	11	367	160	76	22	23	27	17	6	4
T. Klang Wiang	3	62	448	140	137	19	24	24	23	5	8
	4	38	380	141	126	18	26	29	21	4	6
	5	50	416	111	81	19	28	28	22	3	4
	6	32	421	96	78	22	21	26	18	4	4
T. Pong Sanuk	4	34	393	149	105	21	29	26	18	4	6
AREA 2											
T. Na Pung	1	49	338	150	105	17	28	26	19	4	6
	2	73	442	179	147	17	28	25	26	5	8
	3	99	442	161	140	17	26	26	26	5	8
	4	56	315	117	109	19	28	27	17	3	5

NOTE: The data are based on information received from 591 individual households, by questionnaire survey in April 1967. The yield data depend upon householders' assessments of area planted and the volume of harvest for each crop, and should be regarded as suggestive rather than definitive statements of yield for rice and peanuts. Peanut yields were probably overstated in many instances, while the rice yields are probably more reliable.

(d) Finally, table 12.5 attempts an assessment of annual per capita income. Here the salient features are the low levels of net per capita income for the median-income person in each village, the fairly low contribution of crop sales to cash income, and the high contribution made by nonfarm work in every village.

AN ATTEMPT AT ECONOMIC DEVELOPMENT

When the pitifully low returns from the Thai supplementary swiddens in Nan are considered, perhaps the best that can be said is that returns could not fall much lower. This may have some advantages, as well as disadvantages, when economic development is being attempted.

The Thai-Australian project was established in 1967 by the Department of Land Development, Ministry of National Development, acting on recommendations made the previous year after a survey of land use, land tenure, farm production, and household incomes in 67 sample villages of northern Thailand. The first recommendation, based on survey evidence of the diminishing length of short-cycle swidden cultivation in Nan and other provinces, proposed the setting up of a land-use research station and a pilot land-development operation, with the ob-

TABLE 12.5 Amount and Sources of Annual Household Income for Swidden Households in Villages of Areas 1 and 2, Changwat Nan (figure 12.1), 1966

Administrative Village (*Tambon* Name and Village No.)		No. of Swidden Households	Estimated Median Net Income (*baht* per capita)	Sources of Household Income Including Value of Crop [a] Consumed (%)						Used by H/h
				Sold for Cash						
				(a)	(b)	(c)	(d)	(e)	(f)	
AREA 1										
T. Ai Na Lai	1	20	734	20	13	1	9	36	5	17
	2	63	417	12	10	1	13	28	3	33
	3	5	292	10	–	–	26	20	–	44
T. San	7	11	632	12	17	2	7	21	2	39
T. Klang Wiang	3	62	769	11	8	–	4	50[b]	7	20
	4	37	638	15	5	1	5	32	19	23
	5	50	585	25	11	3	10	15	2	24
	6	32	633	19	6	2	11	33	3	27
T. Pong Sanuk	4	34	608	29	20	2	4	12	–	33
AREA 2										
T. Na Pung	1	48	536	19	13	1	5	21	4	38
	2	73	494	11	10	1	4	22	3	48
	3	99	425	7	7	1	7	30	5	44
	4	56	325	4	14	2	8	28	2	41
	5	44	533	13	8	1	5	24	7	43

NOTE: These data are based on a questionnaire survey in which heads of households were asked for estimates of cash income and expenditure over one year, in each of the main sectors of income and expenditure. The value of goods consumed was calculated for crops retained for domestic consumption and seed, and deductions made from gross household income for expenditure on seed, livestock, etc., in order to arrive at estimates of net household and per capita income. Although the accuracy of the data is such that it provides only a very general guide, consistency is evident in the high proportion of household income contributed by *non farm labor* and subsistence production.

[a] Key to sources of cash income: (a) from the sale or barter of crops; (b) from the sale or barter of buffalo, cattle, poultry, and pigs; (c) from the sale or barter of household products; (d) from paid farm labor (on another farm); (e) from nonfarm labor; (f) other income, including rent of land or equipment, profit from business, gifts, etc. The percentages have been rounded.

[b] The very high proportion of income attributed to non farm labor in Village 3, Tambon Klang Wiang, is explained by the fact that this village is part of the *amphur* Sa district town.

jective of accelerating the transition from swidden to permanent-field cultivation. During the two years beginning in May 1967, the research station was set up on 200 *rai* of middle-terrace soils at Amphur Sa (Nan Province), and in 1969 2,500 *rai* of adjoining swiddens and swidden regrowth were cleared, cultivated, and allocated, with legal title, to 320 farm households in the nearby villages (see figure 12.1).

In the long term, the success of this project will depend on the results of research on crop rotation and the maintenance of soil fertility, either under permanent rainy-season cropping, or with a green-manure phase included in the rotation. But at this early stage, land development for villagers has in many respects been initially the greatest challenge. Land clearing and cultivation have involved related issues of op-

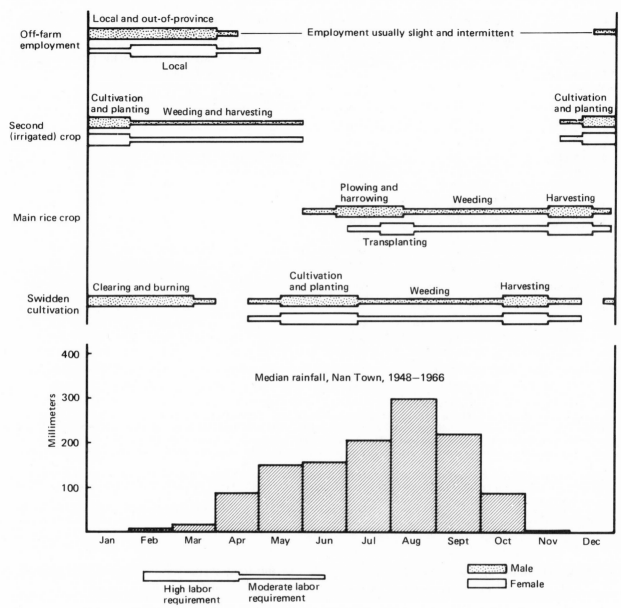

FIGURE 12.2 Farmer labor employment in the lowlands of Nan Province.

timal timing, benefit-cost ratios with different blends of mechanical equipment and villager participation, the question of cost sharing by villagers, issues of farm size and farmer tenure, and, of course, the fundamental logistics of any land-development enterprise. Some of these matters are discussed by Charley and McGarity in chapter 13.

What are the likely results of the project? Is the area likely to revert to swidden cultivation, owing to a combination of vegetation regrowth, decline in soil fertility, and deterioration of soil structure? An ultimate reversion will be likely, of course, unless problems of soil depletion under permanent cropping can be overcome. Alternatively, is the middle-terrace terrain likely to be depopulated as a consequence of land speculating entrepreneurs purchasing land from the initial smallholders, thereby adding to the landless group? What may be the consequences of refocusing farmers' attention on the lowland fields, if irrigation eventually allows multiple cropping there? And what, in turn, may be the wider implications of the project for other provinces of Thailand and other agencies concerned with economic development?

Many of these questions are still unanswerable. All of them, however, center to some extent upon villagers' attitudes to their land in the early years after its sudden transformation from swiddens to plowed fields. If economic incentives are too weak, then farmers' interests in fertilizers or recommended crop sequences will soon fade, and they will certainly be responsive to the offers of persons prepared to move into extensive commercial farming on the terraces.

A guide to the profitability of farming on the terrace soils is provided by a report of the cash returns from the villager-operated research farms on the Land Development Research Station at Sa in 1967. Six annual crops were

planted: upland rice, maize, cotton, peanuts, mung beans, and sesame. All six crops were familiar to farmers and all had a known local market. Results with three different fertilizer treatments (nitrogen and phosphorus applied singly and in combination) showed no substantial improvement over yields obtained without fertilizer, *in the first year of effective cultivation*. On the basis of these results a recommendation of "no fertilizer" was given to farmers for the first year after plow cultivation, which in most instances was the rainy season in 1969. This recommendation meant that it was unnecessary to implement immediately an arrangement for farmers to obtain "production credit" from the Agricultural Bank, using as collateral their land titles. But the same initial research results indicated the need for a major research effort into the reasons for poor response to fertilizer applications, and for poor nodulation of legumes, especially peanuts. Work in these and other areas of plant nutrition has begun (see chapter 13).

The yields and cash returns for crops on the Sa research farms, grown without added fertilizer in the first year after plow cultivation, are shown in table 12.6. The most spectacular results and those which particularly impressed villagers were the yields of upland rice: a mean yield of 406 kg/per *rai*, compared with about 150 kg/per *rai* on swiddens in the same locality. Plow-cultivated upland rice fields produced more than the nearby irrigated rice fields! The possibility of maintaining yields and cash returns at this level from the terrace farms depends, of course, on the success of the research now in progress concerning fertilizer needs, plant selection, and crop rotations. But if, for example, net cash returns of only 250 *baht* per *rai* are maintained under permanent land use over the next few years, the transformation

TABLE 12.6   Yields and Related Cash Returns under Rainfed Conditions for Crops Grown on the Same Land with Continuous Cropping and without Added Fertilizer, Sa (Nan) Research Station, 1967, 1968, 1969

	Cotton	Mung Beans	Rice	Maize [a]	Peanuts
Yields (kg per *rai*)					
1st Year (1967)	175	153	406	428	100
2nd Year (1968)	127	178	302	101	185
3rd Year (1969)	96	69	222	55	108
Cash returns (*baht* per *rai*) [b]					
1st Year (1967)	610	406	325	342	171
2nd Year (1968)	443	472	242	81	316
3rd Year (1969)	335	183	178	44	185

NOTE: Although all crops were grown without fertilizer, an important variable from year to year was the amount and distribution of rainfall in the growing season between April and October. In 1968 the rainy season began early and in 1969 the rains stopped unusually early, with dry conditions in September and early October. Nonetheless, the expected yield decline reflecting nutrient run-down under continuous cropping is very evident, particularly in regard to rice. Sesame was planted in 1967, but failed owing to heavy rain just before harvest.

[a] Maize planted in 1967 was Q962, an Australian hybrid. In subsequent plantings a "synthetic" American variety has been preferred. Farmers in Changwat Nan are not familiar with hybrid seed and are accustomed to retaining seed after harvest.

[b] The cash returns are actual gross returns to the farmers at harvest, including the harvest value of the subsistence rice crop at 80 *satang* per kg. No fertilizer costs were involved, and only cotton was sprayed, at an estimated cost of about 100 *baht* per *rai*.

from rice swiddens cultivated once in three years to permanent-field cultivation will mean an increase of 400 percent in the value of annual crop production, per unit area of former swidden land.

What will this mean to the livelihood of a village household? Taking the average household with swiddens in Village No. 2 of Tambon Ai Na Lai, for example, the extent of terrace land cultivated by the household will have changed from approximately 3.4 *rai* in one year to 7.0 *rai* in the next. Assuming, rather generously, a net return of 150 *baht* per *rai* from the former swiddens, and 250 *baht* per *rai* from the new farmland, the contribution to household income will have increased by 243 percent from 510 *baht* to 1,750 *baht*. As the average household with swiddens in this village had a net per capita income, from all sources, estimated from the results of interviews in 1967 at 417 *baht* per

annum, the result of the change to permanent-field cultivation would be an increase in net per capita income of 53 percent. The increased inputs required from the householder to achieve this improvement would amount mainly to the labor of farming an additional 2.6 *rai*. This may be a more serious requirement than it would initially appear to be, because of intense weed growth and because some householders with lowland fields may wish to work in their wet-rice fields when they ought to be planting "up above," on the terraces.

At the present time, one can be only cautiously optimistic about the longer-term success of this project concerned with the transition from a low-yielding swidden system to more productive permanent-field farming. Clearly, it is highly localized on gently sloping terrain which allows fairly low development costs, and it has been greatly helped by an array of factors including the enthusiasm of villagers to participate in a development process which upgrades the productivity of this marginal farmland.

But two questions stand out. If a permanent improvement can be effected in the productivity of this river terrace land (and there is a large amount now being used by swiddeners), to what extent can there be a carryover upslope to the hill swiddens of Thai, Lua', Karen, and others living in the foothill environment? And, if an improvement in the swidden sector of the householder's economy can be achieved, why not also in other sectors: in the production from the wet-rice fields, in the development of dry-season cropping under irrigation (perhaps by field wells, utilizing the high dry-season water-table), and in the in-

creased use of rural manpower in seasonal off-farm jobs and the establishment of better links between villagers and employment opportunities?

This leads me, in conclusion, to suggest two basic approaches to economic development of the swidden and nonswidden areas of northern Thailand: first, the need for a *farmer-centered* approach that assesses the actual benefits which local villagers are likely to derive from any development proposal; and second, a holistic approach, rather than a piecemeal one, to the improvement of rural incomes—an approach that takes into account *all* the ways in which the incomes of rural households are derived in a particular area, and ways in which each sector can be improved.

13

Soil Fertility Problems in Development of Annual Cropping on Swiddened Lowland Terrain in Northern Thailand

J. L. Charley
J. W. McGarity

Viewed from the standpoint of geographic range, the most remarkable feature of swidden cultivation is its flexibility. Although now mainly a phenomenon of tropical and subtropical environments, the essentials of the technique have also been used in the past in temperate areas along the margins of settled agricultural communities where land was in the process of development for clean cultivation or pastoral use. It is also broadly based in an ecological sense, as it spans a wide climatic spectrum, a diversity of soils, and a complex array of vegetation types. Many different crops are grown under shifting cultivation, many rotations are adopted, and a great variety of separate crop-fallow combinations can be used even on a single site with a specific set of environmental characteristics.

Despite such room for maneuver, swiddening carries the common requirement of a minimum natural fallow period if it is to be self-sustaining in the sense that yields of a chosen crop hold steady across the span of a succession of crop-fallow cycles. For a given site and crop sequence this minimum recovery period is the one that will yield the greatest return in the long term and maintain the site at a fertility level not too far below the equilibrium condition of the un-

disturbed site. Lengthening a minimum fallow may in many instances return higher crop yields at the individual harvests, but the aggregate yields should be less than when the ecosystem is being tapped on the shorter, optimum cycle. Truncation of the minimum rest period inevitably results in declining productivity, and the longer such reduction is continued, the longer the fallow necessary for the system to regain its original equilibrium biomass and functional efficiency. Further, if swidden cycles are tightened and continued in this frame for too long a time, the risk of permanent damage is greatly increased, particularly with respect to crucial soil resources. Such is the broad theory that has met considerable direct and indirect testing against the reality of yield, and for which there is a good understanding of the natural functional processes involved (chapters 6–9).

In the following pages an outline is given of the more important of these processes and their role in maintenance of soil fertility and site productivity. The specific case of over-swiddened terrace areas in northern Thailand is examined in some detail as an illustration of the biological problems encountered when attempts are made to improve production on such run-down land by introduction of mechanical land-preparation and fertilizer technology.

THE GENERALIZED SWIDDEN CYCLE

The beginning of a swidden cycle can be taken as the end of a fallow when the regrowth is about to be cut, dried, and fired. At this time total nutrient content of soil and standing crop in a well-managed rotation is at a maximum for the specific time span adopted in the cycle. At the burn, a high percentage of the nitrogen and sulfur reserves of the felled vegetation will be lost into the atmosphere, but virtually all phosphorus in the ash remains within the system; so too, the content of metallic nutrient cations will be maintained. These elements are added directly to the soil surface in ash, and constitute a significant natural fertilizer increment which is positionally and physiologically available because of its concentration and inorganic form. Organic nutrient reserves of the immediate topsoil are similarly affected by the burn, at least to the extent that they are made more readily susceptible to microbiological transformations and mineralizations at the onset of rain (chapter 7).

At the commencement of the rainy season, soil biological activity is stimulated and the system begins to work on the capital accumulated during the fallow. Changes in nutrient status are initiated through crop withdrawal, through surface transport of insoluble ash and organic residues from the site, through leaching of soluble ions, and by way of carbon dioxide production from soil respiration. Run-down is most marked for carbon and nitrogen, particularly in the early phase when labile organic materials are undergoing the flush of decomposition so characteristic in soils which have been dry for a protracted period and are then wetted at tropical temperatures. This decomposition is usually well underway before the planted crop is established, and in consequence much of the inorganic nitrogen resulting from oxidation of organic nitrogen can be subject to leaching because there is little in the way of an established root system to intercept it in the profile. Sulfate is similarly mobile and easily leached, especially when the soil material is coarse textured. Fortunately, phosphorus, which is the most significant element in the long term, does not leach appreciably, as it quickly forms insoluble compounds by precipitation and adsorption reactions. Phosphorus is notable in this respect, and fortunately so, because it is one essential element that is not added to natural systems either by biological mechanisms or as simple fallout from the atmosphere or as cyclic salt. For practical purposes, all phosphorus in an ecosystem must have come from soil parent material.

Leaching losses are probably quite small once the crop is established to the point of having a root system which explores the bulk of the biologically active surface horizons. They should continue small until the end of the rainy season, when leaching temporarily ceases. Accordingly, once crops and weeds are well established, the major nutrient loss pathways are likely to be crop withdrawal and erosion of surface soil.

The beginning of the dry season marks the end of nutrient removal from the site, except that some nutrients already taken up by crops will be removed at harvest. In general, however, nutrient capital actually taken from the site in plant products is usually a relatively minor consideration.

The final phase of the rotation is taken up with regrowth of native vegetation. This may begin after one or several years of monospecific or mixed cropping when the swidden is abandoned and the system begins to move in the direction of reestablishment of equilibrium with its environment. If the rotation is well chosen, regrowth begins quickly from stumps and shoots remaining from the previous felling (see chapters 6 and 9). On the other hand, if the cropping period has been overdone and control of regrowth excessive during the rainy season, then viable residues from the last fallow may be so thinned out that reestablishment from seed may be the sole means of restoring the original species complex (chapter 11). This is slow in comparison with regrowth from stumps, as the latter begins with established root systems capable immediately of bringing to the plant top nutrients drawn from the subsoil. Consequently, it is important that cropping never be carried to the point where vegetation of the fallow is slow to reappear; not only does this deflect the system too far below the equilibrium and so lengthen the recovery time, it also increases the likelihood of erosion and serious change in chemical and physical soil properties. Furthermore, as the intensity of utilization in a given crop period increases, so also does the risk of dominance by weeds such as *Imperata*.

Well-chosen rotations can undoubtedly be repeated many times, perhaps indefinitely, without soil resources being permanently impaired. But this is the ideal case, one which is becoming increasingly difficult to realize as population pressures demand either that more virgin forest be put under shifting cultivation or that existing rotations be shortened in order for more crops to be grown in a given time span. Commonly, the latter is the only alternative available. In consequence, large areas that were once productive and stabilized under adequate fallows are now run down and probably beyond natural recovery to a forest vegetation, except in the long term.

In the cycle outlined above, continuity at steady yields hinges on soil chemical and physical deteriorations of the cropping phase being made good through natural agencies during the bush fallow, and by way of physical movements of essential nutrients effected by deep-rooted tree species of the regrowth. Nitrogen and organic carbon are the two elements whose gross amounts show greatest change over the full cycle, and it is the effectiveness of biological fixation of these elements from atmospheric sources that determines whether or not the system will be self-maintaining. For the remaining macro- and micro-nutrient elements, it is mainly a question of the fallow concentrating enough of them in the standing vegetation and biologically active surface soil for there to be an adequate supply after the burn.

In many parts of Thailand, but especially in northern provinces such as Nan, increasing population pressure and the consequent demand for more intensive use of upland areas have resulted in widespread reduction of bush fallow periods to a point which is clearly below the stable yield minimum. On terrace land which would seem to require a regrowth fallow period of about 10 years in order to stabilize yields, swiddening is now commonly operating on a three- to four-year cycle, and crop yields have fallen accordingly. Chapman, in chapter 12, has described the social and economic implications of this progressive change, as well as the mechanics of the land development project which has been implemented in an attempt to resolve the basic problems of the Thai swidden cultivators caught in this setting of increasing population, shortening fallows, and falling yields. It remains, therefore, to round out the account of the project by considering some of the characteristics of terrace soils which present problems for the agronomist who attempts to do with crop rotations and fertilizers what the bush fallow of the swidden cycle does naturally.

LANDSCAPE CHARACTERTISTICS

Much of Thailand is covered with unconsolidated sedimentary deposits in areas of low relief. Four levels of sedimentation are at present recognized: alluvial plain, low terrace, middle terrace, and high terrace. The most fertile and productive agricultural soils are found on the lower areas and the poorest on the higher terraces. The distribution of the major great soil groups is determined by the sedimentation pattern. Thus alluvial or paddy soils with varying textures and degrees of mottling are usually found on recent alluvium on the lowland flood plains. Low terraces, on the other hand, are characterized by low humic gley soils with some textural horizon differentiation (Bt) and strong hydromorphic mottling. At the higher elevations of the middle terraces, soils are generally better drained with red-yellow podzolics and latosols predominating. In lower situations of the middle terraces, however, low humic gleys and grey podzolic and lateritic soils are usual. On the high terraces, which are often strongly dissected, the major soils are red-yellow podzolic and reddish brown lateritic.

SOIL MORPHOLOGY

The general pattern of distribution described above applies to the Nan valley. Here, the most extensive upland unit is middle terrace, and on this level soils range from those with both podzolic and latosolic characteristics to those with distinct podzolic and hydromorphic features. On the Thai-Australian Land Development (T.A.L.D.) experiment station, at Sa and adjacent areas which have been cleared for farms, the topographic sequence is from red-yellow podzolic soil on the highest gravelly terraces to a red latosolic (intergrading to a red-yellow podzolic), derived in part from high-terrace colluvium, and passing downslope to a grey podzolic soil with or without laterite.

The great soil group nomenclature used here requires explanation. The soils of the upper slopes have been mapped as Yasothon and Mae Rim series, which are red latosol and red-yellow

podzolics, respectively. The absence of a pale A2 and the presence of a generally earthy fabric and red colors would appear to distinguish these latter soils from the usual modal concept of red-yellow podzolic soils. In Australia such soils are classified as red earths. In Southeast Asia there is uncertainty as to their classification.

Continuing down the middle terrace toposequence to less readily drained sites, soils with pale A2 horizons develop, while at the lowest catenary position the soils developed are light colored throughout, with a strong, sporadically bleached A2 horizon. These profiles are weakly hydromorphic and remain poorly drained during the wet season; they have been named grey podzolic and are common problem soils in Southeast Asia. Plinthite (laterite) may be present in the top 100 cm of the profile or not at all. These lower members have been named San Pa Tong or Korat series.

Analytical data to accompany the following morphological descriptions are set out in table 13.1.

MORPHOLOGY OF THE RED-YELLOW LATOSOL (YASOTHON SERIES)

Profile Description for Sa 1 Site

0–5 cm A11	Very dark brown (7.5 YR 2/2M, 10–7.5 YR 4/2–3/2D) sandy loam; weak medium crumb to medium subangular blocky; weak surface crust on bare surfaces; crushing to powdery single grain; roots common; pH 6.2; changing clearly and smoothly to:
5–10cm A12	Very dark brown and dark brown (7.5 YR 2/2 and 4/4 M, 10–7.5 YR 4/4 and 3/4 and 5/4 D) sandy loam to loam; weak medium subangular blocky, to massive; friable moist, hard setting dry; porous, earthy fabric; pH 6.0; changing clearly and smoothly to:
10–15 cm AB	Dark brown and very dark brown (7.5 YR 4/4 and 4/2 M, 10–7.5 YR 4/4 and 4/3 D); sandy clay loam; massive, apedal dry; friable moist, very hard dry; containing soil materials mixed by soil fauna from horizons above

TABLE 13.1 Chemical Properties and Clay Mineralogy of Latosol (Sa 1) and Grey Podzolic (Sa 8) Soil Profiles

Genetic Horizon	Depth (cm)	Carbon (%)	Nitrogen (%)	Clay (%)	pH (1:1 H$_2$O)	Cations and Exchange Capacity (milli-equivalents per 100 g)					Base Saturation (%)	Clay Minerals in Profile
						Ca	Mg	K	Na	CEC		
Latosol												
A1	0–5	1.51	0.09	5	5.9	4.8	1.2	0.3	0.2	9.6	68	Kaolin +++
A12	5–10	1.05	0.08	8	4.9	2.8	1.0	0.1	0.2	6.3	65	Interstratified[a] +
AB	10–15	0.70	0.06	8	4.7	1.3	0.7	0.1	0.2	6.0	38	Illite +, in upper
B1	15–40	0.47	0.05	17	4.2	0.5	0.3	0.1	0.2	4.9	22	part of profile
B21	40–70	0.25	0.06	22	4.2	0.4	0.1	0.04	0.2	4.3	16	Trace of feldspar
B22	70–90	0.19	0.05	22	4.7	0.4	0.1	0.04	0.2	3.9	18	throughout
B23	90–140	0.15	0.05	26	4.7	0.4	0.2	0.04	0.2	4.0	20	
Grey Podzolic												
A11	0–10	0.82	0.10	9	6.0	2.8	0.7	0.1	0.1	4.7	77	Kaolin +++
A12	10–25	0.39	0.06	11	6.0	1.5	0.4	0.04	0.1	3.8	53	Interstratified ++
A2	25–40	0.24	0.05	13	5.4	0.9	0.4	0.03	0.1	3.0	47	Illite, trace
AB-B1	40–50	0.19	0.04	16	5.0	0.6	0.3	0.04	0.1	3.6	44	Quartz present
Bg	50–105	0.14	0.04	20	5.0	0.5	0.3	0.03	0.1	4.4	33	
C	105–130	0.14	0.05	23	5.1	0.8	0.3	0.04	0.1	4.4	52	

NOTE: Chemical data: G. Arnott, Soils Division, Department of Land Development, Armidale, N.S.W. Clay mineralogy: Department of Agronomy, University of New England, Armidale, N.S.W., Australia.
[a] Vermiculite-mica, randomly interstratified.

and below; pH 6.0; changing clearly and irregularly to:

15–40 cm B1   Reddish brown (5 YR 4/4 M, 5 YR 4/1–5/6 D); light sandy clay; massive apedal; friable moist, very hard dry; earthy fabric, clay skins lining some earthworm channels, porous with many voids due to termite and earthworm activity; pH 5.5; changing gradually over a wavy surface to:

40–140 cm B2   Yellowish red (5 YR 4/8 M, 5 YR 5/8 D); medium sandy clay; massive with some weak medium crumb and medium subangular blocky due to termite and earthworm activity; nonsticky subplastic clay, slightly hard dry with inclusions of A horizon material in voids, porous earthy fabric; becoming more massive with depth; pH 5.1; changing gradually to:

140–210 cm B3   Red (2.5–5 YR 5/8–4/8 M, 5 YR 5/8) medium sandy clay as above; pH 4.5.

CLASSIFICATION:

Thailand Great Soil Group	Red Latosol
Australian Great Soil Group	Red Earth
Australian (Northcote)	Gn 2.11, Red Earth
USDA 7th Approximation	Halplustox

MORPHOLOGY OF THE GREY PODZOLIC (SAN PA TONG SERIES)

Profile Description for Sa 8 Site

0–10 cm A11   Very dark brown (10–7.5 YR 2/2 M, 10 YR 6/1–5/1 D) sandy loam; weak medium crumb, with subangular blocky worm casts 1–3 cm on surface; crushing to single grain; nonsticky, very friable moist, but slightly hard dry; noncoherent, earthy fabric, with numerous worm casts and voids, porous; with some mixing of soil material from horizons below; roots present; pH 6.0; clear wavy boundary to:

10–25 cm A12   Brown (7.5 YR 4/2–5/2 M, 10 YR 6/1–5/1 D) sandy loam; weak medium crumb to fine subangular blocky in worm casts, crushing to single grain; becoming massive; porous with termite voids; nonsticky, friable moist, slightly hard dry; noncoherent earthy fabric with some clay skins along worm channels, with mixing of A11 and A2 material; pH 5.5; clear to gradual, broken boundary to:

25–40 cm
A2

Brown moist, light grey to white dry (7.5 YR 5/2 M, 10 YR 6/1 and 7/1, 7.5 YR 6/1 D); individual nests of white grains (sporadic bleach); sandy loam to light sandy clay loam; massive breaking to weak medium crumb and fine granular; slightly sticky, friable moist, very hard dry; some clay skins on peds but generally coherent earthy fabric with some rough faced peds; porous with large termite channels (5 cm); roots few; pH 5.0; clear, smooth to irregular to:

40–50 cm
B1

Brown (7.5 YR 5/2 M, 7.5 YR 7/2 D/pinkish grey) sandy clay; fine to medium subangular blocky crushing to single grain; slightly sticky, very friable, slightly hard; porous with fine micropores, earthy fabric; some mixing of cast material from below; pH 4.7; changing through a gradual smooth to irregular boundary to:

50–105 cm
Bg

Brown mottled (7.5 YR 5/3 M, 7.5 YR 7/2, 6/6, 5/4, 5/6 D) light clay with sand; moderate fine to medium subangular blocky, fine granular crushing to single grain, with increasing proportion of peds; sticky, slightly hard; porous earthy fabric; mottling due to iron segregation; roots few, porosity somewhat less than horizon above; pH 4.5; clear smooth boundary to:

105–130 cm
D

Brown (7.5 YR 5/3 M, 7.5 YR 7/1–7/0 D) gravelly sandy loam; massive; sticky clay between rounded white and black quartz gravel.

CLASSIFICATION:

Thailand Great Soil Group	Grey Podzolic (hydromorphic)
Australian (Northcote)	Gn 2.91, Grey Earth
USDA 7th Approximation	Oxic Dystropept

All the above soils which have been examined to date show evidence of intense earthworm and termite activity, often to such an extent that many of the peds in the otherwise apedal soil mass are portions of earthworm excretive casts. As a result of this mixing of material from different horizons a noticeable mottle is produced. This effect has not generally been recognized in soil descriptions, apparently to avoid confusion with mottling effects consequent on poor internal drainage.

The reversal of the downward leaching effects on clay movement and nutrient elements by the mechanical movement of soil materials caused by soil fauna is probably the major factor in the development of gradational rather than duplex profiles. The magnitude of movement can be estimated from the density of the soil "buttons" of worm excreta remaining on the surface at the end of the wet season. These vary from 1 to 3 cm in height, and, although they may not completely cover the previous soil surface, they are commonly sufficiently dense to all but obscure it (photo 127).

The presence of termites is usually indicated by numerous pockets of frass which mark the location of old tree roots, and by fine galleries running down a meter or more. However, the most dramatic evidence of their importance in soil development are the large termitaria scattered over the surface, particularly in poorly drained middle terrace situations (photo 128). Chemical analysis of these mounds has shown that the soil material is notably higher in total nitrogen and organic matter than surrounding soil, but the most impressive difference in composition is the massive accumulation of calcium carbonate in the mound core. In the example shown in photo 128, this lime begins about 0.5 meter in from the mound surface and extends to approximately 2.5 meters below the general level of the surrounding surface. The significance of this local concentration is more apparent when it is remembered that the termitaria are set in a matrix of acid soils with only a little exchangeable calcium, certainly no free lime.

Although mainly a feature of ecological interest, the calcium carbonate of termite mounds may prove to be a useable source of agricultural lime should this fertilizer be found necessary for satisfactory growth of crops such as peanuts. Commercial lime is not readily available in northern Thailand, whereas termitaria occur in abundance in the project area and are easily reduced to fine powder with a bulldozer.

EROSION

Dispersive soil surfaces are common in middle terrace terrain, a thin layer of sand up to 1 cm in thickness being a common feature after heavy rain, particularly early in the wet season before crop and weed cover protects the surface from raindrop impact. In most soils the underlying subsurface material is somewhat massive, particularly in the grey podzolics, and infiltration is normally quite restricted once the first few inches of the profile are wetted. As a result, the infrequent very heavy rains of the wet season can do great damage if the soil has been disturbed by cultivation, particularly if they fall around planting time when the soil has been recently worked. In consequence, even though the relief is gentle, most middle terrace areas cleared for cultivation require contour banking and similar soil conservation measures.

NUTRIENT STATUS OF TERRACE SOILS
NITROGEN

Total nitrogen analyses of surface samples from a range of terrace sites in the northern provinces of Nan, Phrae, Lampang, and Chiang Mai are summarized in figure 13.1A. These span a wide range of sites from near-virgin bush to badly overworked swiddens. Surprisingly, however, there is no clear evidence in the individual results of a consistent difference in nitrogen status between degenerate ground and adjacent scrub regrowth. Most likely, this reflects limited sampling at each site and the marked variation in nitrogen status which can occur in samples collected only a few meters apart. An instance of such lateral heterogeneity, which could have an important bearing on crop experimentation on these soils, is shown in figure 13.1E, representing the frequency distribution of the means of a collection of five samples taken from each of 84 subplots of a crop rotation trial. Similar variation has been encountered on all experimental sites which have been examined in detail. It is not clear whether this is the result of cropping history, litter-fall halos of the original trees that covered the swiddens, or the effects of microtopography. So far there is insufficient information to say whether or not the same applies to other nutrients, but this would be expected solely on the grounds of traditional swidden practice, where felled vegetation which remains after the first burn is stacked and burned in heaps to leave a pattern of ash beds.

In addition to the scattered sampling represented in figure 13.1A, three widely separated project areas on middle terraces have been examined in some detail to compare surface nitrogen levels and patterns of change with depth. The comparisons are shown in figures 13.2 and 13.3, respectively. These data show a reasonably uniform pattern of surface nitrogen values in accord with the more generalized spot survey. Nonetheless, there are significant differences in content between separate project areas, which could be important in terms of crop response.

A feature of the profile distributions worth noting is the marked surface concentration common to all areas. Almost all soils show this accumulation as a reflection of nitrogen turnover and localization of most biological activity near

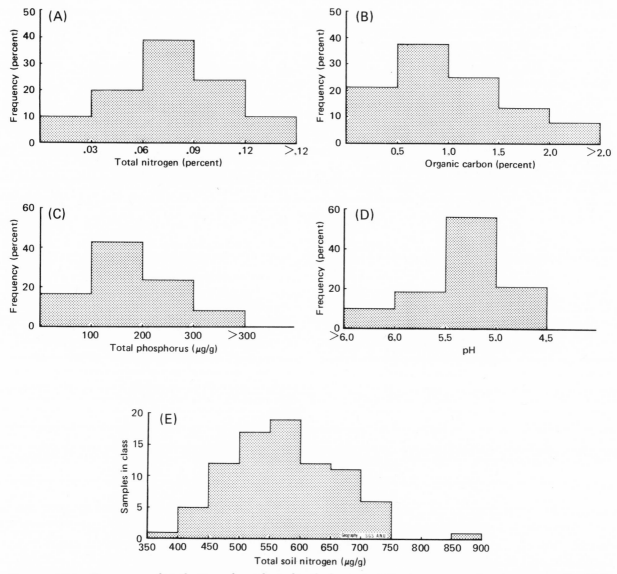

FIGURE 13.1 Frequency distributions for selected soil characteristics in a comprehensive range of middle terrace soils of Nan, Phrae, Lampang, and Chiang Mai provinces: (A) total nitrogen; (B) organic carbon; (C) total phosphorus; (D) pH; (E) total soil nitrogen.

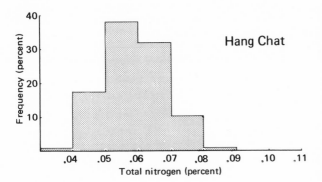

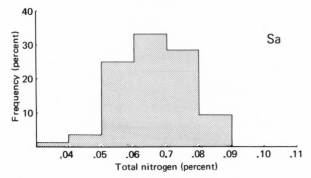

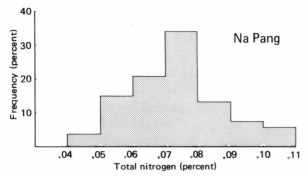

FIGURE 13.2 Frequency distributions of total soil nitrogen content in surface sample (0–7.5 cm) collections from middle terrace terrain of the Hang Chat, Sa, and Na Pang project areas.

the surface, but it is generally most pronounced in soils toward the lower end of the fertility spectrum. Thus it is best illustrated in sandy soils of warm, wet climates and in all desert soils; the terrace data represent a fairly marked case.

By itself, total nitrogen content is of limited use, as it merely states the concentration of this element, not the biological reactivity of the reserve nor its susceptibility to loss either by crop withdrawal or leaching. Nonetheless, a detailed knowledge of soil nitrogen status is important in two major respects: first, as a possible predictive guide in assessment of land capability if clearing is contemplated and, second, as an essential measure of initial nutrient level from which changes induced by fertilizer and crop practices can be detected and their significances gauged.

Despite the complication of a considerable range of values between and within sites, there is no question but that middle terrace soils of northern Thailand are very low in total nitrogen and that husbanding of this crucial resource will remain a central issue in any agronomic work aimed at maintenance of stable crop yields.

PHOSPHORUS

As in the case of nitrogen, there is surface accumulation of phosphorus in the profile reflecting the influence of litter turnover by the original vegetation and regrowth fallows, but the effect is not as marked nor as consistent. What is significant, however, is that approximately half the reserve of phosphorus is incorporated in the organic fraction, a component of the total pool which is essentially unavailable to plants until mineralized by microorganisms. Surprisingly, crops have not responded to dressings of superphosphate to the extent originally expected on the basis of the analytical data. Nevertheless, it is more than likely that deficiencies of this element will develop in later years, particularly in legumes; in this respect, it is interesting to note that terrace soils tested in pot experiments usually show up as phosphorus-deficient when peanuts are the test plants.

Preliminary laboratory work has shown that the more ferruginous acid soils have a marked

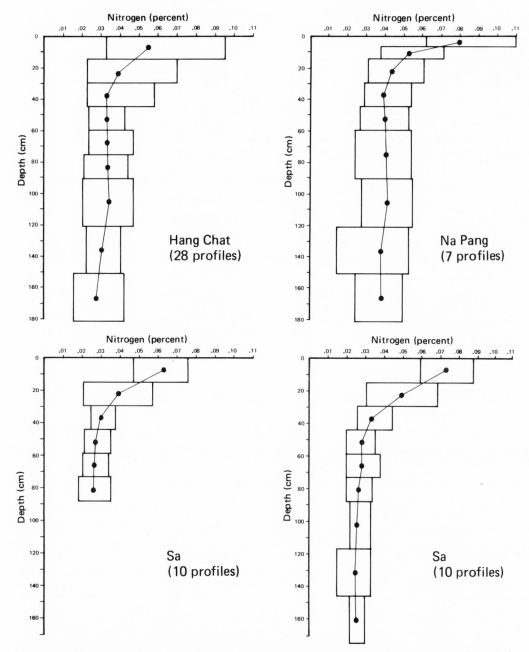

FIGURE 13.3 Depth functions of total soil nitrogen content showing averages *(dots)* and ranges of variation *(bars)* encountered in soil profile collections from middle terrace terrain of the Hang Chat, Na Pang, and Sa project areas.

ability to fix phosphorus and a strong buffering capacity for this element. It is not yet known whether this is a common characteristic or typical only of the iron-rich materials.

The phosphorus analyses available are limited in number, but they come from a wide range of terrace areas. Thus, while they are much less comprehensive than the nitrogen results, there is little doubt that further work will support their evidence of very low phosphorus status in middle terrace soils (figure 13.1C).

ORGANIC CARBON

A striking feature of terrace soils under virgin forest or dense regrowth is the virtual absence of a litter mat on the surface despite the large annual litter fall. Rapid disappearance of organic residues can be partly attributed to fire and partly to the activity of soil fauna, but the evidence of the organic carbon and C/N ratio analyses (figures 13.1B, 13.4) suggests also that microbial respiration proceeds vigorously during the wet season. Otherwise the gross amounts of organic matter in the soil surface would be higher and the C/N ratios wider.

Some newly cleared terrace soils have C/N ratios high enough to indicate that mineral nitrogen may be immobilized for some time after the beginning of the rainy season, but crop responses in early experimental work and rice growth on unfertilized but well-cultivated farm fields suggest otherwise. In fact, general observations and the data currently available imply that maintenance of organic reserves in these soils will be difficult because of the rate at which residues are decomposed by the microflora.

pH AND EXCHANGEABLE IONS

All middle terrace soils are mildly acid to acid in the immediate surface (pH 6.0–5.5) and strongly acid in the subsoil, pH occasionally

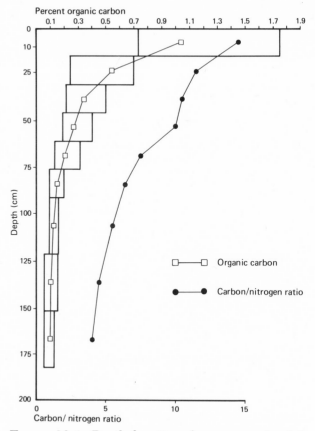

FIGURE 13.4 Depth functions for mean carbon/nitrogen ratio *(dots)*, mean organic carbon content *(squares)*, and range of variation in organic content *(bars)* in soil profiles from middle terrace sites of the Sa project area.

falling to less than 4.5. The high weathering of the environment and siliceous parent deposits are further reflected in low base saturation (less than 50%) and low cation exchange capacities (less than 15 m.e./100 g of clay). Kaolinitic clay minerals predominate, but sesquioxides are important mineral constituents, often in amounts which could influence phosphate fixation appreciably.

Under swiddening it is unlikely that deficiencies of calcium, magnesium, or potassium would ever be serious in relation to nitrogen or phosphorus supply, as ash from firing provides a localized concentration of these elements and an increase in surface pH which is probably adequate for a least one year of cropping. Nevertheless, under clean cultivation and annual cropping, additions of these elements may be necessary, especially when nitrogen fertilizers are used. In this respect, there are indications from crop trials that calcium supply may be limiting development of peanuts, as the percentage of "pops" and poorly developed kernels is high.

OTHER ESSENTIAL ELEMENTS

At present there is no analytical information for other important macronutrients or trace elements. It is clear, however, that some, such as sulfur and molybdenum, are in low total supply in several of the major middle terrace series. Relatively severe deficiencies have been detected in pot experiments with peanuts as the test species.

SOIL BIOLOGY

MINERALIZATION OF ORGANIC NITROGEN

One of the most unexpected features of initial cropping on project farms and experimental plots has been the excellent early growth of upland rice. In most instances this vegetative response has been carried through and realized in higher grain yields, yet it is the color and vigor of crops in their first six to eight weeks of growth which is most remarkable when it is remembered that the soils used had previously been regarded as overworked and were returning very low swidden yields. The contrast between a poor swidden crop and a good one on mechanically cultivated project farms is evident in photos 129 and 130. Although the comparison is not entirely valid in that the swidden rice is only four weeks old while the other is seven

weeks from planting, it is quite apparent that the former is a much inferior stand and will remain so.

Physical disturbance, long-continued drying, and high temperature are all influential in promotion of biological activity when the soil is subsequently wetted, and their effects are particularly well documented in soils literature. Thus, as project operations include the first thorough physical breakup that terrace soils have ever had, improved rice yields on unfertilized farm plots might reasonably be attributed, at least in part, to enhancement of mineral nitrogen production early in the rainy season. If this is indeed the case, the excellent rice yields which have been obtained without use of fertilizers in early years on developed farms can only be described as the "mining" of a limited total nitrogen pool. The ability to reap such short-term rewards is of advantage to both farmers and the project operation itself, as it provides the opportunity to generate a cash surplus in the first year that can later be used to obtain fertilizers for subsequent legume crops, which have the potential of fixing atmospheric nitrogen symbiotically and so restoring soil reserves. Exploitation of organic nitrogen reserves need not have serious long-term consequences provided production represents a high percentage recovery by the crop of the total pool of mineral nitrogen released by microorganisms during the wet season. But if efficiency is low and loss by leaching of soluble nitrogen is appreciable, repeated stimulation of biological activity could lead to a degree of nitrogen depletion which would make recovery to a level for maintenance of adequate yields a difficult agronomic problem in the existing economic setting. As far as grain removal is concerned, the drain on reserves is small; for example, the mean rice yield of 2,500 kg/ha obtained on experimental farms in 1967 represents a withdrawal from the site of about 40 kg of nitrogen per hectare, whereas the top 5 cm of Sa middle terrace soil contains something like 1,300 kg N/ha of surface.

In view of the above, it is of some importance to know the extent and pattern in time of mineralization in the early weeks of the wet season when the major flush of biological activity can be expected. The magnitude of potential leaching losses depends very largely on the relative production of the ammonium and nitrate forms of mineral nitrogen. The former is retained in the profile to a considerable extent by adsorption on exchange surfaces, while the latter is completely soluble and therefore easily washed out by heavy rain. Because the terrace soils are fairly acid it would be anticipated that nitrification is limited and mineralization mainly a matter of ammonium ion buildup. However, immediate surface soil is commonly in the physiological pH range for active nitrification (figure 13.1D), and this is the zone where organic nitrogen concentration is highest. Accordingly, if an active population of nitrifiers exists in the topsoil, nitrate could constitute a significant fraction of the inorganic nitrogen pool.

In order to resolve this question, a collection of 10 profiles taken from newly cleared project sites in Nan and Lampang was tested for mineral nitrogen production under aerobic incubation conditions. The results from this experiment are summarized in figure 13.5. The data cannot be taken as accurate measures of production rate in the field because the laboratory method sets conditions as near to optimal as possible and these seldom apply for any length of time in the natural situation. Nonetheless, the results do give a fairly reliable indication of the balance between ammonium and nitrate production. They show that the broad cross section of terrace soils included are all active nitrate producers in the surface, but that the organisms involved are of small importance below about 15 cm. Though

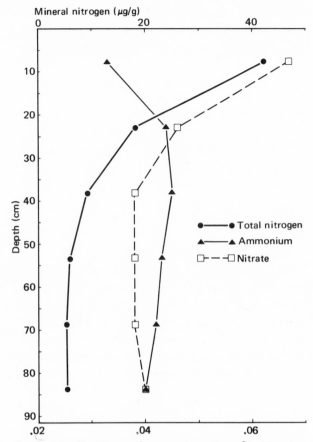

FIGURE 13.5 Mean changes in mineralization activity with depth, in samples taken from 10 profiles of low nitrogen, middle terrace soils of the Sa project area; production of nitrogen in the form of ammonium and nitrate during nine weeks of aerobic incubation.

ammonification predominates throughout most of the profile, the degree of nitrification which takes place in the immediate surface would almost certainly be sufficient to constitute a loss risk if heavy rains came prior to establishment of a dense crop root system.

Under swidden conditions the course of mineralization in these soils is probably very similar to that which occurs after clearing and cultivation, except that the stimulation due to disturbance would be absent. The difference between the two land preparation procedures with respect to potential leaching of soluble nitrogen should nonetheless be marked, as established root systems already exist to some extent in swiddened ground, and rapid regrowth of native species following initial rains ensures active uptake of nutrients shortly thereafter.

Just as soil nitrogen can be depleted by leaching when organic forms are oxidized to the nitrate ion, so also can sulfur be lost when organic compounds of this element are converted to sulfates by the activity of microorganisms. In this case, however, leaching loss is potentially more serious because, unlike nitrogen, sulfur is not returned to the soil by natural agencies to anything like the extent which is possible for nitrogen through symbiotic fixation by legumes. The evidence from pot experiments is that the sulfur status of middle terrace soils is already low enough to cause acute deficiency symptoms in relatively high-demand crops, such as some legume species. This condition might therefore be expected to worsen under clean cultivation farming where leaching should be increased.

LEGUME NODULATION

In 1968 and again in 1969 a survey of peanut and mung bean nodulation was carried out in crops grown on terrace swiddens, permanent upland fields, and wet rice bottomlands, with the objective of determining whether ineffective nodulation could be a reason for the generally low yields returned by these potentially productive species. Plants were dug in a great number of fields scattered over most of the major terrace areas in the northern provinces, but none could be described as well nodulated. All were nodulated to some extent, yet the color, size, and distribution of nodules over the root systems indicated either that native strains of *Rhizobium*

in terrace soils are only marginally effective in nitrogen fixation, or that host plant nutrition is sufficiently poor to prevent an effective symbiosis.

From any viewpoint, maintenance of an adequate soil nitrogen status will always be a problem facing intensified agricultural development of any terrace areas because the economic limitations mentioned previously are likely to put restraints on the amounts of fertilizer which can be recommended to farmers with some confidence of acceptance. For this reason, determination of crop culture conditions necessary for satisfactory yields and effective nitrogen fixation is of immediate importance.

Early experimental work seemed to indicate that the solution to the nodulation problem was little more than inoculation of seed with an appropriate strain of *Rhizobium*, together with a modest application of agricultural lime. Subsequent work in the field and glasshouse has shown that soils of the middle terrace series differ with respect to microbial and nutritional influences on nodule formation. Thus, significant increases in nodule development and dry-weight accumulation have been obtained with peanuts grown in pots following additions of lime, phosphorus, sulfur, molybdenum, and inoculum, but the pattern of response to these five treatments in terms of main effects and interactions has not been consistent between soils collected from different middle terrace locations. Accordingly, it is not possible at this stage to make a general recommendation that can be applied with absolute confidence to all of the major soil series so far encountered on middle terraces. Nevertheless, as phosphorus and sulfur deficiencies are widespread, and lime pelleting of inoculated seed is a simple and inexpensive procedure, light applications of superphosphate and the use of treated seed are likely to be worthwhile in all situations, even though some components of the additions may be unnecessary on particular soils. On the most acid soils, light applications of agricultural lime may also be beneficial as nut-in-shell yield increases of 25 percent have been obtained from superphosphate-treated peanut plots following surface broadcasting of calcium carbonate. Although these yield responses have not yet been converted to nitrogen increments, it is quite obvious from the few plant analyses which have been completed that inputs sufficient to sustain a following crop of rice are being realized provided all trash is returned to the ground and incorporated into the organic nitrogen pool of the soil. Photo 131 gives a general indication of the growth response which can be expected when all conditions are favorable for active nitrogen fixation.

CROP TRIALS

When the T.A.L.D. project began in 1967 a large demonstration and research trial (Sa 1) was started at the Sa experiment station. This trial was set up with two quite separate objectives: first, and more important at the time, to serve as a demonstration to farmers of what might be done with middle terrace soils using the standard crops of the area; and second, to provide the first information on fertilizer responses and nutrient rundown in these soils when they are taken out of a swidden cycle into a clean cultivation, annual-cropping system.

In order to give the greatest possible appearance of legitimacy, the experimental area was subdivided into four "farms," and these were handed over to local farmers to operate as their own, with no inputs other than labor called for and all produce going to the owners. This experiment was subsequently repeated on the same plots for three successive years, and, while there were shortcomings in its design and management which rule out use of the results for anything more detailed than preliminary assess-

ments of soil potential under cropping, its demonstration function has been remarkably successful.

The most interesting features of the results (figure 13.6) are the high rice yields in all treatments in the first year and the rapid rate of yield decline shown by cotton, maize, and rice over the three years, notably on the control plots. The legume yields were erratic and did not show consistent trends or clear responses to fertilizers. Seasonal differences may explain the peanut and mung bean yield increases of 1968, as this was a more favorable year than the previous one.

In the general area of the experiment, rice yields on swiddens were apparently in the range 600–1,200 kg/ha. Yet on unfertilized land which had been cleared and thoroughly prepared the return in the first year approximated 2,500 kg/ha. Thereafter, yields fell dramatically but even after three years without fertilizer they remained at or above the top swidden yields.

Later field experiments on a range of different sites have given good initial rice crops. Similarly, the first farms developed and planted at Sa returned yields well above swidden results. Thus it is now standard practice to advise farmers not to use any fertilizer in their first year of cropping on project-developed land. With minor exceptions this recommendation has proved itself and probably contributed to farmer acceptance of the project as a whole. Later demonstrations of use of fertilizer on farms already cropped several times to rice have given clear visual proof of the advantages of the light sulfate of ammonia dressings, and this follow-up practice is expected to be incorporated without resistance into the recommendation pattern.

Of the other crops commonly grown in the area, cotton and maize have been discouraged at this stage, the first because it is relatively difficult agronomically and requires considerable

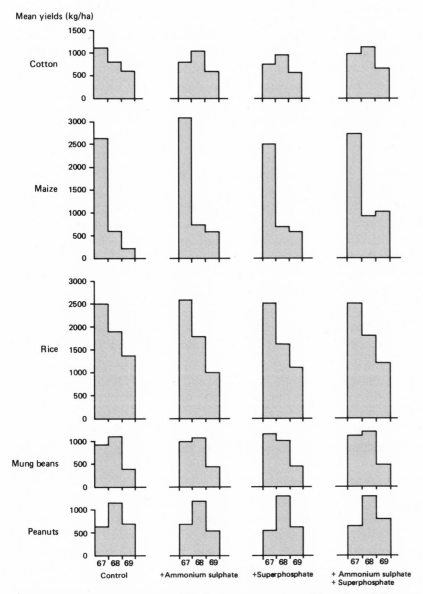

FIGURE 13.6 Mean crop yields (kg/ha) on over-swiddened middle terrace soils of the Sa experiment station following clearing and cultivation for three successive years. Histograms show mean yields for 1967, 1968 (when fertilizers were applied), and 1969, for different crop and fertilizer combinations. Note the initial yields of cotton, maize, and rice on control plots, and their subsequent decline.

cash outlay for disease and pest control, the second because it is unreliable on the terrace soils, poorly priced on the local market, and hard on these erosion-prone soils. Peanuts and mung beans have therefore attracted most attention; both have a ready local market, are well priced, and capable of good yields. More importantly, however, they are looked to as a source of "free" nitrogen in rotations with rice.

Despite a fairly comprehensive program of research, rainy-season yields of peanuts have been disappointing and not greater than the 1,200 kg/ha nut-in-shell obtained in the second year of the Sa 1 trial. Inoculation of seed with *Rhizobium* and application of superphosphate have not been effective, even though pot experiments on the same soils have demonstrated marked deficiences. On the other hand, field experimentation with hand watering in the dry season has shown that very satisfactory results can be obtained from the crop with careful band placement of superphosphate and surface broadcasting of lime. Under these conditions nut-in-shell yields approaching 4,700 kg/ha have been recorded on small plots given both fertilizers, while plots with lime only gave approximately 2,100 kg/ha.

Examination of peanuts from a wide range of sites has shown a very high percentage of "pops" and poorly filled, shriveled kernels, clear evidence that calcium nutrition is inadequate for seed development on unamended soils which have been cropped several times. Further, plumules with black margins, another indication of calcium deficiency in fruit formation, may be found in seed samples from upland and lowland fields. It is not surprising, therefore, that nut-in-shell yields have been increased substantially by applications of lime to the fruiting zone of peanuts supplied with banded superphosphate. In the absence of superphosphate, surface lime is ineffective. Whether or not the same responses can be obtained on farmers' fields remains to be seen, as accuracy of placement of superphosphate with respect to seed and placement of surface lime with respect to the fruiting zone appear to be quite critical.

A deficiency in boron may also be limiting production. Addition of this element has not given responses in pot experiments, but the typical "hollow-heart" symptom has been noticed in some seed samples.

While peanuts remain something of a problem crop on the terrace soils, results with mung beans planted late in the rainy season have been quite encouraging. This species yields well and appears to be more reliable than peanuts. Given correct treatment it forms nodules freely and is undoubtedly capable of an effective nitrogen input to the soil. A further advantage is that farmers usually plant this crop following harvest of early rice or peanuts, thereby getting two crops in one season. If it follows peanuts, there is the possibility of two nitrogen increments through symbiotic fixation. Because of the above advantages, the species holds great promise as a cash crop. In consequence, once reliable cultivation and nutritional practices have been determined for middle terrace soils, a marked expansion in current plantings can be expected. However, although the potential value of the species seems to be appreciated by local farmers, the low yields and high labor requirement of serial picking at a time when the major rice harvest is underway may more than outweigh the good market price of the crop.

A number of other crop species have been introduced on experimental plots for purposes of observation and evaluation, but as yet little has been done to determine their yield capability. The whole emphasis to date has been on rice, peanuts, and mung beans as these are well known to farmers and seed supplies are readily obtainable.

CONCLUSION

Land-use change that entails removal of all trees and tree regrowth potential from a swidden constitutes a fundamental ecological modification with far-reaching implications for subsequent cropping. Destruction of the larger, deep-rooted trees and shrubs, which comprise the fertility restoration potential of the swidden cycle, inevitably means that the chemical inputs of the bush fallow, and the nutrient redistributions which result from litter turnover and the slash-and-burn, are eliminated, and other means must be looked to for maintenance of soil fertility. An entirely different input strategy involving cash outlay is unavoidable if satisfactory yield level and stability are to be achieved. Unfortunately, however, situations in northern Thailand which call for such basic alteration of land use are commonly those whose economic setting is least likely to allow the necessary expenditure. Accordingly, success of agronomic innovation is not simply a question of resolving the technicalities of the particular situation, but a matter of answering cropping problems in ways that are economically realistic. This is not unusual, of course. Such economic restraints apply in virtually every agricultural endeavor. But when the context is a subsistence economy, the restraints imposed on agricultural research are much more formidable and allow much less room for maneuver. Complicate the situation further by attempting the fundamental ecological change on terrain whose soils occupy the lower end of the fertility spectrum and the problem begins to appear insoluble.

Despite appearances, successful cropping of the middle terrace areas in northern Thailand may be achieved relatively simply and inexpensively if the major input requirement of nitrogen can be had by means of the same process which operates in a bush fallow. Symbiotic fixation of atmospheric nitrogen by crop legumes may under favorable circumstances reach a level sufficient to meet the needs of a following rice crop.

Although the soils are deficient in a number of essential elements, research to date has indicated that relatively minor additions of a simple fertilizer mixture may be adequate for effective nodulation of peanuts and mung beans. If this result can be successfully transferred to the more exacting conditions of farmers' fields, and providing retained nitrogen is not seriously depleted by leaching in the following rainy season, then one of the major requirements will have been met in part. It is unlikely that a continuous rice-peanuts rotation can maintain a reasonable yield level, but this is not essential. Several consecutive years under legumes could be substituted as these crops are very profitable when yields are good.

Other elements which are naturally restored to the surface soil under swiddening must of necessity be supplied in fertilizers, yet this too may not involve a great cash outlay if part of the income from high yields of unfertilized rice in initial cropping can be set aside for purchase of fertilizer in the second year of cropping.

Overall, middle terrace terrain presents a complex problem for agricultural development aimed at annual cash cropping. Not only are the soils nutritionally extreme, but seasonal variability is high and the erosion hazard ever present. Nonetheless, there is every indication that a reasonably stable agricultural economy can be worked out for these areas provided the basic objective of development is stability of yield moderately above that of swiddening, not the pursuit of crop potential in relation to environment. Once basically reliable fertilizer and planting practices have been developed for several of the major terrace soil series, it will no doubt be possible to adjust these practices to obtain more favorable crop responses for the investment in fertilizer. In the early stages, however, it would seem advisable to minimize the degree of technological change asked of farmers who have had little if any experience with fertilizers or modern cultivation and planting methods. By proceeding slowly with agronomic change, modifications of traditional practice are more likely to be accepted and the degree of economic risk imposed on farmers by outlays for fertilizer and other materials held to a reasonable level. Such, anyway, has been the general philosophy of agricultural innovation on the T.A.L.D. project areas; it remains to be seen whether it can lead to a stable farming scene significantly more prosperous than an economy based on swiddening.

14

The Fermented Tea *(Miang)* Economy of Northern Thailand[1]

F. G. B. Keen

The geographical distribution of the tea tree *(Camellia sinensis)* covers extensive areas of mainland Asia's uplands. East and west it has been found from Assam to the southern hills of eastern China along approximately latitude 29°N, while from northeastern Burma at about longitude 98°E, it spreads southward through Yunnan, the Shan States of Burma, northern Thailand, and Laos to the hills of southern Viet Nam (Harler 1964:4). From these origins it has been taken to many parts of the world, including Africa, southern India, Sri Lanka, and South America, where it has long maintained popularity mainly as the source of the beverage.

It is generally believed that present-day strains of tea originated from three primary types: the China variety which is small-leafed and bushy, the Assam type which has large, glossy leaves, and the Cambodian type with "long, narrow, turned-up leaves" (Harler 1964: 5). Commercial strains of tea and even many "wild" types are hybrids of these basic plants.

Tea grows freely and apparently "wild" in northern Thailand, but in the light of the very considerable human migrations which have taken place in Southeast Asia over the last two or three millennia it is impossible to say for certain how far man has been responsible for its presence. The plant is rarely more than 5 meters high, with large, smooth, shiny, and slightly serrated leaves, bearing characteristics of both Assam and Cambodian strains.

Both soil and climate in northern Thailand are suited to the needs of tea (from a production viewpoint), as the growing rhythm induced by the wet and dry monsoons and the somewhat acid soils help improve the flavor (Harler 1964: 23, 45).

The practice of fermenting tea leaves by steaming them and then storing them away in some manner which excludes air, such as in pits or sealed baskets is widespread throughout the original homeland of the tea plant. Green tea is an old traditional drink in China and Japan, where the tea leaves are most commonly dried after the fermenting period is over, and then prepared for consumption by pouring boiling water over the leaves. In Burma and Thailand, where tea is drunk primarily by urbanites, it is also prepared and used quite differently in each case, in its own distinct way.

The people of the Shan States of Burma, and

the Northern Thai people make fermented or "pickled" tea for consumption within their own countries. In Burma the product is called *leppet-so*. The inhabitants of Tawngpeng, one of the northern Shan States, grow tea in significant quantities in hill country, at altitudes of between 1,000 and 1,500 meters. It is processed by individual farmers into *leppet-so* and then sold at Kyaukme, about 110 km away by road, where its trade is the sole business for 40 or more brokers (Harler 1964:207). Therefore it is a product of some value and importance.

The Shan method of processing the leaf and the manner of consumption are very different from the Northern Thai system. The leaves are placed in wooden containers which have a plaited bamboo base. These are stood over a pot of boiling water for 10 minutes or so and the contents then thrown on a mat and kneaded for 10 minutes. The leaves are then placed in a pit about 1.5 meters in diameter and 2 meters deep, lined with bamboo mats and banana leaves. Nowadays this pit is often made of concrete. Steamed and kneaded leaf is added as it is processed, and the pit's contents are weighted down by planks with stones on top. This *leppet-so* is allowed to ferment in the pit for a minimum of 10 days but may remain there for six months or more, just as in Western countries green fodder is preserved as silage.

The product is packed for sale in bamboo baskets which hold 50 kg or so. They are first smeared with cattle dung and lined with banana leaf to exclude air. Small quantities of *leppet-so* for home use may be rammed into hollow bamboo stems. According to custom, different types and qualities are classified by the time of the year when the leaf was picked and the part of the pit in which it was preserved.

Before being eaten, the *leppet-so* is washed in salted water. Then it is prepared as a salad with oil, garlic, onions, dried prawns, and so on.

Among the Northern Thai tea producers, whose operations are the main concern of this paper, the product is called *miang*. The leaves are steamed for a much longer period, two hours or so, and fermentation takes place in the sealed bamboo containers in which the *miang* is sold. In northern Thailand it is often consumed as a part of social custom, like cigarette smoking or beer drinking. When visitors come or when the family is seated together in the evening, the *miang* is passed around from one to the other. A jar of coarse salt and sometimes a condiment such as chopped peanuts goes with it. Each person takes a small bundle of leaves, rolls them up into a wad like chewing tobacco with a lump of salt in the center, and pops the lot into his mouth. Both men and women use it daily.

LAND TENURE IN THE *MIANG* ECONOMY IN NORTH THAILAND

In terms of labor and land, *miang* production is the major tree crop economy of upland Chiang Mai Province, perhaps even of the northern Thailand hills if we except forestry itself. For example, in the area of 205 sq km set aside for resettlement of "hill-tribes" in Chiang Dao District there were, in October 1969, 30 villages of Northern Thai people occupying uplands, with a total of 2,416 people. Of these, 24 villages comprising 1,382 people were almost wholly dependent on *miang* for their livelihood (Oughton and Imong 1970, table II; see above, pp. 202–204 for further details).

The customary method of establishing a *miang* orchard, at least in the past, has been simply to clear the forest from around already growing trees. Thus, an "orchard" may be only a winding path, perhaps 6 meters wide, cut through the forest for several hundred meters, wherever the tea trees may be growing. In recent years a few people have begun to augment their "wild" trees by planting seedlings, either nursery raised or transplanted from the forest. This practice tends to block out the fields into more orthodox shapes.

Government policy will probably work toward encouraging this practice, as the authorities have recognized the increasing presence of Thai people in the uplands. This land is strictly forest reserve, and it is illegal to occupy or use it (chapter 3). However, since 1960, new regulations have empowered district officers to grant usehold titles and charge an annual tax on former forest reserve uplands. The tax is 3 *baht* (US 15 cents) per *rai*, and titles follow the lowland system for occupation of new lands by farmers (see chapter 3). There are four separate kinds of title to rural land in Thailand, three of which, as usehold titles, are obtainable by upland settlers. None of these titles permits the user to *sell* or transfer the land or the right to use it to anyone outside his family.[2] The fourth, outright ownership, is not granted in the hills.

Except where titles are involved, neither the size of the field nor the number of trees is of great significance to the proprietor of a *miang* orchard. What is important is the knowledge of precisely which trees are his, because the annual yield of particular trees may vary from a single *kam* (double handful, the unit of production) or less, up to 130 *kam* for a well-grown 20-year-old tree. For this reason the farmer is always aware of the exact location of his field boundaries, no matter how irregular they are, rather than of the size of his fields. It is not realistic to try to estimate typical yields per unit area, because of variations in yield per tree and also because of the great variations in tree density in orchards where a great part or perhaps all of the stock includes simply wild trees growing naturally. Thus most producers have a clear expectation, based on experience, of a total yield for the season, but no other interest in the dimensions of their orchards.

This approach is reflected in the system of renting, which is based on a share of the yield. The central figure in the system is the *pawliang*. Literally this means "father who feeds us," but in Northern Thai the connotation is quite different. It is used to describe three types of people: a landlord, a money-lender, or any outstandingly rich man. In the same way, the term *maeliang* is applied to a woman who fills any of these roles.

The *pawliang* receives a traditional customary proportion of rent, described as "two-thirds of the second picking." Tea leaves for *miang* are picked four times a year; the second picking is the largest, yielding about one-third of the total annual harvest.

There are three main categories of *pawliang* in the *miang* economy. First, there is the one who represents to all *miang* orchardists the ultimate symbol of success. He is the successful peasant who, through hard work in his *miang* orchard, aided perhaps with good luck, has saved the money to buy lowland paddy fields and rent out his tea trees to some less fortunate fellow. This is the basic objective in taking up a *miang* orchard. People with no paddy fields on the plains have a traditional hope in North Thailand. They may go the hills to "seek their fortune," so that they can return and buy paddy land. Most will live out their lives in the hills, but the successful few keep alive the ideal for the rest (Van Roy 1971).

Another type of *pawliang* is one who has acquired some kind of government title to the land on which the peasants live. He is usually a businessman who holds a government lease. In some cases he acquired this before, and in other cases after, the villagers who pay him rent occupied his land. He also receives the traditional rent portion referred to above.

Both of the above types of people renting out land receive in reality a larger share than the nominal one because they are paid on the basis of the full value of the *miang* with none of the very considerable production and freight costs deducted.

The most rapacious, and unfortunately the most common, *pawliang* is the money-lender. The usual technique is to lend money, especially it seems, to young married couples. When the borrowers are heavily in debt they are invited to go to the hills and produce *miang* for their creditor, very often on land over which he already exercises some control. Theoretically these poor folk receive a little less than the basic producer's price, but in practice a great many of them get advances of rice and almost nothing else, while all that they produce goes directly to the *pawliang*. The reason for buying the debtor's *miang* at below the normal price is said to be that in these cases the *pawliang* must pay all cash outlays himself, as his tenants usually will not have cash. He must therefore allow for the expense of getting the *miang* to market. However, the combination of low prices for *miang*, high interest, and high prices for advances of rice and other essentials make it extremely difficult to get out of debt.

There is a fourth kind of person to whom rent may be paid, though he is not a *pawliang* in the eyes of the villagers. Some peasants grow old in the village, without sons or daughters to carry on the work in the *miang* orchard. These people may let the trees to another villager, year by year at a rental paid in *kam*, and agreed upon between the two parties, not necessarily the customary payment of "two-thirds of the second picking."

TECHNIQUES AND COSTS OF *MIANG* PRODUCTION AND MARKETING

The tea trees are allowed to grow to their normal height of about 5 meters; so makeshift bamboo ladders are needed to pick the larger ones. A ladder is usually just a notched pole leaning into a forked branch, for the picker to stand on. The pickers, both men and women, go to their work carrying a large basket and a small bundle of thin bamboo strips *(tawk)* about one cm in width with which to tie the leaves into the small, fist-sized bundles called *kam*. Pickers of average skill can pick about 50 *kam* per day, for which the usual payment is 10 *satang* per *kam*. Thus the picker expects to earn 5 *baht* for a day's wage. (One *baht* = US$0.05; 1 *baht* = 100 *satang*.) This is only about half the "normal" average wage for a laborer in unskilled work in North Thailand, where scales of wages run from approximately 4 *baht* per day for women, to 10–12 *baht* for men doing hard work. However the work is considered easy, and expert pickers can pick up to 100 *kam* if the leaf has been good.

Labor for picking comes from the family—husband, wife, and older children—augmented by workers who live in the village. There are usually several families in a *miang* village who neither own nor rent orchard land and are entirely dependent on day labor. In addition to picking, the fieldwork consists of keeping other varieties of trees cut down to facilitate movement and to ensure that they do not compete with the tea.

Another important task is cutting and transporting the firewood necessary to operate the *hai* (leaf steamer). Whether the owner of the orchard cuts his own firewood or not depends on many factors, such as his age, the scale of his operations, and his capabilities. Firewood must be cut into lengths of about 2 meters and then split with wedges into convenient sizes for burning; about 100 sq cm in section is considered suitable. Some farmers employ laborers to fell the trees and chop or saw them into lengths, whereupon they will split them and transport the firewood home themselves. Others have the cutting and splitting done and provide their own transport. People who are no longer able to work hard pay to have their firewood delivered, while a few carry out the entire operation themselves.

As in all aspects of this very old traditional industry, there is a scale of charges which do not seem to have varied in the memory of the people operating with them. Apparently the inflationary economy, which has doubled rice and meat prices in the towns between 1965 and 1970, has not yet reached the Chiang Mai *miang* villages. At the place where it is cut, the firewood is worth about 600 *baht* per thousand pieces. Cutting logs into lengths is valued at 25 *satang* per cut, logs being chosen at around 30 to 40 cm diameter, which seems to suit both parties. At this rate, a laborer cutting logs can earn about 12 *baht* per day, but if he is lucky enough to be employed to split the logs as well, he may earn up to 30 *baht*. It is common in the Chiang Dao area for certain ethnic minority people such as Hmong, who are recognized as skillful woodsmen, to be employed in this work.

Thus the *miang* industry provides employment for local workers in addition to those living in *miang* villages. Transport costs vary with distance to be carried, but can add as much as 300 *baht* to the cost of a thousand sticks of firewood. The usual method is to use pack cattle, as most *miang* villages are located above and beyond the services of wheeled vehicles.

Processing of the leaf is carried out at night by the family. The *hai* does double duty as the living-room fire in the house. The term *hai* is applied to the whole apparatus from fire pit to wooden steamer. It consists of a fire pit about 2 meters or more in length by 0.5 meter wide and deep. At one end a large iron boiler rests on two iron bars placed across the pit. The fire is lit

under the boiler, and the firewood lengths are pushed under as they burn. The *hai* has made an important difference in the structure of *miang* village houses, as compared with those of rice villages. Rice village houses are built clear of the ground, with room beneath for livestock, storage, and so forth, but houses in *miang* villages are built on the ground, with a platform for sleeping only about one meter above ground level.

Toward evening, pickers begin bringing in the day's bundles of leaves *(kam)* to be counted. The fire is lit, and the *kam* are packed tightly into a wooden barrel that has a base of bamboo mesh. It is placed over the iron boiler, and the top is covered over with banana leaf or sacking to keep in the steam.

After about one and a half hours, the barrel is removed and the *kam* tipped out on the floor of the house. Here they are untied, resorted, usually into slightly smaller bundles as the family seeks to increase its profit, and tied again with a pure white *tawk* about 2 cm wide. Great care is taken to protect these *tawk* so that they do not become discolored, as this reduces the attractiveness of the product. The *kam* are then carefully packed in large bamboo baskets *(tang)* specially made for the purpose, and lined with banana leaf. A *tang* holds about 330 *kam*, the actual number being written on a small piece of bamboo fitted into the lid of the *tang*. Once packed, they are left to ferment for an indefinite period, usually determined by the time it takes to accumulate a load for transport to market.

The manufacture of accessory objects for the *miang* industry—narrow picking *tawk*, wide packing *tawk*, and the *tang*—provides money-earning employment for numbers of people in both upland and lowland villages. The only requirement is a steady supply of bamboo. Young boys cut the bamboo into the appropriate lengths with their machetes and bring it home to the elderly men and women, who sit all day splitting the bamboo into *tawk* which the *miang* growers will buy for 4 *baht* per thousand. The *tang*, which an experienced person can make at the rate of one a day, bring 8 *baht* each. There is a regular market for these goods, as very few *miang* households are able to produce their own. The reason for this seems to be that much of the picking is still within the capabilities of the elderly folk in *miang* villages, so that their time is already occupied. Children in the villages spend part of their time gathering the wild banana leaf which is used for packing.

Transport of the *tang* to market is by pack cattle, or occasionally by packhorses, usually owned by some of the villagers. One *tang* is slung on each side of a beast over a packsaddle, and long lines of animals are a common sight on the mountain tracks, carrying *miang* to lowland market towns. For many people who lack their own pack animals, this is a further production cost. Freight rates are computed at 25 *baht* per day per thousand *kam*, and as each beast carries a little more than 600, it earns about 16 *baht* per day, probably twice what its owner could make by laboring.

Cattle are far more commonly used than horses. When not working, they graze among the tea trees on the native grasses, which thrive in the sunlight let in by removal of the forest. The animals help to keep the land clear while finding their own food, and they are permitted to roam freely on any person's land. This is another example of the peasant proprietor's concept of ownership being directed toward specific trees rather than to the land areas within which they grow.

Once the *miang* reaches a village or small town at the road end, it may be sold there, but alternatively it may be picked up by motor truck or bus and transported to a larger center. Freight rates by motor vehicle are much lower than those for cattle-back transport. The bulk of the loads will go to the *pawliang* of the particular village from which it comes. This man's role in the marketing organization is that of wholesaler. He buys from the independent growers, and takes delivery of the *miang* produced by his unfortunate debtors. Because *miang* can be purchased at most town and village shops and restaurants anywhere in northern Thailand, there is a great variety of retail outlets.

The price system shows little if any variation. An independent grower receives 50 *satang* per *kam* and pays all expenses including freight to the wholesaler. Indebted growers receive nominal prices of 30–40 *satang*, but in practice they receive advances of rice, salt, and other minimal necessities, such as essential clothing, in lieu of payment. The wholesale price seems to be standard at 1 *baht* per *kam*, while the retail value is 1.50 *baht*.

There appears to be no way by which the indebted grower can cheat his *pawliang*, who controls the market outlets and who, as a wholesaler, knows the amount that individual growers have produced. Every *tang* bears the name of the producer and the number of *kam*, so it is easily checked.

THE ECONOMICS OF *MIANG* AT THE FAMILY LEVEL

The population and land tenure situation for three villages for which we have detailed information is summarized in table 14.1. Pang Ma O was settled as early as 1890, but it also contains recent landless migrants from the valley; Mae Ta Man Nawk was settled at least by 1930, but 70 percent of its population are migrants who arrived after 1958; the longest-term resident of Mae Ta Man Nai arrived in about 1958.

TABLE 14.1   Land Tenure and Resources in Three *Miang* Villages

| | Village | | | |
	Pang Ma O [a]	Mae Ta Man Nawk	Mae Ta Man Nai	Total
Number of families:				
Total	36	10	13	59
Who own *miang* orchards	11	3	6	20
Who own part, rent part	2	1	2	5
Who rent only	20	4	3	27
Who neither rent nor own	3	2	2	7
Who own cattle	9	1	2	12
Who own no cattle	27	9	11	47
***Miang* land area (hectares):**				
"Owned" by villagers	28.00	11.04	16.96	56.00
Rented from absentee	52.16	8.96	10.56	71.68
Used without title			0.32	0.32

[a]Only about 85 percent of the land is occupied, the balance being steep slopes.

The table indicates that 39 of the 59 families (66%) are dependent partially or wholly on tenancy or wage labor for access to productive resources. The following brief descriptions suggest how the tenancy arrangements operate in the *miang* production system at the level of the primary production unit, the family.

About 1925 a Bangkok businessman applied to the government for a 50-year land lease in this locality for the purpose of establishing a dried-tea factory. The lease was granted, but the factory was never built because of financial difficulties. The 52.16-ha area now claimed under the lease includes the greater part of that occupied by Pang Ma O village, which was certainly in existence for many years before the lease was granted. The law recognizing usehold rights as a result of prior possession did not then exist (see chapter 3). The effect of the lease has been to allow the agents of the owner to come each year from Chiang Mai to collect the rent, payable in cash, calculated as the value of two-thirds of the second picking, at 0.5 *baht* per *kam*. The re-

mainder of the land, 28 hectares, is held under one or another variety of individual usehold titles by individual villagers (see note 2). The portion of the village area held by individual farmers represents either expansion into the forest fringe or purchase from the leaseholder of the right to claim a part of his leased land under title from the district office. This has been done in at least eight cases.

The people of Pang Ma O say with pride that "our village has no *pawliang*," by which they mean that other than paying rent, they have no obligations to the landowner, and can sell their *miang* wherever they want, to their best advantage, and for cash. The benefit of being able to do so is the difference between a price of 35 *satang* per *kam* sold through the *pawliang* and 75 *satang* per *kam* when sold to retailers in Chiang Mai.

A detailed study of the receipts and expenditures of one family shows the relative complexity of the economics of *miang* production on the family level. The family consisted of the hus-

TABLE 14.2   Receipts and Expenditures for a Pang Ma O Family for the Year 1968–1969

Receipts (baht)		Expenditures (baht)	
Sale of *miang* (20,000 *kam* @ 0.75)	15,000	Rent (4,740 *kam* @ 0.75)	3,555
Wages from picking	2,000	Wages for picking leaf	4,000
Wages from cutting firewood	600	Purchase of firewood	600
		Freight, firewood	200
		Freight, *miang*	1,200
		Balance (net return)	8,045
Totals	17,600		17,600

band and wife, both in their early thirties, the husband's younger brother, age 26, and four young children from 5 to 11 years. They had lived in Pang Ma O for 12 years and had use-rights over a field of 1.60 hectares, of which 0.32 hectare was producing tea, while young tea and coffee were being planted on the remainder as rapidly as seedlings became available. The family also rented 1.28 hectares, from which they derived their main harvest. They were cutting their own firewood as they cleared excess timber from their land.

The husband kept a written record of his receipts and expenditures from year to year. They owned no cattle and had to pay to have their firewood brought to the *hai*, as well as to have their *miang* carried to the road. The figures refer to the 1968–1969 season.

The family picked a total of 20,000 *kam*, of which 4,000 came from their own land and 16,000 came from the rented orchard. The family picked 10,000 *kam* and employed pickers for the additional 10,000. Processing consumed 1,000 pieces of firewood. The *miang* was transported to the road by cattle and thence to Chiang Mai by bus, where it was sold at 75 *satang* per *kam*. This family is one of the fortunate few who can organize the transport and sale of their product, bypassing the middlemen. For an investment of only 10 *baht* to transport

1,000 *kam* by bus to Chiang Mai, they can realize an additional 250 *baht* on the sale of the *miang* over the sale price to the landowner, or 400 *baht* over the sale price to a local money-lender.

Receipts and expenditures for the family were as shown in table 14.2. For this family of seven the per capita net income was 1,045 *baht* (US$52.25). A family that owns its own land and cattle can earn much more than this, but such families are rare. Picking wages in Pang Ma O and neighboring villages are about double those in other *miang* villages because there is a tea plantation within 3 km of the village that hires pickers at one *baht* per kilo. This works out to be about twice as much as the normal wages paid in areas at a greater distance from this source of employment.

Two *pawliang* control all rented land in Mae Ta Man Nawk and all the rented fields in the land of Mae Ta Man Nai, with the exception of one field rented to a young man by an elderly villager. This latter arrangement illustrates the type of tenancy which is arranged between two villagers.

The man who rents out the land, a man in his sixties, who had lived in Mae Ta Man Nai for 22 years, held title to 4.16 hectares of *miang* orchard—all wild trees. His wife was much younger than he, and of their five children only one was of working age. His orchard was too large to manage with his household labor alone, and for years he had rented 1.92 hectares to a younger man who had no other field. The tenant picked an average of 20,000 *kam* per season, for which he paid 2,500 *kam* as rent. The leaf was delivered green to the *rentier's hai* for him to process and sell. Picking and transport were the responsibility of the tenant. Both parties understood that if the tenant planted more tea trees, any increase in yield would not affect the rent, and if the yield decreased, the same would apply. There was nothing in this arrangement to inhibit the tenant from increasing his production, and some incentive to maintain or increase it.

By contrast, the oppressive practices of the *pawliang* are illustrated by another case. A tenant who came to the village in debt five years previously rented 2 hectares from his creditor. He picked an average of 18,000 *kam* per season from this, and paid rent nominally amounting to 2,000 *kam*, delivered to the *pawliang* in Mae Taeng. The remainder of the harvest had to be sold through the *pawliang* at the price of 35 *satang* (only US 1.75 cents). The entire proceeds of this sale went for interest and payments on the original debt. The *pawliang* allowed his debtor only the bare necessities of subsistence and kept the balance of the payments; he had been doing so for five years.

When questioned, the tenant could not (or would not) divulge the current state of his indebtedness, but concluded that he must increase his production to escape from debt. In an attempt to do this he had established a tea nursery when he first arrived in Mae Ta Man Nai, and two years later he had a closely planted orchard of 0.32 hectare. He expected to take his first small harvest in 1971 but, because of his debt, he would still have to sell his *miang* through the

same channels, at the same low price. He had no title to his nursery, nor had he yet applied to the district office for one, believing his application would be successful when he could face the district officer with a *fait accompli*, whereas he might be refused if the nursery was not yet producing.

Another case illustrates further the difficulties posed by a combination of high interest and low returns on produce sold through the creditor. A villager in Mae Ta Man Nai purchased a 1.04-hectare *miang* orchard on credit from the *pawliang* for 9,000 *baht* (US$450). He had harvested an average of 12,000 *kam* per year over six years, a total of 72,000 *kam*. Under the usual arrangement, he delivered the entire crop to the *pawliang* in Mae Taeng against the advance of the necessities of life. This system was to continue until the debt was paid. Our informant, the head of the family, told us he still owed 2,000 *baht* (US$100) after six years. Using Grist's figures (1959:367) for average rice consumption, and rather generously allowing double the retail cost of middle-grade rice as the total value of advances made to the family, it was calculated that 14,000 *baht* (US$700) had been repaid as interest and capital on the original amount of 9,000 *baht*. As this amount had reduced the sum owed by 7,000 *baht*, the rate of interest must have been at least 20 percent on the full value of the debt.[3]

It is apparent that investment on the part of money-lenders, in cases like those which have been described, is not in land or improvements, but in people. The land properly belongs to the state and has not been and cannot be bought. The *pawliang* has acquired only a usehold interest and has not improved it by clearing or planting. His investment is clearly in the person to whom he has lent the money. The Thai government is striving to bring education to all children in Thailand. It is appropriate to reflect on the possible future reaction of these impoverished people as they become educated and can better understand the true nature of such business transactions.

From the foregoing description it can be seen that the *miang* economy is a traditional, and strongly institutionalized, operation. The circumstances surrounding the stages of production, sale, and consumption are highly conventionalized, and expectations regarding all of these aspects are widely understood.

Theoretically, producers of *miang* are illegal occupiers of the forest reserve, though the fact that lowland population growth forces people to move to the uplands has been officially recognized in the last decade through the granting of usehold titles. Justifiable concern is felt in government circles that increasing occupancy of the uplands is being accompanied by rapid and continuing forest destruction.

MIANG CULTIVATION AS A SYSTEM OF FOREST USE

It is appropriate to consider the *miang* economy from several standpoints. As a destroyer of the forest, how does it compare with other upland agricultural systems? In terms of the population that it will support per unit area, how does it compare with possible alternatives? Finally, as it is deeply institutionalized, how much flexibility does it have? That is, could the people involved adapt their existing resources to a possible serious decline in demand for *miang*, which might, for instance, accompany social change in Thailand? From the national viewpoint, the first two questions are vital, the third perhaps equally so in the context of political unrest which accompanies economic problems almost everywhere.

As a tree crop, it would seem that by defini-

tion tea has certain advantages in terms of forest preservation. It is a plant that grows naturally in the forest, needing only judicious thinning to ensure that it will thrive. However, two factors militate against the continuing existence of the forested landscape.

Cattle are essential to the industry in the present circumstances, and they rapidly eat out the forest around the tea. (Fortunately, they do not like the tea leaves.) In appearance the *miang* orchards range from those where the forest is so thick that the tea trees can be found only by careful observation, to those which have no vegetation but the tea trees themselves and neatly cropped grass. The older and more established the village, the cleaner are its orchards. Unfortunately, there has been no compelling reason in the past to interest the peasant in close planting his orchard on small areas. As already mentioned, a high proportion are not planted at all, merely cleared around the trees where they happen to be most numerous in the forest. The result of this system of land use is that in most long-established villages there is very little vegetation on the cleared, cattle-grazed hillsides to reduce run-off during the wet season.

A second important cause of the steady denudation of forest is the unceasing and considerable demand for firewood. This takes the common species and, owing to the traditional system of letting informal contracts for the cutting of the logs, the firewood is cut from mature trees. Thus the demand for firewood eliminates the best forest specimens and also the trees that are important as suppliers of seeds for the future.

Specific evidence for the depletion of forest by a *miang* village is provided by Pang Ma O, a well-established village of 36 families set in steep mountainous country in Amphoe Chiang Dao, 19 km from Chiang Dao town. Here, about

TABLE 14.3 Population and Occupied Area in Three *Miang* Villages

Village	Population	Occupied Area (ha)	Area per Head (ha)
Pang Ma O	173	64.32	0.372
Mae Ta Man Nok	35	20.16	0.576
Mae Ta Man Nai	41	27.84	0.679
Totals	249	112.32	Mean 0.451

85 percent of village land is actually in *miang* orchards; the remainder is forested land in the steepest gullies. It is commonly understood among *miang* producers that 20,000 *kam* per year is a reasonable goal for production by a family. A conservative estimate of 15,000 *kam* per year for 30 of the 36 families, multiplied by the empirically derived estimate by *miang* producers of one piece of firewood for 20 *kam*, implies an annual burning of 22,500 pieces of firewood. Repeated observation and measurement, supported by the expectations of woodcutters, suggests a figure of 66 pieces per tree as a reasonable average; so annual use is equivalent to about 375 trees. The pieces of firewood average about 0.02 m³; so a total of about 450 m³ per year is used for 64.32 hectares of non intensive *miang* orchard cultivation.[4] While this is not a vast amount, its significance increases when the quality of the trees is taken into account, together with evidence for rapid growth in the number of *miang* producers. In the group of 24 *miang* villages studied in the Nikhom Chiang Dao Survey Area, including Pang Ma O, 9 have come into existence during the last 20 years.

Depletion of mature forest by *miang* producers is probably a more serious problem in the more recently settled villages. Pang Ma O is an old, established village settled for at least 80 years by *miang* producers, according to local people, and it is now entirely surrounded by other *miang* villages which restrict its expansion. In younger villages, where expansion is less limited, the area occupied by a household is often much larger than the average at Pang Ma O, and the depletion of forest may be considerably greater.

Evidence for this contrast in forest depletion rates between older and younger villages is set out in table 14.3, comparing Pang Ma O with two small and more recent villages (Mae Ta Man Nawk and Mae Ta Man Nai) which are located about 15 km northwest of the district town of Mae Taeng. In these two hamlets, only half a kilometer apart, the mean duration of settlement in 1970 was 7.5 years for Mae Ta Man Nai and 12.8 years for Mae Ta Man Nawk. Despite the relatively recent settlement, most households in Mae Ta Man Nawk are tenants or part-tenants, and a large part of the *miang* area is held under tenancy arrangements, as in Pang Ma O. In the two villages with the smaller populations, however, the *miang* area per capita was considerably greater than in Pang Ma O (table 14.3), suggesting that encroachment on forest land by more recent *miang* producers is proceeding more rapidly than the overall average might indicate. Presumably, this higher rate in newer villages will continue for some time, until the shortage of forest land or other restrictions lead to more intensive land use.

TABLE 14.4   Human Carrying Capacities of Various Upland Economies in the Chiang Dao Area

Village	Ethnic Group	Total Population	Land-Use Type	Fallow Period	Total Land Area per Head (ha)
Huay Tadt	Christian Lahu	200	upland rice swiddens coffee plantations	10 yrs nil	1.164 [a]
Pa Khia	Hmong	303	upland rice opium poppy	10 yrs 5 yrs	2.264 [a]

Parts of
  Pang Kyt and
  Pang Huay Tadt
	Northern Thai (laborers)	258	commercial dried tea plantation	nil	0.246 [b]

Pang Ma O, Mae Ta Man Nawk, Mae Ta Man Nai	Northern Thai	249	*miang* orchards	nil	0.451 [c]

[a] Including fallow.
[b] Information by courtesy of the managing director, Highland Tea Co., Chiang Mai, January 1970; assistance gratefully acknowledged.
[c] Not including land required for fuel production (see text and note 4).

MIANG AND OTHER FOREST FARMING SYSTEMS

There are only two other upland land use systems in this region with which the *miang* economy can be compared for relative density of population. These are the commercial dried tea industry and swiddening. Swiddens in the region are used in several different farming systems: for subsistence and cash crops, for subsistence only, and as a supplement to lowland wet-rice cultivation. The last type will be ignored in this reckoning as it is not clear just how many people are supported by supplementary swiddens, and in any case they are often neglected and yield very poorly (see chapters 12, 13).

Table 14.4 shows relative population densities, under the three different forms of upland land use, present in or near the area bounded by the Chiang Dao Hill Tribe Settlement Area *(nikhom)*. It is apparent from these data that the *miang* economy is capable of supporting a higher density of population than any form of swidden economy, even one such as that of the Lahu village, which is relatively efficient and supported by plantations to provide the cash income.

The commercial plantation employing laborers would seem to be the most efficient of all the existing alternatives if judged solely on the population density that it can support per unit area. At present it does not represent a true alternative to *miang* production, however, because of very limited opportunities for employment.

Population densities based on subsistence swiddening economies are likely to be *less* rather than *more* than those shown in table 14.4 if based on a wider area of sampling, for Kunstadter gives figures of 2.88 and 3.04 hectares per person for Karen and Lua' people in Mae Hong Son Province (chapter 6). Yields of upland rice recorded by Kunstadter (812.50 kg per ha) are much lower than those of the 1969 harvest recorded for Huay Tadt (1418.75 kg per ha) and Pa Khia (978.17 kg per ha). Allowing for this variation, the figures presented seem reasonably consistent with each other (for additional comparisons of values of various upland economies, see chapter 1).

The relative degrees of forest destruction caused by the several types of upland land use considered here are less easy to measure. Presumably the closely planted commercial tea plantation is a satisfactory substitute for native forest from the point of view of water and soil retention, so that it need not be considered as a hazard in this sense. On the other hand, swiddening varies a great deal in technique. Zinke (chapter 7), measuring erosion in Lua' swiddens, suggests an erosion rate as low as one mm per decade where firebreaks are cut, fallow periods are carefully maintained, and great care is taken to maintain maximum regrowth. At the other extreme, some swiddeners cultivate their fields to exhaustion, permit fires to spread, burn off indiscriminately, and in fact so destroy the forest that they must quite frequently migrate to new areas (Keen, chapter 10 and 1966:24–28). In these cases whole landscapes are transformed into tropical grass savanna in the space of one or two decades. At its worst, swiddening as a form of upland land use is therefore much more destructive to the forest than is *miang* production. At its best, swidden cultivation may be preferable area for area, but against this must be set the much greater land area required for a given population to cultivate swiddens than to produce *miang*. Thus, if the forest is regarded as an alternative resource, to supply timber for industry, the *miang* economy once again is superior to swiddening in permitting a greater density of people in smaller areas.

FUTURE PROSPECTS

Further expansion to provide for population increase within villages such as Pang Ma O will have to take the form of a more intensive pattern, that is, more tea trees per unit area. As

even the longest-established villages are beginning to change from the system of exploiting only the wild, chance-sown trees, there is certainly scope for at least doubling the number of trees in even the most densely growing present-day orchards.

A more difficult question to answer is how long growth in the *miang* market is likely to keep pace with the increases in production resulting from net in-migration. Fifty-seven percent of the households in the 24 *miang* villages surveyed within the area of the Chiang Dao *nikhom* have moved into them during the last 10 years; and while many of these families consist of only a young couple, they probably represent a rate of increase in *miang* village population rather greater than the national average, and much of the incoming population is of the working-age group on arrival. Even if no decline in per capita consumption of *miang* occurs in North Thailand, it is most probable that the ratio of producers to consumers is increasing. This implies a future decline in per capita income for the producers and a corresponding need for alternatives.

The possibility of decline in per capita consumption of *miang* is highly relevant to future market prospects. Data from a sample survey carried out in 1970–1971, while not conclusive, suggest a possible reduction in future demand (table 14.5). The figures indicate that while almost all northerners over the age of 25 use *miang* (actually 161 out of 164), only just over half of the younger group use it. On the other hand, only about one-fifth of immigrants from other parts of Thailand adopt the habit. From this sample study it would be possible to argue that consumption could decline because of increasing mobility of the population, as well as the changing tastes of younger people. It is interesting to note that of the 132 people of all categories who filled in the part of the question-

TABLE 14.5 *Miang* Consumption by Adults in Chiang Mai Province
(Sample Survey 1970–1971)

Place of Birth	Age Group	Consumers as % of Total	Number Interviewed
Northern Provinces	under 25 yrs	52.11	71
	over 25 yrs	98.17	164
Other parts of Thailand	under 25 yrs	23.73	118
	over 25 yrs	16.11	242
		Total	595

NOTE: The survey sampled people resident in Chiang Mai Province, both rural and urban. Birthplaces included 8 of the 12 northern provinces and 33 from the northeast, center, and south of Thailand. The survey was carried out with the assistance of the Faculty of Agriculture, Chiang Mai University, and the Tribal Research Centre.

naire giving reasons why they did not use *miang*, 80 stated that they disliked the taste or smell, 49 were unfamiliar with it, while only 2 in each case regarded it as too expensive or old-fashioned. Perhaps other refreshers such as chewing gum are now competitors.[5]

It can be argued that the *miang* economy has the characteristic weakness of monocultures in its vulnerability to adverse changes in any phase of production or marketing. Harler suggests that this characteristic applies to the tea industry generally, and especially to the commercial plantation system, requiring high investment in the processing sector (Harler 1964:246, 247). He cites the peasant tea grower of South China as being in a stronger position through growing his own subsistence crops as well as tea (1964: 246–247; cf. Pelzer's analysis of cash and subsistence cropping in Indonesia, chapter 14).

The *miang* industry in North Thailand is mainly a peasant monoculture, beset with fairly serious indebtedness and marked by an almost complete absence of any form of subsistence cropping in its most concentrated areas. However, on the positive side, the level of investment in either land or processing plant is very low by any standard. Farmers who are not in debt and who have not had to buy their orchards have in-

vested very little but their labor, except perhaps in cattle, which are easily liquidated assets. A less tangible but possibly more important asset is their general familiarity with other forms of agriculture. They produce *miang* because it appears in their circumstances to be the best alternative, not because they know no other crop. Another significant advantage is the frequent contact of the *miang* villages with the lowland plains. This contact is both human and commercial; people go to the market towns to visit their relatives or the temple, as well as to buy and sell goods.

Overall, the *miang* economy should perhaps be seen as lacking *diversification*, but not flexibility, as there is certainly no evidence of a conservative clinging to a way of life centered around a single economic activity. The problem is that of finding alternatives through which to diversify, rather than of overcoming resistance to innovations.

There could be a limited potential market in supplying leaf for the dried tea industry. At the present time a few *miang* producers in Chiang Dao *nikhom* sell a small amount of surplus leaf to the tea factory in their vicinity, at prices which are roughly similar to the possible earnings from *miang*. In this case the market is

TABLE 14.6 Intensification of Tea Production, 1938–1960

	Area Planted (thousands of ha)		Production (millions of kg)	
	1938	1960	1938	1960
World	864	985	485	969
India and Pakistan	340	363	205	365

SOURCE: Data from Harler (1964:251) converted to metric units.

small, as the company concerned has sufficient land to grow leaf for what it estimates as the potential market. As yet most of the company's land has not been brought into production, and in the future the peasant growers may be able to compete successfully against its development costs.

The potential market for dried tea in Thailand could possibly be increased by a greater level of government protection. As of 1970, tea blenders were required by law to use at least 25 percent of local leaf in packaged tea, but if this proportion were to be increased the local industry would benefit. Experience in other countries does not indicate that this could be enough to provide a market for a greatly expanded area of planting, as the supply could very easily come from more efficient and intensive cultivation of existing orchards, or even from a reduced area in production. Table 14.6 shows the degree to which tea cultivation has been intensified in other countries during the last few decades.

As shown in table 14.5, while tea acreage increased very little between 1938 and 1960, production has about doubled, and this has happened on commercial plantations. Potential increase per unit area must therefore be very great in North Thailand where many growers are still simply picking the wild plants.

Expansion of the tea industry in Thailand is probably limited to the national market. In the export field the situation does not indicate any great increase in demand. The circumstances are peculiar in that the great tea *producers* are not the great per capita *consumers*. The annual consumption is 10 lbs per capita in the United Kingdom, 7.5 lbs in New Zealand, 7 lbs in the Irish Republic, 6 lbs in Australia, but only 2.5 lbs in Ceylon (Sri Lanka) and 0.75 lb per person in India (Harler 1964:254). The countries of high per capita consumption are those with relatively smaller populations and slower growth rates; that is, there is no reason to expect any rapid growth in the export market.

CONCLUSION

The opportunities for development and diversification can be summarized as follows:

1. Consolidation of *miang* orchards onto smaller, more densely planted areas, preferably toward the lower size limits of the existing ones. This would help reduce the destruction of forest on steep slopes, which is essential for the protection of soil and watershed resources. Some modification in local interpretation of land laws would be required in order to accomplish this.

2. Diversification of the economy to include other crops and more livestock (with careful attention to problems of overgrazing). Greater emphasis should be placed on supplying subsistence needs as a way of reducing the almost absolute vulnerability to possible changes in the monocrop market.

3. Improvement of credit and marketing organization to ameliorate the problem of indebtedness of the *miang* producers without losing the expertise of the *pawliang* wholesalers, who form an essential link between producer and consumer.

4. Introduction of perpetual woodlot plantations of fast-growing trees for fuel. Again, this would require a change in interpretation of the land laws but might appeal to the *miang* pro-

ducers on the basis of reduction in fuel costs, especially as fuel becomes scarce in the vicinity of the villages.

Reviewing the total situation, we may conclude that the *miang* economy shows a degree of flexibility in that leaves for *miang* and dried tea are interchangeable. There is also scope for greatly intensifying production and at the same time reducing the total area under tea, but the eventual market for tea is probably limited. There is no reason to think that the *miang* producers would resist soundly based attempts to diversify their economy, and, in view of the rapid rate of population growth through migration from the lowlands, there is every reason to assume that such diversification will become increasingly necessary as time passes.

NOTES

1. This chapter is a revised and edited version of a paper delivered at the Seminar on Contemporary Thailand, held at the Australian National University, 6–9 September 1971. A different version, together with a number of case studies, was published in 1972 by SEATO, Bangkok, under the title "Upland Tenure and Land Use in Northern Thailand."

For six months, from October 1969 to April 1970, the author was granted a SEATO Research Fellowship in North Thailand, during which time he carried out the research reported here. The author expresses special appreciation for the assistance and excellent advice given by the director and staff of the Tribal Research Centre, Chiang Mai, during the course of the study.

2. In the first stage, a man wishing to occupy and use a piece of land may apply to the district office for a title *(bai chong)* which gives him permission to use the land temporarily for agriculture. If he improves it and makes it productive to the satisfaction of the district officer, he may be granted a second title *(naw saw sam)*, which gives him the right to use the land and hand it on to his own family in perpetuity. It was recognized that many people occupied reserved forest before the regulations were established in 1960, and so a third variety of title *(saw kaw neung)* was established, similar to that of the *naw saw sam*, in cases where development which should have been carried out under a *bai chong* title was carried out without benefit of any title.

3. The stringency of these conditions for the debtor who has no access to land for subsistence crops is readily apparent. It should be remembered that rice is commonly borrowed at 50–100 percent interest in some parts of northern Thailand, as in the hills of Mae Sariang District (see chapter 6). The extraordinary difficulty of extricating oneself from a burden of this sort is easily imagined.—P.K.

4. At the rate described above, about 583 trees, or 699.629 m^3 of lumber, are used for each square kilometer of *miang* orchard per year. Khemnark et al. (1972) estimate that 12,882.76 m^3 of lumber of the required size is present per sq km in the Hill Evergreen forest of the Chiang Dao Hill Tribe Settlement. This means that each sq km of *miang* would consume the lumber from one sq km of Hill Evergreen forest in about 18.4 years. The forest might be able to replace this biomass during this period, but the quality of the lumber would not be as good as that prior to cutting (see chapter 16, table 1, n.2).—P.K.

5. An alternative explanation and prediction might be as follows: Assume that *miang* consumption is largely a habit of older Northern Thai people. Assume that the habit is more easily acquired during youth than at an advanced age. Then the newcomers arriving when they are young are more likely to pick up and continue the habit than are their elders. The figures of table 3 might support this argument, since they show a reversal of the age distribution of *miang* consumers in migrants from other parts of Thailand, as compared with those born in the North. Among the migrants, the highest proportion of *miang* users is in the younger age groups.—P.K.

15

Swidden Cultivation in Southeast Asia: Historical, Ecological, and Economic Perspectives

Karl J. Pelzer

HISTORICAL AND ECOLOGICAL PERSPECTIVES

Shifting cultivation is sometimes regarded as a regional phenomenon of Southeast Asia, but in fact it is a pantropic agricultural system found around the globe. It is useful to take an ecological approach to the study of this agricultural system, to look at its interplay with the environment, and to consider something of its history and potential. Swidden cultivation may well be the oldest system devised by man for use of his ecosystem that involves the combination of systematic cultivation of tree, root, and/or seed crops, and the primeval practices of hunting, fishing, and gathering. Thus, as Harris (1969:4) points out, an ecological approach to the development of shifting cultivation may also yield the most valid insights into the origin of agriculture.

In Southeast Asia, early man found himself in one or another of the many varieties of forest ecosystems: evergreen tropical rainforest, semideciduous forest, deciduous forest, montane forest, sandy littoral forest, mangrove forest, and so on. Tropical forests are characterized by large

numbers of species and a rapid turnover of organic materials, both in plants and in herbivorous and carnivorous animals. Among the animal populations, the more primitive organisms such as worms and insects, and the simpler plants such as bacteria and fungi play important roles in the rapid breakdown and decomposition of woody plant matter.

The swidden system may appear to be less sophisticated and is usually much less specialized than the other widely used agricultural systems in Southeast Asia—the wet-field lowland rice system and the plantation system. Nonetheless, swiddening as traditionally practiced has one unique and distinguishing feature. So long as the population density is below the system's carrying capacity, most swidden cultivators live in the forest with a relatively balanced ecosystem. They live in harmony and in intimate relationship with the forest, which provides food, medicines, ornaments made of flowers or seeds, fibers for clothing, bark for walling of houses or flooring or the making of baskets, gums, resins for incense and for caulking boats, wood oils, tannin for making cutch, dyes, fuel, (especially charcoal), leaves for roofing (such as *atap*) or shingles (made from the leaves of *Nipa fruticans*), and wood for construction of shelter, boats, tools, and weapons (Cobban 1969).

After the swidden cultivator clears a patch of forest for temporary production of crops, the forest tends to reoccupy the clearing. He may deliberately plant seeds of trees in such a clearing in order to speed up the reforestation. Many swidden cultivators develop balanced ecosystems, able to persist in the same locality for many generations, so long as the human population density is low and extensive burning, weeding, grazing, or other forces that interfere with successional processes are kept out of the old clearings.

In the course of development of food-producing economies, man began to pay special attention to a smaller number of plants than were his concern at earlier stages. A wide range of undomesticated plants was reduced to a much smaller number of domesticated root and/or seed crops, and these were further restricted with the development of monocrop systems. The successful swidden cultivator who is in balance with his environment manipulates the ecosystem of the forest, rather than transforming it drastically. He alters "selected components without fundamentally modifying its overall structure" (Harris 1969:6).

Sauer has speculated that the progenitors of the Southeast Asian swidden cultivators were fishing folk living along fresh waters. He postulates fresh rather than salt water because seaside vegetation contributed little to the inventory of domestic crop plants (Sauer 1952:23–24). "It may well be that among the earliest domesticates were multi-purpose plants set out around fishing villages to provide starch food, substances for toughening nets and lines and making them water resistant, drugs and poisons.

Food production was one and perhaps not the most important reason for bringing plants under cultivation" (Sauer 1952:27). For example, fiber, food, medicine, and magic and ceremonial color all come from the same plant, *Cordyline fruticosa* Goeppert (= *C. terminalis* Kunth., a species of the family Liliaceae). The Javanese eat the very young shoots cooked as a flavoring with rice. The sweet lower part of the swollen saccharine rhizome is also eaten (Burkill 1935: 671–672). Plants of the red-leafed races of *Cordyline* are grown at the four corners of a house.

There is evidence that the earliest important crop plants of Southeast Asia may have been root crops such as taro (*Colocasia esculenta*) and yam (*Dioscorea alata*). Burkill speculates that the yam must have evolved in Southeast Asia east of the Bay of Bengal. Its closest relative is *Dioscorea persimilis*, found in deep forests. Both taro and yam preceded rice (*Oryza sativa*) in Southeast Asia. Both were taken by man out into the Pacific and became staples on the high and low islands. The first migrations took place earlier than the development of upland and lowland rice (Pelzer 1945:6–7; Sauer 1952:32–33). Other early root crops of Southeast Asia were birah (*Alocasia macrorrhiza*), arrowroot (*Canna orientalis* and *Canna edulis*), and *Curcuma*, a genus of rhizomatous herbs of the ginger family, some of which yield starch or Indian arrowroot, others turmeric, used as a coloring material and as a condiment. *Curcuma domestica*, known as turmeric, is a domesticate of Southeast Asia, but it is not known to occur in the wild state, indicating very early domestication. The term birah is used from Atjeh to the Philippines where the plant is known as *biga*, and becomes *piga*, in Guam and *via* in Fiji (Burkill 1935 vol.1:106–107). Root crops have the great advantage to their cultivators that they store starch, that they are able to survive prolonged dry or cold seasons, and that they do not have to be harvested when ripe and stored, as do seed crops, but can be left in the ground until needed for consumption.

The second type of crops of tremendous importance to the swidden cultivator are the perennial giant herbs, bushes, vines, and trees, such as banana species *(Musa)*, papaya *(Carica papaya*, a New World plant), coconut palm *(Cocos nucifera)*, jackfruit *(Artocarpus integer)*, mango *(Mangifera indica)*, durian *(Durio zibethinus)*, candlenut tree *(Aleurites moluccana)*, stinkbean tree *(Pithecellobium lobatum)*, and santol *(Sandoricum koetjape)*.

The cultivation of root crops and some tree crops is technically quite different from that of seed crops in that many of the former can be grown from eyes and cuttings, that is, reproduced asexually, while the seed crops require sexual reproduction. Seed crops, such as rice, millet *(Setaria italica)*, and Job's tears *(Coix lacryma-jobi)*, tended to displace root crops as the primary sources of starch in the economy of swidden cultivators as they spread throughout Southeast Asia. Today, most of the Southeast Asian swidden farmers raise both cereals and root crops in their swiddens. The Pacific islanders, on the other hand, cultivate only root and tree crops. Theirs is a grainless agriculture (Pelzer 1947:75–81), an indication that their ancestors left the Southeast Asian mainland and islands after the domestication of tree and root crops, but prior to the development of seed grain crops.

Many swidden cultivators tend to imitate the natural ecosystem by planting mixed assemblages of root crops, herbs, climbers, shrubs, trees, and such grains as maize and upland rice. Harris notes that "swidden cultivation and fixed-plot horticulture . . . come closer to simulating the structure, functional dynamics and equilibrium of the natural ecosystem than any other agricultural systems man has devised" (Harris 1969:6).

Swidden cultivators of Southeast Asia who depended primarily on root crops for their starch were more or less tied to river banks, seashores, or the edges of swampy areas. These sites were not only highly suited for the cultivation of root crops, but also had abundant supplies of animal protein (Harris 1969:13; Sauer 1952:24–28). Seed crops such as upland rice, millet, and Job's tears, and much later, maize from the New World, made possible the great expansion into the uplands and mountainous sections of Southeast Asia.

Many of the root crops are shade loving; so the early swidden cultivator did not have to clear the forest extensively. Only with the domestication of seed crops did this necessity arise.

As Vavilov pointed out, Southeast Asia is one of the early centers of plant domestication and development of agriculture, and the burden of this development was carried by swidden cultivators (Vavilov 1926; Sauer 1952: 24–32). In the course of millennia, the Southeast Asian swidden cultivators learned to manipulate the foodstuffs which they gathered, produced, and harvested and eventually were able to improve tropical foods, to produce foods from wastes, and to convert natural raw materials into useful products (Stanton 1969:465).

Even a cursory examination of the swidden systems of Southeast Asia reveals a great variety of systems which reflect differences in physical geography and culture, and their interactions (Spencer 1966). A particular system may reflect such geographic features as extreme isolation or proximity to a navigable river, the coastline, or an all-weather highway giving the cultivator easy access to distant markets. The combination of favorable location with an ecosystem conducive to the cultivation of such tree crops as rubber, coffee, benzoin, and coconuts, or of a vine such as pepper, enabled the Indonesian swidden cultivator of Sumatra and Kalimantan to gain a remarkably high level of international economic importance. By contrast, except for opium growers, swidden cultivators of the Burmese, Thai, or Laotian hills play minor international economic roles. What a road can do in stimulating cash crop production of vegetables can easily be seen along the road from Tapah to the Cameron Highlands of West Malaysia, where hill people carry baskets of ears of maize and other vegetables to the roadside to sell to Chinese middlemen, who in turn take their purchases by car or truck to the lowland settlements.

ECONOMIC PERSPECTIVES: INDONESIA

The incorporation of the swidden cultivators into the economy of their respective countries and the provision of social services to the upland minorities have become an important challenge for all Southeast Asian governments. It has been customary in much of Southeast Asia to think of swiddeners at best as remote hill people with no relevance to the national economy, or at worst as despoilers of the national forest and land resources (e.g., Dobby 1954:349). While these views may be true for some swidden cultivators of the Asiatic tropics, they definitely do not apply to the majority of the swidden cultivators of Indonesia and should never be stated in such categorical terms. Spencer (1966), who examined the systems of shifting cultivation of Southeast Asia in considerable detail, seems to fail to appreciate the economic significance of the Indonesian shifting cultivator. Kroon (1969:556) points this out in his review of Spencer's book remarking that "the paucity of information on shifting cultivation in Sumatra and Borneo may

perhaps explain why the relationship between rubber growing and shifting cultivation in these regions escapes the author's [Spencer's] attention. . . . The various aspects of this phenomenon should be of interest to economists, anthropologists and geographers."

Like other countries of Southeast Asia, Indonesia has a great variety of agricultural systems which can be grouped under two major categories: permanent-field agriculture and shifting-field, or swidden, agriculture (Pelzer 1958:126). Both categories divide further into many systems and subsystems which in turn may combine, in that the same cultivator may use some of his land permanently and some only intermittently. Permanent-field and shifting-field cultivation systems are unevenly distributed in Indonesia. The permanent wet-field (sawah) system is prevalent in Java except for a small number of districts in the southwest corner of the island (Kools 1935) where swidden cultivators hold out with great tenacity. It is also of importance in Bali and Lombok, on the shores of Lake Toba, in the coastal lowlands of Atjeh, and in the Minangkabau highlands of Sumatra. Geertz (1963: 12–14) has divided Indonesia into the sawah region of Java, Bali, and West Lombok, which he calls Inner Indonesia, and the remainder of the archipelago, which he refers to as Outer Indonesia. In Outer Indonesia most of the agriculturally used land comes under swidden cultivation in one of its numerous variations. The Indonesian shifting cultivator's food supply is not all gained from working a ladang, or swidden. Since time immemorial and up to the present day, food gathering in the forest, hunting, and fishing contribute varying shares to the household larder. In addition the forest furnishes the swidden cultivator with a great variety of materials for use in his daily life, including wood, rattan, fibers, dyestuffs, wood oils, resins, and poisons. He may collect some of these materials in excess of his domestic needs and therefore have them for sale or barter.

Inner Indonesia, especially Java, is largely deforested. Forests by now account for less than 20 percent of Java's land area. The land has been converted to *sawah*, or wet-rice fields; *tegalan*, or dry fields; *pekarangan* compounds, or mixed garden land surrounding farm houses and villages; and *tanaman keras perkebunan*, or perennial-crop plantations. By contrast, two-thirds of Outer Indonesia is still forest covered. Far less of this than is commonly believed is primeval forest. Most forests are of the second-growth *belukar* type which may have been cleared innumerable times thoughout the ages to serve as swidden land (Pelzer 1963:122–123).

Both Inner and Outer Indonesia have been drawn into world trade in different periods and to varying degrees. In the nineteenth century, during the days of compulsory cultivation of export crops, the center of action was located in Java and involved mainly *sawah* cultivators, except for Sundanese in the Preanger highlands of West Java whose swidden cultivators, ever since the beginning of the eighteenth century had been compelled to plant coffee on hillsides on a large scale. The so-called Preanger system of coffee cultivation by swidden cultivators continued through the nineteenth century. During the two centuries of compulsory coffee cultivation, the Sundanese swiddeners were systematically coerced to change over from swidden to permanent-field cultivation of their food crops. Prior to 1700 the Sundanese of the Preanger highlands had neither *sawah* or *pekarangan*, but practiced swidden cultivation and were inclined to escape excessive pressure and exploitation by moving into sections of the highlands outside the reach of the administration. The Dutch insisted on the development of irrigation systems with the introduction of the Javanese type of wet-rice fields and the planting of fruit trees in the villages, in order to end once and for all the traditional practice of shifting both fields and settlements at frequent intervals, and to turn the Sundanese into sedentary permanent-field tillers (De Haan 1910, vol. 1:31–32, 116, 371, 375, 376; vol. 4:463).

Since the end of the nineteenth century Java's main concern has been the production of food crops for domestic consumption. This has developed into a discouraging, if not nightmarish, race between population growth and intensification of agriculture. As a result, Java's smallholders have been able to contribute less and less to the export sector of the economy, and the island depends more and more on support from Outer Indonesia in the form of food and of foreign exchange to be used for the purchase of food imports (Pelzer 1963:130–132).

In sharp contrast to Inner Indonesia, Outer Indonesia has plenty of room for expansion of cultivation by enlarging the swidden area in response to market demands. For centuries the swidden cultivators of areas blessed by easy access to markets because of their location near coastlines, on or near navigable rivers, or, in modern days, near highways permitting motorized transport of bulky goods have contributed export commodities, among which perennial vine, bush, and tree crops play a leading role. These crops include pepper, benzoin, coffee, copra and other coconut products, and above all, rubber.

The swidden cultivators of Sumatra, Kalimantan, and the Sulawesi region have been able to fit these perennial crops successfully into their agricultural systems and have thus become a vital element in the economic development of the country. This process was a relatively easy one because of the low population densities prevailing in most of Outer Indonesia and the abundance of cultivable land, fertile enough for the raising of tree crops although frequently not as fertile as the young basic volcanic soils of Java tilled by *sawah* cultivators. Easy access to land and to markets, suitable ecological conditions, and a highly flexible agricultural system placed the swidden cultivators in an infinitely better position than the *sawah* tillers of Inner Indonesia to be dynamic and enterprising and to utilize new opportunities as they arose (Geertz 1963:144–152). The Javanese finds himself locked in the *sawah* system, which acts as a straitjacket. His farm is small to start with, on an average less than one hectare, and tends to shrink in size with each new generation. He does not want to use his *sawah* for growing anything but wet rice during the rainy season. During the dry season he can grow a variety of crops including vegetables, root crops, and maize, but with the next rainy season he is back to his staple crop. In contrast, the peoples of Outer Indonesia by and large enjoy more elbow room and can fit perennial crops into their system with very little or no cash expense and small effort, since they clear their swiddens for growing their staple and secondary food crops. Together with the latter they can plant tree crops such as benzoin, rubber, and coconut palms, which can be interplanted for a second year certainly, and possibly even for a third year. This interplanting automatically provides protective maintenance while giving a return for the labor input, and allows the trees a head start over the competitive *belukar* (secondary growth), which can be controlled by occasional slashing. After a few years (seven or eight in the case of rubber and benzoin) the cultivator can begin harvesting. Only in exceptional instances do these new tree crops displace the annual swidden, although there may be a slight drop in hill rice and maize pro-

duction, especially at times of low rice and maize prices and high cash-crop prices (van Gelderen 1961:131; Fickendey 1941:98).

PEPPER

Of the perennials grown by Indonesian swidden cultivators, pepper was probably the first to enter world trade. This spice reached the Mediterranean in ancient times via either the Persian Gulf or the Red Sea, coming at that time from the Malabar coast of southern India, its probable original home. From there the vine was spread quite early into the humid parts of Southeast Asia, where it became established in Sumatra, Kalimantan, Malaya, and West Java. According to Burkill, "it is quite probable that the Hindus, who made kingdoms in Java between 100 B.C. and, say, A.D. 600, took [pepper] to Malaysia, and we may rest assured that its cultivation in the Archipelago is at least as old as that" (Burkill 1935, vol. 2:1777). In the early days pepper vines were probably cultivated in small numbers in farmyards, but when this spice became a trade commodity the swidden cultivators began to plant it systematically in their swiddens. The descriptions provided by Eschels-Kroon and Marsden in the eighteenth century clearly show that the practices of the Sumatran pepper growers have not changed during the past 200 years and were in all likelihood the same for the previous centuries (Eschels-Kroon 1781:34, and Marsden 1811:131–136, for the eighteenth century; Rutgers 1949:631–633, for the twentieth century). When a swidden cultivator wants to develop a pepper garden he looks for good forest soils covered by primeval or at least really old second-growth forest, which he cuts and burns. In the fields with his upland rice, he plants cuttings of coral tree, or *dadap* (*Erythrina* sp.), at intervals of 8 by 8 feet (2.5 by 2.5 meters). The coral trees serve as support for the pepper vines, which are planted at the base of the coral trees after the rice harvest (photo 132). After some weeks the young vines are taken down from their support trees and buried, with only the tops showing, in a shallow furrow dug by hand around the tree. This practice provides additional roots, and with increased vigor the pepper vines climb the coral trees again and begin to bear their first crops in the third year. The coral trees are pruned from time to time to prevent excessive shading. The pepper vines reach their prime in the seventh or eighth year, after which the yields decline. The gardens are usually exhausted after about 15 years and revert to *belukar*. By the time the first pepper garden is on the decline the swidden cultivator may start a second garden, which will be in production when the first one is abandoned.

During the eighteenth century, when both the Dutch and British East India companies maintained trading posts and garrisons along the west coast of Sumatra from Singkel to South Sumatra, the swidden cultivators of Sumatra were forced to plant and maintain 1,000 pepper vines per family (or 500 per unmarried adult male) and to accept a discouragingly low and inadequate price for the pepper. Because of lack of economic incentives, both the Dutch and British administrators had to inspect the pepper gardens annually, on which occasions they punished cultivators who neglected their gardens (Marsden 1811:139–143). Sir Stamford Raffles, as lieutenant governor of Bencoolen, after experiencing considerable difficulties in obtaining the expected quantities of pepper, recommended to his superiors that the forced delivery of pepper at inadequate rates be abolished and the growers "be allowed to cultivate pepper or not at pleasure" (Lady Raffles 1830:297; Bastin 1957:85–87, 128–130). While the Dutch and British could obtain the desired quantities of

pepper only by using coercion, American traders found it easy to buy large quantities of pepper along the west coast of Atjeh, where swidden cultivators were willing to produce pepper in response to attractive prices which the Americans were willing to pay. The American traders could pay higher prices than the British and the Dutch since they had no garrisons and administration to maintain (Gould 1956).

At the beginning of the nineteenth century pepper cultivation spread to the east coast of Sumatra in the states of Langkat, Deli, and Serdang. Wealthy local chiefs hired Karo Batak swidden cultivators to start pepper gardens. The latter planted dry-field rice, maize, tobacco, or beans between the young pepper vines and received rice, salt, and agricultural implements from the chief (Anderson 1826:260–261).

The Atjeh pattern of developing new pepper gardens in the nineteenth century seems to have differed from the South Sumatran pattern of today in that the chieftains, or *uleebalang*, borrowed money from Chinese merchants to support the pepper growers during the early phase (Siegel 1969:16–19). In Atjeh, too, catch crops were grown as long as the vines permitted intercropping.

Today the Lampong region of South Sumatra is the leading pepper producing area of Indonesia. Some production figures for the period before the Second World War are shown in table 15.1.

Data for the late 1960s (table 15.2) show that over 50 percent of the pepper production is not accounted for in export figures. This difference is apparently due mainly to smuggling, not home consumption. The outer islanders resent the high taxes paid compared with the low revenue returned by the central administration and use this method to retain a larger portion of the profits of local labor.

TABLE 15.1   Pepper Production of
             the Lampong Districts
             of South Sumatra

Year	Tons
1928	13,000
1930	18,000
1932	12,000
1934	26,000
1936	47,000
1938	37,000

SOURCE: Dutch East Indies 1939, The Export Crops
of the Netherlands Indies in 1938, p. 230.

TABLE 15.2   Pepper Production and Exports, Indonesia, 1960s

	Plantations and Smallholdings				Smallholdings (percent)	
	1960	1961	1966	1967	1960/61	1966/67
Area (thousands of hectares)	34	35	40	43	100	100
Production (thousands of tons)	12	24	49	49	100	100
Exports (thousands of tons)	13	19	21	22	100	100

SOURCE: Data from International Bank for Reconstruction and Development.

BENZOIN

Both Eschels-Kroon and Marsden reported that Batak swidden cultivators in the mountains between the west coast and the Toba Plateau were planting seeds of the benzoin tree (Styrax benzoin and S. paralleloneurus) in their swiddens in the eighteenth century. The Arab traveler Ibn Battuta, who visited Sumatra in the fourteenth century, mentioned benzoin among the export products of the island. At first, the Sumatran swidden cultivators tapped wild benzoin trees for the resin. But repeated tapping kills the trees and to make certain that they did not run out of them they began, we do not know how early, to place seeds of the benzoin tree in the ground together with the upland rice when they planted their swiddens (Eschels-Kroon 1781:62; Marsden 1811:154). The young seedlings need shade, which the rice plants provide during the first four or five months. After the rice has been reaped, fast growing weeds and belukar provide the necessary shade. After about seven years the trees can be tapped by cutting triangular wounds into the wood. These wounds are arranged in vertical rows up the tree to a height of 7 meters or more (Burkill 1935, vol. 2:2143–2144). The wounds fill with benzoin, a balsamic resin (kemenyan of the Malays, hamindjon of the Toba Batak, or gum Benjamin)

TABLE 15.3 Production of Benzoin in Tapanuli and Palembang, Sumatra

| Years | Average Production per Year (in tons) | |
	Tapanuli	Palembang
1926–1928	3,848	903
1929–1931	3,707	591
1932–1934	4,088	570
1935–1937	4,713	476
1938	5,080	276

SOURCE: Koppel 1950: 682.

that is used for incense, medical preparations, and perfume. For centuries various grades of benzoin were shipped from Barus. More recently Sibolga on Tapanuli Bay on the northwest coast of Sumatra has become the main export harbor. The Palembang area of South Sumatra is the second, but less important, *kemenyan* producing district.

The benzoin tree reaches its maximum yield after three years of tapping and continues to yield for another five, so that the trees have an economic life of about eight years. The trees are tapped twice a year. The total production of Tapanuli and Palembang ranged from about 4,700 tons in the mid-twenties to 5,300 tons in 1938 (Brans 1935) (see table 15.3).

COFFEE

The coffee tree, introduced into Southeast Asia (Java) in 1699, was the third perennial which the Indonesian swidden cultivators fitted into their agricultural systems. As mentioned above, the Dutch forced Sundanese cultivators to plant coffee on a large scale in the eighteenth and nineteenth centuries. Whenever permitted, they interplanted food crops and thus realized a return during the two years before the young coffee trees began to produce.

The Sumatran swidden cultivators did not become acquainted with coffee until the early nineteenth century. Neither Eschels-Kroon, whose report was published in 1781, nor Marsden, whose knowledge was from the 1780s to 1811, knew of coffee cultivation in the island. But by 1829 Padang was already exporting 40,000 *pikuls* of coffee. After 1850 the Dutch forced coffee production in Sumatra, compelling the cultivators to transport it to the coast and sell it at low prices. This caused great hardship. After about 1880, coffee production expanded as a result of improved prices and facilities for transport. The South Sumatran swidden cultivators of the Palambang and Lampong residencies have developed an extensive swidden coffee industry with *robusta* coffee. They plant upland rice and/or maize together with young coffee seedlings in their swiddens. During the second year they produce another crop of rice or maize and/or sweet potatoes. In the third year the trees produce their first coffee crop. The size of an average swidden is about one hectare and has about 2,000 trees. An average swidden, or *bidang*, produces 500 kg of coffee in the third year, 900 kg in the fourth, and 500 kg in the fifth year. After that, second-growth forest takes over and is left untouched for from 8 to 20 years before the cycle is repeated (Paerels 1949:111– 112). The swidden cultivator plants a new coffee garden every second or third year and thus has the possibility of harvesting a cash crop every year besides his food crop (Pelzer 1945:25). *Robusta* coffee exports from Sumatra in the prewar years are shown in table 15.4.

Table 15.5 indicates that some coffee is grown on plantations, though most is grown by small-holding swiddeners. Part of the difference between production and export figures is due to local consumption, though some is due to smug-

TABLE 15.4 Robusta Coffee Exports from
            Sumatra, 1925-1939

Year	Metric Tons	Year	Metric Tons
1925	31,500	1934	44,600
1926	41,400	1935	47,800
1927	51,000	1936	64,300
1928	64,800	1937	61,000
1932	64,500	1938	50,400
1933	44,100	1939	44,600

SOURCE: Paerels 1949:93. Sixty to 80 percent of this coffee came
from Pelambang and Lampong.

TABLE 15.5   Coffee Production and Export, Sumatra, 1960s

	Plantations and Smallholdings				Smallholdings (percent)	
	1960	1961	1966	1967	1960/61	1966/67
Area (thousands of hectares)	270	281	315	330	85	88
Production (thousands of tons)	98	97	136	136	80	86
Export (thousands of tons)	43	67	98	82	88	76

SOURCE: Data from International Bank for Reconstruction and Development.

gling for the same reasons as those suggested for pepper.

COCONUT PALM

The coconut palm has been called one of nature's greatest gifts to man, being a source of oil, nonalcoholic and alcoholic beverages, vinegar, fruit, vegetable food, fiber, medicines, leaves for basketwork, roofing material, household utensils, charcoal, and wood—to mention the most important uses (Burkill 1935, vol. 1:611–617). Prior to the development of large-scale demand for coconut oil and copra there was no reason to plant more coconut palms than were necessary to satisfy the domestic demand. This changed drastically during the later part of the nineteenth century, when copra found a market in the expanding soap and margarine industries of the mid-latitudes. Beginning in the 1880s the Menadonese, as well as islanders living between Menado and Mindanao, began to plant coconut palms on a large scale. Sangirese and Menadonese swidden cultivators planted young coconut seedlings together with upland rice and maize. They could grow food crops between the young palms for a second and a third year (Reyne 1948:465–666, 471–474), thereby getting a return for the labor involved in the maintenance of the immature groves. Beside rice and maize the cultivators interplanted derris, peanuts, soybeans, pineapple, tobacco, and cotton. In Sumatra swidden cultivators inter-

TABLE 15.6   Copra Exports from Indonesia, 1883–1939

Year	Value (guilders)	Period	Tonnage (metric tons, 5-year average)
1883	35,600	1891–1895	43,000
1885	305,000	1896–1900	60,000
1887	341,000	1901–1905	111,000
1889	1,955,000	1906–1910	198,000
1890	2,045,000	1911–1914	247,000
		1915–1920	233,000
		1921–1925	353,000
		1926–1930	425,000
		1931–1935	460,000
		1936–1939	557,000

SOURCE: Data from Reyne 1948:519.

TABLE 15.7   Coconut Production and Export, Indonesia, 1960s

	Plantations and Smallholdings				Smallholdings (percent)	
	1960	1961	1966	1967	1960/61	1966/67
Area (thousands of hectares)	1,610	1,540	1,904	1,972	100	100
Production (thousands of tons)	1,239	1,361	1,350	1,320	100	100
Export (thousands of tons)	169	251	119	316	100	100

SOURCE: Data from International Bank for Reconstruction and Development.

planted *robusta* coffee, bananas, and even cacao. Before the war, up to 95 percent of the copra production in Indonesia came from smallholders, and a very high percentage of the exports came from the swidden regions of Celebes (Sulawesi) (44 percent in 1939) and Sumatra (28 percent in 1939), so that the two areas accounted for about 72 percent of the 1939 exports. Table 15.6 shows the growth in value of the copra industry of Indonesia for the period from 1883 to 1890, and in tons for the period from 1891 to 1939. Between 1890 and 1940 the export expanded no less than thirteenfold.

By the 1960s, all coconuts were reportedly being produced by smallholders, as is shown in table 15.7. This table also shows the relationship between production and consumption of coconuts in Indonesia. In the recent past there has been much smuggling of coconuts to Mindanao, especially when the value of the rupiah on the black market was low. Because the Indonesian currency and economy were stabilized in the late 1960s, the amount of smuggling has fallen off.

RUBBER

Rubber *(Hevea brasiliensis)*, a South American tree, was introduced into Southeast Asia in 1876. Systematic planting of this tree did not get under way until about 1900, in response to the rapidly growing demand for rubber and the resulting high prices. Chinese and European capital started the first rubber plantations in Malaya and Indonesia, but it was not long before peasants began to plant the tree. During the years of high rubber prices (1909–1912) Indonesian swidden cultivators in Djambi, Sumatra, and West Borneo planted rubber seeds together with their food crops in newly cleared swiddens.

The idea was brought into these districts by Indonesians who had spent some time in Malaya, and also by Chinese traders who traditionally purchased forest products, such as gutta-percha, jelutong, rattan, and dammar, and could see the technical possibility of fitting rubber into the agricultural systems of the swidden cultivators. Chinese traders quickly recognized the potential for rubber and are reported to have encouraged its production among swiddeners by distributing rubber seeds at cost, and even below cost, in the expectation of future trade in rubber. In 1910–1912 the price of 1,000 seeds was one guilder (Luytjes 1925:26).

There is no doubt that the Chinese trading community contributed more to the growth of the smallholder rubber industry than did the government. As a matter of fact, in the early days Europeans were of the opinion that *Hevea* was not suited for cultivation by peasants. Instead they held that proper maintenance, tapping, and latex preparation could be provided only by Western-managed plantations. Government officials repeatedly advised smallholders

against growing rubber and recommended instead the planting of *Ficus elastica* (Gelder 1950:428:31; Ozinga 1940:237, 262). Fortunately, despite the pessimism in government circles, the swidden cultivators of Sumatra and Borneo continued to convert swiddens into rubber gardens. They commonly planted a catch crop for a second, and even a third, year between the rows of the young rubber trees, thereby delaying the development of second-growth forest trees or invasion of *Imperata cylindrica*.

Not until 1925 did the Department of Agriculture order a survey of the smallholder rubber industry in Sumatra and Borneo in order to obtain basic data about the nature of the industry and methods of production, processing, and trade (De Bevolkingsrubbercultuur 1925–1927). The investigators were very much impressed by the ease with which swidden cultivators became the owners of rubber gardens. By 1925 the Indonesian cultivators, stimulated by the high rubber prices resulting from the Stevenson Restriction Scheme (which directly affected only the British territories), were engaged in large-scale planting (Bauer 1948). Communities which had only small cash incomes at the beginning of the century were earning hundreds of thousands of guilders by the late 1920s. Table 15.8 shows the quantities and value of export crops produced by Tapanuli swidden cultivators in the first half of the decade and clearly demonstrates their economic importance. In the following years rubber production expanded further until in 1938 a total area of 61,000 hectares was in rubber and exports reached 4,000 tons; this was below production capacity on account of the restriction scheme (Dutch East Indies 1939: 117).

It is frequently claimed that the swidden cultivator and smallholder simply followed the model set by the rubber plantation, and it is

TABLE 15.8 Benzoin, Coffee, Rubber, and Copra Exports from Tapanuli, 1920–1925

Year	Benzoin		Coffee		Rubber		Copra	
	Tons	Guilders	Tons	Guilders	Tons	Guilders	Tons	Guilders
1920	1,590	1,448,000	2,499	2,348,000	1,095	568,000	241	102,000
1921	1,507	1,396,000	1,897	1,617,000	1,541	1,002,000	81	20,000
1922	1,760	1,460,000	2,544	2,160,000	1,778	1,331,000	61	12,000
1923	1,964	1,736,000	1,892	1,522,000	1,115	1,532,000	55	14,000
1924	1,999	1,799,000	2,112	1,878,000	1,764	2,173,000	32	6,000
1925 [a]	825	718,000	929	939,000	1,216	1,532,000	2	4,000

SOURCE: De Bevolkingsrubbercultuur in Nederlandisch-Indie, vol. V, C. P. Brook en H. W. J. Doffegnies 1926:4.
[a] Figures from January through May.

assumed that this model was a suitable one. Actually, the first smallholders began planting rubber before the first plantation had reached the production stage. Futhermore, the smallholders planted rubber trees far more closely than did plantations, and for a long time sold their rubber more often in the form of thick cakes or slabs of unmilled latex, rather than in the form of ribbed sheets as sold by plantations (photo 133). Finally, smallholders avoided the costly mistake of planters and did not practice clean weeding with its concomitant soil erosion.

I called attention above to the fact that the swidden cultivator interplanted food crops during the second and sometimes the third year, a practice condemned, and therefore avoided, by the planters. However, even here we may see a change in the future. I learned in 1968 that the agronomists in the experiment station of Guthrie Company in Seremban, Malaysia, were conducting experiments with intercropping of rubber and oil palm during the initial years in order to reduce the cost of development of new plantations. Crops which could be used include cassava, upland rice, maize, castor beans, soybeans, peanuts, mung beans, velvet beans, patchouli, citronella, and sesame (Tan Hong et al. 1968; see also Lim and Barlow 1968).

It can be pointed out that swidden rubber groves are, ecologically speaking, closer to the second-growth forest than are plantation rubber groves because of closer planting distance (photo 134), which results in deeper shade and higher humidity, both conducive to more rapid bark recovery, and reduces growth of weeds without the need for weeding. Intuitively, the native chose the correct way, which the European rubber planter learned only slowly to follow (Rutgers 1925:833 as cited by Gelder 1950:749). The planter had to learn by trial and error that the rubber tree in the long run benefits from the belukar, which grows along with the young rubber, and that the planter's intensive clean weeding was harmful and nearly led to the failure of rubber cultivation (Van Gelder 1950:448). In short, the swidden cultivator has proven the better practical ecologist. It is true that all too often he is a poor and unskilled tapper and damages the cambium, but it also took the planters years to develop the presently accepted tapping technique (Burkill 1935, vol. 1:1171–1173). The big new rubber development schemes in Malaysia have had trouble as a result of failure to give follow-up supervision to tappers. The new and delicate varieties of rubber tree require careful tapping if their maximum yields are to be maintained. These varieties have a potential yield of 3,368 kg/ha, as

TABLE 15.9 Rubber Trees and Rubber Hectarage Held by Indonesian Growers (1936, 1937, and 1938 census figures)

Territory	Number of Cultivators	Number of Trees	Number of Hectares Planted
Sumatra			
Atjeh	13,017	5,854,000	8,359
East Sumatra	58,508	38,359,000	41,924
Bangkalis	62,698	28,130,000	34,771
Tapanuli	67,004	50,874,000	60,715
West Sumatra	38,677	18,546,000	24,029
Riouw	36,171	29,227,000	46,928
Banka	27,394	14,305,000	14,107
Djambi	43,189	72,714,000	69,509
Palembang	139,287	152,757,000	179,941
Bencoolen	3,895	1,195,000	2,803
Lampong	4,956	4,520,000	6,198
Borneo (Kalimantan)			
West Borneo	113,249	87,796,000	108,022
South and East Borneo	180,345	78,155,000	83,830
Celebes (Sulawesi)			
Menado	48	23,000	51
Total	788,438	582,365,000	681,187

SOURCE: Dutch East Indies 1939, The Export Crops of the Netherlands Indies in 1938, pp. 116–117.

compared with the 505 kg/ha yields of older varieties. Because of the high development costs, potential gains will be lost unless the trees survive for a long period.

In 1938 the government ordered registration of all rubber holdings in Inner as well as Outer Indonesia. This clearly revealed that rubber had become a smallholder crop only in that part of Java where swidden cultivation had survived. That island had only 8 million rubber trees on approximately 16,000 hectares. By contrast, Outer Indonesia had 582 million trees on 681,000 hectares owned by no fewer than 788,000 smallholders. By 1940 the rubber area had increased to 714,500 hectares. Table 15.9 gives data on the geographic distribution of smallholder rubber. It is apparent that rubber is practically limited to Sumatra and Borneo, the

two huge Indonesian islands ecologically best suited for rubber. Table 15.10 estimates the year of planting of the pre-World War II rubber area. One-fourth of the prewar rubber area was planted prior to 1925. No less than 495,000 hectares, or 69 percent, were planted after 1924 but prior to the signing of the International Rubber Agreement which temporarily curtailed the planting of rubber but allowed replanting of over-aged stands.

Table 15.11 gives pertinent data on area, production, and export of rubber for both plantations and smallholdings and estimates the percentages attributable to smallholders. The area planted to rubber has increased markedly, but production has not kept pace with the increase in area. About 25 percent of Indonesian rubber production is now on nationalized (formerly

TABLE 15.10 New Rubber Planted Annually in Indonesia, 1925–1940

Year of Planting	Outer Indonesia (hectares)	Inner Indonesia (hectares)
Prior to 1925	181,000	7,086
1925	111,000	1,917
1926	115,000	3,532
1927	91,000	1,839
1928	72,000	1,157
1929	53,000	317
1930	25,000	143
1931	11,000	34
1932	3,000	16
1933	14,000	3
1934	5,000	5
1939	16,500	406
1940	17,500	365
Totals	714,500	16,820

SOURCE: Gelder 1950:467.

TABLE 15.11 Rubber Production and Export, Indonesia, 1960s

	Plantations and Smallholdings				Smallholdings (percent)	
	1960	1961	1966	1967	1960/61	1966/67
Area (thousands of hectares)	1,855	1,867	1,904	1,922	79	80
Production (thousands of tons)	679	699	700	695	63	76
Exports (thousands of tons)	468	657	680	620	88	76

SOURCE: Data from International Bank for Reconstruction and Development.

Dutch) plantations or foreign-owned plantations. Production on these large holdings is relatively low.

CONCLUSIONS

In 1960 the five smallholder crops, pepper, benzoin, coffee, copra, and rubber, accounted for no less than 40 percent of the value of *total* Indonesian exports, including mineral products (Pelzer 1963:142, table 2). The bulk of these smallholder exports are produced by swidden cultivators who annually clear a forested area for the raising of their food crops. This practice makes these growers less vulnerable to economic setbacks due to serious drops in commodity prices, while at the same time they make a most impressive contribution to the *export* sector of the economy, exceeding in this respect the *sawah* (irrigated land) cultivators of Java.

There are a number of implications of the Indonesian case study for the development of shifting cultivation in Thailand and elsewhere in the tropics. It is obvious from the success of Indonesian swiddeners (as well as from the relative economic success of Hmong and other opium cultivators in Thailand) that cash cropping is possible in swiddens. It also appears that swidden farmers are flexible and will accept innovations in crops and techniques of cultivation if the economic incentives are clear.

In Indonesia, and perhaps in other areas including Thailand, the swidden cultivators may be in a better position to innovate in the direction of cash crops than are the irrigated agriculturalists who are already trapped by a limited land base and a population explosion. On Java 70 million people depend on farms averaging only 0.5 hectare, and almost all of this area is required for subsistence crops under a very intensive, technically and socially intricate cultivation system. Agricultural innovation in this "involuted" system is extremely difficult because of the many technical, legal, and political implications. By contrast, more land area is available to swiddeners, allowing them to produce both subsistence and cash crops. There is more safety in this "dual economy" for the swidden cultivator, since he is thus not completely at the mercy of fluctuating international commodity prices for his livelihood.

It is clear from the Indonesian case that tree crops allow a greater intensity of land use, through intercropping and obtaining a cash crop in what is ordinarily thought of as the "fallow" period of the swiddens. It is also clear that a certain amount of technological development must take place in order to adapt crops to a new environment, and that schemes involving technical changes will suffer, and perhaps be defeated, unless there is adequate management and education of the farmers and processors.

Of course the Indonesian system cannot be transferred directly to Thailand because of important differences in climate, population density, and ethnic diversity. Sumatra, for example, has high rainfall, well distributed throughout the year, and thus resembles southern, much more than northern, Thailand. Although the specific crops which have been grown successfully in Indonesia might not be appropriate in the shifting cultivation areas of Thailand, the principles of their use could be applied. Perennial tree crops could be interplanted with subsistence crops. The Indonesians have had advantages of transportation and access to the sea that are not available to the swidden cultivators of northern Thailand, who are located far from seaports. The economy of the northern Thailand valleys has already been dramatically altered by the construction of all-weather roads, and a similar transformation might take place if roads were available in the hills. Opportunities for development of the upland areas exist, but they will require investment in the form of transportation systems, technical experimentation, adequate testing in pilot projects, extension of knowledge to farmers, marketers and processors, and coordination among the various concerned government departments.

PART V

CONCLUSION

16

Alternatives for the Development of Upland Areas

Peter Kunstadter

HISTORY AND FARMERS IN THE FOREST

The distribution and size of Southeast Asia's population is the result of long-term historical processes, including agricultural innovations and their social correlates. The prehistory of Southeast Asian agriculture is not yet fully known, but there is evidence that man has tended plants in northern Thailand for at least 12,000 years (Gorman 1969, 1971a, 1971b; Yen 1977). Social and agricultural developments since then have been associated with increased population size, a concentration of population in the lowlands, and increasing social, economic, and cultural differentiation between hill and valley people. The foothills and hills, whence come the most ancient indications of agriculture, are now much less densely populated than the valleys, but population pressure, indicated by environmental deterioration, is becoming common in the hills.

Several trends in the agricultural history of northern Thailand are similar to developments in other parts of the world. As agriculture has evolved, the tendency has been to concentrate on uniform environmental settings and on increased control of the variability within them: clearing the forest to allow sunlight to reach the cultivated crops uniformly, leveling and diking the soil to equalize water distribution and retain rainwater, irrigating to remove the uncertainties of rainfall, selecting uniform seed to insure uniform plant characteristics, using pesticides to reduce unwanted flora and fauna, using tillage, fallow techniques, or fertilizer to reduce variations in soil fertility, and planting only one variety per field to allow mechanical rather than individualized cultivation.

The latest series of changes has been the development of modern methods of plant breeding, chemical fertilization, weed and pest control, and mechanical cultivation. This revolutionary technology has greatly expanded food production in the lowlands, but has had little effect in the swidden areas, save to make them even more marginal economically. Modern agricultural technology has required much more environmental control than traditional technology, and this has been cheaper and simpler in the flat irrigable plains.

Another tendency in attempts to simplify the environment has been to use fewer plant species. The transitional ecological zones which were probably important to early cultivators because of their environmental and species diversity are not favored by modern farmers precisely because of this diversity. Early farming was carried out in locales where a profusion of species was present and involved the domestication of many different species, the tending of additional semi-domesticates, and collection of a wide variety of undomesticated species. Subsistence swiddening has retained these characteristics (chapters 6, 15), while modern farming has emphasized a reduced number of cultivated species and has practically eliminated the collection of nondomesticates (cf. Harris 1972: 182ff.).

The ultimate stage in management and simplification of the environment has been monocropping, as seen in plantations, or concentration on one "super crop" which provides carbohydrates and calories even though it may be of limited nutritive value. The reduction in number of species cultivated may mean greater efficiency in use of human labor or machines, but it means a reduction in the variety of the subsistence products, and/or involvement in supracommunal economic networks (worldwide in the case of cash crops such as rubber, sugar, or opium) for the marketing of the cash crop and purchase of staples.

The increase in agricultural productivity has been accompanied by an increase in population associated with the reduction of famines as environmental fluctuations are dampened, and by basic public health measures. Whatever the cause, in those areas where productivity and population have increased, a declining proportion of the population is directly involved in agriculture.

Increased population density resulting from greater productivity decreases the availability of "wild" products, such as game and fish, as sources of protein. Ultimately this forces man to live lower on the food chain (substituting plants for animals as a source of protein), or to manage an even greater portion of the food chain (raising feed for livestock, and raising livestock for food or to sell to others for food), or to import animals from areas of lower human population density (as the lowlanders buy pigs, cows, buffalos, and elephants from the hill villagers).

Despite the relatively slow pace of technological change in the swiddening areas, the upland population is growing rapidly. This is the result of disease control and famine control in the lowlands and the consequent reduction of epidemics spreading to the hills, and of migration from bordering countries. The sustained growth and the consequent large size of the hill population in recent years has been unprecedented and has been accompanied by a series of changes in the balance between man and the environment.

Swiddeners have modified the landscape extensively, but as compared with lowland farmers they have exerted only limited control over the environment. The chief ecological effect of swiddening is the temporary replacement of forest cover with cultivated plants and the long-term succession to fire-resistant species of uncultivated plants. The details of these effects are related to the distinction between cash-cropping farmers using a long cultivation—very long fallow cycle like that of the Hmong (chapters 10, 11), and the primarily subsistence swiddeners with a short cultivation—long fallow cycle such as that used by the Lua' and Karen farmers (see chapters 6, 9).

Cash cropping is clearly an extension of the lowland economic system, and is dependent on lowland markets for disposal of its products. In general the subsistence swiddeners have been much more conservative in modifying the environment than have the cash croppers. Cash crop farming is often confined to a relatively limited number of species, as compared with subsistence swiddening. Cash croppers may become agricultural specialists whose economy depends on others for basic supplies and equipment, and even food staples and credit. Their production system may involve such extensive environmental changes that it is not even theoretically self-sustaining, as the techniques involved may prevent forest regrowth which is essential for restoration of soil fertility (chapter 11).

By contrast, subsistence swiddeners cultivate a large number of species (chapter 6) in an agricultural system which probably resembles closely that of much earlier days, and which was theoretically self-sufficient before population increase and limited land resources overtook them.

The appearance of self-sufficiency of the subsistence swiddeners today may be deceiving. Despite the absence of technological change and relatively limited contact with the market in the agricultural sector, many subsistence swiddeners are already bound inextricably to the larger lowland-based economic system. Their combination of technology and land resources, given increased population, is insufficient to provide subsistence without the supplement of wage labor. Cash is increasingly important to them as they are exposed to the desires and needs of an economy with manufactured goods. Still, within their villages, they maintain their traditional social structure: almost everyone is a farmer, and the villages continue to be organized around the social aspects of swidden farming even after wage labor becomes an important supplement to income. The small nonagricultural population within subsistence swidden communities (school teachers, occasionally traders) is exogenous, and the impulses for

change come largely from outside, not from within.

Present-day swidden communities can be seen as reduplicating, and perhaps exaggerating in a restricted setting, the conditions of many postcolonial nations. Population growth has preceded basic technological and social changes, and traditional solutions to economic problems are no longer adequate. Meanwhile the resources of the swidden areas (lumber, minerals, some agricultural products) are siphoned off to the benefit of an external economy, with little or no effect on the development of the local area nor improvement in the life of the local people.

INACCURACIES IN STEREOTYPES OF SHIFTING CULTIVATORS

The descriptions of swidden cultivators in this book should modify some stereotypes concerning shifting cultivation. It is clear that the population of swiddeners in Thailand contains a large proportion of Thai as well as "hill tribes" (chapters 12–14; cf. Judd 1964). It is also clear that the majority of the swiddeners do not grow opium; in fact, most of them are subsistence rice farmers. The descriptions of their cultivation systems show that many of them are conscious of conservation practices and, at least until overwhelmed by population increase, have managed to maintain their soil resources and to live in communities in the same locale for many generations.

Despite the fact that these people benefit from many generations of accumulated wisdom, they are not bound inflexibly by tradition. Many of them have shown themselves to be adaptable to changing conditions and responsive to new opportunities in terms of crop plants (New World crops, introduction of improved varieties), cultivation techniques (irrigation where the terrain permits), and new sources of income (wage work and cash crops). They are clearly responsive to opportunities for increasing their income through rational economic activity, and this is perhaps the greatest source of optimism for their future.

ESTIMATING THE BENEFITS OF FOREST LAND USE

Increasing population pressure implies the need for more intensive land use in northern Thailand. Cash cropping and wage labor (for example, in lumbering) have been suggested as potential solutions to the problems of rising population pressure and rising expectations of rural upland populations. Opium has been a major cash crop in the highlands, but its production is illegal and increasing governmental and international efforts are directed at suppressing opium production and trade. Opium producers, who are already familiar with many aspects of marketing cash crops, might seem to be good candidates for the development of a non-narcotic cash economy. Some reports suggest, however, that farmers who attempt to substitute rice or maize (land-extensive swidden crops) for labor-intensive opium as a cash crop may quickly be faced with a land shortage (Miles 1967; Scholz 1969). The reason for this is clear when we compare rice with opium on a unit area basis (see table 16.1). This implies that care must be taken to select new cash crops that will produce levels of subsistence and income similar to or better than the present systems, as measured per unit of land area, per unit of time, and per capita.

The benefits of alternative types of land use in upland areas can be compared on the basis of available studies, but with due caution because these studies were not made by identical methods. In any analysis of costs and benefits we must ask the questions: benefit to whom? and

are *all* the costs in the entire economic-ecological system accounted for?

Successful subsistence swidden cultivators in a self-contained, balanced ecosystem support themselves using their own work supplemented by solar energy and photosynthesis which power the recycling and replacement of essential chemical nutrients through the forest fallow cover and the crops. Such a system is balanced to the extent that its resources are either nonconsumable (the future availability of solar energy is not affected by swiddening) or self-renewing (soil nutrients recycled through the forest fallow or replaced by weathering of soil parent materials), and its products are not removed from their position in the ecosystem. Analysis of Lua' and Karen systems shows that, although these groups may at one time have had balanced economies, the balance has been lost due to increased population, reduced fallow time, and possibly the necessity to export products which can no longer be recycled in the local ecosystem. The cash-crop economies described in chapters 12–14 also appear to be unbalanced. The implication of the studies by Chapman and by Charley and McGarity is that without fertilizer, agronomic systems such as those practiced by the Northern Thai swiddeners cannot be self-sustaining. The need for fertilizer implies participation in the cash economy, and successful application of fertilizer will accelerate the tendency to involve these farmers in an increasingly large economic system.

Modern economic systems, requiring fossil fuel, are not even theoretically in balance, although for the short run the balance may be simulated by exchanging money for fossil fuel. Even this balance may be more apparent than real for the national economies within which no fossil fuels are produced. Lack of self-containment can be seen, for example, in the modern lumber industry, which depends on fossil-fuel powered trucks and tractors to haul logs to the sawmill. Although such energy sources will undoubtedly influence the relationship of upland to lowland economies, we can disregard them for present purposes as being outside the economic-ecological system of the forest. Other energy costs, which are within the forest ecosystem, such as feed for elephants used in hauling logs, or logs for the fires necessary for cooking *miang* must be included in the total costs of the system.[1]

Likewise we should look carefully at the distribution of the benefits. In a pure, balanced subsistence swidden system, the farmers bear all the costs (their own labor) and receive all the benefits (their own produce). Substituting any cash economy, such as lumbering, for subsistence agriculture means involving the forest farmers in a much larger economic system. Although the value of the product may increase, as measured by national income accounts, the farmers no longer receive all the benefit (sale price of the logs). They receive only the sale price of their labor, usually unskilled, which is a very small portion of the total market value of the lumber. In assessing the effects on their standard of living a further caution must be considered. In giving up subsistence agriculture the forest dwellers will be forced to purchase their staples, and these are sold in remote areas at notoriously high prices. Thus their labor must bring in substantially more than the market value of their subsistence crops in order to allow for costs of transportation of their food from market to point of consumption. Sabhasri (chapter 8) has calculated that lumber production (for saw logs and charcoal) would be more profitable in terms of market value than the present level of rice production for the Lua' of Pa Pae, but at present there is neither market nor trans-portation for these products, nor is there an adequate locally available substitute for Lua' subsistence products. Similar calculations have been made in the Chiang Dao area for the value of forest products as shown in tables 16.1 and 16.2.

THE BENEFITS OF FORESTRY

Table 16.1 shows the gross value of the lumber and agricultural products per square kilometer in a number of different ecotypes and economic systems. Figures in the second column represent the gross value of the "standing crop," that is the market value assuming the crop was cut and sold in one year, with no deductions for costs of production, transportation, or marketing. This figure is the same as the annual gross value in continual or annual cropping systems, but not for forest lumber or forest fallow systems where, in order to determine the carrying capacity, the value of the standing crop must be divided by the number of years required to reproduce the crop, as shown in the fourth column. A range of estimates is required here because the length of regrowth cycle varies in different environments and with different cultivation systems. Also there is evidently a range in production. The third column of table 16.1 shows estimates of these ranges on an annual basis. The lower values in the third column can be interpreted as reflecting a change from an ecological-economic system in which land is unlimited to one in which land is completely occupied. From the standpoint of some cash-crop swiddeners, this may not yet be the condition under which they are operating. From the standpoint of the demographically oriented economist, land shortages already exist.

The next step is to consider the benefits of forestry to the local people, by estimating their receipts from the economic system. Since sub-

TABLE 16.1   Gross Total and Gross Annual Values of Various Ecotypes and Crops

Ecotype or Crop	Gross Total Market Value of Standing Crop (baht/km²)	Gross Annual Market Value of Standing Crop (baht/km²)	Years between Harvests
Hill Evergreen	2,326,369	38,773–77,546	30–60
Mixed Deciduous with teak	4,668,063	77,801–155,602	30–60
Dry Evergreen	6,119,289	101,988–203,976	30–60
Dry Dipterocarp	2,194,991	36,583–73,166	30–60
Dry Dipterocarp with pine	2,005,660	33,428–66,855	
Miang [a]	1,250,000	1,250,000	
Commercial tea and other planta- tions	2,500,000	2,500,000	
Irrigated rice	125,000–203,250	125,000–203,250	1
Swidden rice	65,625–149,375	6,563–49,792	3–10
Swidden opium	660,156–2,437,500	66,016–812,500	3–10
Pine plantation [b]		218,750–437,500	20
Teak plantation [c]		468,750	60

SOURCES: Yield estimates for forest ecotypes from Khemnark (1972:15, 26); for miang and tea from Keen (chapter 13) and Oughton and Imong (1971:5); for irrigated rice from Kunstadter (chapter 6, table 5 in this book), 20–30 tang/rai @ 10 baht/tang; for swidden rice (chapter 1, table 2 in this book), 10.5–23.9 tang/rai @ 10 baht/tang. Estimates for opium from Walker (1970, vol. 2:501), 4.15 kg/ha; Geddes (1973, 1976:183), "conservative estimate" 1.3 kg/rai; Punyasingh (cited in U.N. Survey Team 1967:59), 1.3 kg/rai; Miles (1967:20), 4.8 kg/rai; value figures at observed sale price of 812.5 baht/kg (Walker 1970:501).

[a] See chapter note 1.

[b] Estimated value is derived from figures supplied by the Division of Silviculture, Royal Forest Department. Pine seedlings are planted at about 100 per rai and later thinned to about 50 trees per rai. After 20 years the yield should be between 25 and 50 m³ of lumber. The price at the mill must be less than 280 baht per m³ in order for the mill to operate profitably, according to U.N. Development Plan estimates. See text for further explanation.

[c] Estimated value is from Faculty of the Social Sciences, Chiang Mai University (n.d.), based on a 60-year cycle.

sistence and cash-crop swiddeners generally consume or sell most or all of their own produce, the entire benefit (gross annual value) can be assumed to go to them. This is not the case in lumbering or in the miang and tea industries. Khemnark et al. (1972) give figures for gross value and harvesting cost of lumbering in the different ecosystems of the Chiang Dao Hilltribe Settlement (nikhom). We have used their estimates to calculate the benefit to local inhab-

itants, assuming that only unskilled jobs are available to them (this is the predominant pattern in the area), and that the principal payments to local people would be for girdling teak trees, felling trees, and hiring elephants to drag logs to lumber road heads, from which point they would be taken by tractor or truck to the sawmill. Khemnark et al. estimate that roads could be built within an average of one km from the felling sites, and that the cost of hauling one

TABLE 16.2   Potential Benefits to Workers in Various Forest
             Ecotypes and Upland Economies

Ecotype or Crop	Potential Total Payments to Un-skilled Workers (*baht*/km²)	Potential Annual Payments to Un-skilled Workers (*baht*/km²)
Hill Evergreen	837,431–1,030,724	13,957–34,357
Mixed Deciduous with teak	869,483–1,100,133	14,491–36,671
Dry Evergreen	2,130,246–2,621,841	35,504–87,395
Dry Dipterocarp	537,136–661,090	8,952–22,036
Dry Dipterocarp with pine	613,438–755,000	10,224–25,167
Miang[a]	180,000–502,875	180,000–502,875
Tea	1,000,000 +	1,000,000 +
Irrigated rice	125,000–203,250	125,000–203,250
Swidden rice	65,625–149,375	6,563–49,792
Opium	66,016–812,500	66,015–812,500
Pine plantation[b]		26,875
Teak plantation[c]		1,170 +

SOURCES AND NOTES: Potential benefit to workers in forest ecotypes is calculated from figures in Khemnark et al. (1972), arbitrarily estimating payments for labor and elephant hire at 80–100 *baht*/m³ of teak and 65–80 *baht*/m³ of non-teak. The lower benefits represent the lower labor costs on a 60-year cutting cycle, the higher benefits represent higher labor costs on a 30-year cycle. Some of these figures are unrealistic; for example, the potential benefit from the Dry Evergreen forest is not high, given the high transportation and cutting costs in comparison with the market value of the wood. Thus there is little incentive for commercial exploitation of this forest type. Likewise the upper limit of potential benefit for opium is probably much too high as an estimated average, because fallow requirements may be greater and Miles' estimate of opium production, on which the upper limit is based, is considerably higher than other estimates. Source of the estimate for benefit to workers in the *miang* economy is Keen (1970, Appendix, pp. 6, 15). Source for tea plantations is Khemnark et al. (1972:39). This is a minimum figure derived from the cost of picking alone; transportation, weeding, and pruning would add to this amount, assuming that all this was done by debt-free wage laborers.

[a] Benefits considered on the basis of requirements of the total ecosystem should allow for approximately 2 km² of Hill Evergreen forest, or its equivalent, to supply fuel for cooking the *miang*. No estimates are available for fuel requirements in the tea industry.

[b] Total benefits to workers is in terms of wages in this amount. Workers have no access to agricultural land within the plantation. Figures are derived from information supplied by Silviculture Division, Royal Forest Department, based on a 20-year cycle.

[c] Benefits include 1,146 *baht* in direct wages. Figure does not include indirect benefits (water, electricity, schools) or value of subsistence products to the villagers who have access to agricultural land. Figures are derived from Faculty of the Social Sciences, Chiang Mai University (n.d.).

cubic meter of lumber is approximately 50 *baht* (1972:22–24). They list other costs—surveying, road construction, tractor or truck hauling, stumpage fees, overhead, capital, and interest (none of which would go to local people)—but give no estimate of costs for these items. In constructing the estimates in table 16.2 we have assumed arbitrarily that the average cost of unskilled labor might be between 15 and 30 *baht* per cubic meter for non-teak, and double that for teak. Teak is more expensive to cut since each tree must be visited twice, once for girdling, and again two years later for felling.

Using figures from Khemnark et al. (1972:21, table 5, Appendix) for species distribution in the different forest ecotypes, we have calculated the labor payments as shown in table 16.2. Swidden rice production is described in chapters 6, 9, and 12; opium production in chapter 11.

THE BENEFITS OF *MIANG* AND TEA GROWING

Figures on income of *miang* and tea growers are calculated from reports of Keen (1969, 1970, and chapter 14), and Oughton and Imong (1971), who discuss income of workers in these activities, after they have paid for rent, fuel, transportation, and other costs. An important feature of the *miang* industry as it exists today in northern Thailand is the high proportion of farmers who work rented land or who are otherwise heavily in debt to creditors who both market the *miang* for the producers and sell the farmers staples. Credit costs are very high in this area, and it is as difficult here to escape from debt as it is elsewhere in rural Thailand.

This condition recalls a previous caveat, that the cost of food and other essentials brought into areas of low population density and poor transportation are very high. In considering plans for development of the area, it should be assumed

that payments to workers outside the main market areas must be high enough to compensate for these high costs.

Substantial numbers of people in the hills now contribute to their own support by subsistence activities. The question must be asked whether an equivalent standard of living can be maintained with a switch to a cash economy, or whether a transitional economy—mixed cash crop plus wage labor plus subsistence farming—should be encouraged as a cushion against higher costs for staples in remote areas, and against fluctuation of market prices of the upland cash products. The Indonesian example described by Pelzer (chapter 15) suggests the wisdom of this strategy if sufficient land is available.

BENEFITS OF TEAK PLANTATIONS

The Forest Industry Organization (FIO) of Thailand has developed a "forest village system" which is a modification of the *taungya* system (Faculty of the Social Sciences, Chiang Mai University n.d.). They currently operate 10 teak plantations in northern Thailand, on a 60-year cycle. Each plantation unit clears and plants 1,000 *rai* per year. Villagers are recruited for this program in family groups, with a limit of 100 families for each plantation. The villagers do not get title to the land they are working. The village sites may be moved from time to time within the 60,000 *rai* of the plantation. To date there has been a fairly high rate of turnover among residents within the one village studied, Mae Moh in Muang District, Lampang Province. Two-thirds of the household heads were from the Northeast while only one third were from the North. In other words, the village is accommodating twice as many people from outside the region as from within it.

Each household, with an average of about two adult workers, is obliged to clear and plant 10 *rai* to teak per year. The teak seedlings are planted on a 4-meter by 4-meter grid, and the plantation workers are allowed to cultivate their own plants between the teak trees for two years after the plot has been cleared. Actually most of the villagers have been cultivating in other places, as have commercial farmers (who must pay 20 *baht* rent per *rai* per year for the privilege). In addition to allowing the villagers to plant subsistence or commercial crops (which is the only benefit villagers receive in the normal *taungya* system), water, electricity, and schools are provided free of charge (annual cost to FIO per *rai* for these services is not clear). Each family is paid 20 *baht* per *rai* for clearing and up to 20 *baht* per *rai* for planting, providing that 95 percent of the seedlings survive, plus another 20 *baht* per *rai* for weeding after harvest time. After three years, in which the family has cleared and planted 30 *rai*, they receive a 1,500 *baht* bonus (50 *baht* per *rai*). Subsequently they get a 500 *baht* bonus every year they clear and plant at least 10 *rai*. Thus the total cash income for doing all these chores is 110 *baht* per *rai* per year, or 1,100 *baht* per family per year. In addition they may plant subsistence or cash crops and work for wages doing additional weeding on contract. The average family income at Mae Moh village in 1973 was 4,306 *baht* (735 *baht* per capita) compared with the Thai average of 941 *baht* per capita in farm families (Faculty of the Social Sciences n.d.:14–15). About 55 percent of this was from wages and bonuses and the remainder from sales of crops. Few families were actually growing subsistence crops, and their value was not measured.

Value of the teak to FIO at the end of the 60-year cycle was estimated to yield about 8.4 percent per annum on the investments in labor and social services. Although this is not considered an adequate commercial profit, and although

theoretically this system (at 100 families per 60,000 *rai*) will support fewer people than the pine plantation system, the villagers are probably better off under the FIO program, which is designed to solve rural social and economic problems as well as to produce teak for sale. Also it has been recognized that at least in the early stages of teak planting, more than 100 families can be supported. Thus a mixture of teak and cash crops is actually grown, and in the year studied the average income for the villagers was almost four times the amount paid for the nominal 10 *rai* cleared and planted per household.

A detailed study of the economics of this system has not been done from the standpoint of the villagers. For them the important question is whether they can do an adequate job of weeding both the trees and their crops. This village study suggests they cannot do both, as additional labor is hired on contract to help with the weeding of the trees. Apparently individuals or families concentrating on teak do not have time to grow crops, and vice versa, in part because of the time it takes to get to the farms, which are often distant from the site of the teak plantations (Faculty of the Social Sciences n.d.: 25–26, 28).

The amount of land per person, an average of 100–120 *rai*, is considerably more than is currently used by Lua' and Karen subsistence swiddeners in Mae Sariang District (chapter 6), who averaged between 18 and 19 *rai* per person, including fallow land and unused "reserved" forest. Thus, if the system is economically feasible, it can support a human population density only one-fifth or one-sixth as great as subsistence swiddening without lumber production. The benefit to the villagers would be greater than in pure subsistence swiddening, and there would be an increment to the national income as well. The net profit (after deducting costs and interest on costs) from the lumber produced on teak plantations in an 80-year cycle is estimated by the Royal Forest Department to be about 40,000 *baht* per *rai*, equivalent to about 500 *baht* per *rai* per year (312,500 *baht* per km²) on a sustained-yield basis; figures used in the Faculty of the Social Services study give about 468,750 *baht* per km². To this amount should also be added the value of the crops, which might range between 1,100 and 8,300 *baht* per km² per year, depending on swidden yields and the length of time each swidden was actually cultivated.

BENEFITS OF PINE PLANTATIONS

The Royal Forest Department's pine plantation scheme (chapter 4) has not been operating long enough to accumulate complete figures, but they estimate a 20-year cycle, with a total payment to unskilled labor during that period of approximately 855 *baht* per *rai*, or about 43 *baht* per *rai* (26,875 *baht* per km²) per year. An additional 50 *baht* per *rai* would be paid for harvesting the trees at the end of the growing period, and this work might be done by unskilled local labor, giving a total payment of 905 *baht* per *rai*, or about 45 *baht* per *rai* (26,875 *baht* per km²) per year. This is the entire benefit paid to the villagers, whose swidden land is being absorbed into the pine plantation and who are not allowed to cultivate subsistence crops within the plantation area.

The assumption is that wage labor will be substituted for subsistence agriculture. If one figures an average requirement of 2 *baht* cash per person per day (a minimal amount), a family of five to six people, without access to agricultural land for subsistence farming, would require about 6,000 *baht* cash income per year, the equivalent of wage-labor income from about 130 *rai* (at 45 *baht* per *rai* per year), or about 24 *rai* per person. This is about 25 percent more

than the land now used by Lua' and Karen villagers in subsistence farming, and thus represents a major decline in the intensity of land use for the local people. The total value of the product would be much higher than that from subsistence farming (estimated at less than 350–700 *baht* per *rai* per year, roughly equivalent to the yield from a teak plantation). The difference between the value of the product delivered at the mill and the wages paid to unskilled workers represents costs of machinery, supplies, insurance against fire and other losses, interest, transportation, and wages paid to skilled and salaried employees who are not locally recruited. The total annual costs for this scheme are estimated to be about 1,000–1,500 *baht* per *rai* (625,000–937,500 *baht* per km²), of which only about 45 *baht* goes to the local unskilled laborer.

Although the scheme may aid the general economic development of the nation, it appears to contribute nothing to solving economic problems of the upland population. According to available figures, none of the forestry development plans will simultaneously increase cash or total income and increase the carrying capacity of the land for the local inhabitants. They will be able to receive the benefits of development only if they share opportunities for skilled and technical employment and receive a larger portion of the profits from the sale of their products.

INCREASING THE BENEFITS OF FOREST LAND USE

We can generalize from the findings of the research on which this book is based to describe the limits under which forest farmers operate. Keen's discussion (chapter 11) of tensions between different sectors of the local economies is helpful in understanding this situation. Any self-sustaining economy requires a balance between a number of factors, including availability and productivity of labor, availability of land and other essential resources, and the costs of production and distribution, including subsistence costs. The forest farming systems we have described must also balance the needs for production with the needs for renewal of essential soil nutrients. As we have seen, several traditional strategies exist for approximating this balance, including manipulation of the cultivation-fallow cycle and temporary or permanent migration into unoccupied land or into other economic systems. Increases in population, declining productivity, decline in availability of land, increased psychological ties to the market economy, and increased costs of purchased items relative to agricultural products have upset what has been a relatively self-sustaining local economic system.

Forest farming in northern Thailand, as practiced by a very diverse set of people, is relatively labor-intensive. There is often underemployment in agriculture during the dry season, and often a shortage of labor when maximum concentration of work is required (planting, harvest). When fallow requirements are included, yields, relative to those from permanent irrigated fields, are low per unit of land and per unit of labor. The people are relatively poor, with little ability to accumulate capital for productive use. In general they have only traditional claims to their land, without legal or political support in case of infringement. Their agriculture is subject to high local and annual variability (see tables 1.2, 6.6) and high risks due to the natural variability of their environment and their limited control over important environmental conditions including their social environment. In other words, they are relatively poor and powerless in the face of increasing stress on their economic systems.

Population pressures are now operating in both the valleys and the hills, with the result that increasingly marginal upland areas are subject to slash-and-burn clearing and cultivation, both by hill and valley dwellers. The increased pressure on upland resources is reflected in the lowland economy by shortages of lumber and damage to watersheds upon which the irrigated valleys depend, and by surpluses of unskilled labor. This situation no longer represents a stable balance between people and natural resources.

If the objective is to return to a stability in which resources are regenerated as fast as they are consumed or destroyed, and in which there is an opporunity for all the people to benefit from national economic development, several conditions will have to be met. Agricultural productivity will have to be increased, the numbers of people depending on forest farming must be restricted, and alternative sources of income and subsistence must be available to the forest farmers.

In general the proposed solutions for bettering the conditions of forest farmers have been to provide technical innovations to attempt to "fix up" subsistence farming through introducing improved strains of pigs or chickens or field crops, or to concentrate on the introduction of a single cash crop, for example, as a substitute for opium. What is clearly implied in the descriptions of swidden systems in this book is that the economic and ecological problems, of which the conditions of forest farmers are symptoms, are regional in nature. This suggests that successful solutions may have to be regional in scope, rather than being confined to the communities of hill cultivators and their specific agricultural techniques.

Emphasis has often been placed on exports, to the exclusion of production for local markets. Because of the environmental diversity in the hills and the fact that upland dwellers now support themselves largely through subsistence agriculture, because of the past history of boom and bust in monocropping for the world market, and because of the familiarity with wage work of a large segment of swiddeners, it would seem more appropriate to seek to produce a variety of cash crops for a variety of markets, and to strengthen, at least temporarily, the subsistence sector through introduction of more efficient techniques, and to expand wage-work opportunities.

The favorable conditions of soil, ready access to transport, and favorable markets found in Indonesia may not exist elsewhere in Southeast Asia. Nonetheless, Pelzer's examples (chapter 15) encourage us to believe that swidden farmers, with very limited external governmental or commercial control, can contribute in a major way to the national economy, under the proper conditions. Numerous examples of rational economic behavior among swidden farmers in northern Thailand suggest that these people can and will respond to economic incentives for changing their agricultural systems.

Although this book has concentrated on agricultural aspects, the solution of these problems will require attention to wage-labor opportunities and population planning as well as to improving the techniques and the economics of farming.

STRATEGIES FOR DEVELOPMENT OF FOREST FARMING AREAS

Development of the swidden areas is complicated by the fact that the environment is much more varied than that in which irrigated agriculture is practiced, with altitudes ranging from 250–300 meters up to 2,500 meters, with concomitant variations in temperature, rainfall, soil types, native vegetation, and crop pests. These areas are also occupied by a much greater variety of peoples, including speakers of many different dialects of four or five major language families, who live in small, scattered, sometimes impermanent villages. These variations make any development in the hills more difficult and costly than in lowland areas, which are all relatively similar in environment, to which access by road can be relatively cheap and easy, and which are occupied primarily by Northern Thai speakers (and some Karen).

Possibilities for improving the balance between population and production in the upland areas may be outlined as follows.

INCREASE PRODUCTION

1. *Increase the area under cultivation.* The size of the population which can be accommodated in hill areas is determined both by the size of the area available for cultivation and by the potential productivity of that area. There is no measure of these variables now because no complete survey of land use, land types, or land capabilities has been made (see chapter 5; Weizman 1971:3; Keen 1972). What is needed is a revision of land capability evaluation which is updated as technological change increases potential productivity, and which is not limited to irrigated rice farming. The impression gained from flying over, driving through, or walking in the hills of northern Thailand is that land is already fairly densely settled and that there are few remaining unexploited areas suitable for agriculture under present techniques. Quantification of these impressions is essential for rational planning. Most swiddeners could clear much more land than they now cultivate annually. As shown in preceding chapters, forest farming in northern Thailand is labor-intensive, and the heaviest labor requirement is not in the spectacular events of clearing and burning the forest, but rather in the continual weeding throughout the six-month rainy season. This, as

well as scarcity of land, limits the area which can be effectively farmed with existing technology unless truly under-utilized land is found; adding to the amount of land cultivated annually will not increase production, and may actually lead to a decline in productivity.

2. *Increase the ratio of cultivation to fallow.*

(a) Decrease the length of fallow between periods of cultivation. Where this has been tried in upland fields without modern fertilizers and tillage techniques (chapters 12, 13), decreases in length of fallow time leads to declining productivity and may make the land unsuitable for further cultivation for many years due to replacement of forest with herbaceous vegetation. Where modern technology is available, however, this may be a solution to increasing the production per unit of land (chapter 14).

(b) Increase length of cultivation between fallow periods. Most subsistence swiddeners cultivate only one year before returning their fields to fallow. Where cultivation is prolonged, as in some areas of Viet Nam, production declines in successive years (see chapter 1, table 1.2). Some Hmong farmers cultivate subsistence crops and opium for several years on the same sites, but this is followed by abandonment of the fields for very long fallow periods.

(c) Multicrop in cultivated areas during annual cultivation. Most cultivation takes place during the rainy season, but the vigorous growth of weeds after harvest and the continued growth of some crop plants into the dry season (cotton, opium, peppers, tobacco) suggests that a greater portion of the year might be devoted to cropping if proper varieties were selected and tillage techniques were developed to make use of soil moisture available at the end of the rainy season. Careful evaluation of this procedure would be required to insure that it did not interfere with regeneration of the fallow vegetation, which serves a multitude of ecological and economic functions.

(d) Increase the utility of fallow areas. Pelzer (chapter 15) has described the extensive use of fallow areas for commercially important production in Indonesia. Although the species he discusses might not be appropriate for northern Thailand, the idea deserves systematic investigation, as does Keen's suggestion (chapter 14) of incorporating woodlots or rapidly growing trees as a source of fuel into the fallow or uncultivated portions of the cycle. This suggestion is similar to the *taungya* system except that it emphasizes products of benefit directly to the farmer, rather than to the forest industry. Little research has been devoted to increasing the efficiency of the fallow portion of the cycle through selection and planting of appropriate species for nitrogen fixation, nutrient cycling, and so forth, although this is the logical analog of green manuring practices on annually cultivated fields.

(e) Irrigate the upland fields. Irrigated fields in upland areas are far more productive per unit of area (when fallow requirements are allowed for) than are swiddens. They also require less labor once they have been cleared and leveled and the irrigation ditches have been dug. Hill people have already developed much of the uplands that can easily be irrigated, but an aerial photographic survey might reveal additional upland areas that could be irrigated. There are several limiting factors in upland irrigated farming which make it inherently more difficult to develop than lowland irrigated farming. One is that upland catchment and storage areas are much smaller, thus subject to more variation in availability of water than in lowland areas, and the possibilities of winter (dry season) cropping are much more limited. Second, and perhaps most important, most hill people lack the capital or means of acquiring capital to invest in the expensive job of terracing; the available areas for terracing are unlikely to be large enough to produce economies of a scale that would be attractive to large development schemes. Thus any program of expanding irrigated farming in the hills would have to include a system of financing the improvements through either grants or loans at rates which could be repaid.

3. *Increase the efficiency of cultivation.*

(a) Improve crop varieties. High-yield varieties have been successfully developed for use in lowland parts of Southeast Asia, but little effort has been devoted to improving upland crops. This is an inherently difficult job because of the greater variability of the hill environment, but some work is now being done on this possibility (chapter 10).

(b) Increase labor efficiency. Improvements in productivity of farm labor in the lowlands have resulted from supplementing human effort with machines and with chemical fertilizers and pesticides. No doubt these innovations could be applied in the hills, with suitable modification, but the expense would be greater in the hills due to variability of the terrain and other features of the environment, as well as lack of transportation. Under existing conditions, even the simplest modern technical devices are far too expensive for the average upland farmer, and the costs of modern technology, including fuel and agricultural chemicals, are bound to increase in the forseeable future. Thus this form of technology-intensive or energy-intensive development will be of no utility in the hills unless economic conditions change radically there, either through improvement of the economic

position of the uplanders, or, as is more likely, by intrusion of investors from the lowlands. Improved health in the lowlands may also have contributed to greater per capita production there. It is clear even to a casual observer that poor health limits agricultural production in hill villages, but improved health also carries with it the possibility of even more rapid population growth. The balance between population growth due to better health and increased productivity due to the same cause is not understood, and it deserves further study for practical and humanitarian reasons.

4. *Change purpose of cultivation.* Upland farmers are predominantly subsistence rice or maize growers, with some cash cropping, especially of opium and tea, among some groups. Although in many ways opium is ideally suited to the upland environment, its future as a cash crop is in doubt because of its ecological and moral consequences (chapters 10, 11). The market for tea is probably limited to local Thai consumption (chapter 14). Other possibilities are being explored for changing the basic orientation of upland agriculture from subsistence farming to cash cropping and livestock herding. It is too early to tell if these are ecologically or economically feasible. Obviously any such reorientation would imply major social changes for hill people, related to the nature and system of ownership of their resources (see below).

INCREASE THE VALUE OF PRODUCTS OR RESOURCES

1. *Increase farm prices.* Theoretically, the position of upland farmers could be improved if farm prices increased relative to other costs. It has been government policy to maintain relatively low prices to the farmers, but even if this policy were to change it is unlikely that an increase in agricultural prices would give much

benefit to people who are essentially subsistence producers and have little surplus for sale. The only way they might benefit is through sale of specialized crops well adapted to their environment, the sale of which could supplement their subsistence. As indicated above, additional activities associated with new crops must fit the present schedule of subsistence farming, that is, require little labor in the rainy season.

2. *Increase land values.* Chapman and his colleagues (chapters 12, 13) have suggested the importance for economic development of resolving in favor of the farmers the ambiguities of upland farm ownership. This will require a change in basic government policy. An adequate legal model has yet to be worked out which would accommodate both the communal aspects of traditional upland village land use and the needs for individualized title if upland fields are to be used as security for loans. Major changes in the social life of upland villagers are implied in any formalization or change in the current land laws.

3. *Increase price of farm and forest labor.* Present farm wages are low, and perhaps declining, due to seasonal and local oversupply. Wage rates could rise if labor demands increased or supplies declined, but this is unlikely in the face of rapid population increase without much accompanying industrialization. Wages might also rise if agricultural and forest product prices should rise, but only if the portion going to the farmer rises. It seems evident that the price of unskilled labor in the forest developments (see above pp. 295–298) is too low, and again this would seem to be in part a matter of government regulation.

IMPROVE DISTRIBUTION

1. *Decrease costs of distribution.* Distribution costs are high in hill areas where roads and markets are not well developed. In general there are no shops in villages where cash cropping is unimportant. Villagers depend on itinerant peddlers or trips to town to buy manufactured items. They must take their livestock and surplus rice to town for sale (at high transportation cost) or wait for a buyer to come through the village. Improved transportation will be an essential feature of upland development if it is to involve anything beyond continued subsistence agriculture or opium farming. Improved transportation brings with it risks of exploitation by lowlanders, and any plan for networks of roads in the hills should be coordinated with securing title for the uplanders to the land they have customarily used (see below).

2. *Decrease loss in storage.* Storage is an essential aspect of the swidden economy in northern Thailand, where the entire annual rice crop is harvested within one or two months, and where annual variations in yields may be extreme. Major losses occur during storage due to rodents, insects, and spoilage. These losses presumably could be minimized through development and use of better storage techniques. Reducing loss in storage could lead to an increase in productivity, especially in the critical months before harvest during a lean year, when a farmer whose family has eaten all their rice must spend much time looking for rice to purchase, and then carrying it back to his home.

DECREASE POPULATION PRESSURE

1. *Encourage temporary or permanent migration out of the hills and discourage migration into the hills.* Although there has been some international migration into the hills of northern Thailand, it is apparent that much of the population increase has resulted from a surplus of births over deaths, plus some migration from the northern Thai lowlands to the hills. A pattern of migration from hills to lowlands also exists, both for temporary wage work and for resettlement.

Virtually nothing has been done to discourage movement of lowlanders into the hills, or to encourage resettlement or temporary employment of hill people in the lowlands. To the contrary, government policies have often resulted, at least temporarily or indirectly, in increased migration from the lowlands to the hills, either through failure to provide adequate resettlement areas for people displaced by dam and reservoir construction, or through failure to employ hill dwellers rather than lowlanders in the various development projects in the hills.

2. *Balance births and deaths.* Although it is evident that hill populations are growing as a result of natural increase at rates equal to those of the lowlanders, little effort has been made to extend birth control to the upland peoples, except by a few missionary groups. The skills required for a birth control program in the hills are more complex than in the lowlands because of the ethnic mixture in the hills, but stopping population growth in the hills should be a major priority.

SOCIAL IMPLICATIONS OF AGRICULTURAL DEVELOPMENT

All suggestions for improvement of the economic situation of forest farmers have social implications. One of the most important concomitants of the introduction of cash crops, especially those which require long-term investment, such as tree crops, is a change in the nature of land ownership customs. In swiddening communities, land is often treated as either a free good, to be claimed temporarily during cultivation (Akha, Hmong), or as a community resource to be reallocated annually by village leaders (Karen, Lua'). Where long-term investments are made, the nature of ownership and control can be expected to change, a situation analogous to changes in land customs when irrigated agriculture is introduced into swiddening

communities. Acquisition of permanent rights in land will become important and valuable; leadership based on kinship and authority to reallocate community resources will be eroded as relationships determined by money and control of labor and individually held land become more important (Kunstadter 1966). Relationships between people and land will change from the situation in subsistence farming where land beyond the amount required for subsistence is of no utility and labor is organized on a kinship or reciprocal exchange basis, to a situation in which land is valuable as an asset potentially leading to greater cash income, which can be exploited because of the availability of wage workers. The large-scale introduction of cash cropping (and de-emphasis on subsistence agriculture) may thus result in an increase in the number of wage workers who are underemployed or seasonally unemployed, who will be available to the general labor market and who will feel less attachment to their home communities than do residents of swidden villages.[2] Thus, unless crops are labor-intensive throughout the year, an expansion of cash cropping in the hills may lead to an increase of dry-season job seekers in the valley.

Cash cropping alone probably cannot be an answer to the needs of economic development in the hills. If the cash crops are land-extensive (maize, forest plantations with low value per unit area per year and low requirements for labor) they may actually increase the need for land among the upland population. If the cash crops are land-intensive, with high value per unit area per year and high ability to absorb labor, they may attract lowland investors with greater economic capabilities than the uplanders and increase the pressure on the land to the detriment of people already in the hills, as in the tea and *miang* growing areas.[3] Furthermore, the noncultivated land requirements (as for firewood in the processing of *miang*) must be considered, as must the need for increased income due to higher staple prices, when evaluating the total land requirements for cash-crop economic systems.

Cash cropping separates work from subsistence, since the crops must be sold and then food must be purchased before it can be eaten. Cash cropping may require higher investments in time, labor, equipment, and supplies than does subsistence farming. These conditions imply a need for capital accumulation or credit. To date, investment credit at reasonable rates has been almost completely unavailable to upland farmers, many of whom live barely above the subsistence level. Credit is often unavailable even to lowland farmers, who may have title to their land to pledge as security.

Given the legal uncertainties of ownership and lack of title to land in the hill areas, the major form of collateral in securing loans is unavailable to upland farmers. Thus the successful introduction of cash cropping for hill farmers will require innovation in land laws (chapter 3) and in credit facilities, or may mean that all development in the hills will have to be done by the government or by lowland-based individuals or organizations with access to credit. The social and political consequences of development must be considered in planning a successful program. A policy is required which will give the cultivators control over the land they have traditionally farmed, as is being done in the Thai-Australian Land Development project (chapters 12, 13), or risk the creation of an impoverished, unhappy, landless hill population. Of course, the development of cash cropping also involves the development of marketing and transportation networks, which may require governmental assistance or participation.

Opportunities for productive investment among subsistence farmers in upland areas have been limited. The same set of ethics that enables villagers to call on one another for exchange of labor in production often allows poorer people to borrow from richer ones to such an extent that richer ones cannot accumulate capital. There are no banks or savings accounts, and opportunities for investment of surplus are limited to durable consumer goods (silver jewelry, brideprice or dowry goods, etc.) or perhaps livestock, which, because of scarcity of fodder, can be kept only in small numbers. There is little or no chance of making an investment that will increase the productivity of upland resources except where irrigation is possible and irrigated fields can be bought or constructed. Other investments include elephants (used primarily in the lowlands) or lowland irrigated fields (which are then rented out on a sharecrop basis).

Where cash cropping is practiced, surplus income may be invested in hiring additional labor for crop production. Storing surplus subsistence crops may be difficult because of pressures from kinsmen, as well as the perishable nature of most upland commodities. In these respects the opium farmers have reached a much higher stage of development, and their type of mixed cash and subsistence economy (chapter 11) may be instructive as to the kinds of economic organizations which can result from cash cropping.

Despite the fact that the northern hills are located within the national boundaries, the problems of the farmers in these forests are analogous to problems of social and economic development in colonies.[4] Economic and political conditions are increasingly beyond the control of local inhabitants, as they become encompassed in a wider social and economic system. They are becoming relatively poorer as compared with people in the Bangkok-dominated society. The resources they traditionally have thought of as their own, resources which once were largely ignored by outsiders, are now considered by the larger society to be essential to the well-being of the nation. Economic "development" which has taken place has been largely extractive (mining, lumbering with inadequate reforestation), and the benefits of these enterprises have gone out of the hill areas, not to the hill residents. The common tendency of developing nations to drain the resources of the hinterlands for the benefit of the central region is seen here even more clearly than in the provincial lowlands. Thus it is not surprising that economic conditions of the hill people have not improved as rapidly as among the lowlanders despite the declared objectives of the Thai government's development plans to reduce rural-urban and regional income differentials. It is hard to see how these differentials might be reduced as long as policies similar to those followed by colonial powers in their colonies are applied to the northern Thailand hills. To the contrary, it seems that the history of impoverishment and stagnated development characteristic of the colonies may be repeated in up-country Thailand. If so, the effects will surely be felt most severely in the marginal regions.

What would be the consequences of different policies with regard to control of upland resources? There seems to be no alternative to allowing upland dwellers to share in determining what will become of themselves and the land which they have occupied for generations, and giving them a major share in the benefits to be derived from these resources. If hill people are allowed an equitable share in exploitation of these resources, it will be in their interest to conserve them. If they are deprived of an equitable share, given the scarcity of land and the pressure of population, the hill dwellers will have no choice but to attempt to make their living as well as they can knowing that they do not control the land they cultivate. The history of tenancy, whether in the South of the United States, in Latin America, Indonesia, or elsewhere in the world, has shown that this is a policy which lowers productivity and destroys land resources.

For years it has proved impossible to control the destruction of the forest, despite ever-increasing numbers of laws and personnel. Perhaps now it is better to recognize that most of Thailand's forest resources are on their way to destruction, and to attempt to save that portion of upland resources in which there are easily recognized common interests of both hill and valley dwellers. Soil and its vegetative cover are essential to both. Given the existing population pressure, perhaps the best that can be hoped for is to conserve these two essentials and at the same time allow the hills to support a sizeable number of people through improved systems of upland agriculture.

Such a policy would mean assigning title of the land to the traditional inhabitants, restricting new settlement in the already overpopulated hills, encouraging the limitation of births, encouraging migration out of the hills and wage work for hill dwellers, while encouraging social and technical innovations to increase the value of hill land and the perception of this value by dwellers in the hills.

One key to successful development in the hill areas is to recognize that population pressure has reached the point where it is no longer possible to have extensive game preserves, profitable lumbering, and colorful "untouched" hilltribes. The wild animals are almost gone, lumbering has been carried on for years with inadequate reforestation, and the hill people are changing rapidly.

The best hope of preventing a complete wasteland in the hills is to give the hill people a sufficient reason to preserve their resources, and the ability to do so. Conservation concepts will be easily understood by people like the Karen and Lua', who have made permanent villages in the hills and who have practiced conservation within the boundaries of what they recognize as their own territory. People like the Akha or perhaps the Hmong or Yao will have more difficulty in learning that land is not a free good, that in fact it is a valuable and limited resource. The essential problem is to convince these people that despite appearances there is no more "free" land.

Preservation of the land base of upland communities is an essential feature of a successful program to preserve upland resources. Each individual in the community must recognize that it is in his best interest not to sell land to outsiders. The issue is not that they should be *unable* to sell it, but that *they should realize the benefits of keeping it.* The consequences of failure to anticipate the ecological and social concomitants of radical changes in land use and land ownership abound in the modern world. Rapid and cheap sale by American Indians of their allotted land led to the destruction of the Indian communities, the perpetuation of an impoverished minority, and the creation of Dust Bowl conditions through over-exploitation of land resources, resources which the Indians had preserved for thousands of years. This tragedy need not be repeated in northern Thailand.

NOTES

1. The *miang* industry depends on the burning of wood for fuel. Keen indicates the normal size for pieces of firewood is about 100 cm² cross section by 2 meters, or 0.02 m³, and indicates that for a village with 64.32 hectares of *miang*, approximately 22,500 logs, equivalent to 450 m³ of firewood, are used annually. This is equal to a rate of 699.6 m³ of firewood per km² of *miang* (see chapter 14). Khemnark et al. (1971:81) give a total of 12,882.76

m³ of lumber from trees of 10-cm girth or more in the Hill Evergreen forest from which the *miang* growers cut their fuel. Assuming that all species of trees were used for firewood, this means that one km² of *miang* would use all the lumber on a square kilometer of Hill Evergreen forest in a period of 18.4 years. If the forest were cut on a sustained yield basis, each square kilometer of *miang* would require two or more square kilometers of Hill Evergreen forest, even at the relatively low intensity of cultivation now practiced. If younger, smaller trees were satisfactory, the same amount of firewood could be harvested in about half the time (or half the area), assuming forest production at Chiang Dao resembles that described by Sabhasri (chapter 8).

2. People like the Hmong and Yao may be an exception to this prediction. Despite long-term commitment to cash cropping (opium), few of these people have become involved as workers in the labor market, perhaps because they conceive of themselves as *employers* rather than employees. Unlike the Karen and Lua' who have entered the wage-labor market for several generations, the Hmong are reputed to have strong feelings against being employed by anyone. Nonetheless, Keen (1969:3 and chapter 13) has reported that Thai *miang* producers hire Hmong workers in the Doi Chiang Dao area to chop firewood.

3. The concept of a land-intensive economic system implies a time dimension as well as a spatial one. Opium cultivation is highly land-intensive on an annual basis, if the need to acquire more land when the soil is locally exhausted is disregarded. When fallow requirements are included, opium cultivation is seen to be much less land-intensive, but despite its spatial mobility it is still labor-intensive. Large numbers of people must be assembled, organized in a small (if temporary) space, and rewarded for their work, even if this assemblage must be moved from time to time. The social organizational effects may resemble those in a truly land-intensive system, and, in terms of economic turnover, it may be more intensive than irrigated agriculture despite its needs for fallow (see table 16.2). The differences between figures in the left- and right-hand columns of tables 16.1 and 16.2 indicate the effect of the time dimension on the economic value of the activity per unit area, and thus are a measure of the land-intensity of the activity including the time dimension.

4. The following description, taken from Myrdal's (1968) discussion of the history of Asian economy, reveals the accuracy of the analogy. If we substitute "northern Thailand," "central Thai," "Bangkok," etc., for Myrdal's

"South Asia," "British," "foreign," etc., the comparison would be more pointed.

In South Asia, the processes of capital accumulation and spread were frustrated. The plantations, like the mines, remained enclaves in largely stagnant economies while the initial impulses failed to trigger cumulative and self-perpetuating growth. . . .

The expansion of peasant growing of cash crops undoubtedly meant an increase in monetization. But in India much of the money went to pay the new taxes imposed by the British authorities. Furthermore, the rise of peasant cash crop production in India was apparently at the expense of food output. . . . the resulting increase in total crop production was hardly sufficient to keep pace with population growth. [P. 448]

Spread effects were also vitiated inasmuch as expansion of output of cash crops by native growers did not in general imply the use of new technology. . . .The increase in production meant . . . a rising demand for food by the growing indigenous population. The profits from the export trade went almost entirely to foreign commercial firms and were regularly remitted abroad. [P. 449]

The development of plantations was initiated and controlled by foreigners. Managerial functions and ultimate control were in the hands of aliens. Dividends and a large part of the salaries were remitted abroad, or used to purchase foreign goods rather than to stimulate demand on the local market. . . . Although expansion gave rise to a demand for local labor, it was for the most part a demand for unskilled labor; more highly skilled workers were brought in from outside. [P. 449]

Not only did the higher salaries go to (non-local) managers and foremen; much of the wages of unskilled labor also went to workers imported from other South Asian countries . . . so that even part of the incomes accruing to low-paid workers on the estates was sent back to their families at home rather than translated into demands for locally produced commodities. [P. 450]

A further aspect of the plantation system that strongly bolstered the enclave structure . . . was the fact of segregation and discrimination. Had the European owners, managers or skilled workers . . . come in close contact with the natives, a diffusion of skills would almost certainly have taken place and a much larger group of indigenous personnel would have acquired the requisite abilities. . . . But the fact of European ownership and control in primitive regions meant a wide separation between the European upper caste and the masses of unskilled workers. . . . This was less a matter of "race" or even racial prejudice, at least at the start, than a very real difference in modes and levels of living and, more generally, cultural characteristics. [P. 450]

. . . As the factories in the home country required abundant and cheap raw materials from the colonies, manufacturing industry in the colonies was inhibited. The result was a lopsided economy precisely suited to the stimulation of manufacturing in the metropolitan country. [P. 455]

Photographs

Photographs are in sequence roughly according to the first reference in the text, starting with different types of vegetation and terrain. A series showing Lua' and Karen economic systems begins with the swidden cycle, followed by irrigated farming and gardening in this hill environment, and then illustrates the processing and use of agricultural products and other subsistence activities. Contacts between upland and lowland economies are illustrated next. Subsequent series show Hmong farming, the Thai-Australian Land Development Project, and swiddeners producing export crops in Indonesia.

All photographs are by Peter Kunstadter unless otherwise indicated.

1. Coniferous forest with pine-dipterocarp association. Tree at left is *Dipterocarpus obtusifolius*; the conifer is *Pinus kesiya (P. insularis)*. On the Hot–Mae Sariang highway, 35 km west of Hot. (Photo by Tem Smitinand)

2. Dry Evergreen forest. Dark stem is *Hopea odorata*; large stem at right is *Lagerstroemia balansae*. (Photo by Tem Smitinand)

3. Moist Mixed Deciduous forest at Wang Kham, Mae Hong Son. Teak *(Tectona grandis)* predominates. (Photo by Tem Smitinand)

4. Dry Mixed Deciduous forest at Khun Yuam, Mae Hong Son. Large tree in center is *Terminalia alata*. (Photo by Tem Smitinand)

5. Dry Deciduous Dipterocarp forest along the Hot–Mae Sariang highway. (Photo by Tem Smitinand)

312

6. *Kha* grass *(Imperata cylindrica)* well established in disturbed upland forest. The tall grass at right is *Themeda arundinacea*, trees are oaks *(Lithocarpus* spp.). Doi Pae Poe, Mae Hong Son, elevation ca. 1,400 meters. (Photo by Tem Smitinand)

7. Swidden just before harvest. Sorghum ripening in foreground; rice awaiting harvest in middle ground. Lua', Pa Pae, October 1968.

8. Piles of rice straw remain in harvested swidden; new swiddens have been cut and are drying in middle and background. Photo taken from about 20 meters to the right of photo 7. February 1968.

9. Undergrowth, third year after cutting swidden. *Imperata cylindrica* and *Saccharum spontaneum* (tall flowering grass) are competing with coppiced shoots; *Schima walichii* at left foreground. Pa Pae study site, February 1967. (Photo by Tem Smitinand)

10. Seven years after cutting swidden, grasses are already suppressed by coppiced shoots. Pa Pae study site, February 1967. (Photo by Tem Smitinand)

11. Vegetation in swidden just before recutting, 10 years after previous cutting. The tall grass in bloom is *Saccharum spontaneum*. Pa Pae study site, February 1967. (Photo by Tem Smitinand)

315

12. Swidden shortly after planting. Rice has sprouted in clumps, and weed growth is vigorous; tall stakes in the center are for pole beans; horizontal logs laid along contours retard soil slippage. Lua', Pa Pae, May 1967.

13. Fallowed swidden. Ground cover has been restored by vigorous weed and coppice growth from stumps. Same site as photo 12. March 1968.

14. Doi Chiang Dao karst formation 60 km north of Chiang Mai. Irrigated rice fields and orchards at lower right; patches of swiddens on lower gentle slopes; opium swiddens on steep slopes closer to the top. January 1970.

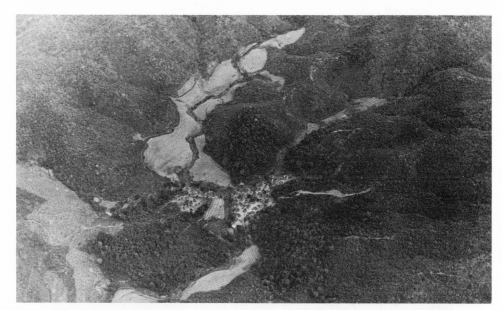

15. Lua' village of Pa Pae, surrounded by small patches of old forest. "Old forest" study site just to right of village; at lower right, swiddens cut in 1962; at lower left, swiddens cut in 1967; irrigated fields line the streams. Spring 1969.

16. Northern Thai village in heavily swiddened foothills of high population density area. Note scattered orange orchards. Nan Province, January 1970.

17. Abandoned swiddens cut by Karen in low population density area west of Hua Hin. January 1970.

18. Hmong village of Mae Tho, Mae Sariang District, Mae Hong Son Province, surrounded by clean-cultivated opium and maize fields. April 1971.

319

19. Northern Thai and Hmong swiddens in mature teak forest, 15 km south of Mae Chaem, Chiang Mai Province. February 1970.

Preparing Swidden Fields

20. Each field user makes a small offering to the field spirits and reads the omen from a chicken's gall bladder to determine if he should cut his field in this location. Lua', Pa Pae, January 1967.

21. Swiddeners top large trees to keep them from shading the fields; small trees are felled. Lua', Pa Pae, January 1967.

22. Swiddens are cut in coherent blocks, and the slash is left to dry for about six weeks before burning. Karen, Laykawkey, March 1968.

23. Lua' villagers clear and sweep a wide firebreak to prevent the swidden fire from spreading into fallow areas. March 1967.

24. Burning, the most dangerous phase of swiddening, requires both ritual and practical measures to keep the fire under control. Lua' elders make sacrifices and chant to the spirits of the fields on the day the swiddens are fired. March 1967.

25. Lua' man in foreground holds the taboo sign he will plant in his field before beginning cleanup of swiddens as soon as the fire burns out; in the middle ground are bamboo poles split for the flooring of field shelters. Pa Pae, March 1967.

26. Karen man holding bamboo water tubes stands on the roof of his house, prepared to defend it against embers from the swidden fire. In foreground a squirt gun made of a bamboo section lies in a water trough. Note bamboo bellows under house to right. Laykawkey, March 1968.

27. As swidden fire burns near Laykawkey, Karen woman, standing in front of posts for a new house, winnows salt, using magic to prevent wind from blowing fire into village. Laykawkey, March 1968.

28. Slash before swidden fire. Lua', Pa Pae, March 1968.

29. Slash after swidden fire. Temperature probes were buried in this field. Lua', Pa Pae, March 1968. See page 144.

30. Lua' woman chopping and piling logs for reburning. Pa Pae, March 1968.

31. Reburn scar with ash and scattered charcoal. Pa Pae, April 1967.

32. Logs are placed to mark swidden boundaries; some erosion is apparent along pathway. Lua', Pa Pae, April 1967.

33. Logs across a narrow valley at the foot of swiddens retard erosion. Such locations may be made into wet rice terraces if there is enough water for irrigation. Lua', Pa Pae, April 1967.

34. Log and brush frameworks in well-watered places reduce erosion and support squash vines. Lua', Pa Pae, April 1967.

35. Maize is one of the first crops to be planted, often before the slash has stopped smoldering. Lua', Pa Pae, March 1967.

36. Making a hole with an iron-tipped digging stick, a Karen woman plants cassava in her swidden before beginning to clean and reburn. Laykawkey, March 1968.

37. Lua' farmer offers chick, egg, rice, liquor, cotton, etc., to his ancestors and to spirits of the fields before planting swidden. Pa Pae, April 1967.

38. Young Karen men jab shallow holes in the soil with long iron-tipped bamboo planting sticks; women, children, and old men follow, throwing a few rice grains in each hole. Laykawkey, April 1968.

39. Lua' farmers use the same swidden planting techniques as the Karen. Pa Pae, April 1967. (Compare photo 118.)

40. After finishing planting her swidden a Karen woman splits the planting pole, props it against a tree, and scatters water around the field while praying for rain. Laykawkey, May 1968.

41. Weeding is a back-breaking job. Scraping and chopping with the L-shaped weeding tool disturbs only the top few centimeters of the soil. Lua', Pa Pae, June 1967.

42. Bundles of weeds dot the swidden surface after the first weeding. Lua', Pa Pae, June 1967. See also photo 48.

Protecting the Fields and Crop

43. Lua' farmers set rows of deadfalls into a low bamboo fence and bait them with a few rice grains, to kill rats as the rice begins to grow. Pa Pae, June 1967.

44. In mid-growing season Karen farmers invoke the spirits to protect the rice and promote a bountiful harvest. Laykawkey, June 1968.

45. Wild pigs or bears may raid the fields as the rice begins to ripen. A Lua' farmer installs a water-powered gong to frighten them away. Pa Pae, October 1967.

334

46. Lua' villagers try to protect their rice against rats by tying slippery bamboo leaf-sheaths around the rice barn posts. Note firewood piled under barn and tobacco planted in right foreground. Pa Pae, December 1967.

47. Fields are fenced to keep out cattle. Lua' farmers have built a stile where the fence cuts across the village path. Pa Pae, June 1968.

48. Logs laid by farmers along contours are effective in reducing erosion in swiddens. Lua', Pa Pae, June 1967.

49. After the swidden soil is thoroughly moistened by rain, Lua' farmers may transplant rice seedlings to insure even spacing throughout the field. Pa Pae, June 1967.

50. Rice ripens in September and October, and harvest begins in the lower, moister parts of the fields. Lua', Pa Pae, October 1967.

51. Farmers select small bunches of rice as they ripen and cut them with a small sickle, propping them up to dry on the stubble. Karen, Laykawkey, October 1968.

52. Women carry big bundles of rice sheaves and lay them carefully at the edge of the threshing floor. Karen, Laykawkey, October 1968.

338

53. The ritual owner of each Karen field must thresh the first bundles of rice. Early in the morning they twine threshing ropes of rice straw, and set up an altar on the right side of the threshing floor. They kill a chicken to honor the rice soul and smear its blood and feathers on the threshing mat and altar to encourage the rice soul to stay there. Laykawkey, October 1968.

54. After fastening a few rice sheaves to the altar, the Karen farmer offers a little rice liquor to the rice soul. Laykawkey, October 1968.

55. As the harvest begins, Lua' men offer rice, yams, peppers, chicken, eggs, cotton yarn, turmeric, and cowrie shell "money" to their ancestors, their wife's ancestors, and to the spirits of previous field owners. Pa Pae, November 1967.

56. Most of the grain is knocked loose by beating the sheaves against the threshing mats; the rest is freed by beating the straw with threshing sticks. Karen, Laykawkey, October 1968.

340

57. The straw is kicked off to the side of the threshing floor, where it has accumulated into large piles by the end of the day. Karen, Laykawkey, October 1967.

58. Children start young to learn the techniques of harvest. Karen, Laykawkey, October 1968.

341

59. Sometimes, especially when the rice is not quite dry, it is freed from the straw by rubbing with the feet. Lua', Pa Pae, October 1967.

60. Villagers do the first cleaning of the rice at the threshing floor, sorting through by hand, stirring with feet, and blowing the straw away with a winnowing fan. Karen, Laykawkey, October 1967.

61. For a second cleaning, Lua' farmers carry the rice up a ladder built for the purpose and pour the rice out, fanning it as it drops to the winnowing floor. Pa Pae, November 1967.

62. Rice is measured and the harvest counted at the winnowing floor; it is stored temporarily in the field shelter. Lua', Pa Pae, October 1967.

63. Lua' farmers keep count of the yield by making a bend in a notched stick for each basketful. Karen farmers keep count on strips of bamboo. Pa Pae, October 1967.

64. Karen farmer harvests a yam he has planted in his swidden. Laykawkey, October 1968.

65. The rice is carried back from the temporary barns to the village. Lua', Pa Pae, November 1967.

66. A few families have elephants to help carry rice from the swiddens. Karen, Laykawkey, November 1968.

67. Early in the morning of the day after the last rice has been carried back to the village, having picked a few flowers to provide seed for next year's field, two Lua' farmers squat by a dismantled winnowing ladder and summon their families' souls to return with them to the village, lest they get lost from their bodies and cause illness. A pile of straw burns in the background to light their way. Pa Pae, December 1967.

Irrigated Fields

68. Terraces are carved with hand tools out of the slopes at the bottom of swiddens. Lua', Pa Pae, June 1967.

69. Simple irrigation dams of sticks, brush, and mud are rebuilt each year. Lua', Pa Pae, June 1967.

70. Irrigation ditches are cleaned and repaired before the heavy rains start. Lua', Pa Pae, June 1967.

71. As soon as they can get a little water to their fields, the farmers hoe and flood a seed bed, and then carefully smooth the soil to receive the seed. Lua', Pa Pae, June 1967.

72. A farmer throws seed onto the surface of the water after it clears. Lua', Pa Pae, June 1967.

73. Some irrigated rice varieties are germinated in dry nurseries, often dibbled into small sections of abandoned swiddens. Although this requires more seed, it avoids the need for special preparation of the irrigated seed bed, and saves all the irrigated area for the crop. Note luxuriant regrowth in abandoned swidden seven months after harvest. Karen, Laykawkey, June 1968.

74. Fields must be thoroughly wet before they can be plowed. This Lua' farmer tried farming in the dry season of 1967–1968, but despite adequate water his yield was quite low. Pa Pae, December 1967.

75. After plowing, the dikes must be cleaned and repaired. Lua', Pa Pae, June 1967.

76. The thoroughly soaked, plowed fields are harrowed to break up the larger clods. Karen, Laykawkey, June 1968.

351

77. Karen women and children pull rice seedlings from a swidden nursery for transplanting in an irrigated field. Laykawkey, June 1968.

78. The terraces are flooded and transplanted. Note rice nursery in swidden at left and poles piled up to dry for firewood *(left foreground)*. Lua', Pa Pae, June 1967.

79. The transplanters twist the tops off the rice seedlings and thrust three or four plants into the mud. Karen, Laykawkey, June 1968.

80. The weeds float in irrigated fields and the farmers pass their hands between the rice clumps to pull them out. Karen, Laykawkey, July 1968.

353

Processing and Consuming

81. Karen woman pounds rice with a foot-powered pestle to remove the hulls, a daily chore in these villages where there are no mechanical rice mills. Laykawkey, December 1968.

82. Lua' woman tosses rice in a winnowing tray to remove the chaff after the hulls have been loosened by the mortar and pestle. Chickens and pigs, attracted by the sound of the mortar, come looking for spilled grains. Pa Pae, December 1967.

83. Rice is the center of every meal, as well as an essential feature of every ceremony. A Karen father summons the souls of his wife, children, son-in-law, and grandchildren by tapping a bamboo rod on the rice tray, before taking part in a ritual meal at which the people's wrists will be bound to keep bodies and souls together. Laykawkey, January 1968.

84. Karen youth offers home-brewed rice liquor to maiden at lunch time during harvest. The girls at first customarily refuse to drink, feigning disinterest in this courting ritual. Laykawkey, November 1968.

Garden Produce, Tobacco, and Other Minor Crops

85. Pa Pae villagers carefully fence their dry-season village gardens to keep out pigs and chickens. Lua', Pa Pae, January 1967.

86. Lua' man flips water over his onions and mustard greens from an irrigation ditch using a half section of bamboo. Pa Pae, March 1968.

87. Lua' man peels dried garlic bulbs, grown in village gardens. Pa Pae, December 1967.

88. Sugarcane is grown in village gardens. Karen, Laykawkey, June 1968.

89. To insure fertility of mango trees, Pa Pae villagers tie women's skirts around the trunks. Pa Pae, May 1968.

90. Karen woman slices tobacco onto a drying rack. Laykawkey, December 1968.

91. Lua' woman sets tobacco out to sun-dry on her porch. Numbers on house post are records of malaria spraying. Pa Pae, December 1967.

92. Lua' woman picks chili peppers in swidden garden. Rice sheaves are drying in background; lemon grass *(Cymbopogon)* grows in right foreground. Pa Pae, November 1967.

93. Beans, which are grown in swiddens, ripen at the time of the rice harvest and are an important supplement to the diet. Karen, Laykawkey, November 1968.

94. Job's tears *(Coix lachryma-jobi)* of two varieties, round and long, are planted in small quantities and are used primarily for children's necklaces. Lua', Pa Pae, November 1967.

95. Karen woman removes seeds from swidden-grown cotton. Laykaw-key, February 1968.

96. Karen woman fluffs the ginned cotton with a bow before spinning. Laykawkey, February 1968.

97. Karen woman spins cotton thread. Laykawkey, January 1969.

98. Lua' woman binds cotton thread with dye-resistant strip of leaf before dyeing to produce sets of *ikat* warp thread for weaving blue-and-white pattern into skirts. Pa Pae, March 1968.

362

99. Karen woman weaves on backstrap loom. Laykawkey, January 1969.

Collecting Firewood, *Imperata* Grass, and Other Forest Products

100. Karen maiden chops firewood in a newly burned swidden. Firewood, gathered mostly in current or old swiddens, is the primary source of fuel for all upland villages. Laykawkey, April 1968.

101. Collecting firewood and carrying it back to the village is a regular chore for women. Lua', Pa Pae, 1967.

102. Lua' man ties bundles of dried *Imperata cylindrica*, cut in a fallow swidden cultivated four years previously. Pa Pae, January 1968.

103. Lua' maidens carry bundles of *Imperata* grass back to the village for weaving roofing shingles. Pa Pae, December 1967.

365

104. Lua' boy weaves roofing shingle of *Imperata* grass. Pa Pae, March 1968.

105. Putting new shingles on roof of Lua' house. Pa Pae, January 1967.

106. Lua' man strips bark, to be chewed with betel, from an oak tree growing in the Dry Dipterocarp forest near Pa Pae, February 1967.

107. Lua' man makes rice storage basket of split bamboo. Pa Pae, September 1967.

367

Fishing

108. Lua' women are using dip nets. Fishing supplies small amounts of protein for the diet. Pa Pae, June 1967.

109. Lua' villagers are netting and grasping for fish under rocks after building temporary small dam to divert water from one section of the stream. Pa Pae, December 1967.

110. Karen man repairs a knife blade. Laykawkey, December 1968.

111. Karen craftsman repairs the barrel of a muzzle-loading caplock gun, using a stone-weighted pump drill. Laykawkey, December 1968.

112. Pa Pae villagers sell rice to merchant in Mae Sariang town. December 1968.

113. Lua' peddler from La'up has brought *miang* (fermented tea), canned fish, and salt from the Mae Sariang market to sell in Pa Pae. December 1967.

114. Pwo Karen men from the Dong Luang area take temporary wage work harvesting dry-season valley rice near Mae Sariang. May 1969.

115. Lua' men from Chang Maw village doing hydraulic mining for tin at Baw Keo, Amphur Samoeng, Chiang Mai Province, January 1967.

116. Karen family from Laykawkey *(center)* buying tobacco in the Mae Sariang market. Some of the market women are Northern Thai, others are Lua' who moved from the mountains many years ago. Note dipterocarp wrapping leaves. January 1969.

117. Lua' girl, the daughter of migrants from a hill village, rolls dipterocarp leaves, collected in the foothills east of Mae Sariang town, for sale as wrapping leaves in the Mae Sariang market. Ban Phae', Mae Sariang, February 1969.

118. A Pa Pae Lua' woman who has married and moved to the valley, and transformed herself into a Northern Thai. (This is the same person shown in photo 39 as a Lua' planting a swidden.) July 1971.

119. Karen elephant driver moving logs near highway in Mae Sariang. May 1969.

120. Northern Thai making charcoal in earth-mound oven for sale in Chom Chaeng market, Chiang Mai; wood was cut from open forest growing on middle terrace lands. July 1970.

121. Hmong house in Tak Province. (Photo by F. G. B. Keen)

122. Hmong swiddens, Tak Province. Elephant grass (*Saccharum* sp.) has replaced the forest after intensive cultivation. (Photo by F. G. B. Keen)

123. A Hmong swidden about 70 km west of Hot on the highway to Mae Sariang. Main crops are maize *(upper left)* and potatoes *(upper right)*, some of which are marketed along the highway. Note water running from bamboo tube above and to right of house; storage house covered with squash vines; house built on posts in Northern Thai style. August 1970.

124. Hmong woman hoeing potato field. Note deep cultivation and soil slippage. Compare Lua' and Karen weeding (photos 41, 42). Km 70, Hot–Mae Sariang Highway, August 1970.

125. Hmong, resettled in lowlands of Sayaboury Province, Laos, working irrigated rice field. July 1968.

126. Karen addict smoking Hmong opium in his empty rice barn. May 1968.

377

127. Worm casts almost cover soil surface at end of rainy season, showing importance of worms in mixing soil and counteracting effects of leaching. Size is indicated by one-*baht* coin (27 mm) on right. Middle terrace soils, Sa District, Nan Province. (TALD photo)

128. Dissection of medium-size termite mound on San Pa Tong soil, middle terrace level, Sa District. The light coloration of the floor and spoil is due to a high concentration of calcium carbonate. (TALD photo)

129. Growth of upland rice on well-prepared but uncultivated swidden, middle terrace, four weeks after planting. No fertilizer was applied. Compare with photo 130. Sa District, Nan Province. (TALD photo)

130. Rice and peanut growth on mechanically cleared and cultivated land, seven weeks after planting. No fertilizer was applied. Compare with photo 129. Sa District, Nan Province. (TALD photo)

131. Experimental plots showing response of peanuts to banded super-phosphate and surface-broadcast agricultural lime; plot 15 treated, plot 14 control. Dry weight increase at the stage illustrated represents a gain of approximately 250 percent on the control. Hang Chat Experiment Station, Lampang Province. (TALD photo)

Swidden Export Crops

132. Indonesian rubber plantation smallholder plants pepper vine at base of coral tree in his swidden. (Photo by Karl Pelzer)

133. Densely planted rubber of Indonesian smallholder. (Photo by Karl Pelzer)

134. Indonesian smallholder rubber cakes awaiting shipment to mill via readily accessible water transport. (Photo by Karl Pelzer)

References[1]

Anderson, John
　1826 *Mission to the East Coast of Sumatra.* Edinburgh: Blackwood.

Anonymous
　1969 "Effect of fire and water losses at Mae Huad forest, Amphur Ngow, Lampang province." Forestry Research Bulletin No. 6. Bangkhen, Bangkok: Kasetsart University, Faculty of Forestry.

Anonymous
　1969 "Watershed management research on mountainous lands at Kok-Ma, Doi Pui, Chiang Mai." Conservation Research Bulletin No. 1. Bangkhen, Bangkok: Kasetsart University, Faculty of Forestry, Department of Conservation.

Asian Development Bank
　1969 *Asian Agricultural Survey.* Seattle: University of Washington Press.

Bastin, John
　1957 *The Native Policies of Sir Stamford Raffles in Java and Sumatra.* Oxford: Oxford University Press, Clarendon Press.

　1960 "The changing balance of the early Southeast Asian pepper trade." Papers on Southeast Asian Subjects, no. 1. Singapore: Eastern Universities Press.

Bauer, P. T.
　1948a *Report on a Visit to the Rubber Growing Smallholdings of Malaya, July to September 1946.* London: Her Majesty's Stationery Office.

　1948b *The Rubber Industry: A Study in Competition and Monopoly.* Cambridge: Harvard University Press.

Bertrand, P.
　1952 "Le conditions de la culture du riz dans le Haut Donnai (Viet Nam)." *L'Agronomie Tropicale* 7(3):266–275.

Bhagwati, Jagdish
　1966 *The Economics of Underdeveloped Countries.* London: World University Library.

Bhodhacharoen, Wanchern, Malee Sundhakhul, Poonsook Atthasampunna, and Chaiyuth Klinsukhont
　1970 "Effect of forest fire on soil microbial

---

[1]With respect to laws of Thailand, apart from the Civil and Commercial Code which was originally drafted in English, there is no official publication of Thai laws in English. Official publication in the Thai language is in the *Government Gazette.*

flora." Research Project No. 27/1, Description of Tropical Dry Evergreen Forest Ecosystem, Tropical Environmental Data (TREND). Cooperative Research Programme No. 27. Unpublished manuscript. Bangkok: Applied Scientific Research Corporation of Thailand.

Bhruksasri, Wanat, and G. A. Oughton
1970 "Research priorities in hill-tribe development." Paper presented for the Seminar on Shifting Cultivation and Economic Development in Northern Thailand. Mimeographed. Chiang Mai: Tribal Research Centre.

Bordsen, Marcus C.
1968 "Report on the 1967 meter square measurements of rice yields to Mr. Keopraseuth Meksvanh, provincial agriculture chief, southern region, Pakse." 24 January 1968. Typescript. Pakse, Laos: IVS/AGR.

Boserup, Ester
1965 *The Conditions of Agricultural Growth.* Chicago: Aldine Publishing Co.

Boulbet, Jean
1966 "Le Miir, culture itinérante avec jachere forestière en pays Maa', région de Blao-Bassin de Fleuve Daa' Dööng (Dông Nai)." *Bulletin de l'École Français d'Extrême Orient* 53(1):77–98.

Brans, P. H.
1935 *Sumatra-Benzoë.* Amsterdam: N. V. D. B. Centen's Uitgevers-Maatschappij.

Burkill, I. H.
1935 *A Dictionary of the Economic Products of the Malay Peninsula.* 2 vols, 1966 reissue. Kuala Lumpur: Ministry of Agriculture and Cooperatives.

Central Hill Tribe Welfare Committee
1963 *Hill Tribe Development and Welfare in Thailand.* Bangkok: Ministry of the Interior.

Chapman, E. C.
1967 *An Appraisal of Recent Agricultural Changes in the Northern Valleys of Thailand.* Bangkok: Department of Land Development.

Champsoloix, R.
1960 "Le ray dans quelques villages des Hauts Plateau du Viet Nam." In *Raports du Sol et de la Vegetation,* G. Viennot Bourgin, ed., pp. 46–62. Paris: Masson et Cie.

Cobban, James L.
1969 *The Traditional Use of the Forests in Mainland Southeast Asia.* Papers in International Studies, Southeast Asia Series, no. 5. Athens, Ohio: University of Ohio.

Conklin, Harold C.
1954 "An ethnoecological approach to shifting agriculture." In *Readings in Cultural Geography,* Philip L. Wagner and Marvin W. Mikesell, eds. Chicago: University of Chicago Press.

1957 "Hanunoo agriculture, a report on an integral system of shifting cultivation in the Philippines." FAO Forestry Development Papers, no. 12. Rome.

De Bevolkingsrubbercultuur in Nederlandisch-Indie.
1925– *Rapporten Uitgegeven door het Departe-*
1927 *ment van Landbouw, Nijverheid en Handel in samenwerking met het Native Rubber Investigation Committee.* Weltevreden: Dutch East Indies, Department van Landbouw, Nijverheid en Handel.
I. Pekelharing, N. R. *Djambi.* (1925)
II. Luytjes, A. *Zuider en Oosterafdeeling van Borneo.* (1925)
III. Loos, H., and D. Ven Beusichem. *Westerafdeeling van Borneo.* (1925)
IV. Warren, C. N., and B. Van Staalduinen. *Palembang.* (1925)
V. Brook, C. P., H. W. J. Doffegnies, and Zomede C. G. Slotemaker. *Tapanoeli en Sumatra's Westkust.* (1926)
VI. Slotemaker, C. G. *Riouw en Onderhoorigheden, Oostkust van Sumatra en Atjeh en Onderhoorigheden.* (1926)

VII. Luytjes, A. *Eindrapport.* (1927)

Dessaint, Alan Y.
1971 Lisu migration in the Thai highlands. *Ethnology* 10(3):329–348.

Dobby, E. H. G.
1954 *Southeast Asia.* London: University of London Press.

Durrenberger, E. Paul
1971 "A socio-medical study of the Lisu of northern Thailand: Ban Lum, Amphur Mae Taeng, Changwat Chiang Mai." Mimeographed final report. Chiang Mai: Tribal Research Centre.

Dutch East Indies, Centraal Kantoor voor de Statistiek
1939 *De Landbouwexportgewassen van Neder-landsch-Indie* [The export crops of the Netherlands Indies in 1938]. Bulletin of the Central Bureau of Statistics, no. 175. Batavia: Landsdrukkerij.

Edgar, A. T.
1958 *Manual of Rubber Planting (Malaya).* Kuala Lumpur: Incorporated Society of Planters.

Encyclopaedisch Bureau
1931 *De Pepercultuur in de Buitenbezittingen.* Batavia: Landsdrukkerij.

Eschels-Kroon, Adolph
1781 *Beschreibung der Insel Sumatra, besonders in Ansehung des Handels, und der dahin gehorigen Merkwurdigkeiten.* Hamburg: Carl Ernst Bohn.

FAO Committee on Forest Development in the Tropics
1967 "Report of the first session (18–20 October)." Rome: FAO.
1969 "Shifting cultivation in tropical forests, summary. Paper no. FO: FDT 69/2, July 1969." Presented at the second session (21–24 October) Rome: FAO.

Faculty of the Social Sciences, Chiang Mai University
n.d. "A case study of the forest village system

[c.a. 1975] in northern Thailand." Mimeographed. Chiang Mai: Chiang Mai University, Faculty of Social Sciences.

Fickendey, Ernst
1941 *Eingeborenenkultur und Plantage*, vol. 4. *Mitteilungen der Gruppe Deutscher kolon-ialwirtschaftlicher Unternehmungen.* Berlin: Walter de Gruyter.

Freeman, J. D.
1955 *Iban Agriculture.* Colonial Office Research Studies No. 18. London: Her Majesty's Stationery Office.

Geddes, William R.
1954 *The Land Dyaks of Sarawak.* Colonial Office Research Studies No. 14. London: Her Majesty's Stationery Office.
1970 "Opium and the Miao: A study in ecological adjustment." *Oceania* 41(1):1–11.
1973 "The opium problem in northern Thailand." In *Studies of Contemporary Thailand*, R. Ho and E. C. Chapman, eds. Canberra: Australian National University, Monography HG/8, Department of Human Geography.
1976 *Migrants of the Mountains: The Cultural Ecology of the Blue Miao (Hmong Njua) of Thailand.* Oxford: Oxford University Press, Clarendon Press.

Geertz, Clifford
1963 *Agricultural Involution: The Process of Ecological Change in Indonesia.* Berkeley and Los Angeles: University of California Press.

Gelder, A. Van
1950 "Bevolkingsrubbercultuur." In *De Landbouw in den Indische Archipel*, C. J. J. van Hall and C. van de Koppel, eds., vol. 3, pp. 427–475. The Hague: Van Hoeve.

Gelderen, J. Van
1961 "The economics of the tropical colony." In *Indonesian Economics: The Concept of Dualism in Theory and Policy*, pp. 118–164. The Hague: W. van Hoeve.

Gorman, Chester F.
1969   "Hoabinhian: A pebble-tool complex with early plant associations in Southeast Asia." *Science* 163:671–673.
1971a   "The Hoabinhian and after: Subsistence patterns in Southeast Asia during the late Pleistocene and early Recent periods." *World Archaeology* 2(3):300–320.
1971b   "*A priori* models and Thai prehistory: A reconsideration of the beginnings of agriculture in Southeast Asia." Unpublished manuscript. Dunedin, New Zealand: University of Otago, Department of Anthropology.

Gould, J. W.
1956   "Sumatra: America's pepperpot, 1784–1873." *Essex Institute Historical Collections* 92(2):83–152; (3):203–251; (4):295–348.

Grist, D. H.
1959   *Rice.* 3rd ed. London: Longmans.

Haan, F. De
1910–   *Priangan. De Preanger-Regentschappen*
1912   *onder het Nederlandsch Bestuur tot 1811.* Batavia: G. Kolff.

Hallett, Holt S.
1890   *A Thousand Miles on an Elephant in the Shan States.* Edinburgh and London: Wm. Blackwood and Sons.

Hamilton, J. W.
1965   "Ban Hong: Social Structure and economy of a Pwo Karen village in northern Thailand." Ph.D. thesis, University of Michigan, Department of Anthropology.
1976   *Pwo Karen: At the Edge of Mountain and Plain.* American Ethnological Society Series. St. Paul, Minnesota: West Publishing Co.

Harler, C. R.
1964   *The Culture and Marketing of Tea.* 3rd ed. London: Oxford University Press.

Harris, David R.
1969   "Agricultural systems, ecosystems and the origins of agriculture." In *The Domestication and Exploitation of Plants and Animals*, Peter J. Ucko and G. W. Dimbleby, eds., pp. 3–15. Chicago: Aldine Publishing Co.
1972   "The origins of agriculture in the tropics." *American Scientist* 60(2):180–193.

Hinton, Peter
1973   "Population dynamics and dispersal trends among the Karen of Thailand." In *Studies in Contemporary Thailand*, R. Ho and E. C. Chapman, eds. Canberra: Australian National University, Monograph HG/8, Department of Human Geography.

Hirst, Eric
1974   "Food-related energy requirements." *Science* 184:134–138.

Iijima, Shigeru
1970   "Socio-cultural change among the shifting cultivators through the introduction of wet rice culture—a case study of the Karens in northern Thailand." Kyoto: Memoirs of the College of Agriculture, Kyoto University (No. 97, Agric. Econom. Ser. No. 3).

Izikowitz, K. G.
1951   *Lamet: Hill Peasants in French Indo-China.* Etnologiska Studier 17. Goteborg: Etnografiska Museet.

Jones, Delmos J.
1967   "Cultural variation among six Lahu villages, northern Thailand." Ph. D. dissertation, Cornell University.

Jørgensen, Anders Baltzer
1976   *Swidden Cultivation among Pwo Karens in Western Thailand.* The Lampang Field Station, a Scandinavian Research Center in Thailand, 1969–1974, Reports, edited by Søren Egerod and Per Sørensen. The Scandinavian Institute of Asian Studies, Special Publication No. 5, pp. 275–288.

Judd, Laurence C.
1964   "Dry rice agriculture in northern Thailand." Southeast Asia Program, Data

Paper No. 52. Ithaca, N. Y.: Cornell University.

Kalland, Arne
1976 *Carrying Capacity of Shifting Cultivation of Northern Thailand and Some Implications.* The Lampang Field Station, a Scandinavian Research Center in Thailand, 1969–1974, Reports, edited by Søren Egerod and Per Sørensen. The Scandinavian Institute of Asian Studies, Special Publication No. 5, pp. 289–297.

Kandre, Peter K.
1971 "Alternative modes of recruitment of viable households among the Yao of Mae Chan." *South-East Asian Journal of Sociology* 4:43–52.

Keen, F. G. B.
1966 "The Meo of northwest Thailand." Wellington, New Zealand: Library of Victoria University. M. A. and Honours thesis.
1969 "The miang village of Pang Ma-O, Chiang Dao district, Chiang Mai province." Nikhom Doi Chiang Dao Resources and Development-Potential Survey, Report 3. (Adapted from an Interim Field Report to the Tribal Research Centre by F. G. B. Keen.) Chiang Mai: Tribal Research Centre.
1970 "The fermented tea *(miang)* economy of northern Thailand." Appendix: "Four case studies of miang villages." Unpublished manuscript.
1972 "Man-land relations." *The Nation*, 23 March, 11; 24 March, 11. Bangkok.

Khao Phanit [Commercial News]
1969 Special issue (in Thai). Bangkok.

Khemnark, Choob, et al.
1972 Project "Forest production and soil fertility at Nikhom Doi Chiang Dao, Chiang Mai Province." Project Leader: Mr. Choob Khemnark. Associates: Mr. Sathit Wacharakitti, Mr. Sanit Aksornkoae, Mr. Tawee Kaekla-iad. Consultants: Dr. Sanga Sabhasri, Mr. G. A. Oughton, Dr. James A. Chalmers. Forest Research Bulletin No. 22. Bangkhen, Bangkok: Faculty of Forestry, Kasetsart University.

Kickert, Robert W.
1969 "Akha village structure." In *Tribesmen and Peasants in North Thailand*, Proceedings of the First Symposium of the Tribal Research Centre (1967), Chiang Mai, Thailand, Peter Hinton, ed., pp. 35–40. Chiang Mai: Tribal Research Centre.

Komkris, Thiem, et al.
1969 "Effect of fire on soil and water losses at Mae Huad forest, Amphur Ngao, Lampang province." Forest Research Bulletin No. 6. Bangkhen, Bangkok: Kasetsart University, Faculty of Forestry.

Kools, J. F.
1935 *Hoema's Hoemablokken en Boschreserves in de Residentie Bantam.* Wageningen: H. Veenman Zonen.

Koppel, C. van de
1950 "Benzoe." In *De Landbouw in den Indische Archipel*, C. J. J. van Hall and C. van de Koppel, eds., vol. 3, pp. 654–685. The Hague: Van Hoeve.

Kroon, A. H. J.
1969 Review of Spencer, J. E.: *Shifting Cultivation in Southeastern Asia. Tropical Abstracts* 24(8):556–557.

Kunstadter, Peter
1966*a* "Irrigation and social structure: Narrow valleys and individual enterprise." Paper presented at the Pacific Science Congress, Tokyo. Mimeographed abstract in proceedings of the congress.
1966*b* "Residential and social organization of the Lawa of northern Thailand." *Southwestern Journal of Anthropology* 22:61–83.
1967 "The Lua' and Skaw Karen of Maehongson province, northwestern Thailand." In *Southeast Asia Tribes, Minorities and Na-*

tions, P. Kunstadter, ed., vol. 2, pp. 639–674. Princeton, N. J.: Princeton University Press.

1969a "Hill and valley population in northwestern Thailand." In *Tribesmen and Peasants in North Thailand*, Proceedings of the First Symposium of the Tribal Research Centre (1967) Chiang Mai, Thailand, Peter Hinton, ed., pp. 69–85. Chiang Mai: Tribal Research Centre.

1969b "Socio-cultural change among upland peoples of Thailand: Lua' and Karen—two modes of adaptation." Proceedings of the Eighth Congress of Anthropological and Ethnological Sciences (1968), vol. 2, pp. 232–235. Science Council of Japan, Tokyo.

1970 "Cultural patterns, social structure, and reproductive differentials in northwestern Thailand." Paper presented at Symposium on Culture, Family Planning and Human Fertility, at the American Anthropological Association Annual Meeting, San Diego, November 1970.

1971 "Natality, mortality and migration of upland and lowland populations in northwestern Thailand." In *Culture and Population: A Collection of Current Studies*, Steven Polgar, ed., pp. 46–60. Carolina Population Center, Monograph 9, University of North Carolina at Chapel Hill. Cambridge, Mass.: Schenkman Publishing Co.

Kunstadter, Peter, Sanga Sabhasri, and Tem Smitinand
1978 "Flora of a forest fallow farming environment in northwestern Thailand." *Journal of the National Research Council of Thailand* 10(1):1–45.

Lafont, Pierre-Bernard
1959 "The 'slash-and-burn' (ray) agriculture system of the mountain populations of central Vietnam." Proceedings of the Ninth Pacific Science Congress, vol. 7, pp. 56–59. Bangkok.

1967 "L'agriculture sur brulis chez les Proto-Indochinois des hauts plateaux du Centre Viet Nam." Les cahiers d'Outre-mer, *Revue du Geographie* 20(77):37–48.

Leach, E. R.
1954 *Political Systems of Highland Burma*. Cambridge, Mass.: Harvard University Press.

LeBar, Frank M.
1967 "Miang: Fermented tea in northern Thailand." *Behavior Science Notes* 2(2):105–121.

LeBar, Frank M., Gerald C. Hickey, and John K. Musgrave
1964 *Ethnic Groups of Mainland Southeast Asia*. New Haven: Human Relations Area File Press.

Lim Sow Ching and Colin Barlow
1967 "A study of inputs and outputs of selected catch crops on immature rubber smallholdings in West Malaysia." Two parts, mimeographed. Kuala Lumpur: Rubber Research Institute of Malaya, Economics and Planning Division.

Luytjes, A.
1925 "Zuider en Oosterafdeeling van Borneo." In *De Bevolkingsrubber Cultuur in Nederlandisch-Indie*. Weltevreden: Dutch East Indies, Department van Landbouw, Nijverheid en Handel.

Marlowe, David H.
1969 "Upland-lowland relationships: The case of the S'kaw Karen of central upland western Chiang Mai." In *Tribesmen and Peasants in North Thailand*, Proceedings of the First Symposium of the Tribal Research Centre (1967), Chiang Mai, Thailand, Peter Hinton, ed., pp. 53–68. Chiang Mai: Tribal Research Centre.

Marsden, William
1811 *The History of Sumatra, Containing an Account of the Government, Laws, Customs, and Manners of the Native Inhabitants, with a Description of the Natural*

Productions, and a Relation of the Ancient Political State of the Island. 3rd ed. London: J. McCreevy.

Maurice, Albert, and Georges Marie Proux
1954 "L'âme du riz." *Bulletin de la Societé des Études Indochinoises* 29(1–2):129–259.

Miles, Douglas
1967 "Report on fieldwork in the village of Pulangka." Mimeographed. Chiang Mai: Tribal Research Centre.
1973 "Some demographic implications of regional commerce: The case of North Thailand's Yao minority." In *Studies of Contemporary Thailand*, R. Ho and E. C. Chapman, eds. Canberra: Australian National University, Monograph HG/8, Department of Human Geography.

Moorman, F. R., K. R. M. Anthony, and S. Panichapong
1964 "Note on the soils and land use in the hills of Tak province." Mimeographed. Bangkok: Ministry of National Development.

Myrdal, Gunnar
1968 *Asian Drama: An Inquiry into the Poverty of Nations*. 3 vols. New York: Random House, Pantheon.

Nimmanahaeminda, Kraisri
1965 "An inscribed silver-plate grant to the Lawa of Boh Luang." In *Felicitation Volumes in Southeast Asia Studies Presented to His Highness Prince Dhanivat Kromamum Bidyalabh Bridyakorn*, vol. 2, pp. 233–238. Bangkok: The Siam Society.

Oughton, G. A., and Niwat Imong
1970 "Nikhom Doi Chiang Dao: Resources and development-potential survey." Report 2: "Village location, ethnic composition, and economy." Mimeographed. Chiang Mai: Tribal Research Centre.
1971 "Nikhom Doi Chiang Dao: Resources and development-potential survey." Supplement to report 3: "Further data on the native tea *(miang)* economy." Mimeo-

graphed. Chiang Mai: Tribal Research Centre.

Ozinga, J.
1940 *De Economische Ontwickkeling der Westerafdeeling van Borneo en de Bevolkingsrubbercultuur*. Wageningen: N. V., Gebr. Zomer en kuening.

Paerels, B. H.
1949 "Bevolkingskoffiecultuur." In *De Landbouw in de Indische Archipel*, C. J. J. van Hall and C. van de Koppel, eds., vol. 2b, pp. 89–119. The Hague: Van Hoeve.

Pelzer, Karl J.
1945 *Pioneer Settlement in the Asiatic Tropics: Studies in Land Utilization and Agricultural Colonization*. New York: American Geographical Society.
1947 "Agriculture in the Truk islands." *Foreign Agriculture* 2(6):75–81.
1958 "Land utilization in the humid tropics: Agriculture." Proceedings of the Ninth Pacific Science Congress (1957), vol. 20, pp. 124–143.
1963 "The agricultural foundation." In *Indonesia*, Ruth McVey, ed., pp. 118–154. New Haven: HRAF Press.

Phạm-Hoàng Hộ
1970 *Cây-cỏ Miền Nam Việtnam* [An illustrated
1972 flora of South Vietnam]. Bộ Văn-Hóa Giáo-Dục Và Thanh-Niên Trung-Tâm Học Liệu. 2 vols. Saigon.

Pimentel, David, L. E. Hurd, A. C. Bellotti, M. J. Forster, I. N. Oka, O. D. Sholes, and R. J. Whitman.
1973 "Food production and the energy crisis." *Science* 182:443–449.

Raffles (Lady)
1830 *Memoir of the Life and Public Services of Sir Thomas Stamford Raffles*. London: John Murray.

Reyne, A.
1948 "De Cocospalm." In *De Landbouw in den Indische Archipel*, C. J. J. van Hall and C.

van de Koppel, eds., vol. 2a, pp. 427–525. The Hague: Van Hoeve.

Royal Thai Government
1962   Department of Public Welfare records. Bangkok.

Royal Thai Survey Department
1969   Thailand national resources atlas. Supreme Command Headquarters. Bangkok.

Reunyote, Suwan
1967   "The development and welfare scheme for the hill tribes in Thailand." An address by the director-general of the Department of Public Welfare at the Tribal Research Centre, Chiang Mai, August 29, 1967. Bangkok: Department of Public Welfare.
1969   "Development and welfare for the hill tribes in Thailand." In *Tribesmen and Peasants in North Thailand*, Proceedings of the First Symposium of the Tribal Research Centre (1967), Chiang Mai, Thailand, Peter Hinton, ed., pp. 12–14. Chiang Mai: Tribal Research Centre.

Rutgers, A. A. L.
1949   "Pepper." In *De Landbouw in den Indische Archipel*, C. J. J. van Hall and C. van de Koppel, eds., vol. 2b, pp. 620–654. The Hague: Van Hoeve.

Sabhasri, Sanga, Aht Boonitee, Padoem Ratisoonthorn, and Sanit Aksornkoae
1971   Laboratory study of effects of high temperature caused by forest fire on forest flora. Bangkhen, Bangkok: Kasetsart University, Faculty of Forestry. Unpublished manuscript.

Sabhasri, Sanga, Choob Khemnark, Sanit Aksornkoae, and Padoem Ratisoonthorn
1968   Primary production in dry-evergreen forest at Sakaerat, Amphoe Pak Thong Chai, Changwat Nakhon Ratchasima. Research Project 27/2, Report No. 1. Bangkhen, Bangkok: Applied Scientific Research Corporation of Thailand.

Sabhasri, Sanga, and Niwat Ruengpanit
1969   "Huey Kok Ma watershed research, Doi

Pui, Chiang Mai." *The Vanasarn* (Journal of the Royal Forest Department) 27(3): 229–245.

Sabhasri, Sanga, and L. E. Wood
1967   Forest biomass in Thailand. Military Research and Development Command Report No. 67–034. Bangkok.

Sabhasri, Sanga, et al.
1968   "Preliminary study of evaporation and transpiration in dry-evergreen forest at Sakaerat, Amphoe Pak Thong Chai, Changwat Nakhon Ratchasima." Research Project 27/5, Report No. 1. Bangkhen, Bangkok: Applied Scientific Research Corporation of Thailand.

Sauer, Carl O.
1952   *Agricultural origins and dispersals*. New York: American Geographical Society.
1956   The agency of man on the earth. In *Man's Role in Changing the Face of the Earth*, William L. Thomas, Jr., ed., pp. 49–69. Chicago: University of Chicago Press.

Scholz, Friedhelm
1969   "Zum Feldbau des Akha-Dorfes Alum, Thailand." [Contribution to the shifting-cultivation of the Akha village Alum, Thailand]. *Yearbook of the South Asia Institute*, Heidelberg University, 1968/69, Band 3, pp. 88–99. Wiesbaden: Otto Harrassowitz.

Siegel, James T.
1969   *The Rope of God*. Berkeley and Los Angeles: University of California Press.

Spencer, J. E.
1966   *Shifting Cultivation in Southeastern Asia*. University of California Publications in Geography, vol. 19. Berkeley and Los Angeles: University of California Press.

Spielmann, Hans J.
1967   "Lahu Sheleh and Lahu Na of northern Thailand." Preliminary report to the National Research Council of Thailand. Unpublished manuscript. Bangkhen, Bang-

kok: National Research Council of Thailand.

Stanton, W. R.
1969 "Some domesticated lower plants in Southeast Asian food technology." In *The Domestication and Exploitation of Plants and Animals*, Peter J. Ucko and G. W. Dimbleby, eds., pp. 463–469. Chicago: Aldine Publishing Co.

Staub, William J., and Melvin G. Blase
1971 "Genetic technology and agricultural development." *Science* 173:119–123.

Steinhart, John S., and Carol E. Steinhart
1974 "Energy use in the U.S. food system." *Science* 184:307–316.

Tadaw, Saw Hanson
1961 "The Karens of Burma: A study in human geography." In *Studies in Human Ecology*, George A. Theodorson, ed., pp. 496–508. Evanston, Ill. and Elmsford, N. Y.: Peterson and Co.

Tan Hong, Yeow Kheng Hoe, and
M. M. Chandapillai
1968 "Possibilities of intercropping." Mimeographed. Seremban, Malaysia: Chemara Research Station.

Thai Geographical Dictionary
1963 Bangkok: Rajabhanditsathan.

Thailand
1962 Civil and Commercial Code. Compiled by Prasobchai Yamali and Watana Ratanawichit. Books 1–6. Bangkok: Wichit Nilapaichit.
n.d. Forest Act of B.E. 2484 (1941), as amended by the Act of B.E. 2503 (1960).
n.d. Land Code.
n.d. National Reserved Forest Act of B.E. 2507 (1964).
n.d. Nationality Act of B.E. 2508 (1965).
n.d. Promulgation of Land Code Act of B.E. 2497 (1954).

Thailand, Department of Public Welfare
1966 "Report on the socio-economic survey of hill tribes in northern Thailand." Bangkok:

Department of Public Welfare, Ministry of the Interior.

Thailand, Ministry of Interior
1956 Declaration of 27 March.

Thailand, National Economic Board
1962 *Population Census of 1960. Whole kingdom.* Bangkok: National Economic Board, Central Statistical Office.

Thailand, Office of the Prime Minister
n.d. *1970 Population and Housing Census.* Changwat series, 76 vols. Bangkok: Office of the Prime Minister, National Statistical Office.

Thailand, Royal Forest Department
1969 "Status and trends of shifting cultivation in Thailand." Bangkhen, Bangkok: Royal Forest Department.

Thomas, K. D.
1965 "Shifting cultivation and production of smallholder rubber in a south Sumatran village." *Malayan Economic Review* 10: 100–115.

Uhlig, H.
1969 "Hill tribes and rice farmers in the Himalayas and Southeast Asia." Institute of British Geographers, *Transactions* 47: 1–24.

United Nations Fund for Drug Abuse Control (UNFDAC)
1974 "UN/Thai programme for drug abuse control in Thailand." United Nations Division of Narcotic Drugs, Progress Report No. 2, July 1973–December 1973. Geneva.

United Nations Survey Team
1967 "Report of the United Nations survey team on the economic and social needs of the opium-producing areas in Thailand." Bangkok: Government Printing House.

Van Roy, Edward
1964 "The miang economy." Mimeographed. Ithaca, N. Y.: Cornell University.
1971 *Economic Systems of Northern Thailand.* Ithaca, N. Y.: Cornell University Press.

Vavilov, N. I.

1926   "Studies on the origins of cultivated plants." *Bulletin of Applied Botany, Genetics and Plant Breeding* 16:1–245.

Walker, Anthony R.

1969   "Red Lahu village society—an introductory survey." In *Tribesmen and Peasants in North Thailand*, Proceedings of the First Symposium of the Tribal Research Centre (1967), Chiang Mai, Thailand, Peter Hinton, ed., pp. 41–52. Chiang Mai: Tribal Research Centre.

1970   "Lahu Nyi (Red Lahu) village society and economy in northern Thailand." Terminal report to the Royal Thai Goverment. 2 vols., mimeographed. Chiang Mai: Tribal Research Centre.

1976   "The swidden economy of a Lahu Nyi (Red Lahu) village community in North Thailand." *Folk* 18:145–188.

Watters, R. F.

1960   "The nature of shifting cultivation." *Pacific Viewpoint* 1(1):59–99. Wellington, New Zealand: Victoria University.

Weizman, H. G., Team Leader.

1971   Third Five Year Plan. Northern Region Development Policies, interim report. Chiang Mai. Northern Region Planning (UNDP Team).

Wharton, Clifton R., Jr.

1969   "Subsistence agriculture: Concepts and scope." In *Subsistence Agriculture and Economic Development*, Clifton R. Wharton, Jr., ed., pp. 12–20. Chicago: Aldine Publishing Co.

Wickizer, V. D.

1960   "The smallholder in tropical export crop production." *Food Research Institute Studies* 1(1):49–90.

Yen, D. E.

1977   "Hoabinhian horticulture? The evidence and the questions from northwest Thailand." In *Sunda and Sahul: Prehistoric Studies in Southeast Asia, Melanesia and Australia*, J. Allen, J. Golson, R. Jones, eds., pp. 567–599. London, New York, San Francisco: Academic Press.

Young, O. Gordon

1962   *The Hill Tribes of Northern Thailand*. 2nd ed., Monograph no. 1. Bangkok: The Siam Society.

1969   *Hill Tribes of Northern Thailand*. 4th ed., Monograph no. 1. Bangkok: The Siam Society.

Index

Numbers in italics refer to photograph numbers.